MW00473334

Religion and Classical Warfare

Religion and Classical Warfare

The Roman Republic

Edited by

Matthew Dillon
&
Christopher Matthew

Pen & Sword
MILITARY

First published in Great Britain in 2020 by
Pen & Sword Military
An imprint of
Pen & Sword Books Ltd
Yorkshire – Philadelphia

ISBN 978 1 47383 431 6

A CIP catalogue record for this book is
available from the British Library.

Printed and bound in England by TJ International Ltd, Padstow, Cornwall

Pen & Sword Books Limited incorporates the imprints of Atlas, Archaeology,
Aviation, Discovery, Family History, Fiction, History, Maritime, Military, Military
Classics, Politics, Select, Transport, True Crime, Air World, Frontline Publishing,
Leo Cooper, Remember When, Seaforth Publishing, The Praetorian Press,
Wharncliffe Local History, Wharncliffe Transport, Wharncliffe True Crime and
White Owl.

For a complete list of Pen & Sword titles please contact

PEN & SWORD BOOKS LIMITED
47 Church Street, Barnsley, South Yorkshire, S70 2AS, England
E-mail: enquiries@pen-and-sword.co.uk
Website: www.pen-and-sword.co.uk

Or
PEN AND SWORD BOOKS
1950 Lawrence Rd, Havertown, PA 19083, USA
E-mail: Uspen-and-sword@casematepublishers.com
Website: www.penandswordbooks.com

Cover illustration: A detail of the Altar of Domitius Ahenobarbus. The Roman god of war, Mars Ultor, stands to the left of his altar. A Roman official pours a libation on the altar, prior to presiding over an animal sacrifice to the god. Marble; 122–115 BC; Field of Mars (Campus Martius), Rome.

> Our [Roman] empire was made vast by those commanders who were obedient to religious practices. Furthermore, if we wish to contrast our Roman ways with those of foreign races, while we are equal – or even inferior – in all other ways, it is the case that, in the practice of religion, that is to say, in the worship of the gods, we are vastly superior.
>
> Cicero, *On the Nature of the Gods* (*De Natura Deorum*) 2.3.8

Contents

Abbreviations

Editorial abbreviations

c.	*circa* (about or approximately, used for dates)
ed. pr.	*editio princeps* (the first editor of an inscription, papyrus or manuscript)
F, FF	Fragment, Fragments
sv, svv	*sub vide*, see under

Abbreviations of Ancient Sources

Amm. Marc.	Ammianus Marcellinus (AD 330–*c.* 400) *Res Gestae* (*History of the Roman Empire*)
App.	Appian (AD *c.*95–*c.*165)
Civ.	*Civil Wars*
Hisp.	*Hispanic* [*Spanish*] *Wars*
It.	*Italian Wars*
Lib.	*Libyan* [*Punic*] *Wars*
Mith.	*Mithridatic Wars*
Sam.	*Samnite History*
Apollod. *Bibl.*	Apollodorus (first or second-century AD) *Bibliotheke* (*The Library of Mythology*)
Arnob.	Arnobius (late third/early fourth century AD) *Adversus Nationes* (*Against the Nations*; sometimes translated as *Against the Heathens*)
Arr. *Anab.*	Arrian (second century AD) *Anabasis* (*Journey of Alexander the Great*)
Athen. *Deip.*	Athenaeus (*c.* AD 200) *Deipnosophistae* (*Wise Men at Dinner*)
August. *Civ.*	Augustine *De Civitate Dei Contra Paganos* (*City of God Against the Pagans*)
Aug. *Res Gest.*	Augustus (63 BC–AD 14) *Res Gestae Divi Augusti* (*The Achievements of the Deified Augustus*)

Caes.	Caesar (100–44 BC)
Bell. Gall.	*Bellum Gallicum* (*The War in Gaul*)
Bell. Civ.	*Bellum Civile* (*Civil War*)
Calp*. Ecl.*	Calpurnius Siculus (*c.* AD 50) *Eclogues*
Cass. Hem.	Lucius Cassius Hemina (mid-second century BC) *Annales*
Cato	The Elder (234–149 BC)
Agr.	*De Agri Cultura* (*On Agriculture*), *c.* 160 BC
De Re Mil.	*De Re Militari* (Jordan, H. (ed.), 1860, *M. Catonis Praeter Librum de re Rustica Quae Extant*, Leipzig)
Censorinus *DN*	(Third century AD) *De Die Natali* (AD 238)
Charisius *Gramm.*	(Fourth century AD) *Ars Grammatica* (Barwick, C. (ed.), 1964, *Flavii Sosipatri Charisii Artis Grammaticae Libri V*, Leipzig)
Chron. 354	*Chronograph of 354* (Divjak, J. and Wischmeyer, W. (eds), 2014, *Das Kalenderhandbuchvon 354*, Vienna)
Cic.	Cicero (106–43 BC)
Att.	*Letters to Atticus* 65–43 BC
Catil.	*Against Catiline* 63 BC
Caecin.	*Pro Caecina* 69 BC
Deiot.	*Pro Rege Deiotaro ad C. Caesarem Oratio* 45 BC
Div.	*De Divinatione* (*On Divination*) 44 BC
Dom.	*De Domo Sua* (*On His House*) 57 BC
Fam.	*Ad Familiares* (*Letters to His Friends*) 62–43 BC
Fin.	*De Finibus Bonorum et Malorum* (*On the Ends of Good and Evil*) 44 BC
Font.	*Pro Fonteio* 69 BC
Har. Resp.	*De Haruspicum Responsis* (*On the Response of the Haruspices*) 57 BC
Leg.	*De Legibus* (*On the Laws*) 52–43? BC
Leg. Agr.	*De Lege Agraria* (*On the Agrarian Law*) 63 BC
Leg. Man.	*De Lege Manilia* (*De Imperio Gnaei Pompei*: *On the Command of Gnaeus Pompey*) 66 BC

Nat. Deor.	*De Natura Deorum* (*On the Nature of the Gods*) 45 BC
Off.	*De Officiis* (*On Duties*) 44 BC
Orat.	*De Oratore* (*On Oratory*) 55 BC
Phil.	*Philippicae* (*Philippics*) 44–43 BC
Prov.	*De Provinciis Consularibus* (*Concerning the Consular Provinces*) 56 BC
Rep.	*De Re Publica* 51 BC
Sull.	*Pro Sulla* (*In Defence of Sulla*) 62 BC
Tusc.	*Tusculanae Disputationes* (*Tusculan Disputations*) 45 BC
Verr.	*Verrine Orations* (*Against Verrus*) 70 BC
Curt.	Curtius Rufus (died AD 53) *Historiae Alexandri Magni*
Dio	Dio Cassius (AD *c*. 155–235) *Roman History*
Diod.	Diodorus Siculus (first century BC) *Bibliotheca Historica* (*Library of History*)
Diom.	Diomedes (late fourth century AD) *Ars Grammatica*
Dion. Hal. *Rom. Ant.*	Dionysius of Halicarnassus (60–*c*.7 BC) *Roman Antiquities*
Enn.	Ennius (239–169 BC)
Ann.	*Annals* (Skutsch, O. (ed.), 1985, *The Annals of Q. Ennius*, Oxford).
Hec. Lyt.	Hector (*ROL*: see below)
Eur. *Rhes.*	Euripides (480s–407/6 BC) *Rhesus*
Eus. *Chron.*	Eusebius (AD 260–340) *Chronicle*
Eutr.	Eutropius (AD *c*.350–400] *Breviarium Historiae Romanae*
Festus	Festus (late second century AD) *De Verborum Significatu* (L: Lindsay, W.M. (ed.), 1913, *Sexti Pompei Festi De Verborum Significatu Quae Supersunt cum Pauli Epitome*, Stuttgart)

Flaccus *Mem.* Verrius Flaccus (55 BC–AD 20), *Rerum Memoria Dignarum Libri* (Egger, A.E. (ed.), 1839, *M. Verrii Flacci Fragmenta Post Editionem Augustianam Denuo Collecta: Sexti Pompei Festi Fragmentum*, Paris)

Flor. *Epit.* Florus (AD *c*.74–*c*.130) *Epitome of Roman History*

Front. *Strat.* Frontinus (died AD 103/104) *Stratagems*

Gell. *Noct. Att.* Aulus Gellius (AD *c*.130–*c*.180) *Noctes Atticae* (*Attic Nights*)

Hdn Herodian of Antioch (AD *c*.170–*c*.240) *History of the Roman Empire from the Death of Marcus Aurelius* (AD 180–238)

Hdt. Herodotus (second half of the fifth century BC) *Histories*

Hier. *Ad Iov.* Hieronymus (AD 347–420) *Adversus Iovinianum* (Jerome, *Against Jovinianus*)

Hom. *Il.* Homer (eighth century BC) *Iliad*

Hor. Horace (65–8 BC)

  Epist. *Epistles* (1: 21 BC; 2: 11 BC)

  Od. *Odes* (23 BC)

  Sat. *Satires* (35–30 BC)

Isid. *Etym.* Isidore (AD 560–636) *Etymologies*

John of Lydus *Mens.* (sixth century AD) *De Mensibus* (*Concerning the Months*)

Joseph. Flavius Josephus (AD 37–*c*.100)

  Jew. Ant. *Jewish Antiquities*

  Bell. Jud. *Bellum Judaicum* (*Jewish Wars*)

Julius Exuperantius *History* (fourth or fifth century AD)

Just. *Epit.* Justin (second century AD) *Epitome of the Philippic History of Pompeius Trogus*

Juv. *Sat.* Juvenal *Satires* (AD *c*.65–*c*.127)

Laev. *Erot.* Laevius *Erotopaegnia* (*c*.100 BC) (Courtney, E. (ed.), 1993, *The Fragmentary Latin Poets*, Oxford)

Livy	Livy (59 BC–AD 17) *History of Rome*; *Per.*: *Periochae* (Summaries of the Books)
Lucil.	Gaius Lucilius (180–102 BC) *Satires* (Marx, F. (ed.), 1904–05, *C. Lucili Carminum Reliquiae*, vols i–ii, Leipzig)
Lut. Catul.	Quintus Lutatius Catullus (149–87 BC)
Macrob. *Sat.*	Macrobius (fifth century AD) *Saturnalia*
Mart. *Ep.*	Martial (AD *c.*38–*c.*104) *Epigrams*
Mart. Cap	Martianus Capella (AD 425) *De Septem Disciplinis* (*On the Seven Disciplines*)
Min. Fel. *Oct.*	Minucius Felix (late second or early third century AD) *Octavius*
Naev. *Inc.*	Gnaeus Naevius (*c.*270–*c.*200 BC] *Incertis Fragmenta* (*ROL*: see below)
Obsequens	Julius Obsequens, *Liber de Prodigiis* (*Book of Prodigies*; fourth-century AD epitomator of the prodigies recorded in Livy for 249–11 BC)
Oros.	Paulus Orosius (AD 375–after 418) *Historiae Adversus Paganos* (*History Against the Pagans*)
Ovid	(43 BC–AD 17)
Fasti	*Festivals of the Roman Calendar*
Metam.	*Metamorphoses*
Pac. *Teuc.*	Pacuvius (220–130 BC) *Teucer* (*ROL*: see below)
Paus.	Pausanias (wrote *c.*AD 150) *Description of Greece*
Phlegon *Mir.*	Phlegon of Tralles (reign of Hadrian AD 117–138) *Mirabilia* (*Curiosities*)
Plaut.	Plautus (254–184 BC)
Asin.	*Asinaria*
Amph.	*Amphitryon*
Bacch.	*Bacchides*
Cas.	*Casina*
Capt.	*Captivi*

Epid.	*Epidicus*
Mil.	*Miles Gloriosus*
Truc.	*Truculentus*
Pliny *Nat. Hist.*	Pliny the Elder, *Natural History* (AD 23/24–79)
Pliny *Letters*	Pliny the Younger (AD 61–117)
Plut.	Plutarch (second century AD)
Aem.	*Aemilius Paulus*
Alex.	*Alexander*
Ant.	*Marc Antony*
Cam.	*Furius Camillus*
Caes.	*Julius Caesar*
Cat.	*Cato the Younger*
Cor.	*Coriolanus*
Crass.	*Marcus Licinius Crassus*
Fab.	*Fabius Maximus*
Jul.	*Julius Caesar*
Luc.	*Lucullus*
Mar.	*Gaius Marius*
Marc.	*Marcus Claudius Marcellus*
Mor.	*Moralia*
Nic.	*Nicias*
Num.	*Numa*
Pomp.	*Gnaeus Pompey (Magnus)*
Rom.	*Romulus*
Rom. Quest.	*Roman Questions (Moralia)*
Sull.	*Lucius Cornelius Sulla*
Tib. Gr.	*Tiberius Gracchus*
Polyb.	Polybius (*c.*200–118 BC) *The Histories* (covers Roman history, 264–146 BC)
Prop. *El.*	Propertius (*c.*50–*c.*15 BC) *Elegies*
Ps.-Hyg. *Mun. Cas.*	Pseudo-Hyginus (late first–early second century AD) *De Munitionibus Castrorum* (*On the Fortifications of the Camp*)

Quint. *Inst.*	Quintilian (AD *c*.35–*c*.100) *Institutio Oratoria* (*c*.AD 95)
ROL	Warmington, E.H. (ed.), 1935–1940, *Remains of Old Latin*, vols i–iv, London
RVW	Engels, D., 2007, *Das römische Vorzeichenwesen (753–27 v. Chr.): Quellen, Terminologie, Kommentar, historische Entwicklung*, Stuttgart
Sall.	Sallust (86–35 BC)
Cat.	*The Conspiracy of Catiline*
Hist.	*Histories*
Jug.	*Jugurthine War*
Serv. *Aen.*	Servius (late fourth–early fifth century AD) *Commentary on the Aeneid*
SHA	*Scriptores Historiae Augustae* (late fourth century AD)
Sil. Ital.	Silus Italicus (AD 25–101) *Punica*
Solinus *Coll. Mem.*	*Collectanea Rerum Memorabilium* (*Collections of Curiosities*) (early third century BC)
Stat.	Statius (AD 45–96)
Sil.	*Silvae*
Theb.	*Thebaid*
Strabo	Strabo (born *c*.64 BC, writing in Augustus' reign) *Geography*
Suet.	Suetonius (AD *c*.69–*c*.122)
Aug.	*Augustus*
Calig.	*Caligula*
Claud.	*Claudius*
Dom.	*Domitian*
Iul.	*Julius Caesar*
Tib.	*Tiberius*
Tac.	Tacitus, *Histories* (AD 56–120)
Ann.	*Annals*
Germ.	*Germania*
Hist.	*Histories* (written *c*.AD 100–110)

Tert.	Tertullian (AD *c*.155–240]
Apol.	*Apology*
Nat.	*Ad Nationes* (*Against the Nations*, or *Against the Pagans*)
Spect.	*De Spectaculis* (*Concerning the Spectacles*)
The Digest	(*c*. AD 530) Compilation of Roman law
Tib. *El.*	Tibullus (55–19 BC) *Elegies*
Val. Flacc.	Valerius Flaccus (first century AD) *Argonautica*
Val. Max.	Valerius Maximus (writing in the reign of Tiberius: AD 14–37) *Facta et Dicta Memorabilia* (*Memorable Deeds and Sayings*)
Varro	Marcus Terentius Varro (116–27 BC)
Ant. Hum. Div.	Cardauns, B. (ed.), 1976, *M. Terentius Varro: Antiquitates Rerum Humanarum et Divinarum*, vols 1–2, Wiesbaden
Ling. Lat.	*De Linguae Latina* (*On the Latin Language*)
Vita Pop. Rom.	Riposati, B. (ed.), 1939, *M. Terenti Varronis de Vita Populi Romani*, Milan
Veg.	Publius Flavius Vegetius Renatus (late fourth century AD)
Mil.	*Epitoma Rei Militaris* (*Epitome of Military Matters*)
Vell. Pat.	Velleius Paterculus (19 BC–AD 31) *Historiae Romanae* (*Roman History*)
Vir. Ill.	Pseudo–Aurelius Victor (*c*. AD 350) *De Viris Illustribus Urbis Romae* (*Illustrious Men of Rome*) (Pichlmayr, F. (ed.), 1911, *De Viris Illustribus Urbis Romae*, Leipzig)
Virg. *Aen.*	Virgil (70–19 BC) *Aeneid*
Vitr. *De Arch.*	Vitruvius (first century BC) *De Architectura*
Zon.	Zonaras (AD 1074–1130) *Extracts of History*

Abbreviations of Modern Works, including Editions of Inscriptions

AE	*L'année épigraphique*
Aevum	*Aevum: rassegna di scienze storiche, linguistiche e filologiche*

AJA	*American Journal of Archaeology*
AJAH	*American Journal of Ancient History*
AJPh	*American Journal of Philology*
ANRW	*Aufstieg und Niedergang der Römischen Welt*
ArchClass	*Archeologia classica*
BAR	*British Archaeological Reports*
BICS	*Bulletin of the Institute of Classical Studies*
BMC	Mattingly, H., 1923, *Coins of the Roman Empire in the British Museum (BMC)*, London
CGL	*Corpus Grammaticorum Latinorum*
CIL	*Corpus Inscriptionum Latinarum*
CIL i²	1893–1986, *Corpus Inscriptionum Latinarum. Vol. i: Inscriptiones Latinae Antiquissimae ad C. Caesaris Mortem*, second edition, Berlin
ClAnt	*Classical Antiquity*
CNG	*Classical Numismatic Group*
CPh	*Classical Philology*
Crawford *RRC*	Crawford, M.H., 1974, *Roman Republican Coinage*, Cambridge
CW	*The Classical World*
FGrH	Jacoby, F. (ed.), 1923–58, *Die Fragmente der Griechischen Historiker*, Berlin; Fornara, C.W., 1994, vol. iiic fasc. 1-, Leiden
FHG	Müller, K., *Fragmenta Historicorum Graecorum*, vol. 4, Paris
FRHist	Cornell, T.J., (ed.), 2013, *The Fragments of the Roman Historians*, vols 1–3, Oxford
GRF	Funaioli, G. (ed.), 1969, *Grammaticae Romanae Fragmenta*, Stuttgart
G&R	*Greece and Rome*
Hermes	*Hermes: Zeitschrift für klassische philologie*
Historia	*Historia. Zeitschrift für alte Geschichte*
HRR	Peter, H.W.G. (ed.), 1914, *Historicorum romanorum reliquiae*, vol. 1, second edition, Stuttgart

HSPh	*Harvard Studies in Philology*
HThR	*Harvard Theological Review*
IG iv² 1	*Inscriptiones Graecae* iv, second edition, part 1, Berlin
IG ii²	*Inscriptiones Graecae* ii, second edition, Berlin
ILLRP	Degrassi, A. (ed.), 1957–63, *Inscriptiones Latinae Liberae Rei Publicae*, vols 1–2, Florence
ILS	Dessau, H. (ed.), 1892–1916, *Inscriptiones Latinae Selectae*, vols 1–5, Berlin
InscrIt xiii	Degrassi, A., (ed.), 1937, *Inscriptiones Italiae xiii: Fasti et Elogia*, Rome
Klio	*Klio. Beiträge zur alten Geschichte*
JAAR	*Journal of the American Academy of Religion*
JAH	*Journal of Ancient History*
JBL	*Journal of Biblical Literature*
JDAI	*Jahrbuch des Deutschen Archäologischen Instituts*
JRMES	*Journal of Roman Military Equipment Studies*
JRS	*Journal of Roman Studies*
Latomus	*La Revue Latomus*
MAAR	*Memoirs of the American Academy in Rome*
MEFRA	*Les Mélanges de l'École française de Rome. Antiquité*
Mnemosyne	*Mnemosyne: Bibliotheca Classica Batava*
Nikephoros	*Nikephoros: Zeitschrift für Sport und Kultur im Altertum*
Numen	*Numen. International Review for the History of Religions*
PBSR	*Papers of the British School at Rome*
PEG i	Bernabé, A. (ed.), 1987, *Poetarum Epicorum Graecorum Testimonia et Fragmenta*, Pars i, Leipzig
Phoenix	*Phoenix: Journal of the Classical Association of Canada / Revue de la Société Canadienne des Études Classiques*
RHR	*Revue de l'histoire des religions*
RIB	*Roman Inscriptions of Britain*
RIC	Carson, R.A.G. & Sutherland, C.H.V. (eds.), 1984, *Roman Imperial Coinage*, vol. 1, London
RMPh	*Rheinisches Museum für Philologie*
Scheer	Scheer, E., 1908, *Lycophronis Alexandra. Scholia*, vol. 2, Berlin: 1–398

SE	*Studi etruschi*
Steinby *LTUR*	Steinby, E.M. (ed.), 1993–2000, *Lexicum Topographicum Urbis Romae*, vols 1–6, Rome
Sydenham *CRR*	Sydenham, E.A., 1952, *The Coinage of the Roman Republic*, London
TAPhA	*Transactions and Proceedings of the American Philological Association*
ThesCRA	*Thesaurus Cultus et Rituum Antiquorum*
YCS	*Yale Classical Studies*

Notes on Contributors

Jeremy Armstrong

Jeremy Armstrong is a Senior Lecturer in Ancient History at the University of Auckland. He earned his BA in History and Classical Studies at the University of New Mexico in 2003, and his MLitt and PhD in Ancient History from the University of St Andrews in 2004 and 2009 respectively. He has published on various aspects of early Roman history, archaeology and warfare, including the volumes *War and Society in Early Rome: From Warlords to Generals* (Cambridge, 2016) and *Early Roman Warfare: From the Regal Period to the First Punic War* (Pen and Sword, 2016), as well as editing *Circum Mare: Themes in Ancient Warfare* (Brill, 2016) and co-editing *Rituals of Triumph in the Mediterranean World* (Brill, 2013).

Kim Beerden

Kim Beerden is a lecturer at Leiden University who specializes in the history of ancient mentalities – and especially religion. Divination is an important focus of her research and she is the author of the book *Worlds Full of Signs: Ancient Greek Divination in Context* (Leiden: Brill, 2013), which compares Greek divinatory practices to those in Republican Rome and Neo-Assyrian Mesopotamia. Beerden is currently working on the topic of other ancient ways of dealing with uncertainty about the future.

Matthew Dillon

Matthew Dillon is the Professor of Classics and Ancient History at the University of New England, Australia, and gained his BA Hons and MA at the University of Queensland. His research interests include ancient Greek and Roman religion and how religious beliefs intersected with the workings of these ancient societies. He has written several articles and books on Greek religion, most recently *Omens and Oracles. Divination in Ancient Greece* (Routledge, 2017), as well as textbooks and sourcebooks on ancient Greece and Rome. He is currently working on a monograph project concerning brutality and discipline in the ancient Greek world, with a major focus on Greek warfare. He has also published on Greek epigraphy and society.

Paul Erdkamp

Paul Erdkamp is currently Professor of Ancient History at the Vrije Universiteit Brussel. He earned his doctorate at the University of Nijmegen and subsequently became a research fellow at Leiden University. His research interests focus on the demography and economy of the Roman world, including living standards and food supply. In addition he has published on Republican historiography and Roman warfare. He is author of *Hunger and the Sword. Warfare and Food Supply in Roman Republican Wars* (Brill, 1998) and *The Grain Market in the Roman Empire* (Cambridge University Press, 2005) and edited amongst others the *Blackwell Companion to the Roman Army* (Wiley-Blackwell, 2007), the *Cambridge Companion to Ancient Rome* (Cambridge University Press, 2013) and, with Koen Verboven and Arjan Zuiderhoek, *Ownership and Exploitation of Land and Natural Resources in the Roman World* (Oxford University Press, 2015).

Lora Holland Goldthwaite

Lora Holland Goldthwaite is Professor and Chair, Department of Classics at the University of Carolina, Asheville, and obtained her PhD at UNC Chapel Hill. Her primary research interest is Roman religion, particularly of the Republic. Additional interests include: Roman mythology; other ancient religions, especially Etruscan and Greek religions; the intersections of Greek and Latin literature and material culture; and the history of women in scholarship on Roman religion. Her teaching interests include a range of topics from Homeric epic to Roman comedy. She has two book projects in progress as well as journal articles and conference papers. In 2017, she was a contributor for an exhibition at the Florence Archaeological Museum in Italy on recent finds from Cetamura del Chianti, where she runs the laboratory for archaeological materials during the summer dig season. Her new book, co-edited with Sinclair Bell (Northern Illinois University), is titled *At the Crossroads of Greco-Roman History, Culture, and Religion: Papers in Memory of Carin M. C. Green* (Archeopress, 2018).

Christopher Matthew

Christopher Matthew completed his undergraduate degree in ancient history at the University of New England in 2005 before moving to Macquarie University, Australia, to complete a doctorate examining ancient Greek warfare in 2009. The author of several books and numerous articles on ancient warfare, in 2015 he was awarded the title of Honorary Associate by Macquarie University in recognition of his position as a leading professional with expertise in his field and for his 'demonstrated commitment to excellence, education, and research'. His work has formed the basis of several documentaries and radio interviews, and has resulted in his acting as a historical and creative consultant for museum exhibitions and film projects. He has taught at a number of universities across Australia and has given more than twenty public lectures at various universities, museums and other institutions across the country in recent years. In 2010 Chris took up the position of Lecturer in Ancient History at the Australian Catholic University where he teaches units on the Greek City-States, the Fall of the Roman Republic, Pompeii, Ancient Greek Drama, the Ancient Near East, and the History and Geography of Ancient and Modern Rome.

Brandon Olson

Brandon R. Olson received his Ph.D. in Archaeology from Boston University and is currently an Affiliate Faculty member in the History department at Metropolitan State University in Denver, Colorado. He is an enthusiastic scholar of the ancient world who seeks to combine the historical and archaeological records to explore social issues within the Hellenistic and Roman armies. His relevant publications include 'The Dedication of Roman Weapons and Armor in Water as a Religious Ritual' (2011) and 'Roman Infantry Helmets and Commemoration among Soldiers' (2013).

John Serrati

John Serrati is an adjunct professor in the Department of Classics and Religious Studies at the University of Ottawa. He is also an assistant professor of Classics at John Abbott College in Montreal. He has published extensively on Hellenistic and Roman Sicily, as well as on the role that royal and state economies played in providing elites from the Hellenistic and Roman Republican worlds with the means to wage war. These themes are broadly explored in his latest volume, *Money and Power in the Roman Republic* (ed. with H. Back and M. Jehne, 2016). His current research examines gender and Roman warfare, specifically looking at the role of women in the martial society of the Roman Mid-Republic, as well as the place of war goddesses in the Roman pantheon.

List of Figures

Preface

We editors hope that readers will find *Religion and War in the Classical World. The Roman Republic* useful in understanding the relationship which the ancient Romans of the Republic believed they had with their gods – and those of Rome's enemies – when conducting war. This volume is the second of a three-part series, and was preceded by *Religion and War in the Classical World. Ancient Greece*, and will be followed by *Religion and War in the Classical World. The Roman Empire*. The editors would like to thank most sincerely the Pen & Sword editor Philip Sindell for encouraging this three-volume project. His support and patience have been most appreciated and without him this multi-volume project would not have proceeded.

The editors have aimed to make the volume as easy to use and consult as possible. Many of the authors cited by the contributors are little-known or obscure, even to scholars. It is hoped that the abbreviations list will make clear the various ancient authors, coins and inscriptions being referred to and discussed in this volume. Details are given of editions where the texts of these authors, some unfortunately still not translated into English, can be consulted.

This volume brings together a team of international scholars, from seasoned veterans of academia to newly established young academics. Together, their contributions provide a wealth of information and understanding about the interconnectivity of religious practice and thought in the warfare conducted by the Romans in the Roman Republic (509–27 BC). These papers present a society in which the gods and war were inextricably and indelibly linked.

Chapter 1

Introduction: New Perspectives on Religion and Warfare in the Roman Republic: 509–27 BC

Matthew Dillon

In Roman religious and political thought, it was the favouring of Rome by the city's chief and supreme god, *Jupiter Optimus et Maximus*, in conjunction with Rome's attention to religious matters, that had led to the establishment of the Roman Empire and Rome's ascendancy over the Mediterranean world.[1] For the Romans themselves, their dominion over the known, 'civilized' world, was not only the result of feats of arms or superior strategy, tactics and soldiering. Rather, it was their firm belief that it was the gods who had ordained that the Romans would conquer the world. This aspect of Roman imperialism, and their *imperium* – rule – has received attention from scholars, especially with respect to individual topics such as a Roman general in battle devoting his life to the gods (the *devotio* ritual), when a Roman commander sacrificed himself to achieve victory, and topics such as the declaration of war as a religious ceremony. But there is certainly room for more scholarship about Roman warfare and the beliefs concerning the involvement of the Roman gods in this. In this volume, eight international scholars of Roman warfare examine crucial aspects of Roman warfare and its connection with the gods. The period covered is the Roman Republic (509–27 BC), while a companion volume on the Roman Empire deals with the same themes in relation to the imperial period.

Existing Scholarship on Religion and Roman Warfare in the Republic

In terms of existing scholarship on religion and Roman warfare, there is nothing in English scholarship to compare with Pritchett's *The Greek State at War, volume 3: Religion* (Berkeley, 1979), which surveyed the role played in warfare by Greek religion. In German scholarship, Jörg Rüpke's *Domi Militiae. Die religiöse Konstruktion des Krieges in Rom (Domi Militiae. The Religious Construction of War in Rome*; Stuttgart, 1990) is now three decades old. It remains an invaluable study, dealing with numerous aspects, such as war and the Roman calendar, divination, the religion of the legions, supplications of the gods for victory and the religious ideology of warfare. There is no comparable treatment in English. Where this current volume contributes to scholarship is in bringing together international expertise over a broader range of topics, and dealing with them in more depth, with the focus on the Roman Republic.

Another volume of interest is *The Religious Aspects of War in the Ancient Near East, Greece, and Rome* (2016, Leiden), edited by Krzysztof Ulanowski, in which several scholars deal with various aspects of the beliefs of ancient peoples about the involvement of the gods in warfare. Three essays focus on religion and war in the Roman world, examining the *Ara Pacis Augustae*, the legitimation of warfare in the reign of Antoninus Pius, and soldiers and their religious experience in official cult ceremonies. These are all useful essays, but it is hoped that the current volume will provide, by virtue of its narrower chronological scope, a wider coverage of religion in one part of the ancient world – Roman hegemony and its associated religious and cultic aspects in the Roman Republic.

There are, of course, numerous works on Roman warfare, including several recent 'handbooks' and book series on Greek and Roman warfare. Yet some of these do not have the words 'gods' or even 'religion' in their indices. In these studies, the gods are strangely silent, as if the mechanics and practices of war can be studied as somehow distinct from the religious – and political – ideologies that pervaded the practice of Roman warfare. This is not a criticism, as the aim and orientation of such works are specifically 'secular', exploring the mechanics of military endeavour, rather than its societal and religious constructs. Yet this lack of attention to Rome's gods and the role they were believed to play in Roman warfare and ritual emboldens the editors to hope that this particular volume will be of some utility.

The Stages of Roman War: From Declaring Military Hostilities to the Celebration of the Roman Triumph

Warfare in the Roman Republic was not commenced without due reference to the gods. As a major – and risky – undertaking, the blessing of the gods was considered to be mandatory. Moreover, the permission of the gods to engage in warfare was required. In 'Religion and Roman Warfare in the Middle Republic', John Serrati opens this volume, introducing many key introductory concepts, such as the religious dimension of the declaration of war. In the Roman Republic, warfare and religion were indelibly linked and pervaded every aspect of Roman society. Warfare affected social and economic mobility, politics, conceptions of manhood and citizenship, and even space and spatiality; in all these aspects, religion played a role. From senatorial meetings of the late winter where potential wars for the coming spring would be discussed, to the votes in the *comitia centuriata* to commence hostilities, and the rituals in March to open and in October to close the campaigning season, religion governed the annual rhythm of warfare at Rome, and with it, the year-to-year life of the Roman citizen. The purpose of the Roman state religion was to maintain the *pax deorum* (the peace with the gods), the harmony between the Romans and their gods; doing so ensured the safety and prosperity of the citizen community. Similarly, military action was also viewed as ensuring the safety and prosperity of the populace, and thus all military activity had religious implications. The Romans declared *ius bellum* (just war) through a ritual process conducted by special priests, the *fetiales*, thus ensuring that they did not offend their gods.

Warfare gave rise to another religious phenomenon, that of the *evocatio* ritual, which Matthew Dillon explores in 'Evocatio: Taking Gods away from Enemy States and Peoples'. From Sumerian times, victors were accustomed to take the statues of defeated cities back to their own city, where it was thought the god or gods who were represented by and incarnate in these statues would serve and show favour to their new masters. The Romans developed a sophisticated theology and ritual for removing the statue or statues of gods from their original cities, in the *evocatio*, or 'calling out from' ritual, for which the Latin author Macrobius quotes the formula (*carmen*). The *pax deorum* so intrinsic to the Roman understanding of their relationship with the gods meant not only peace with Rome's gods but also a willingness to invite the gods of enemy states into the Roman pantheon, enticing these gods to abandon their worshippers with the promise of grander worship at Rome: fuller cultic ritual and a better temple than the one they possessed in their original city. The ritual was not simply asking a god to abandon a city but to wage psychological terror on it: to terrorize and strike fear into their current worshippers while the god deserted them.

War was fought with a variety of arms and weaponry, to which individual soldiers could become emotionally attached, and which could serve as votive offerings to the gods in return for the safety of the soldier. In 'The Religious Functions of Roman Arms and Armament', Brandon Olson considers how weaponry could take on religious connotations. At its height, the Roman Army was the most efficient and successful fighting force the world had ever seen. The success of the system derived from many factors, including the various offensive and defensive implements employed by its soldiers. The utilitarian functions of Roman arms and armament are obvious: the objects protected the user and were requisite for offensive manoeuvres. Soldiers found themselves in a unique position, in that the Romans sought to engage in various forms of religious expression, but often stationed far from the epicentre of the Roman cultural milieu: as a result they came to adopt and adapt new rituals to fulfil these needs. Various practices associated with these religious expressions often focused on votive deposition and commemoration, both of which were enacted through some form of engagement with their equipment. Votive deposition in the form of dedications to some form of religious deity in sacred places and the commemoration of posthumous memory represent ad hoc religious practices devised during the Republic by soldiers who were interacting far from their natal homes. Just as Roman religious praxis evolved over time in Rome, so too did it also change in the provinces and frontier zones through the agency of the Roman Army.

Related to the dedication of military equipment was the cult of Rome's legionary eagle, and Christopher Matthew, in 'The Cult of the Eagles', examines how this symbol, one of the most readily associated with the world of ancient Rome, was much more than just a military standard. As the identifying emblem of the Roman military following the reforms of Gaius Marius in the late second century BC, the eagle (or *aquila*) was much more to the soldiers and people of Rome, and assumed all manner of religious characteristics – from displaying prophetic abilities, to having its own festivals, to being the subject of worship and devotion. The evidence that has come down from Roman times demonstrates that, by bestowing such quasi-divine attributes on an emblem that signified, not only the main god of the Roman pantheon, but also the might and power of Rome through its military and its *imperium*, all members of the Roman world were somehow devotees of the 'cult' of the *aquila* regardless of their age, gender or social position – whether they consciously recognized themselves as such, or not.

While the role of women in warfare has been traditionally neglected by scholarship,[2] women did have a specific role to play in the rituals associated with Roman warfare. Lora Holland Goldthwaite, in 'Woman, Warfare, and

Religion in the Roman Republic', examines how the advent of women's studies and related fields has seen the modern understanding of the female role in ancient Roman society undergo dramatic changes. Scholarship by primarily female scholars since the early 1990s has opened new areas of inquiry and is reshaping our understanding of topics that have long been of interest, such as the Vestal Virgins. It is becoming increasingly clear that Roman women at every level of society had a role to play in the nexus of religion and warfare during the Roman Republic, whether written into legends and myths or in real life as attested in literature and material culture. The interplay of women, religion and warfare is especially apparent in the priesthoods of the Early Republic, in public festivals and in the legendary history of early Rome that continued to inform later periods, as well as in the decades of civil unrest during the Late Republic.

War is a desperate time, and sometimes calls for desperate measures and practices which would not ordinarily be countenanced let alone considered. In 'War, Vestal Virgins, and Live Burials in the Roman Republic', Paul Erdkamp explores the phenomenon of the burials of live individuals at Rome in times of military exigency and crisis. The live burials of a Greek and Gallic man and woman in 228, 216 and 113 BC already puzzled the writers in the imperial period. The anachronistic accounts that exist – either apologetic or hostile – offer no evidence on the religious ideas that led to these actions. One modern argument related the live burials of Greeks and Gauls to those of unchaste Vestal Virgins that preceded them. Another argument sees these ritual killings as the direct response to hostile threats in the wake of military disaster. Recently, Várhelyi and Eckstein argued in favour of the latter hypothesis,[3] denying a meaningful link to the live burial of unchaste Vestals. The ancient sources, however, only offer weak support for the link to military disasters. Various writers depict the ritual killing of the Greek and Gallic victims as an act of atonement that was required by the Sibylline Books to restore the *pax deorum* after the polluting act of killing a Vestal Virgin. The ritual killing of a Greek and Gallic couple is linked to Roman concerns about military success, but in a more general sense than as immediate responses to specific disasters. Vestal Virgins played a vital role in the rituals that maintained the *pax deorum* on which Rome's success on the battlefield depended. Hence, unchaste Vestals needed to be ritually expunged, but the trials and deaths of condemned Vestals in themselves caused a grave threat to the *pax deorum*, a pollution that needed to be atoned. In 228, 216 and 113 BC, the ritual killing of the Gallic and Greek couple was ordered by the Sibylline Books in order to expiate the ritual killing of the Vestals that preceded it. This interpretation of the events in these years puts a different light on the link between warfare and human sacrifice, on the religious attitudes to enemies and on the response to pollution in Republican Rome.

Fundamental to ancient religious practice and belief was divination, and as war was one of the most crucial of human endeavours in which the Roman gods were believed to take an active part, the interpretation of omens and prodigies in the context of warfare was taken extremely seriously by the Romans. In 'With the Gods on Their Side: Divination and War in the Roman Republic', Kim Beerden examines divination as a powerful tool in the decision-making process in the context of Republican Roman warfare. *Auspicia, prodigia*, extispicy, dreams and oracles were deemed necessary ingredients for successful battle. When decisions needed to be made they needed to be the right ones, supported by the supernatural. It does not matter what motivations drove the elite to use divination, whether they were 'genuine' or 'political' or had aims of 'stress reduction' or 'manipulation'. Divination was believed to be of crucial importance to both the minds and physical realities of those engaging in ancient warfare – everyday practices of warfare cannot be understood without providing the supernatural with an important role.

The culmination of military activity was the celebration in the city of Rome of major military victories: this was the triumph, or the lesser celebration, the *ovatio*. Jeremy Armstrong, in 'Triumphal Transgressions', explores the nature of the Roman triumph as a transgressive ritual which helped to moderate and delineate the boundary between the civic and military spheres (*domi et militiae*) in Rome. Imbued with an intrinsic tension and part of a complex set of socio–political and religious negotiations, the triumph functioned alongside the institution of *imperium* as part of a system to authorize and regulate military power and control. Going back to Rome's archaic period, both the early triumph and early *imperium* seem to have offered the region's elite a way to bring their extramural military power into the community of Rome – both figuratively and literally. As Rome and its elite developed, both the triumph and *imperium* evolved, with *imperium* increasingly becoming little more than a ritualized confirmation of authority by the late fourth and third centuries BC. The triumph, however, seems to have maintained its role in regulating the boundary between the civic and military spheres until the start of the Empire. Although its purpose and role shifted, the tension and negotiation between these areas (and across the *pomerium*) remained intact, serving as a vital mechanism in the performance of Roman politics in the *res publica*. It was only with the breakdown of the boundary between *domi et militiae* in the reign of Augustus that the triumph seems to have lost its true *raison d'être*, finally transforming into the simple 'victory parade' for which it is sometimes mistaken as part of the propaganda of the imperial family.

All of these essays come together to provide a holistic treatment of the role the Romans assigned to their gods in warfare, and the numerous rituals involving these deities in the context of warfare.

The Roman Gods and 'Empire Without End' (Imperium Sine Fine)

The Roman campaigning season commenced with the double-headed god of openings and closings, Janus (in this aspect being Janus Geminus, 'Twin'). When the doors to his temple in Rome were opened, Rome had declared war, and the doors remained open until peace was secured. As many of Rome's wars were co-terminous, the doors were very seldom closed from the third century BC on. Its doors were the 'Twin Gates of War', which the consul opened when war was declared.[4] Ovid in his *Fasti*, in which he explains to his readers the various festivals and gods of the Romans, day by day for the first six months of the year (he never completed the other six), indicates the significance of the opened and closed doors in an imaginary dialogue he conducts with the god Janus:[5]

> 'But why do you hide in times of peace and open your gates in times of war? Without a moment's hesitation, he answered, providing the explanation I asked for: "So that when the people sally forth to war, my gate is open wide, and so too when they return. I shut up the doors in peace-time, so that peace cannot escape, and under Caesar's *numen* I will be closed for quite some time."'

Caesar's *numen* is a reference to the divine spirit (*numen*) of Caesar Augustus, who boasted that while he governed Rome the doors to Janus' temple, which he notes had only ever been closed twice before since the city was founded (traditionally, in 753 BC), had been closed three times.[6] It was in fact Augustus' great-great-grandson, the emperor Nero, who would also close the doors of Janus' temple and commemorate this on coins, not simply for the message of peace that this conveyed, but for Nero to claim a link with his (divine) ancestor Augustus.[7] The connection between

Janus as opening and closing war is nowhere clearer than on bronze *aes* coins illustrating the two-headed god on its obverse, while on the reverse showing a Roman warship (Figure 1.1).[8] These were minted from during the Punic Wars (264 BC on) and into the 30s BC, showing the relationship between Janus and a crucial component of Roman armament, the fleet. His double head on the coin announces that the context for the reverse of the coin is warfare. In a detail not usually noticed, the small house-like feature on the prow of the Roman warship is in fact a little shrine to the god, carried on the ship, at which the god could be worshipped and his aid invoked as the crew went into battle.[9]

Before the Roman army went to war, it would undergo a *lustrum*, a purification. This involved a *suovetaurilia* sacrifice, quite traditional in Roman religion as a purificatory ceremony. This is depicted on the marble so-called 'Altar of Domitius Ahenobarbus' (Figure 1.2), which in fact is a statue base from Rome's temple of Neptune, with a scene carved on each of its four sides, and dates to sometime in the second century BC. One scene depicts the god Mars (larger than the mortal worshippers, just to the left of centre), armed for war, standing behind his altar, waiting to receive his sacrificial offering. This must be the altar to Mars in the *Campus Martius* ('Field of Mars'). Behind him stand two musicians who would play during the sacrifice to drown out any sounds of ill-omen. Behind them stand soldiers. A censor (one of the two appointed) is touching the altar. Attendants bring up the *suovetaurilia* sacrifice: a sow (*sus-*), a sheep

Figure 1.1: Bronze *aes*. Obverse: laureate head of bearded Janus. Reverse: prow of warship (right), legend: ROMA; after 211 BC. Courtesy of *CNG* 810041.

Figure 1.2: The *lustrum*, purification, scene from the marble 'Altar of Domitius Ahenobarbus', end of the second century BC, length: 147cm; Louvre Ma 975.

(*ov-*) and a bull (*taur-*), hence the name of the sacrifice. One figure – taken to be the second censor – carries a flag, the *vexillum*, an accoutrement of the Roman Army in the field. Once this ceremony was performed, the army could depart Rome, purified for war in a ceremony over which the god of war presided. On the far left is a scene taken to be a registration of citizens, the census which was held every five years by the two Roman censors, which determined to which property class citizens belonged and to which role in the Roman Army they would be assigned (if they had sufficient property).[10]

Janus and Mars were only two of the many Roman gods concerned with war; and given the predilection of the Romans for warfare, it is no surprise that they believed in many deities whose support they trusted they could rely on – if these gods were scrupulously worshipped and venerated. In their descriptions of the Battle of Actium (31 BC), in which Octavian, the future emperor Augustus, defeated the naval forces of Antony and Cleopatra, Roman poets, such as Virgil and Propertius,[11] had gods playing an active part in the victory of Octavian, with the Egyptian gods proving to be no match for the Roman.

Virgil's description of Actium comes in the form of an iconographic prophecy. In Book 8 of the *Aeneid*, he describes how the metallurgical god Vulcan crafted a shield for Aeneas, and on it included scenes of the Battle of Actium – a battle which for Aeneas was several hundred years in the future. Virgil describes how Augustus Caesar was depicted at the head of his fleet, with Senate and People, the Penates (the Roman deities of the household and hence here of the state), 'all the great gods' and Actius Apollo (Apollo of Actium). This victory of Octavian over Antony and Cleopatra at Actium was conceptualized as the victory of the Roman gods against the eastern ones:[12]

'Monstrous gods of every kind and barking Anubis bear arms against Neptune and Venus and against Minerva. In the middle of this struggle, Mavors [Mars] rages, encased in iron, with the grim Furies [Dirae] from on high, and in ragged garment Discordia rushes exultantly, while Bellona with her bloody scourge follows her. Apollo of Actium seeing this, from above was bending his bow. All Egypt and India, all Arabs, all Sabaeans they turned and fled in terror at all of this.'

It was particularly this victory which meant the end of the Roman civil wars. For the successful outcome of this battle for Octavian, representing Rome, the gods were held to be responsible, safeguarding the Roman state from the eastern despotism of a woman. Apollo had a particular hand in the outcome, according to Virgil sinking ten enemy ships, each with one arrow from his bow. Hence Augustus established for him a temple at Actium, and emblazoned him on coinage. A silver denarius depicts Augustus on the obverse and Apollo on the reverse. Augustus is 'DIVI F', the son of the god (Julius Caesar), and is shown bareheaded as a sign of his piety before the gods. Apollo himself is depicted with flowing robes which billow around him as they are wafted by the ocean breeze. He holds his cithara (lyre) and plectrum (he is thus Apollo Citharoedus), presumably in this case to sing of his victory in the naval battle. The exergual letters 'ACT' of course stand for Actium, while 'IMP X' refers to Augustus being hailed as Imperator ten times (Figure 1.3).[13] The particular coin illustrated here was struck at Lugdunum (Lyons) in 15 BC, but another had been struck at Paphos on Cyprus in 22 BC – Augustus hence ensuring that reports of Apollo's aid for him at Actium were widely circulated. An ancient temple of Apollo at Actium was repaired and an existing festival in the god's honour was revitalized by Augustus to celebrate his victory.[14]

While Virgil and Propertius have obviously employed some poetic licence, it does raise the theological question of how the Romans perceived the gods as assisting them in battle. When Camillus vowed to Pythian Apollo a dedication if the Etruscan city of Veii be taken (392 BC), what form did Camillus construe this divine assistance would take? Did he, like Virgil and Propertius in their descriptions of Actium, imagine that Apollo would actually 'put in an appearance' and fight for the Romans, or was it more an exertion of divine will? Presumably, the latter was the case. But the Dioscouri, Pollux and Castor (Greek: Dioskouroi, Polydeukes and Kastor, the sons of Zeus-Jupiter), were said to have been actually present and to have assisted the Romans to defeat the Latins at Lake Regillus in 496 BC.[15] In the *evocatio* ritual, the god deserting its city was asked in fact to take an active

Figure 1.3: Silver denarius. Obverse: Augustus, Divi F, son of the god (Julius Caesar). Reverse: Apollo singing of his role at the Battle of Actium; 27 BC–AD 14. Courtesy of CNG 478846.

role, as seen above: 'upon the populace and community [of the besieged city] fix fear, anxiety, and a forgetfulness.'[16] While this is militarily 'passive' as the deity was not asked to fight against its own people, its psychological assistance was required.

Returning to Actium, Virgil continued his description of Aeneas' shield. Augustus entered Rome in a triple triumph and dedicated in thanksgiving 300 temples to Italy's gods; Roman matrons flocked to the temples worshipping the gods in thanks; around all the altars were the carcasses of sacrificial thanksgiving victims; and Augustus himself, seated at the temple of Apollo, reviewed the tribute of all the nations.[17]

Polybius, the Greek historian who spent time as a hostage at Rome, and then accompanied Scipio to Carthage for the Third Punic War (149–146 BC), saw the growth of Roman power as a single process with a definite result – and he himself did not live to see the expansion of this empire in the spectacular Roman military conquests to the east and west in the first century BC:[18]

'What I have undertaken to record is in fact a single episode, the how, the when, and the means by which the subjugation of the known world to the dominion of Rome occurred, a phenomenon which has a recognisable beginning, a fixed duration, and an end which cannot be disputed.'

Although Polybius does not mention the involvement of Rome's gods in the empire's continued growth, he articulates an idea which the Romans thought themselves. Jupiter, in Virgil's *Aeneid* a century later, makes a specific promise to Venus, the mother of Aeneas, ancestor of the Romans:[19]

> 'I limit the Romans' empire by no boundaries or periods of time;
> I have granted them empire without end [*His ego nec metas rerum*
> *nec tempora pono*; imperium sine fine *dedi*] ... The Romans, masters
> of the world, nation of the toga. This is my decree.'

So entrenched was the religious formulation and ideology that Rome's gods had created and safeguarded its empire, that Augustine in the fourth century AD vehemently attacked it several times in his *The City of God Against the Pagans* (*de Civitate Dei Contra Paganos*),[20] to prove that the Christian God and not the Roman gods had made Rome rule the world: it was God's divine plan, not Jupiter's. Pagans at Rome had in fact been quick to blame the Christians for the sack of Rome by the Goths in AD 410 – the unthinkable had happened and to traditional Romans, the Christians were to blame, for not only neglecting but reviling the worship of the gods who had made Rome great and granted it such longevity of *imperium*. Augustine was spurred on to write his *City of God* precisely by this accusation, writing:[21]

> 'Rome was stormed by the Goths under their King Alaric and felt
> the impact of a great disaster, and the worshippers of the many
> false gods, whom we are accustomed to call 'pagans', attempted
> to attribute this to the Christian religion, and began to blaspheme
> against the true God more sharply and bitterly than ever.'

Ovid has a similar view of empire to that of Virgil's Jupiter: as Ovid articulates it, other countries have fixed boundaries, but Rome has none. He is writing not of boundaries in simply a profane sense, but is discussing the god of boundaries, Terminus. The world of Rome, and the world itself, are one and the same entity.[22] In the *Metamorphoses*, Ovid argues that Caesar, because of his numerous conquests, which he describes, and because he was the father of Augustus (through adoption), deserved to be a god.[23] Tertullian, the Christian author, criticized the various non-Roman gods taken from captured cities and residing thence in Rome, who in return for Roman worship overlook that they are captives and promise the Romans *imperium sine fine*.[24] The idea is not simply, therefore, a literary construct of Virgil, but was an intrinsic aspect of the religious ideology of the Roman construction of their *imperium*, and was recognized as such by Christian authors.

Jupiter's role in Roman warfare is made explicit in the coinage from the crisis of Hannibal's invasion of Italy in 218 BC and subsequent years. The silver Victoriatus series was minted from 218 BC, and continued until about 170 BC. The coin was minted and circulated in southern Italy and was mainly used in the Second Punic War for Roman payments to its Greek allies there (many of whom in fact defected to Hannibal). The message of the coinage was clear: Jupiter as the god of Rome would prevail and Victoria would crown many battlefield victory monuments in the form of captured enemy armour secured to a post (see Figure 1.4).[25] Jupiter's laurel wreath on these coins is particularly relevant as it indicates that he has been crowned as victor: he will defeat the Carthaginians.

Cicero was in no doubt whatsoever that the gods had fashioned Rome and destined it to rule the world, and this was because of Roman piety toward the gods. It was not simply a passive receiving of the gods' favour, but the active cultivation of divine favour and assistance, particularly by Roman commanders:[26]

'Our empire was made vast by those commanders who were obedient to religious practices [*religiones*]. Furthermore, if we wish

Figure 1.4:   Silver Victoriatus. Obverse: laureate head of Jupiter. Reverse: a winged Victoria is placing a victory wreath on a trophy of arms, captured from the enemy. Minted in Apulia, 211–210 BC. Courtesy of CNG 446143.

to contrast our Roman ways with those of foreign races, while in all other ways we are equal – or even inferior – in the practice of religion [*religio*], that is to say, in the worship of the gods, we are vastly superior.

The Romans conceived that Rome was destined, with the support of the gods, to rule over the entire civilized world, for all of time. Rome was not bound by time, as Jupiter promises, and its extent was limitless: the known world. Cicero, as seen, makes a specific connection between the exceptional Roman devotion to the gods, when compared to other peoples, and the extent of their empire. Piety had made Rome great, with the gods supporting without qualification Rome's expansion. The immortal gods watched over Rome and its empire, which would endure forever and through all lands: through all time and all places, delineated neither by chronology nor geography, an immortal empire. Cicero encapsulates the theology of Roman power and empire when he writes: 'It is the immortal gods [*di immortales*] themselves who watch over this city and this empire.'[27] The connection between religion and military success cannot have been made more explicit.

Notes

1. Cic. *Har. Resp.* 19.
2. See now Fabre-Serris & Keith, 2015, but a discussion of women's vital religious role in ancient Greek and Roman warfare is lacking.
3. Várhelyi, 2007; Eckstein, 2012.
4. Vir. *Aen.* 7.607–15 (607: *geminae Belli portae*, with Bellum the goddess of war); also Plut. *Numa* 20.1. V A 12.198. Servius *Aen.* 7.621–22 comments that Virgil is echoing Enn. *Ann.* 225–26 (Skutsch): see Green, 2000: 307 n.12.
5. Ovid *Fasti* 1.277–82, compare with Enn. *Ann.* 225–26 (Skutsch); see also Livy 1.19; Pliny *Nat. Hist.* 34.33; Varro *Ling. Lat.* 5.156, 165; Plut. *Numa* 20.1–2. See Green, 2000: 302–06.
6. Aug. *Res Gest.* 13; Hor. *Odes.* 4.15.4–9, *Epist.* 2.1.255–56; Flor. *Epit.* 2.34.64; Suet. *Aug.* 22; Dio 53.26.5; Orosius *History Against the Pagans* 6.21.11. See for its doors closing: Silberberg–Peirce, 1986: 306–08; Green, 2000.
7. For a description of the temple: Procopius *On the Wars* 1.25; and it appears on several imperial coins; see Platner-Ashby, 1929: 278–80.

8. Figure 1.1: diameter 35mm; *CNG* 810041; Crawford *RRC* 56/2; Sydenham *CRR* 143. Cf. Ovid *Fasti* 1.229–54: Ovid asks Janus why a ship appears on the (reverse of the) *aes* coin with Janus' double-head. Yet the reply the god gives is a false aetiology of Ovid's (that the god Saturn arrived in Italy on a ship). The ship on the coin is a ramming warship and denotes Janus' connection with warfare. Moreover, one Janus *aes* type depicts three ship prows on the reverse: Crawford *RRC* 342/7e.

9. Grueber *CRCBM* 30 incorrectly sees this as, 'the forecastle on the prow is represented with a pointed roof'; it does not, however, in fact appear on ships without Janus on the obverse.

10. For this scene, see Keppie, 2002: 37 fig. 19, 84 pl. 3, 197–98.

11. Prop. *El.* 3.11.41, 4.6.25–70.

12. Virg. *Aen.* 8.698–706.

13. Figure 1.3: diameter: 19mm; *CNG* 478846; *RIC* I 171a.

14. Suet. *Aug.* 18; Dio 50.12.7, 51.1, 53.1.4.

15. Dion. Hal. *Rom. Ant.* 6.13.

16. Macrob. *Sat.* 3.9.8.

17. Virg. *Aen.* 8.714–23.

18. Polyb. 3.1.4–5, compare 1.1.5: in less than 53 years the known world has come under Roman rule.

19. Virg. *Aen.* 1.278–79, 282–83 (Dillon & Garland, 2015: doc. 5.6, pp.209–11); Serv. *Aen.* 1.278 (a disappointingly meagre summary comment). See Kennedy, 1999: 26–31; Dueck, 2003: 215–16; Lowrie, 2003: 58–59.

20. August. *Civ.* esp. his detailed refutation at 4.8, but see also 1.3, 2.19 (specifically quoting the lines of Virg. *Aen.* 1.278–79), 3.3, 3.14, 4.9, 4.13, 4.15, 4.26, 4.28, 5.12 ('the *imperium* of the Romans was not propagated and preserved through the worship of the gods'), 19.12.

21. August. *Civ.* 2.69.

22. Ovid *Fasti* 2.683–84; interestingly, several hundred years later, August. *Civ.* 5.21 makes a point about the god Terminus, who had to move because of the emperor Julian's repulse by the Persians when he invaded across the Roman frontier.

23. Ovid *Metam.* 15.752–64.

24. Tert. *Apol.* 1.26.

25. Figure 1.4; diameter: 17mm; Crawford *RRC* 102/1; Sydenham *CRR* 115.

26. Cic. *Nat. Deor.* 2.3.8. He has a similar sentiment at Cic. *Har. Resp.* 19.
     Cf. Livy 44.1.11–12; Dion. Hal. *Rom Ant.* 2.18.1–2.
27. Cic. *Dom.* 56.143.

Bibliography

Dillon, M.P.J. & Garland, L., 2015, *Ancient Rome. Social Historical Documents from the Early Republic to the Death of Augustus*, 2nd edn, Oxford.

Dueck, D., 2003, 'The Augustan Concept of "An Empire Without Limits"', in Dickhardt, M. and Dorofeeva-Lichtmann, V. (eds), *Creating and Representing Sacred Spaces. Göttinger Beiträger zur Asienforschung* 2–3: 211–27.

Eckstein, A.M., 2012, 'Polybius, the Gallic Crisis, and the Ebro Treaty', *CPh* 107: 206–29.

Fabre-Serris, J. & Keith, A. (eds), 2015, *Women and War in Antiquity*, Baltimore.

Green, S.J., 2000, 'Multiple Interpretation of the Opening and Closing of the Temple of Janus: A Misunderstanding of Ovid Fasti 1.281', *Mnemosyne* 53.3: 302–09.

Grueber, H.R., 1910, *A Catalogue of the Roman Coins in the British Museum*, vol. 1, London.

Kennedy, D.F., 1999, 'A Sense of Place: Rome, History and Empire Revisited', in Edwards, C. (ed.), *Roman Presences: Receptions of Rome in European Culture, 1789–1945*, Cambridge: 19–34.

Keppie, L.J.F., 2002, *The Making of the Roman Army From Republic to Empire*, London.

Lowrie, M., 2003, 'Rome: City and Empire', *The Classical World* 97.1: 57–68.

Platner, S.B. & Ashby, T., 1929, *A Topographical Dictionary of Ancient Rome*, London.

Pritchett, W.K., 1979, *The Greek State at War, volume 3: Religion*, Berkeley.

Rudd, W.J.N., 1983, 'The Idea of Empire in the "Aeneid"', *Hermathena* 134: 35–50.

Rüpke, J., 1990, *Domi Militiae. Die religiöse Konstruktion des Krieges in Rom*, Stuttgart.

Silberberg-Peirce, S., 1986, 'The Many Faces of the Pax Augusta: Images of War and Peace in Rome and Gallia Narbonensis', *Art History* 9.3: 306–24.

Ulanowski, K., 2016 (ed.), *The Religious Aspects of War in the Ancient Near East, Greece, and Rome*, Leiden.

Várhelyi, Z., 2007, 'The Specters of Roman Imperialism. The Live Burials of Gauls and Greeks at Rome', *ClAnt* 26: 277–304.

Chapter 2

Religion and Roman Warfare in the Middle Republic

John Serrati

The subjects of Roman religion and Roman warfare have, separately, continued to spark interest and to receive significant coverage in the secondary literature. Yet, considering that these phenomena were arguably the two most important aspects of Roman culture and society during the Republic, they have only rarely been treated together. In the middle Republic, warfare and religion were indelibly linked and pervaded every aspect of society. Warfare affected social and economic mobility, politics, conceptions of manhood and citizenship, and even space and spatiality; in all these aspects, religion equally played a role. From senatorial meetings of the late winter where potential wars for the coming spring would be discussed, to the votes in the *comitia centuriata* to commence hostilities, to the rituals in March to open and in October to close the campaigning season, religion governed the annual rhythm of warfare at Rome, and with it, the year-to-year life of the Roman citizen. The purpose of the Roman state religion was to maintain the *pax deorum*, the harmony between the Romans and their gods; doing so ensured the safety and prosperity of the citizen community. Similarly, military action was also viewed as ensuring the safety and prosperity of the populace, and thus all warfare, by definition, had religious implications.

The link between warfare and religion can perhaps best be seen in the Roman calendar, which not only revolved around war, but reflected the martial nature of society at Rome. The calendar, or at least the Roman perception of real time, in many ways begins with Aeneas and his arrival in Italy, which was seen as inaugurating a new epoch.[1] In this sense, the figure of Aeneas is, of course, linked with that of Augustus, who likewise sought to portray himself as the founder of a new era. The calendar itself is similarly marked with dozens of anniversaries which served to connect the Romans with the major focal points in what they perceived as their history.[2] Thus, along with a measurement of time, the calendar was a touchstone for memory, and aside from annual religious observances, the main anniversaries which it marked involved warfare. In the middle Republic, the recollection of past triumphs served to pass on ideals of manhood, citizenship and duty, and challenged the citizens of the present to live up to and even surpass the deeds of their ancestors. Equally as important, the calendar marked the annual rhythm of warfare in the Mid-Republic via a series of festivals in March, the opening of both the campaign season as well as the Roman year itself, and October, the last month in which fighting took place. Therefore, the calendar served to steel the Romans for battle through both the triggering of memory as well as a series of religious rituals which acted to prepare the legionaries psychologically for combat.

Religion continued to be an important factor once the campaign had begun and the army was in the field. The gods were always consulted before combat was joined, and a commander ignored an unfavourable omen at his own risk. On campaign, and even in the heat of battle, vows to certain gods would be taken and promises of future dedications made; during a siege, enemy gods might be induced through specific rituals to abandon their people and join the Romans. Afterwards, the interplay between religion and warfare at Rome changed the city itself, as these vows and inducements produced a very significant number of triumphal temples; funded by the plunder taken in conflict and dedicated to gods who were seen as having brought about victory, they became prominent physical memorials to the power of both individual generals as well as the people of Rome. Thus war and religion interacted with each other on a daily basis, as the calendar, the gods and the physical spaces inhabited by their temples and festivals all featured martial overtones. War and religion were part of the rhythm of life in the middle Republic; not only was war itself in part a religious undertaking, but military victory was the primary method of re-establishing order within the Roman divine *cosmos*.

The Calendar and the Rhythm of War at Rome

The calendar at Rome revolved around warfare; in the middle Republic, the year opened with March, which contained a slew of festivals in which the Romans prepared for the coming campaign season. October similarly contained ceremonies which brought the year's warfare to a close. All of this was representative of a time when the Romans went to war with neighbours on an annual basis, and therefore the calendar, beyond measuring the passage of time, also came to sanctify warfare at Rome, as well as to mark its annual rhythm. Moreover, the calendar marked anniversaries of significant battles as well as the dedications of temples which themselves were financed by the plunder taken from successful campaigns. It thus linked together not only disparate periods of time, but equally connected contemporary Romans to their ancestors as well as to the heroes of the city's mythical past. Thus the calendar itself was a *lieu de mémoire* – literally, as it was publically displayed from 304 – since the rituals which punctuated its measurement of time both recalled the glories of Rome's martial past and called upon future generations to imitate their forefathers.[3]

The Roman calendar was largely divided into days marked F (*fastus*, days on which all political, legal and economic activities were permitted) and N (*nefastus*, days on which, because of the observance of certain religious rites, most political, legal, and economic activities were prohibited). A number of surviving calendars also contain other abbreviations alongside the aforementioned two: C, NP, FP, EN, R, QRCF and QSDF; these, however, are significantly less understood. Regardless, January and early March featured a substantial number of days designated F, and even February, despite having several festivals associated with the closing of the year, also had a number of F days in the middle and end of the month. The main reason for the significant number of *dies fasti* in this period is that the Senate and people's assemblies were required to meet more frequently in order to deliberate on the coming campaign season. Therefore, other than the end-of-year rites in February, the later winter months had only a small number of religiously illicit days, specifically because the Romans required this time to plan for war.[4]

While the coming year's operations were being debated in the Senate, any possible declarations of war first had to go through the fetial priests; in theory, the *fetiales* – who appear to have been a common feature in most Latin communities – were the most significant link between warfare and religion at Rome, as it was their college which ensured that a conflict was an *ius bellum* ('just war'), and was thus in line with the *pax deorum*. Once a war was considered *ius* by the *fetiales*, the conflict had been sanctioned by the gods themselves, and victory would be taken as a sign of this divine favour. Successful war, therefore, was vital to the Roman conception of the *cosmos*.[5]

The *fetiales* were responsible for the sanctification of treaties; additionally, when any Roman was condemned for violating the laws of war, the *fetiales* were charged with turning these men over to the enemy. Those thus surrendered were themselves sacrifices for the restoration of the *pax deorum*. Unlike their other responsibilities where they acted on their own, in exercising the former function, the *fetiales* operated at the behest of the government. Five such cases are recorded: three (321, 236 and 137 BC) for making treaties which the Senate subsequently rejected, and two (266 and 188 BC) when Roman magistrates had violated the sacrosanctity of foreign ambassadors.[6] Such practices were rare, however, and the primary function of the *fetiales* always lay with declarations of war. In this regard, their role was purely religious, as they consulted the gods in order to determine whether a potential conflict was *ius* (religiously just or pious).[7] In this rite, one fetial was designated as the *pater patratus* and was empowered to act on behalf of the Roman people. As described by Livy, once the government determined that a foreign people had committed an offence against Rome or one of its allies, the *fetiales* undertook an ambassadorial mission to the potential enemy and demanded recompense, returning to Rome afterwards.[8] In this sense, one could argue that the main role of the *fetiales* was not to initiate war but to maintain peace.[9] Given, however, that no ancient source claims the *fetiales* had to make their demands to any magistrates or representatives of a potential enemy, their role appears to be far more concerned with the performance of proper ritual rather than the avoidance of war itself. The rite clearly existed for the Romans alone and had nothing whatsoever to do with formally notifying the enemy of the coming conflict. All the same, if no recompense were forthcoming, after thirty-three days the *fetiales* returned to the border of Roman or allied territory and there called upon the gods to witness that the Romans had been unjustly treated. The priests thus declared the conflict to be *ius* and ceremonially cast a special spear onto the foreign soil. This rite served as the formal declaration of war on the part of the Roman people.[10] There seems little doubt that the ritual was of great antiquity, and given that Plautus parodies the fetial rite in his play *Amphitryon*, first staged between 190 and 185 BC, must have lasted well into the second century at the least.[11]

The idea of a lack of recompense as being the cause of Roman conflict is embedded within the Latin language itself, as the archaic verb *hostio* means both 'to recompense' as well as 'to fight against'. Ennius even uses the term as a pun, with Achilles promising to recompense his enemies via his weapons (*Quae mea comminus machaera atque hasta hostibitis manu*; You weapons, my sword and my spear, in close combat some recompense will come from my own hand).[12] Pacuvius employs the term similarly, where the character Telamon promises to return (*hostio*) the violence of any enemy in kind.[13] Moreover, the idea that the purpose of warfare was to restore the *pax deorum*, as well as the notion that all conflict was rooted in vengeance, can be seen in the words related to *hostio*, namely *hostis* (enemy) and *hostia* (sacrificial victim). The latter were not merely offerings to the gods out of piety but were given in exchange for something tangible within the human *cosmos*. Thus an enemy was anyone who had not provided Rome with the deserved remuneration for the wrong it had suffered, and enemies who died on the battlefield were themselves offerings which were given to the gods in exchange for a Roman victory.[14]

The fetial rite may very well have originated with the earliest days of Roman state formation; the Gallic sack of 390 BC for the first time allowed something akin to a government to arise in Rome. In the period beforehand, clan-based warlords held much of the power, and Roman legends such as Coriolanus illustrate that such men might form part of the Senate in one year, and then could attack Rome with a private army in the next.[15] But the catastrophes of 390 BC saw several private armies shattered first at the Battle of River Allia and then in the subsequent sack of Rome. After these events, the Senate emerged as the only body powerful enough to defend Rome, and from this point onwards there was a decline in private warfare – in 384 BC Marcus Manlius became the last Roman to be executed for attempting to seize the city with a private force – and an increasing use of troops which had been mustered by and fought on behalf of the state. Thus the *fetiales* and their rite may have been an attempt by the Senate to take control of external violence. Rather than have a private war band strike at an enemy on behalf of the city, the Senate used the *fetiales* to monopolize external projections of violence. As the *fetiales* acted exclusively at the behest of the Senate, their rite symbolized the idea that warfare was now the exclusive domain of the Roman government.[16]

According to Servius, in 280 BC the *fetiales* were unable to perform their ritual declaration of war at the border of enemy territory for the conflict against Pyrrhus due to the distance involved; they therefore acquired a patch of land near the temple to Bellona and henceforth declared that the spear-throwing rite was now happening 'as though in enemy territory' (*quasi in hostili loco*).[17] There is no *a priori* reason to reject this notion, since beforehand, Rome's wars were indeed largely local, and the *fetiales*, even on foot, could have reached a potential enemy, performed their rite and returned to Rome all within the month of February. Appian, however, relates that in 281, the Romans were already engaged in operations against the Samnites when the conflict with Tarentum began. The consul Lucius Aemilius Barbula was issued orders to suspend his current campaign and proceed against the Tarentines. This action on the part of the Romans caused Tarentum to ask for help from Pyrrhos, who invaded Italy and began operations against Rome in the winter of 280 BC, before the traditional opening of the campaign season in March.[18] Thus on both occasions, in 281 and again in 280 BC, the *fetiales* may not have had time to perform their traditional rite at enemy territory; this was in part due to the distance of Tarentum from Rome, but also because in 281 BC the conflict arose within the middle of another war, and in 280 BC operations began during the winter, not allowing the priests a chance to travel. Lacking enemy territory at which to perform their ritual, they therefore consecrated a space near the temple of Bellona and outside the *pomerium* at Rome as foreign soil so that the fetial spear could still be cast, allowing the coming conflict to be considered *ius*, and thus maintaining the *pax deorum*.[19] All the same, this initiated a slow decline in the importance of the fetial college; once Rome's wars came to be further overseas and against more organized powers who had formal means of diplomacy, the *fetiales* ceased to be dispatched in order to demand reparations. There is, however, every indication that the college, although diminished in prestige, survived into Augustan times and perhaps even afterwards, continuing to carry out the rite with the fetial spear at the temple of Bellona.

Once the rites associated with the new year were carried out at the end of February and the beginning of March, the Romans initiated a series of rituals to open the warfare season.[20] Arguably the most important of these, and certainly the longest in duration, were the dances of the *Salii*. These priests were divided into two colleges of twelve members; the *Salii Palatini* undertook their rituals in the name of Mars Gradivus, while the *Salii Collini* did so for Quirinus. The geographical designations linked with their names likely reflects an archaic time before Rome merged into a single urban centre, when the area was still divided into a series of villages which operated with a degree of independence.[21] That the members of the colleges were called *suodales*, the archaic Latin term for retainers or warriors who served a clan chieftain, further testifies to the antiquity of their priesthood, as does the Salian meal at the end of each day's rites, something which likely originated with warriors' feasts in early Rome. The dances lasted the entire month of March and the dancers circulated throughout the city.[22] The priests paraded in archaic military dress and equipment: embroidered tunics cinched with bronze belts beneath robes striped in scarlet and edged in purple; pointed headgear; spears, swords and figure eight-shaped shields called *ancilia* (singular *ancile*), one of which was said to have fallen from heaven, the others being copies attributed to the Mamurius Veturius, whose talents were celebrated in the *Carmina Saliaria* ('Salian Songs').[23] These hymns, which mainly celebrated Mars as well as other martial deities, were sung by the Salian priests as they danced, and were composed in a form of Latin so archaic that the lyrics were already difficult to understand when Lucius Aelius Stilo Praeconinus wrote a commentary on them in the second century.[24] The priests alternated between dancing altogether and dancing in smaller, individual units, a ritual which would seem to mirror the functioning of an actual Roman legion, since the latter could function as a whole or could be broken up into constituent parts. The dance itself was martial, and mimicked the actions of battle; in doing so, the *Salii* illustrated to the youth of Rome the movements which needed to become second nature through vigorous training, and which would someday allow them to fight lockstep in combat with their fellow citizens.

There is little doubt that priests with functions similar to the *Salii* existed in many Italian communities. The leaping warriors on the Plikaśna *situla*, an Etruscan vessel from Chiusi dated to the mid-seventh century, likely represent *Salii*-type figures, as do the men with shields on an Etruscan fourth-century engraved gem (see Figure 2.1).[25] Moreover, a number of Italian communities had celebrations for Minerva in March; in Rome this was

Figure 2.1: Fourth-century BC Etruscan gem showing men, possibly Salian priests, carrying the *ancilia*, shields sacred to Mars and which the *Salii* used in their martial dances. Courtesy of Museo Archeologico Nazionale di Firenze.

undertaken on the first day of the *Quinquatrus* festival. While the other days were dedicated to Mars, the first, on 19 March, was in honour of Minerva, and celebrated skilled craftsmanship and metalworking. Therefore, in the *Quinquatrus*, the Salian dance and *Carmina Saliaria* with its lauding of Mamurius Veturius the blacksmith, Mars and Minerva are intertwined, as she served as the patron goddess of those who made the tools of war.[26]

The *Salii* represent war as controlled violence on behalf of the entire civic community, and their hymns bring routine aspects of civil life such as *ludi*, choral singing, metalworking, military exercise and rites-of-passage into the sphere of warfare.[27] The latter aspect would have been of particular importance, as the *Salii* and their rituals coincided with the *Liberalia* festival on 17 March, where 16-year-old males assumed the *toga virilis* and became full citizens. They thus represented a coming-of-age for young men within the Roman citizen community. As ideas concerning manhood were deeply linked to a male's ability to serve as a Roman soldier and fight in the thick of combat, the initiation into the citizen body made the young men eligible for military service, and they began to participate in the *dilectus*, the annual mustering of men on the Campus Martius for division into army units. The Salian rites, therefore, not only symbolized this manhood, but also served to prepare the young recruits for their first military experiences. And the martial dances did more than open the campaign season for the citizen community; they marked the transition of young males from passive observers to active fighters.[28] Moreover, the presence of dancers known as the *virgines saliae*, as well as a *praesula* (female lead dancer), would indicate that the Salian rite symbolized the coming-of-age for young women as well. This perhaps emphasized females – who birthed and raised the male soldiers – as part of the civic community which was about to go to war.[29]

While the dances of the *Salii* lasted for the entirety of March, individual rituals associated with the opening of the campaign season began in earnest in the middle of the month. The *Equirria* on the 14th and the *Liberalia* on the 17th were both coming-of-age festivals. The former involved young *equites* racing their horses in the Campus Martius; the rite was heavily associated with Mars and has a degree of symmetry with the October *Equus* (*infra* 26).[30] The *Liberalia*, as previously mentioned, was the day where 16-year-old males assumed the *toga virilis* and became full citizens. There may equally have been a rite for girls becoming women on this day as well.[31] The 17th was shared with the obscure rite of the *Agonium Martiale*, where a ram was sacrificed to Mars; Festus tells us that *agonia* was an archaic word for *hostia*, and thus we may perhaps see this as a rite where Rome's enemies were offered up as victims to the god of war.[32] The high point of the war rituals came with the *Quinquatrus* from 19–23 March, the first day of which was dedicated to Minerva and was a celebration of skilled craftsmanship and metalworking, while the remainder were in honour of Mars. The middle days consisted of games and gladiator shows, and the festival culminated on the 23rd with the *Tubilustrium*.[33] This was a purification of the war trumpets (*tubae*) for the coming campaign season.[34] Purification rituals represented rites-of-passage from one state to another; in this case peace to war and then war to peace. They both inaugurated and sanctioned new beginnings. In this context, Charisius speaks of a lustration of arms at the beginning of the *Quinquatrus*, and this likely indicates that an *Armilustrium* took place on 19 March.[35] While an *Armilustrium* did take place in October to cleanse the weapons and close the campaign season, this likely was not meant to cleanse them after the act of killing. As a rule, lustrations happened before battle: there was certainly one before the *dilectus* and the formation of the legions, and then another when the army set off on campaign. There is also clear evidence that the ritual was performed when a commander set foot in camp for the first time.[36] Thus an *Armilustrium* in March to open the campaign season makes sense.[37] The *Armilustrium* in October also took place on the 19th, providing a symmetry between the rites for the beginning and ending of a campaign.

More than anything else, the war rituals contained within the month of March served a psychological purpose. From the new year's rites for Janus on the 1st, to the *Tubilustrium* on the 23rd, to the Salian rites which lasted for the entire month, March was filled with religious preparations for war.[38] The volume and omnipresence of the ceremonies throughout the city would have served to emphasize warfare as a communal endeavour on the part of the Roman citizenry, depicting the city within as a harmonious *domus* as its citizen-soldiers prepared themselves to venture into the hostile *militia*. Moreover, the period would have helped mentally prepare the soldiers to enter battle – something which would likely have been an exciting yet frightening prospect for the younger recruits – as the rituals emphasized manhood, coming-of-age, civic duty and harmony between the Roman people and their gods. Valerius Maximus even says as much, claiming that the purpose of Roman song was to 'make the young more eager to imitate the noble deeds of their elders'. Varro claims much the same thing.[39] Thus, like the war memorials and victory temples with which the city was filled, like the weapons, both personal and *spolia*, which were displayed in family homes, and like the stories of martial prowess which were passed on orally from one generation to the next, the March religious rites also served as a form of societal indoctrination, bonding soldier to society and illustrating the long tradition of which he was now a part. They furthermore reinforced the notion that the individual's ultimate goal was to etch his own name into this tradition by living up to or even surpassing the deeds of his forefathers.[40]

In the autumn, October itself represented the closure of the warfare season and the re-establishment of harmony between Rome and its neighbours; thus the month began with a series of rites at the temple of Fides on the Capitol.[41] On the same day, the *Tigillum Sororium* took place. For the origin of this ritual, Livy and Dionysius both put forth a story whereby the legendary seventh-century Roman hero Publius Horatius was made to pass under a beam (*tigillum*) in order to cleanse himself after he had murdered his sister (*soror*) Camilla. He also erected altars to Juno Sororia and Janus Curiatius, the latter either because he was acquitted of the crime by the *comitia curiata* or because he had recently defeated three members of the *gens* Curiatia in battle, one of whom had been engaged to his sister.[42] This is, however, undoubtedly a folk etymology, as the *Tigillum Sororium* is far more likely to be a purification rite whereby armies returning from the field passed under the beam in order to start the process, culminating in the October *Armilustrium*, where they would be cleansed of the blood and dirt with which they had been stained during battle.[43] Moreover, like some of the rites from March, this also appears to have been a coming-of-age ritual, as the sacrifices at the altar of Janus Curiatius were very likely undertaken when a young man joined a *curia*, while Juno Sororia presided over girls who had reached puberty. Thus the rites of the *Tigillum Sororium* were not only meant to act as a lustration for a returning army, but also to admit to the citizen ranks the young men who had served in their first campaign season and the young women who were now of age to give birth to warriors and become Roman mothers.

Of all the rites to close out the campaign season, the October *Equus*, while perhaps not the most important, was likely the most popular. On 15 October, a chariot race would be held in the Campus Martius in honour of Mars. One horse from the winning team would be sacrificed and its tail then taken by the *Flamen Martialis* to the Regia so that the animal's blood could be sprinkled upon the hearth there. The victim was then decapitated and its head adorned with bread. Festus says that the rite was to ensure good crops, which would fit well with the description by Cato of Mars as a deity associated with fields and agriculture as well as war.[44]

Nonetheless, rites for Mars almost always have a military aspect, and its placement on the Campus Martius as well as the assurance of Timaios that the animal was a warhorse killed with a spear – the weapon sacred to Mars – speaks to its martial associations.[45]

On the same days as the October *Equus* there were other games, known as the *ludi Capitolini*, which provide a symmetry with the events in March, as athletic and equestrian contests were clearly important to the opening and closing of the warfare season. The *ludi Capitolini* were of great antiquity, and Roman tradition held that they were inaugurated either to celebrate the conquest of Veii in 396 BC or, more likely, the defeat of the Gallic assault on the Capitoline in 390 BC.[46] Ennius, in a passage which likely alludes to the games, attributes them to Romulus, and mentions running and boxing as two of the events; some of the contestants, he says, were 'rubbed down with oil, made supple and ready to take up arms', and thus we may infer that the games had martial overtones and featured armed contests as well.[47] There is evidence that the games were for Jupiter Feretrius ('Jupiter who blesses weapons'), a deity of significant antiquity who was heavily associated with the *spolia opima* and had his own priestly college amongst the *fetiales*.[48] Feretrius may refer to the act of striking and killing (*ferio, ferire*) an opponent in battle. More likely, or even alongside this, the name possibly derives from the striking of a treaty. Not only does *icio, icere* refer both to the physical act of striking as well as the concluding of a treaty, but *silex*, or sacred flintstone, was used in the fetial rite when a treaty was struck (*Id ubi dixit, porcum saxo silice percussit. Sua item carmina Albani suumque ius iurandum per suum dictatorem suosque sacerdotes peregerunt. Foedere icto trigemini, sicut convenerat, arma capiunt*; When Spurius had spoken these words, he struck the pig with a sacred flintstone. By their dictator and priests, the Albans likewise pronounced their own formulas and their own oath. When the treaty had been struck, the two sets of triplets, in accordance with the agreement, armed themselves). That the Jupiter Feretrius temple on the Capitoline featured no cult statue and housed only a sceptre and a *silex* would seem to confirm this interpretation.[49]

Finally, on 19 October, an *Armilustrium* took place to cleanse weapons; here, the *Salii* put their sacred shields away for the winter.[50] Thus October was a month dedicated to the closing of the war season; the rites at the temple of Fides began the process by which the Roman community cleansed itself of enemy blood and purified its weaponry. Just as they had taken part in the opening of the campaign season, so the *fetiales*, or at least their paraphernalia, were involved with games in honour of the deity who oversaw treaties and the cessation of the year's hostilities. Afterwards, there were no war festivals between the end of October and the beginning of March. In this sense, the doubling of Mars as both an agricultural deity and a war god is clear, as the campaign season and the farming year were in harmony, serving to regulate life in Rome on an annual basis. These two aspects, war and agriculture, in turn manifested themselves in the Roman calendar, and are similarly reflected in the Roman pantheon.

War and the Roman Pantheon

Roman martial deities covered all aspects of war and society. Mars represented courage, discipline and loyalty on the battlefield. On the level of the aristocracy, he personified strength and strategy in war, as well as victory. His purview was the *militia*, operating beyond the city against Rome's enemies. His doublet Quirinus symbolized the men of Rome as they exercised their political rights in the *domus* of the city. Together, therefore, Mars and Quirinus personified the life of the male citizen in Rome as *quirites* within the *pomerium* and as *milites* displaying their *virtus*, their manhood, outside the walls of the city. Although the worship of Jupiter was of undeniable importance to the Romans, Mars commanded often equal and at times even greater significance. And as the prevalence and frequency of warfare increased at Rome, so too did Mars play a greater role in the city's religious life. While other deities certainly had warlike associations, Mars was the pre-eminent god of the martial culture which had developed by the middle Republic. Of the archaic Capitoline triad, only Mars has a month named after and dedicated to him; he is the only god with a full 'season' of festivals. In his role as both a god of war and of agriculture, and in his doubling with Quirinus, Mars covered virtually every aspect of Roman life, and was therefore a personification of the annual Roman rhythm of farming, political activity, and war.

   Two of our earliest written sources for Mars are the *Carmen Arvale* inscription and the *suovetaurilia* ritual described by Cato.[51] The *Carmen Arvale* inscription is from the early third century AD. The text itself, however, is in archaic Latin and goes back at least to the fourth century BC, and possibly even the sixth.[52] In the hymn, Mars is invoked for protection against agricultural pestilence (*Neve luerue Marmar sins incurrere in pleores*; Marmar, do not allow pestilence and destruction to fall upon the people[53]). The role of Mars in the hymn is as a god of agriculture, and there is no hint of his function as a war deity. This is made clear by the use of *lues*, which refers to agricultural pestilence, and especially by *rue*, which comes from the verb *ruo*, *ruere* and implies destruction in a specific agricultural context; in its earliest form, *ruo*, *ruere* refers to the violent churning up of the earth involved with ploughing, and is related to the word *rustica*.[54] Similarly, Cato invokes Mars Pater for the protection of his lands and his crops.

> 'Mars Pater, I pray and beseech you to be gracious and merciful to me, my house, and my household; for this purpose I have ordered that the *suovetaurilia*[55] be led around my lands, my property, my farm; so that you may keep away, ward off, and remove sickness, both seen and unseen, barren crops and natural disasters, and unseasonable weather; and that you permit my harvests, my grain, my vineyards, and my plantations to flourish and to bring forth good harvests, to preserve the health of my shepherds and my flocks, and give strength and good health to me, my house, and my household.'[56]

Thus, there is no question that Mars in his early mythology has an agricultural function. This can likewise be seen in the etymology of his original Latin name: Mavors, which means 'nourishing man'. At the same time, however, it can also mean 'conquering man', and thus Mars appears to have always had a dual nature as both an agricultural deity and a god of war.[57] Although associated exclusively with agriculture in the passage by Cato, Mars Pater was the name used by Publius Decius Mus in his *devotio* at the Battle of Veseris against the Latins in 340 BC (*infra* note 72).[58] As well, the sacrifices at the Altar of Mars in the Campus Martius on 1 March may have been to Mars Pater Victor, though this is by no means certain.[59] Finally, the intersection between war and agriculture in the god Mars is furthermore evident in the rite of the October *Equus*, a ritual which took place annually on 15 October and helped close the warfare season (*supra* p.26).

In the guise of a war god, Mars was known as Mars Gradivus, with the *Salii Palatini* as his own college of priests (*supra* pp.22–24). Both Livy and Vitruvius speak of a temple to Mars outside the *pomerium*, with the former stating that it was founded in 388 BC. A statement by Servius confirms that this was the temple specifically to Mars Gradivus.[60] This identification is germane as Gradivus is the god Mars when he is representative solely of war. The word *gradivus* may refer to marching, an apt etymology for a temple from which armies departed on campaigns. It can also be translated as 'rampaging', signifying the power of a Roman army and the effect of warfare on the countryside. Equally, however, *gradivus* may refer to the act of physically stepping outside the *pomerium*, furthering the idea of the *pomerium* as the dividing line between the *domi militiaeque*.[61] The structure stood on the outside of the Porta Capena on the Via Appia, in between the first and second milestones from Rome. On account of the temple, this stretch of the Via Appia came to be referred to as the Clivus Martis, and the temple was sometimes called 'Mars in Clivo'. The site served as the muster point for Roman armies who were about to set out on campaign. A temple of this sort dedicated in 388 BC fits well with Roman history; furthering the point made when discussing the *fetiales* (*supra* p.21), in the years and decades immediately after the Gallic sack of the city, the Senate appears to have taken greater control of the city's military forces, eliminating the private, clan-based forces which dominated beforehand. Thus the temple of Mars outside the Porta Capena served as the muster point for armies which were genuinely Roman in character, raised via the *dilectus* and commanded by elected magistrates.[62]

As a war god, the male Mars came to be associated with martial discipline and civic duty; he was the embodiment of *virtus*, a character trait which the Romans saw as innate in themselves. In the Mid-Republic, he was synonymous with battlefield courage as well as the ability to endure the hardships of combat, including death.[63] Mars had no negative aspects to his persona; like *virtus*, he was always viewed as a positive force whose role was to aid Rome's armies and generals.[64] In the Mid-Republic, Mars was not only a god of war but specifically a god of Roman victory, and the latter was brought about by *virtus*. Thus the god was associated with the aspects of war which the Romans most valued in the Mid-Republic. In fact, as the god of courage, battlefield aggression, and conquest, Mars was the very personification of Roman *virtus*, and was thus likewise representative of both citizenship and manhood at Rome during the third and second centuries BC, if not earlier.

Mars represents the Romans when they are marshalled for war outside the *pomerium*. Quirinus, on the other hand, appears to represent Roman males when they exercised their power in the political assemblies within the city. Possibly of Sabine origin, the name likely comes from *co-viri*, or 'men together', referring specifically to this political function. Like Mars, Quirinus also presided over agriculture, as his *flamen* officiated at the *Robigalia*, a festival for a healthy harvest.[65] His consort Hora herself must be an agricultural deity, as her name is related to both the seasons as well as to grain.[66] Yet he was also a god of war; he has his own college in the *Salii Collini*, whose priests, like the *Salii Palatini* for Mars, performed war dances throughout March to open the campaign season (*supra* pp.22–24). Additionally, in the battlefield *devotio* of Publius Decius Mus, Quirinus features in between two war deities, Mars Pater and Bellona, and he is listed amongst other martial deities in a passage by Varro.[67]

Quirinus seems to be connected with the beginning of hostilities; he is invoked in the fetial rite for the declaration of war, and at times is combined with Janus, a god who represents the opening of the campaign season. In this function, he is referred to as Janus Quirinus or Janus Quirini.[68] Janus himself also has aspects of a war deity; the opening and closing of doors was not only associated with the opening and closing of the year, but with the opening and closing of the campaign season as well as the marching of the army beyond the *pomerium*. He is also named, before Jupiter himself, in the *devotio* of Publius Decius Mus.[69] That said, his most famous connection to warfare remains his shrine in the Forum, whose gates were only closed when the Republic was at peace. As Janus, however, is certainly a god who similarly marks the passing of time, the archaic rite of opening and closing the doors of his shrine in the Forum should not be seen as marking the beginning and ending of war, but as symbolizing the beginning and ending of a year. As the former also marked the opening of the campaign season in the Mid-Republic, the rite came to be understood as symbolizing war itself. Thus after the civil wars, Augustus could safely co-opt this ritual in order to claim that the closing of the doors to Janus' shrine illustrated the peace which he brought to the Mediterranean.[70] Beforehand, the doors for the shrine of Janus could not have symbolized peace as such sharp divisions between war and peace did not exist in Mid-Republican Rome; in that era, peace was not seen as the absence of conflict, but as a state of *concordia* brought about by a season of successful war.

While Mars, Quirinus, and Janus may have presided over Roman rituals associated with annual warfare and agricultural rhythms which were them-selves associated with the life of the average male citizen, in between the rituals to open and close war there was the fighting, and this was the realm of Bellona. She personified the idea that warfare stemmed from a Roman desire for vengeance and also served as the primary means for the restoration of the *pax deorum* after the Romans had been wronged. She furthermore represented combat itself, in all of its positive and negative forms. While clearly existing alongside him, Bellona is in some ways Mars' opposite, as he is strategy and she chaos. The passage which most clearly links Bellona to Mars and warfare comes from Varro:

'Bellona, the goddess of war, is said to come from *bellum* or "war"; she was formerly Duellona, from *duellum*. Mars is named from the fact that he commands the *mares*, the males in war, or that he is called Mamers by the Sabines, amongst whom he is a favourite. Quirinus is from *quirites*. *Virtus* or "valour", as with *viritus*, is from *virilitas* or "manhood". *Honos*, meaning "honour or office", is said to be from *onus*, "burden"; therefore *honestum*, "honourable", is said of that which is *oneratum*, "loaded with burdens", and it has been said that, "Burden is the honour which maintains the state." The name of Castor is Greek, that of Pollux likewise from the Greeks; the form of the name which is found in old Latin literature is Polluces, like the Greek Πολυδεύκης, not Pollux as it is now. Concordia or "concord" is from *cor congruens*, meaning "harmonious heart".'[71]

Here, Varro lists nearly every Roman deity and hero associated with war. The order is also very intentional, as the passage begins with Bellona, who by the author's day was associated with strife and chaos, and comes to a close with Concordia, as the ultimate goal of all war at Rome, at least from a religious standpoint, was the maintenance and restoration of the *pax deorum*.

Yet Bellona did not always carry the negative connotations she did in Varro's day. Her role in the archaic Roman pantheon may have been more significant in the days when Mars doubled as an agricultural deity. While she is often interpreted as simply the personification of war or as emblematic of the chaos of conflict, evidence points to a far more nuanced deity who was an important part of the Roman pantheon during the Republic. Firstly, Bellona features prominently as the fifth deity mentioned in the *devotio* of Publius Decius Mus at the Battle of Veseris (Vesuvius) against the Latins in 340 BC, where she follows Mars Pater and Quirinus:

'Janus, Jupiter, Mars Pater, Quirinus, Bellona, Lares, new gods (*Novensiles*), native gods (*Indigites*), you gods who hold both us and our enemies in your power, and you, divine Manes, I invoke and worship you, I beseech and beg your favour, that you fortify the might and bring about the victory of the Roman people, the Quirites, and visit fear, weakness, and death upon our foes. As I have pronounced these words, on behalf of the *res publica* of the

Roman people, the Quirites, on behalf of the army, the legions, and the auxiliaries, I devote the legions and auxiliaries of the enemy, together with myself, to the divine Manes and to the earth.'[72]

With these words, Decius charged headlong into the enemy lines, sacrificing himself to the gods. The battle supposedly turned on this action and the Romans won the day. Decades later, at the high point of a battle in Etruria between a Roman army and a force of Etruscans and Samnites in 296 BC, the Roman commander, Appius Claudius Caecus, made the following vow: '"Bellona, if you grant us victory today, then I hereby vow a temple to you." Having pronounced this, he began to match his colleague (Lucius Volumnius Flamma Violens) in courage, and then the army began to match his, as though the goddess were inspiring him'. As with Decius, this turned the battle and the Romans emerged victorious. Fulfilling the vow, Caecus dedicated a temple to Bellona on 3 June 293 BC; this stood prominently at the north-western end of the Forum Holitorium, next to that of Apollo.[73] Epigraphically, Bellona also features amongst eight other Roman deities whose names are individually inscribed on a series of dishes which have been dated to the mid-third century. These were likely used for libations. Bellona's dish also contains the earliest and only Mid-Republican representation of her (Figure 2.2).[74] Finally, in the early second century, she appears in a list of deities within the prologue to the *Amphitryon* by Plautus.[75]

Moreover, her name itself likely reflects the idea that warfare was viewed with a degree of positivity at Rome during the middle Republic. The older form of Bellona's name, Duellona, as well as the archaic Latin word for war, *duellum*, is almost certainly related to *duo* and signifies a fight between two sides or, perhaps in its most ancient meaning, an instance of single combat.[76] By the mid-third century, though in all likelihood significantly earlier, this began to change to *bellum* and the corresponding Bellona.[77] The etymology of *bellum* is possibly from the description of warfare as *bella acta*, 'good or valorous deeds'. The shift perhaps came about because warfare had by this time come to be seen as the best role for the citizen, something reflected by the contemporary works of Cato the Elder, particularly his preface to the *De Agricultura*.[78] While battle could be negative, war itself, and its corresponding personification in Bellona, could be viewed as a positive undertaking, both on the level of the individual as well as for society as a whole. In every respect, she appears to be a deity who could and did help her adherents, and her powers in war were not to be taken lightly.

Figure 2.2: A libation dish depicting Bellona, the goddess of war. Etruscan red figure terracotta, *c*.250 BC; diameter: 14cm, height: 5.7cm; Louvre K614. Courtesy of Art Resource ART560734.

Bellona is perhaps best known for the aforementioned temple dedicated by Caecus. Here, the Senate greeted returning generals and listened to their petitions for a triumph. As such, there is no question that the temple was *extra pomerium*, close to the very beginning of the Roman triumphal route.[79] As with the aforementioned temple to Mars Gradivus outside the Porta Capena (*supra* p.29), the positioning beyond the *pomerium* was normal for war gods; they specifically operated in the *militia* rather than the *domus*, and any magistrate requesting a triumph would have to do so before crossing the *pomerium*.[80] Indeed, no temple for a deity exercising a function related to war stood within the *pomerium* until that of Mars Ultor (dedicated in 2 BC).[81] After 280 BC, the Columna Bellica in front of Bellona's temple was home to the fetial rite, as the *fetiales* were unable to perform their ritual declaration of war at the border of enemy territory for the Pyrrhic War in that year; in consequence, they acquired a patch of land by the Columna Bellica in front of the temple to Bellona and declared this to be enemy territory (*supra* pp.21–22).[82]

The fetial rite provides a clue to the role of Bellona in Rome's martial pantheon. In framing themselves as victims and in demanding recompense, we can see that the Roman concept of warfare is essentially one of revenge. There is no question that, on a practical level, warfare at Rome was about social prestige and personal enrichment, but on a conceptual level, as illustrated by the speech Livy puts into the mouth of the Samnite general Herennius Pontius after the defeat of a Roman army at the Caudine Forks in 321 BC ('The Romans ... shall not rest until they have wreaked manifold vengeance on your heads'[83]), war for the Romans was seen as the primary method for righting wrongs, bringing about justice, and as stated by Varro (*supra* pp.31–32), restoring *concordia*. Furthermore, it has already been seen how the idea of a lack of recompense as being the cause of Roman conflict is embedded within the Latin language itself, as the archaic verb *hostio* means both 'to recompense' as well as 'to fight against' (*supra* pp.20–21). In this regard, one has to look no further than Lucretia's demand for justice, Dido's curses or the burning of Aeneas' ships to see that females are portrayed as more vengeful in Roman literature.[84] Therefore, the idea of vengeance in Roman conflict fits well with the notion of a female war deity. Virgil even picks on the idea as he associates Bellona with the Furies, three beings whose primary duties were vengeance, justice and the righting of wrongs. As the Romans had conceived of warfare as a form of ritualized revenge since at least the fourth century, Virgil may very well be drawing on an earlier tradition.[85] Thus the pursuit of justice, through warfare may have been Bellona's primary role as a goddess in the Mid-Republic; her wrath on the battlefield was itself the physical manifestation of the fetial rite and, like the Furies themselves, she was the personification of Roman vengeance.

Of course, in between the beginning and the ending of a conflict, there is the actual fighting. Beyond her temple, combat is perhaps the aspect with which Bellona is most associated. Although she could bring her adherents victory and glory, she likewise represented the pains and negativities of war. Despite the multitude of modern, popular works that refer to the Roman Army of the Republic as some sort of 'war machine', killing is not an innate behaviour and comes unnaturally to the majority of humans. This rings especially true for ancient warfare, where the bloodshed was up close and very personal, and where battlefields would have been horribly sonorous, fear-inducing places. In spite of the reputation of Roman soldiers for a sort of stoic toughness and discipline, the psychological trauma of the battlefield must have been very real, and was likely felt even by seasoned veterans accustomed to killing.[86] Given these realities, that the Romans represented battle with a deity other than Mars, the personification of *virtus* and battlefield courage, is hardly surprising. This association with the maelstrom of combat is perhaps responsible for Bellona's dishevelled hair in the only portrait of her from the Mid-Republic (see Figure 2.2).[87] In later sources, she is strongly connected to the chaos, fury, and especially the sound of battle. As with actual soldiers in an actual war, when she enters the field of battle, she is preceded by trumpets, her armour and weapons clang and she shouts with the force of many men.[88] Ovid has her accompanied by 'the clash of arms, the groans of fallen [and] … a sea of blood'.[89] In fact, most of Bellona's imagery has both her and her weapons permanently caked in blood. As opposed to the aforementioned opening and closing of wars, this aspect sees the goddess in perpetual combat.

In both Greek and Latin literature, the washing of the body as well as one's weapons is a highly symbolic gesture which purifies the fighter and removes him from the chaotic realm of war so that he may return, even temporarily, to the everyday world. In the *Iliad*, Andromache prepares a bath for Hector as she awaits his return, and Ares bathes and puts on fresh clothes after combat. Achilles, on the other hand, refuses to bathe following the death of Patroclus, and is thus himself suspended in combat.[90] Similarly, Bellona does not bathe, as she remains on the battlefield. Historical illustrations of this are not only the purification of war instruments via the aforementioned *Tubilustrium* and *Armilustrium* rites, but also the Roman dedication of captured enemy arms after a victory, which were traditionally burnt and offered to a deity. These were normally dedicated to Vulcan, and on more than one occasion were offered to Mars.[91] Yet despite being a goddess of the battlefield itself, Bellona is never recorded as having received such a dedication. This is likely because she was viewed as permanently on the field of war. While Mars might represent war as a communal undertaking by the civic community, winning these wars required a campaign and actual fighting, and Bellona was combat itself.

Religion and the Roman Campaign

Consuls undertook a number of rituals before they processed to the Porta Capena, formally crossed the *pomerium*, and joined their awaiting army at the temple of Mars Gradivus for the coming campaign. Traversing the *pomerium* brought the magistrate from the *domus*, where he mostly exercised civil powers and where his authority was limited, to the *militia*, where his power was based on military command and his *imperium* was largely unrestricted, to the extent that Romans believed it could be wielded over even non-Romans who fell within the magistrate's *provincia* (area of control). Within the *domus*, killing was strictly forbidden, whereas taking a life was permitted in the *militia*. Once outside the *pomerium*, a *lustratio* was then performed to purify the army and its new commander.[92]

On campaign, the consul sacrificed and took auspices at regular intervals, especially before an impending battle. When an army stopped, a *lustratio* would have been performed around the site where the camp was to be built. Once in camp, all tents and facilities were laid out in the exact same order and with absolute precision; small altars may have been placed in central spaces throughout the camp.[93] The *praetorium* (commander's tent) stood in the very centre; in front of the *praetorium* would have stood an altar, and these two spaces would have been consecrated as a *templum*. Here, the commander sacrificed and undertook various rituals for the purposes of divination. Not the least of these would have been the observation of the feeding patterns from the sacred chickens (*pullaria auguria*: 'augury by means of chickens'). These animals were sometimes starved so that, when eventually fed, they would eat so rapidly that they would drop food on the ground, something which was considered a good omen by the *pullarius*, or priest of the sacred chickens.[94] Additionally, *haruspices*, Etruscan priests who specialized in reading the entrails of sacrificial victims, would have travelled with the army and performed rites in front of the *praetorium*. Commanders appear to have genuinely paid attention to these practices, and usually would not offer battle in the face of ill omens. In this regard, the calendar continued to play a role, as certain days were declared to be *atri*, or black, with fighting forbidden if at all possible.[95] Within the camp, religious affairs were not performed in secret, meaning that the rank and file – who believed that part of the commander's responsibility was the correct performance of ritual – would have known if the auspices were either bad or good, and a general risked a great deal if he ordered his troops into battle without favourable signs from the gods. A commander who did so and lost could be accused of impiety, a far worse charge than incompetence, and would have scuttled his chances, and possibly those of his family members, of ever reaching the consulship again.[96] The proper maintenance of ritual was perhaps even more important for an army on campaign, as the soldiers obviously preferred to engage in combat if they believed they were in harmony with the divine *cosmos* and that the gods were on their side. Thus religion served as one of the primary bonds by which a Roman army was held together. The camp constituted a religious space, and the *praetorium* served as its *nexus*. Despite not being within the *domus*, an army on campaign remained part of the Roman religious order, and the soldiers viewed the gods as literally travelling with them.[97]

During pitched combat, commanders could undertake a number of rituals to win the favour of the gods and motivate their soldiers. In a siege, an *evocatio* could be undertaken, whereby an enemy deity would be summoned out of the invested city. A temple and regular worship would be promised in return for the deity abandoning its people and supporting the Romans. Victory for Rome was seen as the ultimate proof that the *evocatio* had been successful, and the cult was then transferred to Rome. However, this is a mysterious practice at best, and although such a ritual is referred to several times within the sources, we know of only a single instance where one was supposedly carried out, and this was from archaic Rome in 396 BC, long before any history was recorded.[98] There seems no *a priori* reason to doubt the existence of such a ritual from one time in Rome's distant past; indeed, it may very well have been an early method of reconciling Rome's pantheon with the diverse deities to be found across Italy. Additionally, Macrobius even claims that a formalized set of rules existed for the rite.[99] Sieges were always difficult affairs, particularly in the time before the existence of artillery, and beyond a dangerous direct assault, a besieging army would have little recourse other than to try to deny the city resupply and at the same time look to the gods for help. However, the later use of the *evocatio* was likely exaggerated by Roman writers who were trying to emphasize the supposedly traditional openness of the Romans to foreign peoples and cults. Moreover, the famous success of the tactic in 396 raises the question as to why it would not have been employed as a rule at every siege, if only for the psychology of one's own soldiers.[100] But clearly this was not so, since at most a case could be made for its successful use on just seven occasions between the fourth century BC and the first century AD, during which time the Romans undertook dozens of sieges.[101]

As seen when discussing Bellona, during battle, a general could perform a *devotio*. The sacrifice of Publius Horatius Cocles at the Pons Sublicius has sometimes been characterized as the first *devotio*.[102] While it has been argued that the practice occurred regularly, had formalized rules and was strictly confined to *imperium*-holding magistrates, in the end, only one such act is known which is actually called a *devotio* – Mus (*supra* p.32) – and nothing in the sources implies either that the practice was so common for formalized rules to exist, or that the rite was in any way confined to magistrates with *imperium*.[103] Nevertheless, a *devotio* only makes sense if it came from an officer of command rank, since lesser soldiers are rarely concerned with overall victory, instead only concentrating on achieving the immediate objectives given to them by the commander. The idea of sacrificing oneself to the gods in return for victory in battle was common in many martial cultures, and may have existed amongst both the Samnites as well as the Germans and the Celtiberians.[104] Thus the ritual is unlikely to be altogether fictitious.

If a conflict proved particularly difficult, or if a war ever endangered the state, then Roman victory was likely to result in the vow and foundation of a temple. On certain occasions, a battlefield vow by an individual general could be undertaken in order to invoke a particular deity, with a temple being constructed afterwards as a manner of thanks. Over eighty victory temples were vowed during the Republic, from the fourth century onwards. These temples came to line the triumphal route, and each successive *triumphator*, in competition with his predecessors, sought to build a larger edifice. They served as focal points for Roman history and collective memory, as each one was a monument to a Roman victory, which would be commemorated through the rites and ceremonies which took place once a year at the temple. The dates for these were marked in the calendar, and thus even the Roman method of reckoning time itself became a repository of collective memory for the military triumphs of the city. Roman victories became so numerous, and the vowing of temples so common, that the practice was actually mocked by Plautus, and in 179 BC the censors began removing older victory memorials as the streets along the triumphal route had become so cluttered that there was no longer room for new generals to set up trophies.[105]

Conclusion

The link between religion and warfare at Rome was not only unquestioned, but vital to the Roman sense of being. Success in war was taken as a sign that the Romans were superior to other peoples in maintaining the *pax deorum*, and thus the gods favoured them with military victories. This was a deeply held belief which serves to explain why the Romans themselves came to hold that their hegemony over the Mediterranean was deserved.[106] In the Mid-Republic, warfare and Rome's agricultural society were deeply intertwined, and both were viewed as fully enmeshed within the Roman concept of *religio*, the means by which the citizens sought to win divine favour while similarly taking the care to avoid divine wrath. While the Romans farmed to live and fought for social prestige as well as to supplement their agricultural income via plunder, both were also religious undertakings, and the rites by which the Romans declared war, opened and closed the fighting season, and which they undertook on campaign were seen as vital to the continued existence of society. Warfare, like agriculture, operated on an annual rhythm which was punctuated and measured by the feast days within the Roman calendar. In theory, the *fetiales* were the most significant link between warfare and religion at Rome, as it was their college who ensured that a conflict was an *ius bellum*, and was thus in line with the *pax deorum*. Once a war was considered *ius* by the *fetiales*, the conflict had been sanctioned by the gods themselves and victory would be taken as a sign of this divine favour. Successful war, therefore, was vital to the Roman conception of the *cosmos*. The use of the *fetiales*, however, waned throughout the second century, as the Romans gradually adopted the mechanisms of Hellenistic diplomacy. The annual rhythm of warfare at Rome was broken in the same period, as larger, more distant conflicts, as well as the growing Mediterranean hegemony, required more than just an annual levy of small farmers to make up the legions. This process was exacerbated by the Marian reforms, which further professionalized the army and laid the foundation for a social order where soldier and civilian would come to inhabit different and increasingly divergent spaces. In the end, through his calendrical reforms, Caesar finally broke the link between the calendar, warfare, and religion. While religion remained important to the professional army of the Imperial period, everyday citizens henceforth no longer interacted with the gods in the militaristic way which had defined the life of their ancestors.[107]

Notes

1. Virg. *Aen.* 7.1–40.
2. Cf. Feeney, 2007: 161–63.
3. Publication of the calendar: Livy 9.46.5; Rüpke, 2011: 39–50. In general, cf. Beard, North & Price, 1998: 1.43–44; Feeney, 2007: 161–63.
4. Fasti Antiates (*ILLRP* 9); Festus 83.6–7, 163.11, 505.7–9L; Ovid *Fasti* 1.45–52; Varro *Ling. Lat.* 6.29; Rüpke, 2011: 44–49. On the mid-Republican calendar in general, cf. Forsythe, 2012: 19–39; Lipka, 2009: 30–51; Rüpke, 1990: 22–28; 2006: 223–25.
5. On the *fetiales* in general, cf. Livy 1.24, 32.6–14, 31.8.3, 36.3.7–12; Serv. *Aen.* 9.52; Beard, North & Price, 1998: 1.26–27, 132–33; Champion, 2017: 83–84; Ferrary, 1995; Rich, 2011; 2013: 559–64; Rüpke, 1990: 97–117; Santangelo, 2008; Warrior, 2006: 58–59; Wiedemann, 1986; Zack, 2001: 1–73; Zollschan, 2011.

6. 321 BC: Cic. *Off.* 3.109; Livy 9.1–12. 236 BC: Amm. Marc. 14.11.32;
    Dio F45; Val. Max. 6.3.3; Zon. 8.18.7–8. 137 BC: App. *Hisp.* 79–80;
    Cic. *Caecin.* 98, *Har. Resp.* 43, *Off.* 3.109, *Orat.* 1.181, 1.238, 2.137,
    Rep. 3.28; Eutr. 4.17; Flor. *Epit.* 1.34.5–7; Livy *Per.* 55; Mart. Cap.
    5.456; Obsequens 24; Oros. 5.4.19–5.11; Plut. *Tib. Gr.* 5–7; Quint.
    Inst. 7.4.12–13; Val. Max. 1.6.7, 2.7.1; Vell. Pat. 2.1.5, 2.1, 90.3. 266
    BC: Dio F42; Livy *Per.* 15; Val. Max. 6.6.5; Zon. 8.7.3. 188 BC: Dio
    F61; Livy 38.42.7; Val. Max. 6.6.3.
7. Cic. *Leg.* 2.21; Dion. Hal. *Rom. Ant.* 2.72.4–5; Livy 1.32.5; Plut.
    Cam. 18.1–3, *Num.* 12.13; Serv. *Aen.* 10.14; Varro *Vita Pop. Rom.* F93
    (Riposati); *Vir. Ill.* 5.4.
8. Livy 1.32.5–14.
9. Wiedemann 1986.
10. Cf. Cic. *Rep.* 2.31; Dion. Hal. *Rom. Ant.* 2.72.6–8; Pliny *Nat. Hist.*
    22.5; Serv. *Aen.* 9.52; Varro *Vita Pop. Rom.* F93 (Riposati).
11. Plaut. *Amph.* 203–10.
12. Enn. *Hec. Lyt.* 192 (*ROL*).
13. Pac. *Teuc.* 377–78 (*ROL*).
14. *Hostio* as to recompense: Plaut. *Asin.* 377; as to fight against: Laev. *Erot.*
    F1 (Courtney); in employing the term as a pun, the aforementioned Enn.
    Hec. Lyt. 192 (*ROL*) and Pac. *Teuc.* 377–78 (*ROL*) capture both
    senses. Cf. Festus 91.7–8, 334.16–19L; Eichner, 2002; Lodge, 1962: 1.723–24.
15. Dion. Hal. *Rom. Ant.* 7.19–65; Livy 2.33–41; Plut. *Cor.* 7.2, 13.3, 14.1,
    26–39; in general, cf. Terrenato, 2011.
16. Marcus Manlius: App. *It.* 9; Diod. 15.35.3; Gell. *Noct. Att.* 17.2.14,
    21.24; Livy 6.19.5–7, 6.18–20; Plut. *Cam.* 36.5–7; Zon. 7.24. Origin
    of the *fetiales*: Rich, 1976: 56–60, 109; 2011: 207–15; 2013: 561–63;
    Rüpke, 1990: 97–117; Walbank, 1985: 101–06; cf. Serrati, 2011: 20–21.
17. Serv. *Aen.* 9.52; cf. Festus 30.14–16L; Livy 1.32.6–14; Ovid *Fasti*
    6.203–08; Suet. *Claud.* 25.5; Ando, 2009: 115–16.
18. App. *Sam.* 17; Zon. 8.2.
19. Beard, North & Price, 1998: 1.132–33; Rüpke, 1990: 97–117; Zollschan,
    2011: 119–44.
20. On the beginning of the year in March, cf. Ovid *Fasti* 3.241–42; Feeney,
    2007: 204–05; Graf, 1997.
21. Livy 1.27.7, 5.52.7; Stat. *Sil.* 6.29; Cornell, 1995: 74–76; Lipka, 2009: 59–60.
22. *CIL* i².1.4.2832a (the 'Lapis Satricanus'); Diom. *CGL* 1.476; Livy
    1.20; Polyb. 21.13.11–13; Cornell, 1995: 74-76; Habinek, 2005: 20;
    Lipka, 2009: 59–60; Vaan, 2008: 570; cf. Virg. *Aen.* 8.275.

23. Dion. Hal. *Rom. Ant.* 2.70–71; Festus 117.13–22L; Livy 1.20.4, 27.7, 5.54.7.
24. Varro *Ling. Lat.* 7.2–3, 26; cf. Diom. *CGL* 1.476; Dion. Hal. *Rom. Ant.* 2.70.2, 4–5 (who emphasizes that the *Salii* generated a large amount of noise); Festus 31.22–24L; Hor. *Epist.* 2.1.86–9; Livy 1.20.4; Macrob. *Sat.* 1.12; Ovid *Fasti* 3.387–88; Plut. *Num.* 13.5; Polyb. 21.13.10–13; Quint. *Inst.* 1.6.39–41; Beard, North & Price, 1998: 1.43–44, 2.126–28; Habinek, 2005: 17–36; Schultz, 2006: 224. On the commentary of Aelius Stilo, cf. *GRF* F1–3.
25. Colonna, 1991: 88; MacIntosh Turfa, 2012: 236–37, fig. 19; Rich, 2013: 543; Schäfer, 1980; Schultz, 2006: 224; Torelli, 1997: 228, 244–55.
26. Festus 446.29–448.4L (who mentions a similar festival amongst the Faliscans); Gell. *Noct. Att.* 2.21; Ovid *Fasti* 3.809; Plaut. *Mil.* 692–94; Varro *Ling. Lat.* 6.14; contra Lipka, 2009: 34–35, 40–41, who argues that the dual festival for Mars and Minerva represents the synoecism in early Rome of diverse groups and their separate religious calendars.
27. Cf. Hor. *Odes* 1.36.12, 4.1.28; Habinek, 2005: 17–36, who stresses that the performance of the *Salii* would have also had an entertainment factor for the Romans.
28. Ceccarelli, 1998: 150–57; Habinek, 2005: 17–20; Sabbatucci, 1988: 53–60, 93–98; Torelli, 1984: 76–78, 106–08; 1990: 93–106; Versnel, 1994—98: 2.329.
29. *ILS* 5018; Aelius Stilo *GRF* F34; Cincius *GRF* F27; Festus 439.18–22L; Beard, 1990: 19–22; Habinek, 2005: 17–18; Versnel, 1994–98: 2.158; contra Torelli, 1984: 76–78, 106–12, who argues that the *virgines saliae* were a case of ritualized transvestitism.
30. Ovid *Fasti* 2.856–62, 3.519–22; Varro *Ling. Lat.* 6.13; Bernstein, 1999; Blaive, 2003; Michels, 1967: 17–18.
31. Festus 103.3–4, 11–13L; Naev. *Inc.* F27 *ROL*; Ovid *Fasti* 3.713–88; Plut. *Mor.* 289a; Prop. *El.* 4.1.131–32; Varro *Ling. Lat.* 6.14. For the possibility that the rite involved women, cf. Plaut. *Cas.* 980. In general, cf. Miller, 2002; Wiseman, 2000; 2008: 84–86, 127–29, 222–24.
32 . Festus 9.15–23L; cf. Macrob. *Sat.* 1.4.15; Varro *Ling. Lat.* 6.14.
33. *InscrIt* xiii.2.104; Ovid *Fasti* 3.809–14; Plaut. *Mil.* 692; Pliny *Nat. Hist.* 35.143; Varro *Ling. Lat.* 6.14, 17; cf. Hor. *Epist.* 2.2.197; Macrob. *Sat.* 1.12.7; Rüpke, 1990: 23–25, 177–79; 2011: 53–54.
34. Verrius Flaccus *Fasti Praenestini* (*InscrIt* xiii.2.17); Festus 310.19–20, 480.25–29, 481.5–6L; Lut. Catul. *GRF* F6; John of Lydus *Mens.* 4.60; Ovid *Fasti* 3.849–50; Varro *Ling. Lat.* 6.14, 5.117; Rüpke, 1990:

24–25. Calp. *Ecl.* 1.67–68 possibly refers to the Tubilustrium. Rüpke, 2011: 26–34 argues that the festival was not of a military nature, and had more to do with the waning moon. However, that the festival day of 23 March was referred to as *feriae* Marti (*InscrIt* xiii.2.104, 123) would seem to confirm the Tubilustrium as a festival associated with the opening of the campaigning season. The name *feriae* Marti, moreover, does not appear to be associated with the name of the month, as the Tubilustrium in May was known as *feriae* Volcano.

35. Charisius *Gramm.* 1.81 Barwick.

36. Cic. *Att.* 5.20.2; Livy 23.35.5.

37. Guittard, 2013: 178; Lipka, 2009: 40; Pascal, 1981: 264–65; Roth, 2009: 61.

38. Polyb. 21.13.11–13.

39. Val. Max. 2.1.10; Varro *Vita Pop. Rom.* F84 Riposati.

40. Roth, 2009: 61–66.

41. Fasti Arvalium (*CIL* vi.2295); Fasti Antiates (*ILLRP* 9); cf. Coarelli, 1974: 45–46. This temple was built only in 254 BC (Cic. *Nat. Deor.* 2.61; Steinby *LTUR* 2.249–52; Lipka, 2009: 136–37), however, ceremonies there supposedly went back to the days before the Republic (Dion. Hal. *Rom. Ant.* 2.75.3; Livy 1.21.4; Plut. *Num.* 16.1).

42. Dion. Hal. *Rom. Ant.* 3.13.4–22; Livy 1.24–26; John of Lydus *Mens.* 4.1.

43. Rüpke, 1990: 24–25; Schilling, 1989: 213.

44. Cato *Agr.* 141.2–3; Festus 246.21–24L.

45. *Chron. 354*, October (*CIL* i² p. 274); Festus 190.11–30, 191.3–8, 246.21–24L; Plut. *Mor.* 287b; Polyb. 12.4b; Timaios *FGrH* 566 F36; Burkert, 1987: 159–60; Devereux, 1970; Guittard, 2013: 178 n.9; Pascal, 1981; Radke, 1990; Rüpke, 1990: 24–28; 2009. Concerning the adornment of the severed head, the suggestion by U.W. Scholz (in his unpublished 1970 *habilitation*, as related in Rüpke, 2009: 108) that *pannus* (cloth) should be read for *pane* (bread) is intriguing. Yet while the October *Equus* certainly had martial overtones, there is no denying that agriculture and the harvest played an equal if not perhaps a greater role. Thus *pane* would have suited the occasion.

46. 396 BC: Festus 430.1–22L; Plut. *Mor.* 277d, *Rom.* 25.6; 390 BC: Livy 5.50.4; Ogilvie, 1965: 740–41.

47. Enn. *Ann.* 1.94–95 Skutsch; cf. Chassignet, 2017: 72–73; Rüpke, 2009: 111. For the games in general, cf. Rüpke, 2009: 111–16.

48. Dion. Hal. *Rom. Ant.* 2.34.4; Livy 1.10.5; Plut. *Marc.* 8.3–5, *Rom.* 16.6–7; Prop. *El.* 4.10.46.

49. Livy 1.24.3–9, 25.1; cf. Enn. *Ann.* 1.32 Skutsch; Festus 81.16–18L; Serv. *Aen.* 12.206. Cf. aslo Festus 266.16–18L; Livy 30.43.9; Polyb. 3.25.6–9; Serv. *Aen.* 1.62, 8.641; Varro *Ling. Lat.* 5.65; Gladhill, 2016: 25–28; Lipka, 2009: 134; Ogilvie, 1965: 110–12; Rich, 1976: 56–60, 109; 2011: 207–15; 2013: 563–64; Richardson, 2008; Rüpke, 1990: 98–99, 111–15; 2009; Scheid & Montremy, 2011: 73–74; Wiedemann, 1986: 486–90; York, 1986: 217; Zack, 2001: 55–59.

50. Fasti Arvalium (*CIL* vi.2295); Fasti Antiates (*ILLRP* 9); Festus 17.28–29L; Livy 37.33.6–7; John of Lydus *Mens.* 4.34; Plut. *Rom.* 23.3; Varro *Ling. Lat.* 5.153, 6.22; cf. Lipka, 2009: 40; Rüpke, 1990: 24–28; 2011: 54.

51. *Carmen Arvale*: *CIL* vi.2104; *suovetaurilia*: Cato *Agr.* 141.2–3.

52. Scheid, Tassini & Rüpke, 1998: 293–302; Scheid, 2015: 99–103.

53. *Luerue*: an archaic compound comprising the dative of *lues* (pestilence) and the verb *ruo*, *ruere* (destroy) (or possibly an archaic version of *ruina*?); *sins*: archaic form of the verb *sino*, *sinere* (allow); *pleores*: archaic form of *plures* (the many, the multitude; *plisima* or *plusima*, which appears in the *Carmen Saliare* (Festus 222.28L; Varro *Ling. Lat.* 7.27), perhaps means the same thing).

54. Cf. Festus 320.7–10L; Varro *Ling. Lat.* 5.134; Vaan, 2008: 530.

55. A compound word describing the three traditional Roman sacrificial victims: a pig (*sus*), a ram (*ovis*) and a bull (*taurus*).

56. Cato *Agr.* 141.2–3.

57. On the etymology of Mars, cf. Vaan 2008: 366. For the earlier, non-military aspects of Mars, in addition to the texts already cited, cf. also *AE* 1995: 248; *CIL* i² 33, 1513, ix.5805.

58. Livy 8.9.1–10.

59. Richardson, 1992: 245; Schultz, 2006: 217.

60. Livy 6.5.8; Serv. *Aen.* 1.292; Vitr. *De Arch.* 1.7.

61. Cf. Dion. Hal. *Rom. Ant.* 2.48.2; Festus 115.6–12L; Livy 22.1.12; Ovid *Fasti* 6.191–92; Serv. *Aen.* 6.860; Beard, North & Price, 1998: 2.370; Scheid & Montremy, 2011: 62–66; Vaan, 2008: 268–69; Ziolkowski, 1992: 101–04, 238.

62. On the temple as the muster point for Roman armies, cf. Livy 7.23.3; Serrati, 2011: 20–21.

63. Balmaceda, 2017: 8–10, 15–26; McDonnell, 2006: 17–24, 29–38, 44–71; Rosenstein, 1990: 95–111; Vaan, 2008: 681.

64. E.g. Enn. *Ann.* 10.326–28 (Skutsch). While *virtus* was viewed as a positive character trait, it could nonetheless be employed for less than noble purposes, e.g. Enn. *Hec. Lyt.* 200 (*ROL*).

65. Ovid *Fasti* 4.911–32; Tert. *Spect*. 5.8, who mentions that the festival was also associated with Mars. Cf. Lajoye 2010: 176–78.
66. Cf. Enn. *Ann*. 1.100 (Skutsch).
67. Livy 8.9.1–10; Varro *Ling. Lat*. 5.73; cf. Ando, 2009: 123–24.
68. Festus 204.13–19L; Hor. *Odes*. 4.15.9; Livy 1.32.9; Lucil. 22 (Marx); John of Lydus *Mens*. 4.1; Macrob. *Sat*. 1.9.15–16; Aug. *Res Gest*. 13; Suet. *Aug*. 22; cf. Lipka, 2009: 74–75; Scheid, 2013.
69. Rites of Janus on 1 March: Ovid *Fasti* 3.135–44; Solinus *Coll. Mem*. 1.35; Rüpke, 1990: 137–41; 2011: 75–79. Though Janus had no *flamen*, there remains a possibility that in some senses, he was viewed as superior to Jupiter in early Roman history: Cato *Agr*. 134.1–4; Macrob. *Sat*. 1.7.19–24; Serv. *Aen*. 7.180, 8.319; Ando, 2009: 178–79; Lipka, 2009: 110–12. *Devotio*: Livy 8.9.1–10.
70. Aug. *Res Gest*. 13; Forsythe, 2012: 28–29; Rüpke, 1990: 136–41; Taylor & Holland, 1952; Taylor, 2000.
71. Varro *Ling. Lat*. 5.73.
72. Livy 8.9.6–8; cf. Ando, 2009: 181–85; Roth, 2009: 62; Versnel, 1976.
73. Livy 10.19.17; cf. *CIL* vi.2.31606, xi.1827 (*InscrIt* 13.3.12, 79); Livy, 10.19.17, 21; Ovid *Fasti* 6.201–09; Orlin, 1997: 28–29, 48–49; Ziolkowski, 1992: 18–19, 47–49.
74. *CIL* i² 2.1.441.
75. Plaut. *Amph*. 43.
76. Cf. Varro *Ant. Hum. Div*. F189 (Cardauns), *Ling. Lat*. 5.73.
77. Plautus uses *duellum* only as an archaism (*Amph*. 189, *Asin*. 559, *Epid*. 450, *Capt*. 68, *Truc*. 483), and the term must have shifted at the very latest just before his birth in order for it to have been antiquated by the time of his writing (cf. Lodge, 1962: 1.210). Ovid uses the term only once (*Fasti* 6.201) and very purposefully: when mentioning the Third Samnite War and the vow of a temple to Bellona by Appius Claudius Caecus. In using the archaic term, Ovid was likely highlighting both the antiquity of the war as well as the goddess.
78. Cf. Astin, 1978: 189–203; Courtney, 1999: 50–53; Gratwick, 2002; McDonnell, 2006: 57–59; Pinault, 1987; Vaan, 2008: 70.
79. Beard, 2009: 92–105, 201, 206; Champion, 2017: 130–42; Versnel, 1970: 132–63; Ziolkowski, 1992: 292–95.
80. Livy 26.21.1, 28.9.5, 38.2, 30.21.12, 31.47.7; Ando, 2009: 116 n.82; Scheid & Montremy, 2011: 62–66.
81. Augustus possibly dedicated an earlier temple to Mars Ultor on the Capitoline in 20 BC (cf. Dio 54.8.2). However, this is most often referred

to as a *templum* rather than an *aedes*, and so the extent to which it was an actual building and not just a consecrated space remains unknown. Therefore, the first war temple within the *pomerium* which can be securely dated is that of Mars Ultor in the Forum of Augustus from 2 BC. Contra Ziolkowski, 1992: 266–68, who argues that several temples associated with war were *intra pomerium*.

82. Cf. Festus 30.14–16L; Livy 1.32.6–14; Ovid *Fasti* 6.203–08; Suet. *Claud.* 25.5; Ando, 2009: 115–16. On the Columna Bellica, cf. Ovid *Fasti* 6.205–08; Serv. *Aen.* 9.52; Ziolkowski, 1992: 18–19, 47–49.

83. Livy 9.3.13.

84. Lucretia: Livy 1.58.5–11; Dido's curses: Virg. *Aen.* 4.584–629; Aeneas' ships: Hellanicus *FGrH* 4 F84.

85. Virg. *Aen.* 8.700–03; cf. Cic. *Nat. Deor.* 3.46; Festus 74.11L; Serv. *Aen.* 4.609; Stat. *Theb.* 1.46–87.

86. On the physical and psychological stresses of ancient hand-to-hand combat, cf. Grossman, 1995: 131–54; Grossman & Christensen, 2008: 30–99, 214–16.

87. *CIL* i 2.1.441.

88. Hor. *Sat.* 2.3.223; Juv. *Sat.* 11.5; Mart. *Ep.* 12.57; Stat. *Theb.* 2.719, 4.9; Tib. *El.* 1.6.45–54; Val. Flacc. 3.60; cf. Scheid, 2016: 128.

89. Ovid *Metam.* 5.154–56.

90. Andromache and Hector: Hom. *Il.* 22.437–46; Ares: Hom. *Il.* 5.905; Achilles: Hom. *Il.* 23.40–46. In general, cf. Grethlein, 2007. I am grateful to Ms Meghan Poplacean for the references to washing in Homer.

91. App. *Lib.* 133; Livy 45.33.1–2.

92. For the rituals undertaken before consuls went to their *provinciae*, cf. Caes. *Bell. Civ.* 1.6.6; Dio 39.39.6; Festus 176.3–15L; Livy 31.14.1, 42.49.1–8, 45.39.11; Varro *Ling. Lat.* 7.37; Rüpke, 1990: 131–46; Sumi, 2005: 35–38.

93. Ps.-Hyg. *Mun. Cas.* 11.

94. Cic. *Div.* 1.15.28, 2.34.72, *Nat. Deor.* 2.9; Linderski, 1986: 2156; Orlin, 1997: 83 n.22. For the sacred chickens, see Kim Beerden's paper in this volume.

95. The most famous of these days was the *dies Alliensis* (18 July), the anniversary of the Battle of the River Allia in 390 BC, where the Gauls crushed a Roman army and afterwards proceeded to sack Rome. However, commanders appear to have largely ignored this restriction (cf. Rich, 2013: 548–49).

96. Cic. *Div.* 1.2, 2.71, *Nat. Deor.* 2.7; Flor. *Epit.* 2.2.29; Front. *Strat.* 1.12.1–2; Livy *Per.* 19, 22.9.7, 42.9, 41.14.7–18.16; Polyb. 1.52.2–3; Serv. *Aen.* 6.198; Suet. *Tib.* 2; Val. Max. 1.4.3.

97. *CIL* vi.331; Cato *De re Mil.* F4 Jordan; Livy 35.48.13, 40.52.5–6, 41.18.5–16, 42.37.12; Plut. *Aem.* 17.6; Polyb. 6.27.1–2; Champion, 2017: 100–03, 111–12, 121, 194–95; Linderski, 1986: 2173–77; Rüpke, 1990: 144–51, 165–83.

98. Dion. Hal. *Rom. Ant.* 13.3; Livy 5.21.1–7, 22.3–7, 23.7, 31.3; Plut. *Cam.* 5.1–2; Val. Max. 1.8.3; for the other mentions, cf. Macrob. *Sat.* 3.9.5–9; Ovid *Fasti* 3.843; Prop. *El.* 4.2.1–4; Serv. *Aen.* 12.841; Gustafsson, 2000: 42–62; Levene, 1993: 182–84; Ogilvie, 1965: 673–75; Orlin, 1997: 62–63, 144–45, who questions whether the ritual was actually carried out in front of the walls of Veii by the dictator Marcus Furius Camillus, or by the Senate in Rome after the victory. For the *evocatio*, see Matthew Dillon's paper in this volume.

99. Macrob. *Sat.* 3.6.9.

100. Verrius Flaccus (*Mem. Dig.* F6 Egger) actually does claim it was performed as a rule at every siege.

101. Cf. Arnob. 3.38; Festus 146.9–12, 268.27–33L; Serv. *Aen.* 2.351; Ando, 2009: 128–38, 181–85, who points out that the ritual was used outside of warfare as well; Champion, 2017: 125–27, 141–43, 203–05, 210–13; Lipka, 2009: 126–27.

102. McDonnell, 2006: 199–200, who also considers the *ver sacrum* as described by Dionysius (*Rom. Ant.* 1.16) and Livy (22.9.10) as a *devotio*; cf. Dion. Hal. *Rom. Ant.* 5.22.3–25.4; Livy 2.10; Polyb. 6.55.1–4.

103. McDonnell, 2006: 199–200 argues, based on Cicero (*Nat. Deor.* 2.10) and Livy (8.10.11), for formalized rules.

104. Samnites: Livy 9.40.10; Germans and the Celtiberians: Val. Max. 2.6.11. On the *devotio* in general, cf. Livy 8.9.1–10; Ando, 2009: 181–85; Champion, 2017: 108; Feldherr, 1998: 85–92; Lennon, 2013: 114; Roth, 2009: 62; Versnel, 1976: 365–410.

105. Plaut. *Amph.* 229–30; Cass. Hem. *FRHist* 6 F43. Cf. Orlin 1997: 11–34, esp. 28–33, 68–69, who stresses that there is no pattern as to why some generals vowed temples for victories, while others did not. He does suggest, however, that the vowing of a temple took some of the credit for the victory away from the individual general and assigned it to a specific god, and as a result, many victorious commanders decided against the practice. And once the temples in question came to be of significant grandeur, cost as well may have been a factor. Cf. also Ziolkowski, 1992: 235–58.

106. Cf. Cic. *Har. Resp.* 19, *Nat. Deor.* 2.8; Hor. *Odes.* 3.6.5; Livy 6.41.8, 44.1.11; Tert. *Apol.* 25; Virg. *Aen.* 756–59, 781–83.
107. Caesar's calendrical reforms: Dio 43.26; Censorinus *DN* 20.4; Macrob. *Sat.* 1.13.12–13; Pliny *Nat. Hist.* 18.211; Plut. *Caes.* 59.1–5; Suet. *Iul.* 40; Feeney, 2007: 151–63, 193–98; Rüpke, 2011: 114–21.

Bibliography

Ando, C., 2009, *The Matter of the Gods: Religion and the Roman Empire*, Berkeley.

Astin, A.E., 1978, *Cato the Censor*, Oxford.

Balmaceda, C., 2017, *Virtus Romana: Politics and Morality in the Roman Historians*, Chapel Hill.

Beard, M., 1990, 'Priesthood in the Roman Republic', in Beard, M. & North, J. (eds), *Pagan Priests: Religion and Power in the Ancient World*, London: 17–48.

Beard, M., 2009, *The Roman Triumph*, Cambridge.

Beard, M., North, J. & Price, S., 1998, *Religions of Rome*, vols 1–2, Cambridge.

Bernstein, F., 1999, 'Die Römischen Ecurria/Equirria: Kriegerische Feste?', *Nikephoros* 12: 149–69.

Blaive, F., 2003, 'Du *Regifugium* aux *Equirria*: remarques sur les rituels romains de fin d'année', in Defosse, P. (ed.), *Hommages à Carl Deroux, IV: archéologie et histoire de l'art, religion*, Brussels: 283–90.

Burkert, W., 1987, *Homo Necans: The Anthropology of Ancient Greek Sacrificial Ritual and Myth*, Bing, P. (trans.), Berkeley.

Ceccarelli, P., 1998, *La pirrica nell'antichità greco-romana: studi sulla danza armata*, Pisa.

Champion, C.B., 2017, *The Peace of the Gods: Elite Religious Practices in the Middle Roman Republic*, Princeton.

Chassignet, M., 2017, 'L'"archéologie" de Rome dans les *Annales* d'Ennius: *poetica fabula* ou *annalium monumentum?*', in Sandberg, K. & Smith, C.J. (eds), *Omnium Annalium Monumenta: Historical Writing and Historical Evidence in Republican Rome*, Leiden: 66–89.

Coarelli, F., 1974, *Guida archeologica di Roma*, Milan.

Colonna, G., 1991, 'Gli scudi bilobati dell'Italia centrale e l'*Ancile* dei Salii', *ArchClass* 43: 55–122.

Cornell, T.J., 1995, *The Beginnings of Rome: Italy and Rome from the Bronze Age to the Punic Wars (c. 1000–264 BC)*, London.

Courtney, E., 1995, *Musa Lapidaria: A Selection of Latin Verse Inscriptions*, Atlanta.

Courtney, E., 1999, *Archaic Latin Prose*, Atlanta.

Devereux, G., 1970, 'The Equus October Ritual Reconsidered', *Mnemosyne* 23: 297–301.

Dumézil, G., 1970, *Archaic Roman Religion*, vols 1–2, Krapp, P. (trans.), Chicago.

Eichner, H., 2002, 'Lateinisch *hostia, hostus, hostre* und die Stellvertretende Tiertötung der Hethiter', in Fritz, M. and Zeilfelder, S. (eds), *Novalis Indogermanica: Festschrift für Günther Neumann zum 80. Geburtstag*, Graz: 101–56.

Feeney, D., 2007, *Caesar's Calendar: Ancient Time and the Beginnings of History*, Berkeley.

Feldherr, A., 1998, *Spectacle and Society in Livy's History*, Berkeley.

Ferrary, J.-L., 1995, '*Ius fetiale* et diplomatie', in Frézouls, E. & Jacquemin, A. (eds), *Les relations internationales: actes du colloque de Strasbourg 15–17 Juin 1993*, Strasbourg: 411–32.

Forsythe, G., 2012, *Time in Roman Religion: One Thousand Years of Religious History*, London.

Gladhill, B., 2016, *Rethinking Roman Alliance: A Study in Poetics and Society*, Cambridge.

Graf, F., 1997, *Der Lauf des Rollenden Jahres: Zeit und Kalender in Rom*, Stuttgart.

Gratwick, A.S., 2002, 'A Matter of Substance: Cato's Preface to the *De Agri Cultura*', *Mnemosyne* 54: 41–72.

Grethlein, J., 2007, 'The Poetics of the Bath in the *Iliad*', *HSPh* 103: 25–49.

Grossman, D., 1995, *On Killing: The Psychological Cost of Learning to Kill in War and Society*, Boston.

Grossman, D. & Christensen, L.W., 2008, *On Combat: The Psychology and Physiology of Deadly Conflict in War and in Peace*, 3rd edn, Mascoutah.

Guittard, C., 2013, 'From the *Curia* on the Palatine Hill to the *Regia* on the *Forum*: The Itinerary of the *Salii* as a War Ritual', in Cusumano, N. et al. (eds), *Memory and Religious Experience in the Greco-Roman World*, Stuttgart: 177–84.

Gustafsson, G., 2000, *Evocatio Deorum: Historical and Mythical Interpretations of Ritualised Conquests in the Expansion of Ancient Rome*, Uppsala.

Habinek, T., 2005, *The World of Roman Song: From Ritualized Speech to Social Order*, Baltimore.

Lajoye, P., 2010, 'Quirinus, un ancien dieu tonnant? Nouvelles hypothèses sur son étymologie et sa nature primitive', *RHR* 227: 175–94.

Lennon, J.J., 2013, *Pollution and Religion in Ancient Rome*, Cambridge.

Levene, D.S., 1993, *Religion in Livy*, Leiden.

Linderski, J., 1986, 'The Augural Law', *ANRW* 2.16.3, Berlin: 2146–2312.

Lipka, M., 2009, *Roman Gods: A Conceptual Approach*, Leiden.

Lodge, G., 1962, *Lexicon Plautinum*, vols 1–2, Hildesheim.

MacIntosh Turfa, J., 2012, *Divining the Etruscan World: The Brontoscopic Calendar and Religious Practice*, Cambridge.

McDonnell, M., 2006, *Roman Manliness: Virtus and the Roman Republic*, Cambridge.

Michels, A.K., 1967, *The Calendar of the Roman Republic*, Princeton.

Miller, J.F., 2002, 'Ovid's Liberalia', in Herbert-Brown, G. (ed.), *Ovid's 'Fasti': Historical Readings at its Bimillennium*, Oxford: 199–224.

Ogilvie, R.M., 1965, *A Commentary on Livy: Books 1–5*, Oxford.

Orlin, E.M., 1997, *Temples, Religion, and Politics in the Roman Republic*, Leiden.

Pascal, C.B., 1981, 'October Horse', *HSPh* 85: 261–91.

Pinault, G.-J., 1987, '*Bellum*: la guerre et la beauté', in Freyburger, G. (ed.), *De Virgile à Jacob Balde: hommage à Mme Andrée Thill*, Mulhouse: 151–56.

Radke, G., 1990, 'October Equus', *Latomus* 49: 343–51.

Rich, J., 1976, *Declaring War in the Roman Republic in the Period of the Transmarine Expansion*, Brussels.

Rich, J. 2011, 'The Fetials and Roman International Relations', in Richardson, J.H. & Santangelo, F. (eds), *Priests and State in the Roman World*, Stuttgart: 185–240.

Rich, J., 2013, 'Roman Rituals of War', in Campbell, B. & Tritle, L.A. (eds), *The Oxford Handbook of Warfare in the Classical World*, Oxford: 542–68.

Richardson, J.H., 2008, 'The *pater patratus* on a Roman Gold Stater: A Reading of *RRC* Nos. 28/1–2 and 29/1–2', *Hermes* 136: 415–25.

Richardson, L., 1992, *A New Topographical Dictionary of Ancient Rome*, Baltimore.

Rosenstein, N.S., 1990, *Imperatores Victi: Military Defeat and Aristocractic Competition in the Middle and Late Republic*, Berkeley.

Roth, J.P., 2009, *Roman Warfare*, Cambridge.

Rüpke, J., 1990, *Domi Militiae: Die Religiöse Konstruktion des Krieges in Rom*, Stuttgart.

Rüpke, J., 2006, 'Communicating with the Gods', in Rosenstein, N. & Morstein-Marx, R. (eds), *A Companion to the Roman Republic*, Oxford: 213–35.

Rüpke, J., 2009, 'Equus October und Ludi Capitolini: Zur Rituellen Struktur der Oktoberiden und Ihren Antiken Deutungen', in Duell, U. & Walde, C. (eds), *Antike Mythen: Medien, Transformationen und Konstruktionen. Festschrift für Fritz Graf zum 65. Geburtstag*, Berlin: 97–121.

Rüpke, J., 2011, *The Roman Calendar from Numa to Constantine: Time, History, and the Fasti*, Oxford.

Sabbatucci, D., 1988, *La religione di Roma antica: dal calendario festivo all'ordine cosmico*, Milan.

Santangelo, F., 2008, 'The Fetials and Their *Ius*', *BICS* 51: 63–93.

Schäfer, T., 1980, 'Zur Ikonographie der Salier', *JDAI* 95: 342–73.

Scheid, J., 1985, *Religion et la pieté à Rome*, Paris.

Scheid, J., 2013, 'Hierarchy and Structure in Roman Polytheism: Roman Methods of Conceiving Action', in Ando, C. (ed.), *Roman Religion*, Edinburgh: 164–89.

Scheid, J., 2015, 'Spéculation érudite et religion: l'interaction entre l'érudition et les réformes religieuses à Rome', in Belayche, N. & Pirenne-Delforge, V. (eds), *Fabriquer du divin: Constructions et ajustements de la représentation des dieux dan'Antiquité*, Liège: 93–104.

Scheid, J., 2016, *The Gods, the State, and the Individual: Reflections on Civic Religion in Rome*, Ando, C. (trans.), Philadelphia.

Scheid, J. & Montremy, J.-M. de, 2011, *Pouvoir et religion à Rome*, Paris.

Scheid, J., Tassini, P. & Rüpke, J., 1998, *Recherches archéologiques à la Magliana. Commentarii Fratrum Arvalium qui supersunt: les copies épigraphiques des protocoles annuels de la confrérie arvale, 21 av.–304 ap. J.–C.*, Rome.

Schilling, R., 1989, 'Roman Religion to 100 BCE', in Seltzer, R.M. (ed.), *Religions of Antiquity*, New York: 193–217.

Schultz, C.E., 2006, 'Juno Sospita and Roman Insecurity in the Social War', in Schultz, C.E. & Harvey, P.B. (eds), *Religion in Republican Italy*, Cambridge: 207–27.

Serrati, J., 2011, 'The Rise of Rome to 264', in Hoyos, D. (ed.), *A Companion to the Punic Wars*, Oxford: 9–27.

Sumi, G., 2005, *Ceremony and Power: Performing Politics in Rome Between Republic and Empire*, Ann Arbor.

Taylor, L.R. & Holland, L.A. 1952, 'Janus and the Fasti', *CPh* 47: 137–42.

Taylor, R., 2000, 'Watching the Skies: Janus, Auspication, and the Shrine in the Roman Forum', *MAAR* 45: 1–40.

Terrenato, N., 2011, 'The Versatile Clans: Archaic Rome and the Nature of Early City-States in Central Italy', Terrenato, N. & Haggis, D.C. (eds), *State Formation in Italy and Greece: Questioning the Neoevolutionist Paradigm*, Oxford: 231–44.

Torelli, M., 1984, *Lavinio e Roma: riti iniziatici e matrimonio tra archeologia e storia*, Rome.

Torelli, M., 1990, 'Riti di passagio maschili de Roma arcaica', *MEFRA* 102: 93–106.

Torelli, M., 1997, 'Appius Alce: la gemma Fiorentina con rito saliare e la presenza dei Claudii in Etruria', *SE* 63: 227–55.

Vaan, M. de, 2008, *Etymological Dictionary of Latin and Other Italic Languages*, Leiden.

Versnel, H.S., 1970, *Triumphus: An Inquiry into the Origin, Development, and Meaning of the Roman Triumph*, Leiden.

Versnel, H.S., 1976, 'Two Types of Roman *Devotio*', *Mnemosyne* 29: 365–410.

Versnel, H.S., 1994–98, *Inconsistencies in Greek and Roman Religion: Transition and Reversal in Myth and Ritual*, 2nd edn, Leiden.

Walbank, F.W., 1985, *Selected Papers: Studies in Greek and Roman History and Historiography*, Cambridge.

Warrior, V.M., 2006, *Roman Religion*, Cambridge.

Wiedemann, T., 1986, 'The *Fetiales*: A Reconsideration', *CQ* 36: 478–90.

Wiseman, T.P., 2000, 'The Games of Hercules', in Bispham, E. & Smith, C.J. (eds), *Religion in Archaic and Republican Rome and Italy: Evidence and Experience*, Edinburgh: 108–14.

Wiseman, T.P., 2008, *Unwritten Rome*, Exeter.

York, M., 1986, *The Roman Festival Calendar of Numa Pompilius*, Frankfurt.

Zack, A., 2001, *Studien zum 'Römischen Völkerrecht': Kriegserklärung, Kriegsbeschluss, Beeidung und Ratifikation Zwischenstaatlicher Verträge, Internationale Freundschaft und Feindschaft Während der Römischen Republik bis zum Beginn des Prinzipats*, Göttingen.

Ziolkowski, A., 1992, *The Temples of Mid-Republican Rome and Their Historical and Topographical Context*, Rome.

Zollschan, L., 2011, 'The Longevity of the Fetial College', in Tellegen-Couperus, O.E. (ed.), *Law and Religion in the Roman Republic*, Leiden: 119–44.

Chapter 3

Evocatio: Taking Gods away from Enemy States and Peoples

Matthew Dillon

When the city of Ur fell to the Elamites in about 1940 BC and lost its brief but widespread empire in Mesopotamia, a scribe of the city penned *The Lament of Ur*, describing how the gods had abandoned the city to its fate.[1] Such a concept became a prevalent one in the ancient world, but nowhere more so than amongst the Romans of the Republican period. They developed a pronounced military ideology in which it was believed that it was necessary to invite the major 'protector' god of a besieged enemy city to abandon its worshippers and come to Rome. This was the *evocatio* ritual, which found its material expression in the transfer of that god's main statue from a captured city to Rome when the city was overcome. The *evocatio* was the 'calling out' of the enemy's god (plural: *evocationes*).[2] Such a god was also asked to take an active role – not simply to abandon and desert the worshippers, leaving them bereft of divine support, but also to strike fear and panic into them. In return for doing so, the Roman commander promised that the god would have an equal or superior place of worship in Rome, and receive worship equivalent to or better at Rome. Roman generals, in attacking cities, might also make a vow to build a temple for a Roman god they prayed to for divine assistance in defeating the enemy.

Working on the premise that gods were powerful allies of their worshippers, the Roman *evocatio* ritual also reflected the Roman tradition that their empire was founded on the goodwill and support of the gods. This Roman attitude was quite different from earlier cultures: in the Near East, gods were not invited to leave their cities. Rather, when a city was captured, the gods of that city were also captured, and taken away to the city of the invader, to serve it. Rome in its campaigns, however, in addition to the pleading of the *evocatio* ritual, did also loot and pillage statues of the gods of enemy peoples, and brought them to Rome. Coupled with this *evocatio* rite was that of *devotio*, which had two aspects: the Roman commander attacking a city would 'devote', or as might be translated, consecrate, and give over a city Rome was attacking to the gods of the underworld, while on the battlefield a Roman general might devote himself and the enemy to the gods of the underworld in return for victory. Successful battles and campaigns in turn required the gods to be thanked for victory, through the ritual of a *supplicatio*. Vows could be made by a general in return for victory – to construct a temple to a particular god, or to dedicate a tithe of the booty of the campaign.

'God-napping' in the Ancient Near East

What could be called statue theft, or what scholars have dabbed 'god-napping', occurred throughout Near Eastern history, and was particularly a practice in Mesopotamia over several centuries. Hittite and Assyrian kings practised this as a matter of course when conquering cities. For example, the statue of the god Marduk, originally in Babylon led a particularly peripatetic existence across the Mesopotamian landscape as different sets of conquerors removed the statue from wherever its current location was to their own conquering city, as described in the *Marduk Prophecy*. The Hittite King Mursili I (1556–1526 BC) took Marduk's statue from Babylon, to whence it was later returned by a Babylonian king.[3] Hittite god-napping, however, had begun much earlier, being first attested in the eighteenth century BC by King Anitta, as recorded in the Anitta-Text. Hittite rulers captured statues of enemy gods and added these to their own Hittite pantheon: these gods were co-opted into the company of those gods supporting the Hittite Empire, but they were also taken away as a means of punishing cities and holding them in subjugation, a policy the later Assyrians also followed. To return to Mursili I, in the 'Manly Deeds' inscription which his son Mursili II narrates, he records how Mursili took the gods of the cities of Aleppo and Babylon back to Hatti. Yet, when he attacked and captured Carcemish in Syria, it is specifically recorded that Šuppiluliuma I did not attack the temples or remove the gods' statues:

> 'When he had conque[red] the city, because [my father was rever]
> ent of the gods, he let no one near the upper citadel of [Kubaba]
> and of the protective deity. He did not intrude into a single one
> of the temples, but rather, he bowed down [to the gods].'

In this case, it has been suggested that Mursili, as he was going to use this city as the Hittite capital of Syria, left the gods in place.[4]

Hebrews and Palestinians were also no strangers to the theft of divine statues: in the case of aniconic Judaism, this took the form of the Ark of the Covenant. The Philistines captured the Ark when they defeated the Israelites at the Battle of Ebenezer. It was then placed in the temple of Dagon in Ashdod, but the next day the statue of Dagon was found on its face before the Ark. The Philistines re-erected the statue, but the next day it was found fallen over again, this time with its head and hands broken off and at the threshold of the temple. The Lord struck Ashdod's people with tumours, and the Septuagint and Vulgate versions add that a plague of rats arose. Consequently, the Ark was then removed to Gath, where another outbreak of tumours occurred; then it was moved to Ekron, but again a plague of tumours occurred. After seven months of affliction, the Philistine diviners predicted that if the Ark was sent back to the Israelites, the tumours would be healed. They advised that a guilt offering was required: a golden tumour for each of the five Philistine kings, and a gold rat for each of the towns and villages.[5] This adds a different dimension to the theft of divine objects: other Near Eastern narratives do not have god-nappers punished, rather in the case of the statue of the god Marduk in the *Marduk Prophecy*, he actually is depicted as acquiescing to his capture and moves. Many centuries later, when Pompey conquered Jerusalem in 63 BC and entered the Jewish Temple, he saw ritual objects that none but the priest might see, as well as 2,000 talents of 'sacred' money: he, however, left all of these in the temple, and ordered it to be purified of his presence. In the next century, when Titus captured and sacked Jerusalem in AD 70, the temple was pillaged and destroyed, and the sacred treasures were taken to Rome and exhibited in his triumph.[6]

Assyria in particular practised the removal of cult statues from cities which they had conquered, as a means of subjugating them fully: cities believed that if the statues of the gods were not present, then cosmic chaos descended on the city, and that it had no divine protection. Several Assyrian reliefs depict the captured statues of gods being transported to Assyria, and one in particular, from Nimrud, shows Tilgath-Pileser III (reigned 745–727 BC) removing the Babylonian Marduk statue.[7] Assyrian kings might also return captured statues: an inscription of the Assyrian king Esarhaddon (r. 681–669 BC) tells how his father Sennacherib (r. 705–681 BC) had captured the gods of Arabia, but now Hazael, king of the Arabs, had successfully asked Esarhaddon for the return of the statues.[8] When statues were 'god-napped', they were removed by the Hittites and the Assyrians so that the captured cities and territories would be without divine protection and assistance (especially if the city revolted), and so that these gods would be added to their own pantheons and become their own gods. Roman ideology towards the removal of the statues of enemy cities was formulated along similar lines.

Greek Divine Statue Theft

When the Greeks conquered other cities, they largely respected the sanctuaries, temples and statues of the gods (there were, of course, exceptions). If a city was captured, the cult statues of its temples were left *in situ*. One major, mythological, exception occurred when Iphigeneia, daughter of Agamemnon, was in Tauris and stole away the statue of Artemis with which Iphigeneia as her priestess had been entrusted, and took it to Brauron in Attica, where it became the centre of a major Athenian cult.[9] A particular saga was attached to some statues made of olive wood. Epidauros experienced a blight on its agricultural land, with nothing growing; it sent an embassy to Delphi, enquiring of the oracle about this, and they were instructed to remedy this by making statues of two fertility deities, Damia and Auxesia. For this, they obtained sacred olive wood from the Athenians in return for an annual tithe. The Aeginetans invaded Epidauros and stole the statues, and the Epidaurians therefore ceased paying the tithe to the Athenians. The latter demanded the return of the statues from the Aeginetans, but were refused, and sent a trireme to collect the statues, but failed. Aegina claimed that the statues refused to leave, even though the Athenians attempted to drag them away when they could not lift them. The statues were said to have changed their appearance when being dragged, to kneeling statues, to signify their absolute intention of staying put.[10] This is an isolated occurrence, however, and generally Greeks did not steal sacred statues from each other, and when conquering each other, left statues of the gods in place. As will be seen, the main exception is in the account of the Trojan War, in which the Greek warriors Diomedes and Odysseus stole the small statue of Athena from the Trojan city.

Chained Gods

Damia and Auxesia, according to the people of Aegina, had bent their knees so that they could not be stolen: mortal worshippers could take a hand in similar processes. Statues might be chained when they were moved for bathing or purification rituals, in order to guard against theft.[11] In one case, the worshippers of Hera on the island of Samos incorrectly believed that their goddess in her statue guise had attempted to run away: henceforth they kept her chained up.[12] Pausanias explains why there was at Sparta an ancient image of the war god Enyalios, chained with fetters: the idea was the same as for the Athenians in the case of their statue of a wingless Nike (goddess of victory) – statues of Nike typically had wings. Enyalios the war god could not run away from Sparta as he was chained there, just as Nike could not fly away from Athens as she had no wings.[13] Both statues were tied up to ensure they assisted the states that worshipped these statues.[14]

The Palladium and the Pignora Imperii ('Pledges of Empire')

According to tradition, the Palladium[15] ('of Pallas' Athena[16]) came from Troy, and thence eventually to Rome: this was a statuette of Athena, in standing pose and armed, in her warrior guise as Athena Promachos ('Armed Athena').[17] Its sacredness was indicated by its origins: after it had fallen from the heavens, it was taken to Troy.[18] There were two distinct narratives about how this statue came to leave Troy for Italy in the reign of Priam. Either Aeneas took it away with him when he fled the city, or Diomedes and Odysseus stole it before Troy was sacked and captured.[19] Ovid knew both versions:[20] Diomedes took it to Italy,[21] or Aeneas did.[22] But the Romans certainly preferred the version involving Aeneas, which connected Rome to Troy and Venus (Aeneas' divine mother).

A silver denarius of Julius Caesar dating to 48/47 BC, struck while he was travelling in North Africa, depicts the theme. On the reverse, Aeneas carries his aged father Anchises on his left shoulder, while holding the Palladium in his right hand. On the obverse of the coin, the head of Venus refers to her being Aeneas' mother. The Julii family claimed descent from Venus, so the coin operated on several levels – stressing this relationship, the piety of Caesar's ancestor Aeneas and his relationship with two goddesses, Athena (Roman Minerva) and Venus (Figure 3.1).[23]

Plautus (254–184 BC) the Roman playwright, in his *Bacchides*, has Troy's capture by the Greeks conditional upon three events: if three *fata* ('fates') were fulfilled. One of these *fata* was the capture of the Palladium, presumably reflecting a Greek play which he had adapted, as well as Greek myth itself.[24] Ovid quotes Apollo oracularizing to the Trojans that, 'Preserve the [statue of] the heavenly goddess, for so you shall preserve the city; she

Figure 3.1:   Silver denarius. Obverse: Venus, Aeneas' mother. Reverse: Aeneas fleeing from burning Troy holding the Palladium in his right hand, while carrying his aged father Anchises on his left shoulder; 48/47 BC. Courtesy of *CNG* 851836.

will transfer, with herself, the place of empire.' Ovid has the statue neglected by Priam; and that this, coupled with Athena's anger at not being judged by Paris to be the most beautiful goddess, led to Athena's willing removal from Troy, taking with her 'the place of empire',[25] so that Rome was the new Troy. Earlier than Ovid, Greek vases and coins show Diomedes and Odysseus stealing the Palladium, and in one case Athena watches with approval.[26]

In Rome, the Palladium received special homage, housed in Vesta's temple in her sanctuary in the Forum.[27] When the temple was burning in 241 BC, the Pontifex Maximus Lucius Caecilius Metellus rescued the Palladium from the flames, calling upon himself punishment if it was a crime for him to enter where no man was permitted to enter: Ovid has the goddess approving his deed, but Pliny has him struck blind.[28] A similar story was situated in Troy when the image was there: King Ilas rescued the Palladium when the temple it was in caught fire, and he was blinded.[29] A related theme of the necessity of purity and correct handling of a divine statue will emerge in the narrative of the removal of the statue of Juno from Veii (see below). While not a case of *evocatio*, the willingness of the goddess to have her Palladium removed from the centre of what had been a mighty empire (Troy) to what would be 'the place of empire', Rome, is pertinent.

Servius, in his fourth-century AD commentary on Virgil's *Aeneid*, listed seven *pignora imperii*, 'pledges of empire', which constituted a guarantee from the gods that the Romans would maintain their empire: all of them were religious in nature. He listed firstly the stone representing the Mother of the Gods, brought from Pessinus in the third century BC when her cult was introduced to Rome (see below). The other six *pignora* were: the chariot taken from Veii at its capture in 396 BC, and mounted on the roof of the temple of Jupiter Optimus Maximus on the Capitoline Hill; the ashes of the Greek hero Orestes; the sceptre of Priam; the veil of Ilione, daughter of Priam; the Palladium (the sceptre, veil and Palladium were said to have been brought from Troy by Aeneas and hence were sacred relics); and the twelve sacred shields the *Salii* priests wielded in their dances to Mars, dating to the reign of the second king of Rome, the religious reformer Numa.[30]

The Magna Mater and Aesculapius come to Rome

This theft by Diomedes and Odysseus, or Aeneas' transference of the cult statue to Italy, did not, however, lead in itself to an ideology of statue transference. But the Romans closely associated a statue of a god with the support of that divinity, in a way which was akin to that of the Near Eastern civilizations, though not so much as for the Greeks. Two cult transfers in particular are important to note in this respect.

In the 290s BC, Rome was ravaged by a plague, and a consultation of the Sibylline Books advised that they enquire of Apollo's oracle at Delphi as to what they should do, which they duly did in 292 BC. The advice of the Delphic priestess, the Pythia, was that they were to go to Epidauros, the major healing sanctuary of the healing god Asklepios, to seek the aid of this god, which they did. Here they requested from the temple authorities that they take back to Rome the cult statue of the god, but these were (understandably) somewhat reluctant. Ovid reports, however, that Asklepios then appeared in a dream to the leader of the Roman embassy, Quintus Ogulnius, to the effect that he would leave his shrine and come to Rome in his form of a giant snake.[31]

Asklepios commonly did, in Greek belief, appear to his worshippers via a dream epiphany, such as the Roman Ogulnius experienced, and this accords with the ritual of the cult. Whether or not the dream actually occurred is not relevant from a historical point of view. Taking a snake from Epidauros as a means of transferring his cult was the main method by which this god's cult spread, and occurred, for example, in the case of both Athens and the town of Halieis.[32] The ship with its snake made its way to the island in the Tiber, where the reptile disembarked, and Asklepios' cult – in his Latin form Aesculapius – was established there. So even though no statue of the god went to Rome, Ovid, as a Roman, conceived of the ritual process here as a process of transference in terms of the god leaving the shrine in his epiphanic form of a snake for a new city, Rome, where he would benefit the inhabitants. Epidauros was not an enemy city, but the procedure was akin to an *evocatio*.

The case of the Magna Mater occurred very much in the context of warfare. In 205 BC, regular showers of stones – which the Romans regarded as a prodigy – were reported, and the Senate consulted the Sibylline Books. The oracular response which was found in the Books required that, 'If ever a foreign enemy invaded the soil of Italy, he could be driven out of Italy and vanquished, if the Idaean Mother were brought to Rome.'[33] Hannibal of Carthage was, of course, the invader at this time. Livy drew a connection between the two instances, having the Romans remembering the precedent of Aesculapius (he employs the Latin form of the god's name) and how he was brought from Greece.[34] The Romans, as they had done in the case of Aesculapius, dispatched an embassy: to Pessinus in Phrygia, where the Idaean Mother was worshipped (Idaean, from Mt Ida in Phrygia, Asia Minor), in the form of a black meteorite. Having obtained the permission of the local authorities, the stone was brought to Rome, along with her local priests (the Galli), and housed in a temple, with an annual festival inaugurated in her honour. Her veneration was considered to be necessary for the eviction of Hannibal and his defeat, which in fact took place in 201 BC at Carthage. The goddess voluntarily came in the sense that the guardians of her stone allowed her to leave.[35] It is not articulated that she played a part in Hannibal's defeat: rather, her presence in Rome was a precondition of that defeat. While later at Rome she was in fact to be represented in anthropomorphic form, this was not the case in 205 BC.

Defining Evocatio

There was, however, a perceived difference between gods who were transferred to Rome from foreign peoples as part of the process of *evocatio*, and the gods involved in a peaceful transfer. Festus the Latin lexicographer defines the difference:[36]

'Foreign cults are those which have either been brought [to Rome] as a result of an *evocatio* of gods during the besieging of cities, or which have been brought in peace-time for certain religious reasons, such as the Magna Mater, from Phrygia, Ceres from Greece, and Aesculapius from Epidaurus. These cults are celebrated just as they are amongst the peoples from whom they have been brought.'

Festus was an epitomator of the work of first-century AD author Verrius Flaccus and his *De verborum significatu*, and so his definition has a decent pedigree. While his account of the Magna Mater is not quite correct (for she had been summoned in times of war in response to an oracle about the defeat of an invader), the distinction is clear: some gods were called out of enemy cities by a specific ritual known as an *evocatio*, whereas others came to Rome as a result of a peaceful process.

Another first-century AD description of *evocatio* occurs in Pliny, and also derives from Verrius Flaccus, whom Pliny specifically cites, indicating that Flaccus himself was relying on other – presumably earlier – authorities:

'Verrius Flaccus points to trustworthy authors to prove that it was the practice, at the very commencement of a siege, for the Roman priests to call forth [*evocari*] the god in whose protection the besieged town was and to promise him that at Rome he would receive even greater worship [*eundem aut ampliorem apud Romanos cultum*]. This ritual has endured in pontifical doctrine, and it is clear that this is why the protecting god of Rome has been kept a secret, in order to prevent any enemy from acting in a similar manner.'[37]

His context is a discussion of spells, magic and divination, and sheds no further light on his information. Romans themselves were keenly aware that this *evocatio* could be practised against them, and so the name of their own tutelary deity was kept secret. Therefore, their deity could not be named and called out by an enemy at Rome's walls, tempted by the promise of more splendid worship. Servius, several centuries later, was aware of this principle: 'By a law of the pontiffs it is ensured that the gods of the Romans are not referred to by their actual names, so that it is not possible to call them out of their shrines.'[38] He goes on to relate that the priests do not name the 'Genius' ('Spirit') of Rome, and refer to Jupiter as 'Jupiter, best and greatest, or if you want to be invoked by any other name'. Elsewhere, Servius reports that Varro had discussed the secret name of Rome and that one Q. Valerius Soranus had been executed for revealing it. Varro may well have been the source for Pliny, Plutarch and Solinus, who also note

Soranus' execution.[39] The process of *evocatio* was not to call out *all* the gods of a city, but the principal one – the deity who had the power to protect the city – the one who, if he or she remained in the city and supported its inhabitants, meant that it could not be taken.

The tutelary deity of the city under siege was tempted, and any misgivings it might have assuaged, by the promise of equivalent – or even greater – worship. The deity needed to be convinced in this way. Moreover, another aspect of the undertaking is clear from Festus' version of Verrius Flaccus – that the deity would be worshipped in the same way and the ritual acts performed in its honour would not change. This is exactly what happened in the case of the Magna Mater, whose veneration was conducted by her priests, brought from Asia Minor, who continued to worship her in their traditional ways (including self-castration, a very un-Roman practice) and to dress in their headdresses and robes and exotic paraphernalia. Roman priests (*sacerdotes*) were responsible for the *evocatio* ritual, but which college of them is not known.

The City of Veii and the Evocatio of the Goddess Juno

Livy understood how the statue of Juno came from Veii to Rome within this context of the first-century AD definition, which probably dated to a much earlier period. Leaving aside for a moment the historicity of the Veii episode, whether an *evocatio* occurred then or not (and there is no real historiographical reason to doubt Livy's record of an *evocatio* at Veii, especially as he is known to be drawing on third- and second-century BC sources for his narrative), how he describes the ritual must be in accordance with the *evocatio* as understood by himself and the Romans in general at the time he wrote his account of the transfer of the Etruscan goddess of Veii to the city of its enemy, Rome. There is a possibility that when the city of Veii was sacked the statue was simply brought as part of the spoils to Rome, with no preceding pre-sack religious rite of the *evocatio*. If so, that tradition was well and truly suppressed in favour of an *evocatio* ritual as described by Livy and which he presumably drew from some earlier source, one of the third- or second-century BC Roman historians.[40] Veii is seen as the classic example of an *evocatio*, with several key and pertinent features.[41]

In 396 BC, the Romans had been besieging Veii for ten years when, according to Livy (drawing on earlier written accounts), the Roman general and dictator Camillus conducted the following ritual:[42]

'A large multitude went forth, filling the camp. Then the dictator [Camillus], having conducted the auspices, came out, ordering the soldiers to arm themselves. "With me leading you," he said, "Pythian Apollo, inspired by your will [*numen*], I advance to the destruction of the city of Veii, and I promise to you a tenth part of the booty. At the same time, Juno Regina, who lives in Veii now, I pray that when we are victorious you will come to us to the city of Rome – which will soon be your city as well, that a temple equal to your dignity might receive you." Having made these prayers, he set out with an overwhelming multitude to attack, from every quarter, the town.'

Livy does not use the term *evocatio*, but the definition of Verrius Flaccus indicates that this is what is being described, and scholarship has always accepted it as such. The invocation to Queen Juno (Juno Regina) follows a traditional ceremony of vowing, in which Camillus promises to dedicate some of the booty from the city – if it is captured – to Pythian Apollo (i.e. Apollo at Delphi). Simultaneously, 'at the same time', he beseeched Juno. This is not a magical ritual of coercion but rather the goddess needed to be persuaded to come to Rome: she was to come willingly, she was not kidnapped. As in the definition, the goddess is invited to Rome where she will receive a fitting temple – which was in fact dedicated at Rome in 392 BC, on the Aventine Hill. The cult title is given as Queen Juno – that this is an approximation of an Etruscan title is probably not the case, but rather reflects that Juno in Roman eyes was the main deity at Veii. Plutarch, in his *Life of Camillus*, writes of the Roman belief that before Juno came to Rome it was but a small and insignificant city, but that Rome rose to greatness afterwards.[43] Related to this is Livy having Camillus stating, when he evokes Juno, that if she comes to Rome it will be *her* city. This, however, was not one of the stated aims of the *evocatio* ritual. Presumably, foreign gods who transferred their allegiance to Rome could be thought of as assisting it, but the primary motive for the ritual was to have the god desist from helping its original city. Even though Camillus – after Veii had been besieged for several years – states that he is about to 'advance to destroy the city of Veii', it was nevertheless crucial that Juno be persuaded not to come to the aid of the city. In the *evocatio* formula, 'I vow that I will build temples and celebrate games for you' is a crucial element. The god was asked to desert its own temples built by the city's inhabitants, and to find a new home, especially to house its statue, at Rome.[44]

An extremely important feature of the *evocatio* which arises out of the ritual discourse of the transference of Juno's statue to Rome is the willingness of this deity to do so – she is not uprooted without her approval. Livy reports that the statue of the goddess was one which only a priest of a certain Etruscan family was allowed to touch, which is a credible enough cultic detail. Young men were chosen from the victorious Roman army, purified themselves and put on white clothing, in order that they convey the statue to Rome. Livy stresses the piety of the statue movers – they are chosen from the young men – and one can probably extend this to mean that they were handsome and therefore pleasant to the goddess' eyes. They were purified and wore the colour of purity – white – and their religious piety and scruples were such that they were reluctant to touch the statue of the goddess. Livy is very particular in stressing these details.

Since they did not want to touch the statue (because of the priestly prohibition). When one of the young men, whether – as Livy asks – divinely inspired or from a youthful sense of fun, asked the statue if she would like to go to Rome, the other young soldiers cried out that the goddess had nodded. This was not incredible from a Roman (or Greek or Egyptian) perspective,[45] because it was believed that statues could indicate a god's will through nodding, or some other sign.[46] Plutarch also knew of a more elaborated tradition, in which the goddess said – in a low voice – that she was willing and ready to go to Rome.[47] Dionysius of Halicarnassus' (brief) version makes it clear how important the affirmation of the goddess was, either at the time of her moving or soon after (or indeed both). His account has one of the young statue movers asking Juno whether she would like to go to Rome and that she answered (in his account) with a loud voice. The young men wanted the question put again, and it was: she answered again, as a double confirmation, obviously so there could be no doubt.[48] As part of this process, Livy stresses that the statue had of course to be moved off its pedestal: but the statue came away easily, showing the goddess' willingness.

For those who were participating in the touching and moving of the statue it was crucial to believe that they did so with the willing and voluntary consent of the goddess – and clearly the Romans after the event needed to have concrete evidence that the goddess was willing to go. Camillus' prayer to the goddess had been answered in that she had not intervened when he entered the city, sacked it and butchered or enslaved its inhabitants. His invitation was a willing self-disempowerment by the goddess, attracted by the prospect of cult in Rome. Here, it was not that the goddess' power for Veii was negated but that the goddess had willingly surrendered it – and that power would now be put to use for Rome's benefit and imperial expansion. Veii also has special significance because it was the first major conquest by the Romans, the first time Rome had defeated a major enemy city and it was the first official introduction of a non-Roman god into the Roman pantheon. This process of *evocatio* was then repeated several times, most notably against another powerful enemy city, Carthage.

Evocatio at Carthage

Carthage provides the next historical occasion for the employment of the *evocatio* ritual.[49] There are two sources for the *evocatio* as conducted by the Romans outside this city, both of which are late: Macrobius, once again, in the fifth century AD in his *Saturnalia*, and Servius in his fourth- to early fifth-century AD commentary on the *Aeneid*.[50] The lateness of the sources has led to some scepticism about the information of these sources,[51] but this is not only unnecessary but neglects Macrobius' introduction of the formula: for he explicitly states that he had taken the 'spell' (*carmen*) of *evocatio* from the fifth book of Serenus Sammonicus' *Secret History*, and that Serenus wrote that he himself had found it in 'the very ancient book' (*vetustissimo libro*) of Furius.[52] Now, given that the context is Carthage, this Furius will almost certainly have been Lucius Furius Philus,[53] consul in 136 BC, who was an intimate of Scipio Aemilianus, conqueror of Carthage in the Third Punic War (146 BC). Some other fragments of Furius' work survive as mentioned by writers such as Macrobius. This 'spell' therefore is of very antique origin (second century BC), and there is no need whatsoever to doubt that this was a historical formula employed by the Romans against Carthage. Furius has recorded in fact the very *evocatio* ritual which Scipio employed at Carthage in 146 BC – historiographical concerns that Macrobius is a late source are therefore invalid as his source was actually contemporary with the sack of Carthage.

Macrobius quotes the actual formula employed by Scipio:

> 'This is the hymn [*carmen*] which is employed to call the gods out when a city is under siege and surrounded:
> 'Whether a god, whether a goddess, in whose protection is the populace and community of Carthage, and of you most importantly, who this city and this people have received under your protection, I beseech and ask all of you for your approval, that you desert the populace and community of Carthage, forsaking its sacred places,

temples and city, and leaving this place, upon the populace and community fix fear, anxiety, and a forgetfulness. And may you come to Rome, to my people and myself, with beneficent spirit, and may it be that Rome's sacred places, temples, and city be more acceptable and more worthy of approbation and that you might be propitious towards myself and the Roman populace and my soldiers. If these matters you bring to pass so that we know and understand them, I vow that I will construct temples and celebrate games for you.'[54]

Most striking to note first of all here is that Camillus, in the ancient sources, does not employ a formula such as this. His words, 'At the same time, Juno Regina, who live in Veii now, I pray that when we are victorious you will come to us to the city of Rome – which will soon be your city as well, that a temple equal to your dignity might receive you', do not utilise Furius' words for the *evocatio* ritual. But Livy was writing a dramatic history, and the full *evocatio* formula might not have been thought appropriate by him in narrating Camillus' rousing speech before the troops. Yet the essential gist is there, especially the crucial element – Macrobius' *evocatio* promises the gods of Carthage temples and games, just as Camillus promised a temple to Juno. What is interesting here is that this *evocatio* before Carthage does not name a particular deity – in fact it also evinces a typical trend of the Romans and their own secret name syndrome (see below), for it calls upon those who protect the people and community of Carthage, 'whether a god, whether a goddess'. Some uncertainty on the part of the Romans as to the identity of the tutelary (protector) deity of Carthage is thus indicated.

What is important is that this god or goddess is indicated to be the deity who is protecting the city and its people, and who has 'been charged' with their protection. This deity has undertaken a particular responsibility which the inhabitants expect her to fulfill – but the Romans call upon the god, literally, to 'abandon' the city and its people. As with Veii, the conquest of Carthage is articulated as a process only achievable through its tutelary deity leaving the city and its people. The god is asked to leave their places, temples and shrines and the city itself, to abandon its sacred locales. A little later in the formula it is asked to come to Rome, to 'our' places, temples, shrines and city. So the deity will do a complete swap and find that these in Rome are 'more acceptable and more worthy of approbation', improving its material and physical surroundings at Rome. Between the request that it abandon these, and the enticement of better places, the Romans request the god not simply to desert but to strike fear and terror into the city and its inhabitants. So unlike at Veii, the god is also asked not simply to leave but to take an active role in harming the people and city which it had previously protected – that is, to turn against its worshippers. Servius, in referring to the *evocatio* formula, has a similar formulation, that the god strike fear and terror into the inhabitants.[55] He also comments that the gods were called out by *evocatio* in order to avoid *sacrilegium* – 'sacrilege'.[56] Unlike in Livy's account of Veii there is here no mention of a cult statue: the god is called forth to Rome, temples will be constructed for it there and presumably a cult statue provided if needed.

Furius records the *evocatio* ritual. Unfortunately, no other historical source does: Polybius and Appian in their accounts of the Punic Wars do not mention it.[57] Yet this is possibly a detail that could be overlooked in their narratives, and Furius did include this in his work – why would he have done so unless the *evocatio* ritual was actually employed at some stage during the Punic Wars? Against a powerful enemy such as Carthage – and this was the third war against it – it would make sound religious – and military – sense. As for historical context, this is provided by Servius, who states that Juno was 'exorated' (*exoratam Junonem*) during the Second Punic War, and that Scipio employed the *evocatio* formula in the Punic War prior to the city's destruction in 146 BC.[58] Servius does not employ the term *evocatio* here, with *exorare* meaning to 'placate', 'to beseech'.[59] As Carthage was defeated on the battlefield, and surrendered without a siege, this explains why the *evocatio* ritual was not employed in the Second Punic War. This Juno was in fact the Carthaginian Talit, called Juno Caelestis by the Romans.

An *evocatio* at Carthage has been called into question not only by the lateness of the sources which mention it (although as seen above, this is not a sound objection on historiographical grounds), but also by an argument that there is no indication that the goddess called out by the ritual, Juno Caelestis, received cult at Rome prior to the reign of the emperor Septimius Severus.[60] But there is in fact no evidence for this proposition.[61] There is no reason to suppose that this *evocatio* did not result in Juno Caelestis finding her place within the Roman pantheon. The testimony is solid second-century BC evidence for the actual formula which Scipio, having imperium, employed.

One final issue: Servius, in discussing the calling out of the gods, is commenting on Book Two of Virgil's *Aeneid* in which the Greeks capture Troy. Similarly, Macrobius, in concluding his discussion of the *evocatio*, specifically quotes the relevant lines of the *Aeneid*: 'All the gods on whom this empire [of Troy] rested have departed, abandoning their shrines and altars.'[62] This is a very typically Roman formulation, and lies at the heart of the *evocatio* ritual, which although not referred to here by Virgil, underlines the crucial significance the Romans placed on the support of the gods in maintaining their own empire, and their belief (reflected in the *evocatio* ritual) that the security and safety of a city and its inhabitants, and any sovereignty these held, rested with the gods. Troy was abandoned by its gods: so it was doomed.

Isaura Vetus: 'Whether it was a God, or Goddess, Protecting this Town'

In 75 BC the proconsul Publius Servilius Vatia captured the town of Isaura Vetus in Asia Minor[63] and set up a votive inscription. He had made a vow to the god of the city, and having captured it, made his dedication, inscribed on stone.[64] Some scholars have seen in this a *possibility* that Servilius had performed an *evocatio* ritual,[65] while others considered that he had *in fact* performed one.[66] The possibility that this was an *evocatio* would mean that the chronological range of known *evocationes*, starting with Veii in 396 BC, and at Carthage in the Punic Wars (146 BC), could be extended down to the first century BC. While tempting, the inscription does not record an *evocatio* as such. Its reference is to a *votum*, a vow: had Servilius made a vow to the god of Isaura Vetus which he fulfilled when he captured the city? If so, he considered that the god, in return for a vow, had abandoned the town. That the inscription is set up at Isaura Vetus, and the block it has been suggested is like a building stone, has led to the supposition that Servilius dedicated a shrine to the god at Isaura Vetus. But that he had destroyed the town (which he also left depopulated), and he would return to Rome after his office expired, probably indicates that he commemorated the victory over the town, and the support of its god, with a public record, but took the god to Rome with him, which would be the typical form of the *evocatio*.

> 'SERVEILIUS · C(aii) · F(ilius) · IMPERATOR
> HOSTIBUS. VICTEIS. ISAURA. VETERE.
> CAPTA. CAPTIVEIS. VENUM. DATEIS.
> SEI. DEUS. SEIVE. DEAST. QUOIUS. IN.
> TUTELA. OPPIDUM. VETUS. ISAURA.
> FUIT *VAC*. VOTUM. SOLVIT.'

'Servilius, son of Gaius (Servilius), Imperator, when Isaura Vetus was taken, having conquered the enemies, sold the captives into slavery. Whether it was a god, or whether a goddess, protecting the town, Isaura Vetus, (Servilius) fulfilled his vow.'

Sei deus seive deast quoius in tutela oppidum Vetus Isaura in lines 4–5 ('whether it was a god or goddess who was protecting this town, Isaura Vetus') has been recognized as being similar to the formula for the *evocatio* at Carthage as quoted in Macrobius,[67] which he took from Sammonicus Serenus, who in turn quoted Lucius Furius Philus writing in the second half of the second century BC, about fifty years earlier than Servilius' inscription: *si deus si dea est cui populus civitasque Carthagi niensis est in tutela* ('in whose protection are the people and community of Carthage, whether it be a god or a goddess'). Servilius was employing the time-honoured ritual of the *evocatio*, though he uses the term *votum*, vow, with the same intent and result as Camillus had used at Veii some 200 years earlier. This is the last instance of the *evocatio* ritual. Servilius' *votum* might in fact have been somewhat unusual, in that the *evocationes* of Veii and Carthage were made against cities of size and military capacity, historically enemies of Rome for many years, over a century in the case of Carthage, tangible enemies of Rome, with which the conquest of Isaura Vetus could hardly compare. One further point, however, is that only dictators such as Camillus and imperators such as Servilius at Isaura Vetus (as the first line of the inscription records) could perform the *evocatio* ritual. This, perhaps, might have been one of Servilius' motives – he was religiously and militarily empowered to perform the ritual which would secure Isaura Vetus for Rome.

Vertumnus, Protecting Deity of the City of Volsinii

Another example which is generally seen as an *evocatio* rests on the evidence of the Roman poet Propertius (*c.* 50–15 BC):[68] that of the god Vertumnus, whose statue was once in the Etruscan city of Volsinii but came to reside in Rome. Vertumnus speaks through Propertius' poetry:[69]

'Vertumnus: A Tuscan am I and from Tuscans I arose, and I do not feel penitent to have deserted the hearths of Volsinii in the time of battle … And you, Rome, gave to my Tuscans the reward of having a street called "Tuscus", even to this day. But grant, divine Saturn, that throughout the ages the toga clad crowd of Rome might pass below my feet. For this crowd makes me happy, nor do I desire an ivory temple: I am satisfied that I have a view over the Roman forum.'

Volsinii was destroyed by the Romans in 264 BC, and the god Vertumnus' statue taken to Rome by its destroyer, the general M. Fulvius Flaccus.[70] Varro reports that Vertumnus was one of the gods introduced to Rome by the Etruscan King Titus Tatius (according to legend, living in the time of Romulus). He was therefore (if Varro is correct) already known and familiar to the Romans before Fulvius' sack of the city. Varro notes too that Vertumnus was the main Etruscan deity.[71] Flaccus 'called out' this god as the principal, tutelary god of Volsinii, in order to aid his conquest of the city. Propertius stresses that the statue of the god which Fulvius brought to Rome did not have its own temple, but did have a view of the Forum from the 'Tuscan Street' (Vicus Tuscus) at the foot of the Palatine hill which Propertius refers to, and with which Varro concurs.[72] And yet a temple of this god existed on the Avertine, and in it was a painting of Fulvius as a triumphator (he celebrated a triumph due to his capture of Volsinii).[73]

Vertumnus, like other gods involved in *evocatio*, as seen in particular with Juno of Veii, was quite willing to come to Rome and feels no 'remorse' at leaving it in 'the days of battle' (i.e. when the city was under attack by the Romans). Propertius conceptualizes his leaving of the city as occurring when the battle was still taking place. This of course was the aim of the Romans in employing the *evocatio* ritual: the god Vertumnus, as the chief god of the city, is construed as deliberately forsaking his city when it was under attack. Propertius has the god satisfied that he has a view of the Roman Forum, the heart of the city, and the god's statue states he has no need for a temple, even though Camillus for Juno at Veii, and the *evocatio* ritual at Carthage, both promised these to the principal god of each of those cities.[74]

It has even been argued that at the siege of Jerusalem, Titus may have employed an *evocatio* just before he captured the city after a lengthy siege.[75] A loud voice was heard from within the Temple, shouting, according to Tacitus, that 'the gods are leaving'.[76] This shows, of course, a lack of understanding of Jewish monotheism. Josephus, the Jewish author writing in Greek, in his *Jewish Wars* – which has a detailed contemporary account of the fall of Jerusalem, including prophecies and omens predicting its capture – includes that priests in the Temple heard a voice like a host saying, 'We are leaving.' Divinity had abandoned the Temple, and hence Jerusalem, to its fate.

Captive Gods

Somewhat at odds with the ceremony of the *evocatio* is that of the phenomenon of 'captive gods'.[77] Ovid in his *Fasti* provides explanations in the form of questions for why the shrine (*delubra*) of Minerva at the base of the Caelian Hill at Rome has the suffix *capta*: *Minerva capta*, 'Minerva captured'. But one question is clearly the correct one: 'Or is it because she came to Rome as a captive at the time when Falerii was conquered? This very fact is proved by an ancient inscription.' The nature of this inscription goes unsaid, but it was 'ancient', and might well have been the dedicatory inscription for the shrine, which detailed how the statue of the goddess came to be in Rome and why the temple was built. Even if the goddess was not 'called out' by an *evocatio*, she was clearly thought important enough to warrant this treatment: this shrine of Minerva of the Etruscan city of Falerii was dedicated when the city was captured and the statue of the goddess brought to Rome in 241 BC. Conquest for the Romans meant total surrender. Hence when Capua was retaken in 211 BC after going over to Hannibal in the Second Punic War, Livy notes that all of the statues in the city were taken to Rome, where they were handed over to the College of Pontiffs to ascertain which were profane and which sacred.[78] Clearly the profane would be sold as booty, while the sacred would find homes in temples and shrines – as captured statues.

But the scope of Roman looting was such that as statues and paintings from conquered Greek cities poured into Rome in the third and second centuries BC, not all statues of the gods, but rather the more famous of them, were housed in Roman temples. Livy, in commenting on the sack and pillaging of Syracuse in 211 BC, under the command of Marcellus, notes that sacred as well as profane places in that city were looted: from this first stemmed, he complains, the Roman passion for Greek art.[79] In 209 BC, Fabius Maximus, having conquered Tarentum, left most of the statues of the gods in the city, but did take home a statue of Hercules, which was then officially dedicated on the Capitoline.[80]

A captured city had forfeited all its belongings, both profane and divine, according to the Christian author Tertullian (AD *c*.155–240), who could remark that the Romans had triumphed over many gods, and he writes that he needs no more proof than the captive statues (*simulacra captiva*) of those gods taken from the enemies of Rome. These captured gods, Tertullian criticizes, allow themselves to be worshipped by their enemies, the Romans, and instead of punishing them, promise them '*imperium sine fine*' – empire without end – as did Jupiter to the Romans in Virgil's *Aeneid*.[81]

While Tertullian as a Christian author is a hostile witness to Roman polytheism, several universal truths about warfare and the gods are illuminated here, and ones which the Romans were conscious of through their *evocatio* ritual. To sack a city is to confront the gods of that city, to attack them.[82] To destroy a city is to destroy its temples, unless a specific attempt is made to avoid this – such as when Alexander the Great parcelled out all the temples of Thebes except what parts were sacred, and spared the priests and priestesses, but sold all others into slavery.[83] Temples and sanctuaries were routinely destroyed by the Romans when they sacked towns and cities.

Minucius Felix (AD 160? –250?) had a similar opinion:[84]

> 'All the things that the Romans hold, occupy, possess: these are the spoils of their audacity. Rome's temples are full of war-booty, looted from the ruins of towns, being the spoils from the gods and the slaughter of priests. Yet this is an insult and a ridicule to serve the religions they have conquered, to capture these gods and then to worship them after the victory.'

Roman ownership of a city's statues followed automatically upon its conquest and looting. The surrendering of a city by its inhabitants also placed its gods at Roman disposal, apparently even since the early, regal days of Rome, if Livy is to be relied on. Tarquinius Priscus (616–578? BC), as king of Rome, received the embassy of the Collatini, a Sabine people, which had come to surrender their city, Collatia, with what seems very much like a formulaic expression as given by Livy:[85]

> 'Collatia's surrender occurred, I [Livy] understand, according to this formulation: The king asked: "Are you here the legates and the speakers sent by the people of Collatia, with the purpose of surrendering Collatia and yourselves?" "We are." "Is the people of Collatia under its own authority?" "Yes." "Do you surrender both yourselves and the people of Collatia, the town, fields, water, boundaries, shrines, utensils, everything divine and human, into my power and that of the Roman people?" "We give it." "So I receive it."'

So here the gods are surrendered to the Romans by the community itself – whereas in the *evocatio*, the principal god is thought of as abandoning the community to its own devices. Surrender to the Romans is absolute – everything of Collatia comes under Roman rule. But here the gods 'stay put' and would continue to be worshipped at Collatia. In connection with the mercy and clemency Scipio extended towards communities in Spain, Livy noted that this was indeed the ancient custom of the Romans.[86]

These divine possessions were not necessarily taken to Rome, but rather were surrendered to it. Plautus, in his play *Amphitryon*, in a description of the Teloboians surrendering to the Thebans, says, 'they surrendered themselves, all their divine and mortal possessions, their city and their children.'[87] An entire community, including its gods, shrines and temples, would upon surrender become the property of Rome. Surrender was complete: even the gods bowed to the might of the Roman conqueror.[88]

When cities were sacked, they were looted. As seen, Pliny has 2,000 statues ransacked by the Romans when they pillaged Volsinii.[89] When enemies were defeated, the same looting took place. Pausanias the Greek geographer, in his *Geography* of mainland Greece, in writing about the sanctuary of Athena Alea in Tegea, in Arcadia, notes that the ancient image of the goddess was taken by Augustus to Rome when he defeated Mark Antony, with whom the Arcadians were allied. In doing so, Pausanias goes on, Augustus was not the first to carry off statues and dedications from the defeated, but was following ancient practices, and he provides a list of examples from the Greek world.[90] Earlier than Augustus, Sulla in Greece had no religious scruples about the religious sanctity of sacred objects and statues.[91] In the East, in the 60s BC, Pompey 'confiscated the statues and other images of the gods' from the people he conquered.[92]

That an *evocatio* occurred at Veii (Juno Regina), Carthage (Juno Caelestis) and Volsinii (Vertumnus) is clear, and Isaura Vetusis (an unknown god) provides, perhaps, a fourth case, whereas evidence for the possible fifth case, of Falerii, is almost non-existent. These four cases date to the Republic, and none to the Empire, with the three main cases dating to the fourth and third centuries BC. This is not an extensive number given the number of cities that Rome conquered and sacked in this period. This could be explained by the vagaries of the historical record: Livy is interested in the case of Veii, but apparently no others, and utilizes it to stress Roman piety. Macrobius' interest records the *evocatio* formula, drawing on an earlier source. Pliny also draws on an earlier source to define the *evocatio*. As with other areas of Roman religion, much has been lost and some survives only by chance.

The *evocatio* was of interest to Roman antiquarians as a ritual which played a key role in the capture of cities, and was doubtless employed many times throughout the Republic, even if this has left but a few traces in the historical record.

The Goddess Juno Sospita Threatens to Abandon the Romans during the Social War

In 90 BC, the year after the tribune Drusus had been assassinated during civil dissension at Rome, and with the Social War (the war against the Italian allies who revolted when denied Roman citizenship in 91 BC, for which Drusus had attempted to legislate) having broken out that year, one of the members of the aristocratic and prestigious Metelli family, Caecilia Metella, reported that she had had a dream: the goddess Juno Sospita had appeared to her to say that she was leaving her temple because it had become polluted. The Senate was informed of this. Prior to this, at the outbreak of the war, a series of portents had been reported to the Senate, the worst of these, Cicero states, being that some silver shields in Juno's sanctuary at Lanuvium had been gnawed by mice: obviously a terrible omen in the context of a war against Rome's allies.[93]

Cicero loosely connects the *prodigia* and the dream, but clearly the Senate must have drawn a close link between them. These *prodigia* and the dream were signs of the gods' displeasure with Rome. While Cicero knows of the dream, it is the fourth-century AD epitomator of Livy, Obsequens, who in his *Prodigium Liber* (*Book of Prodigies*) collected together all of the *prodigia* in Livy, who is the source for the actual substance of the dream. Roman matrons had sullied her temple, when they were meant to be worshipping the goddess, and a bitch had given birth to her litter beneath the statue of the goddess. In her dream, Caecilia had only with difficulty through prayers and supplications persuaded Juno Sospita not to abandon her temple, and had promised to restore the temple building itself to its 'pristine splendour':[94]

> 'Metella Caecilia related that in a dream she had seen Juno Sospita fleeing because her temple had been befouled disgustingly, and that with her prayers she had, with difficulty, persuaded her to remain, and the temple which matrons by their sordid and obscene bodily ministrations had defiled, and in which under the very statue of the goddess a bitch and its litter lived, she

restored to its former pristine splendour, supplications having been held.'[95]

That Caecilia dreamed of Juno Sospita would not have appeared as particularly remarkable from a Roman point of view, for not only did various deities appear to mortals while they slumbered, but Cicero specifically refers to this particular goddess appearing to her worshippers in dreams, as if this was a regular epiphany occurrence.[96] Juno Sospita was not simply a goddess but an important one from a Roman military point of view. The shields which were mice-gnawed in her temple at Lanuvium were almost certainly ones dedicated to her in her temple. Her epithet, Sospita, means 'Saviour'. She was a martial deity, depicted with a spear and shield. Cicero has one of the interlocutors in his dialogue *On the Nature of the Gods* arguing that when Juno Sospita appears in a dream to someone, she does so dressed in a goat's skin, carrying a spear and shield, and with her boots upturned at the toes.[97] She appears so attired on several Roman coins, which also show her with a helmet. A silver denarius minted by the moneyer (minter) Lucius Procilius depicts a bust of the goddess Juno Sospita on the obverse, wearing her goat's skin headdress (Figure 3.2).[98] On the reverse, the martial characteristics of the goddess – and why the Romans would want this goddess on their side in the war against their

Figure 3.2: Serrate silver denarius. Obverse: Juno Sospita with her goatskin headdress. Reverse: Juno Sospita advancing into battle in a *biga* (two-horse chariot), spear at the ready, with shield; an erect bearded snake, her cult totem, is under the horses. The name of the moneyer, L. Procilius, is in the exergue; 80 BC. Courtesy *CNG* 735602.

allies – are depicted. She charges into battle in her *biga* (two-horse chariot), brandishing her spear, carrying a figure-of-eight shield and holding the reins in the same hand, with her goatskin headdress giving her a terrifying appearance.

Caecilia Metella's tomb, in fact, was decorated with two shields, shaped like the ones the goddess is shown bearing on coins, which must be a reference to Juno Sospita's shields at Lanuvium.[99] Her temple at Lanuvium was duly restored, the goddess did not flee and the Roman Senate obviously considered that they had the support of this war goddess in their struggle with the Latin allies.

This discussion has assumed that the temple of Juno Sospita which Caecilia dreamt about was at Lanuvium, rather than that at Rome,[100] where she had received a temple in 194 BC as a result of a *votum* (vow) made by the consul C. Cornelius Cethegus in the Insurian War of 197 BC.[101] This is logical on a number of grounds: it is at Lanuvium that the goddess had her principal and ancient sanctuary, prodigies had occurred there over the years and it was also, technically, while very close to Rome, in Latin territory. The goddess' threat to abandon her temple was thus surely predicated upon, even though not articulated in the sources, her then going over to the Latin side in disgust at her treatment by the Roman matrons. It is possible that if this had not occurred during the Social War there may have been a very different senatorial reaction, but it is apparent that the military crisis meant that Rome was worried that such a goddess would desert the city in such an exigency.

Dionysus abandons Antony

Gods abandoning individuals to their fate in battle is of course a theme in Homer's *Iliad*. For example, the god Apollo abandons Hector moments before Achilles slays him.[102] The Greeks also thought that a defeated city had been abandoned by its gods, as Aeschylus writes.[103] In this vein, Apollo is construed as abandoning the Phoenician city of Tyre before its fall to Alexander the Great in 331 BC, while Herakles on the other hand welcomed Alexander into the same Tyre.[104] And the whole purpose of the Roman *evocatio* was to entice the principle deity out of a besieged enemy city. Virgil provides a Roman counterpart to Aeschylus' comment: the gods of Troy had fled from every altar.[105] When inhabitants abandoned and left a city, naturally they took their gods with them: as the Persians approached their city in the 490s BC, the people of the Greek city of Phocaea in Asia Minor packed up all their possessions, taking with them the statues of the gods from their temples and the dedications in them, as did the people of Myous when they moved to Miletus.[106]

In Republican Rome, the case of a god deserting a favourite is told by Plutarch in his biography of Mark Antony. This occurred during the night of 31 July 30 BC, in Alexandria, and the next day the city fell to Octavian's forces after which Antony committed suicide:[107]

> 'During this night, it is reported, around the middle, when the city was quiet and low-spirited through fear and apprehension of what was going to happen, some melodious sounds of all kinds of musical instruments were suddenly heard and the shouting of a crowd, with Dionysiac cries and satyric leapings, as if a thiasos was clamorously departing the city; their direction seemed to lie rather through the middle of the city towards the outer gate facing the enemy, where the clamour grew loudest and then rushed out. And those who sought to interpret the sign believed that it signified that the god was abandoning Antony – the god to whom he particularly likened and with whom he associated himself.'

Dionysus deserted Antony, but where this story first originated, like all such, cannot be determined. Dionysus as such would not have been a great ally in war, but as Plutarch notes, this was the god with whom Antony had most identified – his favourite god had deserted him, and went out through the gate that led straight to the enemy.

Moreover, when Virgil writes of the struggle of the gods in the heavens above the Battle of Actium on 2 September 31 BC, between Octavian, and Antony and Cleopatra, he must be reflecting Augustan propaganda when he has the 'monstrous gods and barking Anubis' being confronted by Neptune, Venus, Minerva, Mars, Bellona and Apollo of Actium.[108] At Actium, in Greece, there was a temple of Apollo; Neptune, as the god of the sea, would naturally be on the Roman side; while Venus, as Octavian's ancestral goddess, naturally lent a hand, as did the warrior goddess Minerva, the Roman equivalent of the Greek military goddess Athena, who played such a crucial role in assisting the Greeks at Troy. Mars of course is present fighting for Octavian, while Bellona (Figure 2.1) as a goddess of war naturally fights alongside Mars.[109] In the century prior to Actium, Mars, Jupiter and Minerva are shown as triumphant deities of war on a coin of 112–111 BC (Figure 3.3).[110] Virgil ridicules the Egyptian gods through the vehicle of Anubis – the barking, animal god, who is no match for Rome's deities.

Following these lines, Virgil provides a pious portrait of Octavian: he dedicated 300 shrines in Rome to Italy's gods, and before all the altars lay slain sacrificial beasts; at the temple of Apollo he sits and watches his triumphal procession pass by.[111] Servius comments that Virgil here can call the Egyptian gods 'monstrous' (*monstra*) because the Romans had not yet officially adopted Egyptian deities.[112] Octavian, and later as Augustus, was not inimical to foreign deities per se,[113] rather Virgil's lines are programmatic for how Octavian constructed the civil war in the public eye: it was a struggle not between himself and Antony as Romans, but between the Roman state (and hence its gods) and Egypt, symbolized by Cleopatra, and its gods. Similarly, the poet Propertius, also writing like Virgil in Augustus' reign, referred to Cleopatra 'daring to oppose yapping Anubis against our Jupiter'.[114] More fully than Virgil, Propertius in another elegy has Apollo of Actium speaking personally to Octavian (addressing him as Augustus, which name he took in 27 BC) and instructing him to win

Figure 3.3:   Silver denarius. The victorious Roman gods of war: Mars, Jupiter and Minerva. Obverse: a helmeted Mars, with a *bucranium* (bull's head) behind. Reverse: Juno on the left looks on while Minerva, right, with spear and helmet, crowns Jupiter in the centre with a victory wreath; he holds his weapon of war, his thunderbolt, and his sceptre indicating his dominion; he does not require any armour. Moneyer: Gnaeus Blasio, Rome mint, 112–111 BC.

the battle, with Apollo at his side. The god duly participates, and each of his arrows sank ten ships.[115] In this *theomachia* (battle between the gods), Rome's anthropomorphic gods easily defeated the theriomorphic (beast-formed) deities of the Nile.

The Devotio for a City's Destruction, and the Devotio of a Roman General

Macrobius, having quoted the formula for the *evocatio*, writes: 'Once the divinities have been called forth, cities and armies are devoted to destruction with the following words, which only dictators and generals are able to use for the purpose.' This was the *carmen devotionis* (*devotio* prayer), and the ritual's opening lines bear some similarities with the *evocatio* formula. The enemy's people, fields and cities are dedicated to the gods and cursed by the Roman commander, with the intent that this will assure the safety of the general, legions and the army. In essence, it is a prayer that the enemy will die, and not the Romans; that in the bloody struggle of war, the enemy will be substitutes (*vicarii*) for the Romans. Macrobius places this practice in Rome's past, and although there is no evidence for any specific occasion when it was utilized, this could simply be a deficiency in the historical record. Father Dis (Jupiter), Veiovis (underworld [chthonic] Jupiter) and Manes (the gods of the underworld) are the gods called upon to be the agents of destruction.[116]

This is, of course, a very different *devotio*, though related, to that of individual Roman military commanders on the battlefield, which was known as the *devotio hostium*, the devotion of the enemy forces. This *devotio* by an individual commander is known from three specific cases, involving three generations of the same family: P. Decius Mus performed this type of individual *devotio* at the Battle at Mt Vesuvius in 340 BC, as did his son at Sentinum in 295 BC, while in the third generation, his grandson performed the same ritual at Ausculum in 279 BC. Only for the first occurrence is the ritual described in full, by Livy. The omens had been taken, and battle joined, but the Roman left wing began to give way. Decius as general called upon the pontifex maximus, who was present, to recite the ritual words so that Decius could devote himself in order to save the Roman legions. Decius was ordered by the pontifex maximus to put on a toga with a purple border (it is not indicated where this came from: had Decius brought it into battle with the intention of undergoing the *devotio* ritual?). He veiled his head with the toga, with one hand held out from it, touching his chin, then standing upon a spear he recited the ritual formula of *devotio*:[117]

> 'Janus, Jupiter, Father Mars, Quirinus, Bellona, Lares, divine Novensiles, divine Indigites, you deities in whose power are both we and our enemies, and you also, divine Manes, I call upon you and worship you, and I beseech and beg that you will prosper the armed might and victory of the Roman people of the Quirites, and afflict the enemies of the Roman people of the Quirites with terror, trembling, and death ... I devote [*devoveo*] the legions and the auxillaries of the enemy – and myself – to the divine Manes and to the Earth.'

The divine Novensiles were an Italian group of deities, the nature of which is uncertain, the divine Indigites are even more obscure (local deities?), while the divine Manes were the spirits or gods of the underworld. Janus, Jupiter, Father Mars, Quirinus and Bellona were all martial deities and their inclusion is easy to understand. These gods were the ones who in return for the 'gift' of the general's life were believed to undertake the destruction of the enemies of Rome on the battlefield. Decius' *devotio* was a form of human self-sacrifice, in which he promised to give his life in return for the destruction of the enemy: it was therefore a vow (*votum*) in which he surrendered his life. After having performed the *devotio*, Decius ordered his lictors to inform his other consul (Titus Manlius) of this (clearly to encourage him and to announce publicly that the ritual had been performed, helping to ensure its efficacy), and girded his toga in the Gabinian style (*cinctus* [belt] *Gabinus*). This involved using the toga to veil the head (known as *capite velato*, with the head covered, which was required of officiants at Roman religious ceremonies), wrapping it so that one arm could be thrust out through it, so that it formed a girdle or 'belt' around the body.[118] Associated with military rituals, it was the toga worn by one of the consuls when the doors of the Temple of Janus were opened (signifying Rome was in a state of war).[119] Decius then charged into the enemy, spreading consternation, and when he was killed, the enemy took fright, the legions charged and Rome won the battle. His body was later found pierced through with numerous enemy spears.

That only the family of the Decii are recorded to have practised the *devotio* to secure victory is a difficulty. The scholarly surmise is that the formula recorded for Decius Mucius' *devotio* in 340 BC is probably the product of a later age,[120] but this depends on who Livy's source was at this point: he specifically states that he is giving the *devotio* ritual 'in the very same words with which they were formulated, and passed down'.[121] Livy, before finalizing his narrative of this battle, writes that he would like to mention that a general, be he a consul, dictator or praetor, need not devote himself, but could name any enlisted soldier to do so.

To state that the general undertook to commit suicide in the *devotio* ritual in order to be a human sacrifice for the gods involved is incorrect. He was prepared to give his life if necessary, as three generations of one family did. If he died in this battle, well and good, but there were specific provisions made if he did in fact actually survive, even though he had devoted his life and those of the enemy. If he did survive the battle, Livy, continuing his narrative of Decius Mucius' *devotio*, records that an effigy of him was to be buried more than 7ft underground (hence ensuring it was deep enough to have contact with the chthonic gods of the devotion ritual), and a sacrifice made over that spot, which became a *locus religiosus*, which a Roman magistrate could not approach (due to the negative connotations of the man not having been slain in battle). The devoted individual could dedicate his arms to Vulcan or to any other god, but from then on it was impious for him to make any sacrifice whatsoever to any deity. If the spear on which the devoted individual stood was captured by the enemy, then a *suovetauralia* sacrifice to expiate this was to be made to Mars: a pig, sheep and ox. Through this ceremony, the commander made a willing human sacrifice of himself or another soldier, yet with the possibility that the devoted could survive. Presumably its intent, however, must have been to persuade the martial and chthonic gods to accept a human sacrifice of a Roman, and in thanks to cause the enemy to be defeated and die.

Military Vows: Dedications and Temples

Generals on campaign could make several different types of vows (*vota*, singular: *votum*) to an individual god for assistance in battle: the *devotio* was only one such type of *votum*. One of these was to promise a tithe (a portion, usually 10 per cent) of the spoils taken from the enemy, to a god. A vow paid for from booty was, in technical terms, manubial, taken in war, from war booty (*manubiae*). Hence, as seen above, in conjunction with his *evocatio* of Juno Regina, Camillus as imperator vowed to Pythian Apollo a tithe of the spoils from Veii. Throughout the Republic, generals also vowed to build temples, to be paid for from the proceeds of the spoils, to a god, or to stage games, *ludi*, in their honour.

According to tradition, the Temple of Capitoline Jupiter was constructed due to a vow undertaken by Tarquinius Priscus, king of Rome, for Jupiter's assistance against the Sabines, but construction did not well and truly begin until under Rome's last king, Tarquinius Superbus. At his overthrow in 509 BC, the new Roman Republic dedicated the temple.[122] This began a long tradition in the Republic of military commanders dedicating temples to the gods, a phenomenon particularly attested in the middle Republic but which declined markedly after 180 BC, to be revived by Pompey and Caesar.[123] Cicero mentions that generals are allowed to use their *manubiae* to construct temples for the gods.[124]

A few examples will suffice. P. Sempronius Sophus in 268 BC vowed the temple of Tellus when engaged in fighting against the city of Picenum, which had rebelled: an earthquake occurred during the battle, so he placated the earth by vowing a temple to Tellus – the Earth goddess.[125] Rome's initial war against the Carthaginians, the First Punic War (264– 241 BC), was the occasion for temples built for military victories. Tacitus, in a list of temples restored by Augustus, notes that C. Duilius constructed the temple of Ianus (Janus) due to his victory in the naval battle at Mylae in 260 BC, and presumably this was to fulfill a vow to this god.[126] This historian also mentions that Aulus Atilius Calatinus in the First Punic War vowed (here he mentions this point specifically) the temple of Spes (Hope).[127] Also in the First Punic War, when Lucius Cornelius Scipio encountered a storm at sea off Corsica in 259 BC, he vowed a temple to Tempestates (the deity Tempest).[128] Temples were vowed and dedicated by the Senate to Venus Erycina and Mens in 217 BC after the disastrous defeat by Hannibal at Lake Trasimene.[129]

Lucius Furius Purpurio, as praetor, vowed a temple to Vediovis in 200 BC when fighting against the Gauls at the Battle of Cremona; Vediovis' temple (on the Tiber island in Rome) was completed and dedicated in 194 BC. After the battle, 200 wagons of Gallic war-booty had been captured; it is to be imagined that this will easily have paid for the temple. In fact, Purpurio as consul also vowed a second temple to Vediovis, in 198 BC, which was dedicated (on the Capitoline) in 192 BC. His attachment to this god, dedicating two temples to him, is remarkable.[130]

In 191 BC, the temple to the goddess Iuventas which Marcus Livius as consul had vowed at the Battle of Metaurus in 207 BC, in which Hasdrubal was defeated and killed, was dedicated in the Circus Maximus, with accompanying *ludi* (games). Iuventas ('youth') was associated with the age when boys became of age for military service, and hence a military vow to her was appropriate. Livy, the source, also adds an interesting comment: 'By reason of this dedication also ludi (games) were held, and with more intense religious feeling because the new war with Antiochus was imminent.'[131] With a fresh conflict brewing, in Asia Minor, the religious sensitivities of the Roman people, and their belief that divine support was needed in military activity, were aroused. Lucius Porcius Licinius vowed a temple to Venus Erycna in 184 BC while consul, fighting against the Ligurians in northern Italy.[132] This was in fact the second temple dedicated to her (in 181 BC) in Rome, so when it comes to considering why a general might vow a temple to a god, whether or not that god already had one was not always a consideration. This was also the second temple dedicated in 181 BC: the other was to Pietas, which Marcus Acilius Glabrio had vowed at Thermopylai in Greece before the battle against Antiochus there (191 BC).[133] In the twenty years from 194–173 BC, Roman generals built fourteen temples at Rome.[134] It would seem logical that many if not all temples resulted from vows and were financed from war loot, but this is not always explicitly stated by the sources, probably because the sources took this for granted, for why else would a general decide to build a temple, and how would he otherwise pay for it? After 173 BC, by contrast, there was a major slump in building activity by generals, with few temples built by them.[135]

One last vow of temple construction by a general occurred in 101 BC, when the proconsul Quintus Lutatius Catulus vowed a temple to Fortuna Huiusce Diei at the Battle of Vercellae.[136] It was another half century until generals once more built temples. Temple building resulting from war-booty re-emerged when two great individuals wanted to ensure that their personalities had an impact on Rome and wished to advertise themselves through building programmes. Pompey constructed a theatre – the first permanent, stone theatre in Rome, which was dedicated in 55 BC, incorporating a temple of Venus Victrix (Venus Victory), dedicated in 52 BC, and several small shrines, one each to Felicitas, Honos, Virtus and Victoria. These were not, as far as the evidence goes, the results of vows made in the field, but they can only have been paid for by Pompey's extensive wealth resulting from his campaigns, especially in Asia Minor.[137] Pompey had, however, made a vow to Minerva during his campaigns in the East, which he duly fulfilled at the time of his triumph in 61 BC, dedicating to Minerva in her temple a share of the booty from his campaigns.[138]

Caesar, perhaps in rivalry with Pompey, in 46 BC dedicated a temple to Venus Genetrix (Ancestral Venus) in his Forum Iulium, stressing his claimed ancestry from the goddess. Appian records that Caesar made a vow to Venus to build this temple prior to the Battle of Pharsalus (48 BC) against Pompeian forces,[139] and this temple (and the entire Forum) will have been paid for from war booty. Octavian continued this tradition of dedicating temples from war booty. He is in fact quite specific, and states in his *Res Gestae* that he built a temple to Mars Ultor from war booty. He had vowed the temple immediately before the Battle of Philippi (42 BC), and it was completed and dedicated in 2 BC (Mars Ultor was apparently a patient deity),[140] and the standards recovered from the Parthians were housed there (see Figure 5.5). Temples became store-houses for the booty taken from campaigns, and the weapons and arms of the enemy. It was the gods that had decided the battle and allowed the victory, so to them belonged both a share of the booty but also some of the enemy weapons.

For example, in 50 BC a descendant of the five-time consul Marcellus, Marcellinus, as moneyer for the state in 50 BC, struck a denarius issue showing his celebrated ancestor (Figure 3.3). Marcellus, as one of the two consuls in 225 BC, had fought against the Gauls, and prior to battle he, according to Plutarch, vowed to Jupiter Feretrius that he would consecrate to him the most beautiful set of armour from amongst the enemy. When he saw that of the Gallic king, Viridomarus, Marcellus interpreted this to be the armour which he had vowed: the two men met in single combat, and the consul slew the king. On the spot he dedicated the armour, and asked the god's assistance for the rest of the campaign (in which the Romans did in fact achieve victory). Back at Rome, he – as the coin illustrates (Figure 3.4)[141] – carried the king's armour into a temple, which must be that of Jupiter Feretrius.[142] The *triskeles* (Greek 'three legs'), the three-legged emblem, on the lower left of the obverse refers to his sack of Syracuse in 211 BC, as this symbol often appeared on the reverse of Syracusan coins, taking up all that face.[143] The arms of the enemy leader when killed by a Roman were termed the *spolia opima* – the optimum spoils. Only three Romans, including Marcellus (and Romulus), ever achieved this.[144]

Generals vowing ludi to the Gods

Ludi (games) to the gods could also be vowed by military commanders while on campaign.[145] These had an advantage over temples in that they could be organized quickly, were closely associated with the person putting

Figure 3.4:   Silver denarius. Obverse: Marcellus, with the name of his descendant, Marcellinus. Reverse: Marcellus carries a victory trophy into the temple of Jupiter Feretrius, to whom he had made a vow before battle in 225 BC, to dedicate it to the god. Minted at Rome, 50 BC, by his descendant Marcellinus. Courtesy of the American Numismatic Society 1937.158.235.

them on and were always popular with the Roman people. Such games also clearly advertised that the person putting them on had been victorious in a war with the assistance of a particular god.[146] For example, Publius Cornelius Scipio Nasica as praetor vowed *ludi* to Jupiter, while campaigning against the Lusitanians in 194 BC. A pitched battle was fought in which the Lusitanians had at first the better of the Romans and threw them into a turmoil: the battle then became more equal, and at that point Scipio Nasica vowed *ludi* to Jupiter if he should rout and slaughter the Lusitanians. Significantly, in this case it was the commander who needed to pay for these vowed *ludi*. In 191 BC, prior to leaving Rome to campaign against the Boii in Gaul, he requested funds from the Senate with which to stage the vowed *ludi*, but its response was that he could pay for the costs out of his share of the spoils of the campaign or from his private monies. The reason given was that his request was unique and iniquitous (*novum atque iniquum*), but on what grounds is unknown (why he waited until three years after the vow is not made apparent), and whether commanders always had to pay for the *ludi* they vowed is unclear (they had to pay for the temples which they vowed from the spoils of the war); the same pay from booty principle may have held for *ludi*. At any rate, Scipio Nasica celebrated the games over ten days.[147]

Appeasing the Gods after the Roman defeat at Lake Trasimene, 217 BC

Venus Erycina had two temples in Rome. As noted above, one was dedicated as a result of a vow made by the dictator Q. Fabius Maximus after the disastrous Roman defeat at the hands of Hannibal at Lake Trasimene in 217 BC, and was dedicated in 215 BC. Livy states that on his first day as dictator, after the defeat, Fabius advised the senators that 'they must make enquiry of the gods themselves how the divine anger could be assuaged.'[148] Here there is an unambiguous assertion of the Roman religious mentality: the Romans had lost a battle and therefore this was a sign from the gods that they were displeased with Rome. Thus it was necessary to appease them.

Livy provides a long, detailed account of all the religious activities which resulted, clearly drawing on a detailed contemporary account. A decision was reached to consult the Sibylline Books, and Livy notes this was extraordinary as these were usually only consulted when dreadful prodigies occurred. The Board of Ten (*decimviri sacris faciundis*) in charge of these consulted the Books and advised the Roman Senate as follows: the vow (*votum*) made to Mars (this is in fact the first time it is mentioned in Livy) at the beginning of the conflict with Carthage had not been properly performed, and was to be performed again, on a larger scale. Great games were to be vowed to Jupiter, to cost 333,333⅓ bronze asses, and temples vowed to Venus Erycina and Mens, if Rome was victorious and returned the state of affairs to its pre-war condition. A sacrifice of 300 oxen to Jupiter was vowed, as well as the customary sacrifices to the other gods. When the vows had been announced (and this public announcement of the vows was obviously important, to bind the state through the witnessing to the vows), a *supplicatio* was decreed, in which both rural and urban men, wives and children were to participate. This *supplicatio* was a supplication of the gods by prayer.

A *lectisternium* was to be celebrated for three days: this involved six couches being set up, on which statues were placed of the gods Jupiter and Juno, Neptune, Minerva, Mars, Venus, Apollo, Diana, Vulcan, Vesta, Mercury and Ceres. After this, the temples were formally vowed: one to Venus Erycina (completed and dedicated in 215 BC) and one to Mens. The importance of these two temples is indicated by their both being constructed on the Capitoline.[149] Venus Erycina was, literally, Venus of Mt Eryx, in Sicily, where she was a widely worshipped and powerful goddess. Venus was often associated in the Roman mind with military endeavours, and this temple can in a sense be seen as a cult importation, to win this goddess over to the Roman side. Unfortunately, Livy, as with all the temple vows he mentions, does not indicate why a particular god or goddess was chosen for the honour of a temple in a military context.

In addition to these temple vows, *supplicatio* and *lectisternium*, a 'Sacred Spring' (*ver sacrum*) was vowed as part of the overall religious strategy to supplicate the gods: in this case, for victories for the next five years. A sacred Spring was a season of the year in which all the produce – animal or agricultural – was vowed to the gods.[150] Interestingly, despite the detailed arrangements made for the *ver sacrum* as recorded by Livy, in Book 33 he himself states that this vow was performed 'twenty-one years after it was made' in 195 BC: one can only imagine that the state of Rome's agriculture in 217 BC was such that the vow could not be fulfilled, or there were simply too many religious ceremonies to organize. Moreover, because of some irregularity in the *ver sacrum* performed in 195 BC, it was repeated in 194 BC. For 194 BC, Livy provides details as to how long the season of a sacred Spring lasted: it was to involve the sacrifice of all domesticated animals born between 1 March and 30 April 194 BC. The games which had been vowed to Jupiter in 217 BC were now also performed. This twenty-one-year gap between vows and fulfillment can only be explained by Rome's straitened circumstances. The sacred Springs of 195 and 194 BC were the only *veri sacri* mentioned in the historical tradition: it was presumably an ancient rite revived in the terrible crisis after Lake Trasimene in the Second Punic War, but it was never repeated after 194 BC.[151]

Supplicating and Thanking the Gods in Wartime: The Supplicatio Ritual

A *supplicatio*, decreed by the Senate, was in a sense either a propitiation in the hope of success, or a thanksgiving after success. They were particularly associated with military occurrences. Traditionally lasting one to five days (Livy does not mention its length in connection with 217 BC), by the end of the Republic its duration was lengthened to reflect the nature of military success. When this occurred, the *supplicatio* decreed by the Senate was an honour to the commander as much as a thanksgiving to the gods. Worshippers went from temple to temple in the city of Rome, supplicating the gods with prayer. For example, in 295 BC, a *supplicatio* lasted for two days, with large numbers of men and women attending, and the wine for libations to the gods, and incense to be burned in their honour, was provided at public expense.[152]

In 211 BC, with the Carthaginian Hamilcar near the gates of Rome, the women of the city performed a spontaneous, unofficial *supplicatio*. While Livy does not use this term, it is clear that the women did not wait for the Senate's authority before supplicating the gods.[153] Allowing for some dramatic licence on Livy's part, some features can be discerned here:

> 'The wailings of women not only from private houses alone were heard, but, from all directions matrons poured into the public places running around the gods' shrines, with their dishevelled hair caressing the altars, kneeling, their palms held heavenwards, praying to the gods that they would save the city of the Romans from the hands of the enemy, to keep Roman mothers, and their little ones, safe from harm.'

A double victory over the Sabines in 449 BC led the Senate to decree a one-day *supplicatio*, but the people did not think that sufficient, so conducted a further spontaneous *supplicatio* the following day. When news reached Rome that the Carthaginians had been defeated at Zama near Carthage in 202 BC, the Senate decreed a four-day *supplicatio*, and the praetors were ordered to open all the temples in the city so that people had all day to visit them and thank the gods.[154] A *supplicatio* of three days was voted for the defeat of the Gauls at Cremona in Etruria in 200 BC. For the victory of the Scipios over the fleet of Antiochus off Phocaea in Greece in 190 BC, the Senate decreed a *supplicatio* of nine days; the source for this, Polybius, writing in Greek and obviously thinking his Greek readers will need this term explained, helpfully defines it as 'a public holiday observed by all, with a thanksgiving sacrifice to the gods as an offering for the felicitatious success'.[155] In 190 BC, for the Roman naval victory off Myonnesus, the Senate decreed a one-day *supplicatio*, and added a second day as the consul Lucius Scipio had just transferred his army into Asia Minor. Livy notes that this was the first time a Roman army had encamped in Asia Minor, and the second day was so that this 'might turn out prosperously and successful'. Scipio in Asia Minor was to sacrifice twenty full-grown sacrificial beasts on each day the *supplicatio* was being held in Rome. In the following year, 189 BC, the Senate, on the basis of good news from Asia Minor in the war against Antiochus, decreed a three-day *supplicatio* and the sacrifice of forty fully grown beasts.[156] Thanksgiving for victory needed to be given to the gods, for it was believed that military success had come with their assistance. The prayers of a *supplicatio* had to be reinforced by a material gesture, with animals sacrificed to the gods, a 'payment' in kind as thanks.

When Metellus won a victory against Jugurtha, the Senate decreed a *supplicatio* to 'the immortal gods': the city had been in a state of anxiety but was now replete with joy. The gods were to be thanked for an end to Roman anxiety. A commander could actually request the Senate to decree a *supplicatio* for a military victory. Cicero, having defeated some mountain tribes in his province of Cilicia, requested in 50 BC (unsuccessfully) that the Senate decree a *supplicatio* for this. He had, however, received one as consul in 63 BC for his role in the suppression of the Catilinarian Conspiracy, which had ended in Catiline's defeat in a bloody civil war. Cicero himself described how he had proposed and had motions passed for the senatorial decrees of *supplicationes* for Julius Caesar for fifteen days, which were 'intended to be a compliment for the fame and the glory of Caesar'; and also a *supplicatio* for Pompey of ten days, which the Senate increased to twelve, in thanksgiving for Pompey defeating Mithridates and ending the wars in the East.[157] A *supplicatio* was therefore a supplication in times of anxiety and external military threat (or internal in the case of Catiline), especially in the military context, and as a thanksgiving for successful military activity.

A *Lectisternium*: Wining and Dining the Gods

The *lectisternium* ritual (plural, *lectisternia*; *lectum sternere*: to prepare a couch),[158] as with the *supplicatio*, was not exclusively associated with warfare, but as seen in the case of 211 BC could be employed to supplicate the gods in a time of military crisis, as when Hamilcar was close to Rome. It was the role of the Senate to decide that a *lectisternium* be performed, in which all citizens were to participate. In this ritual, the statue of a god was placed reclining recumbent on a pillow or cushion (*pulvinar*) on a couch (*lectum*), and a meal was placed before it (generally several pairs of deities were offered food at the same time), within a temple (the *lectisternium* of 217 BC took place at the Temple of Saturn).[159] Its aim was propitiatory (appeasing the gods for whatever had been done to offend them that brought about the disaster or calamity) or anticipatory (expecting a favourable outcome from the gods), but it could also be as a thanksgiving, in the same manner in which a *supplicatio* could. One was held, for example, when the Magna Mater was brought to Rome, bearing in mind that her arrival was part of a response to Hannibal's continued presence in Italy.[160]

A plague which broke out in 399 BC provides the first historical instance for the celebration of a *lectisternium*, in response to a Sibylline Books consultation. Three magnificent couches were prepared, for six gods (Apollo, Latona, Diana, Hercules, Mercury and Neptune), and banquets set out before them.[161] Gods always dined in pairs on the couches. But military crisis, as in 217 BC, also prompted *lectisternia*: Livy reports that in 326 BC, when the Second Samnite War erupted, the fifth *lectisternium* since that in 399 BC was celebrated, 'to propitiate the same gods as previously'.[162] A *lectisternium* was conducted by the consuls on the orders of the Senate on 1 January 171 BC, when the Roman state was considering war against Perseus, King of Macedon (212–166 BC): the consuls reported that 'the prayers which they had made had gained approval in the sight of the immortal gods, and that for the war, due sacrifice and prayer had been offered.' The *haruspices* (diviners) also reported to the Senate that, 'If any new undertaking were to be essayed, it should be hastened, as victory, triumph, and extension of the empire were forecast.'[163] While *lectisternia* were performed from the fourth century BC on, the one in 171 BC is in fact the last one mentioned in the historical sources. This is not to say that this was the last celebration of it, but seems to suggest that the practice died out soon after the exigencies of the Second Punic War had passed, and the city of Rome itself was not threatened by an external enemy after 171 BC.

Conclusion

The temple of the Roman god Janus, the god of beginnings and endings, was always opened by one of the consuls prior to a war commencing, and closed when all the wars Rome was fighting were over. Janus thus presided over the beginning and end of war, while other gods participated and assisted the Romans in conducting it. Hence Augustus in his *Res Gestae* wrote:[164]

'The temple of Janus Quirinus [Roman Janus], which our ancestors, whenever peace prevailed, made secure by victory, throughout the whole imperium of the people of Rome, both on land and at sea, ordered to be closed and which was recorded before my birth but only twice to have been so closed, in all the time since the foundation of the city, the senate ordered, while I was princeps, to be closed three times.'

Through *evocatio* and *devotio*, Roman military commanders attempted to render a city defeatable. An *evocatio* ceremony was intended not to circumscribe the power of the tutelary deity but to emasculate its power to assist its worshippers completely by 'taking over' the god through this 'calling out ceremony'. Typical of Roman religion, this involved a religious transaction: to persuade the god to betray its people, promises of a better temple and superior worship in Rome were promised. This was not as commercial a transaction as it might seem, for Rome was inviting the god to join the Romans, the 'winning' side, and their ever-expanding empire. Gods were intrinsic to a city – enemy gods needed to be brought on to the Roman side by the *evocatio*, while a city about to be captured had to be devoted through the *devotio*. Commanders made vows to ensure gods worshipped by the Romans would assist in the capture of cities. Much of the religious building in Rome in the middle Republic stemmed from the building activities of Roman generals who had vowed a temple to a particular god in return for its assistance, or a tithe of the spoils. Rome expected its gods to fight alongside its soldiers, and wanted to entice the enemy gods to join it: success in battle was thus predicated on the gods.

Notes

1. Fleming, 2003: esp. 5–7 (trans.).
2. Key discussions of the *evocatio* are the monographs by Basanoff, 1947; Gustafsson, 2000 (with a particular emphasis on the historiography of the accounts of *evocatio* and a detailed discussion of the modern literature); and Ferri, 2010: esp. 29–70, 183–85 (extensive bibliography at 185 n.4); see also Dumézil, 1970: 2.424–27; Ogilvie, 1970: 673–75; Gall, 1976; Berti, 1990: 69–70; Rüpke, 1990: 162–64; Hickson, 1993: 42, 94; Blomart, 1997; Beard, North & Price, 1998: 1.132–34; Turcan, 2000: 97–99; Kloppenborg, 2005: 434–41; Ando, 2008: 128–48; Ferri, 2006; Ferri, 2010a; Hekster, 2010: 611–13; Orlin, 2010: 36–39.
3. See Johnson, 2013; Gilan, 2014: 197–98; Finn, 2017: 37–41.
4. Gilan, 2014: esp. 195, 203; Anitta Text: 195–96; 'Manly Deeds': 196–98; trans.: 198.
5. 1 Samuel 4–6.
6. Pompey: Jos. *Jew. Ant.* 14.4.4 (69), *Bell. Jud.* 1.152; Titus: Jos. *Bell. Jud.* 6–7; sacred items as depicted on the Arch of Titus, Rome, include the menorah, the seven-lamp candelabrum from the Temple.
7. Hundley, 2013: 230–31, fig. 9.2; Johnson, 2013: 113.
8. Luckenbill, 1968: 207–08, no. 518a.

9.   Eur. *Iph. Taur.*

10. Hdt. 5.82–89; Figueira, 1985: esp. 50–51; Trundle, 2019: 26–27.

11. Plut. *Mor.* 279a.

12. Athen. *Deip.* 672c (citing Menodotus of Samos *FGrH* 82 F1).

13. Paus. 3.15.7. A statue of Aphrodite in chains: Paus. 3.15.11. The statue of Eurynome at Phigaleia (Arcadia) was fettered with golden chains: Paus. 8.41.6.

14. The statue of Saturn in the Temple of Saturn in the Roman Forum had its feet bound with woollen restrainers – except when the Saturnalia was celebrated (Macrob. *Sat.* 1.8.5).

15. In Greek, the Palladion. For the Palladion, see Robertson, 1996: 389–427; Gantz, 1995: 642–45. For the Palladium at Rome, see Ando, 2001: 398–99; Ando, 2008: 188–89, 194–95; Praet, 2016: 279–81.

16. Apollod. *Bibl.* 3.12.3.

17. For Athena Promachos, see Dillon, 2019: 93–94.

18. *Iliupersis* (*The Destruction of Troy*, or *The Little Iliad*) *PEG* i F1; Pherecydes *FGrH* 3 F179; Dion. Hal. *Rom. Ant.* 1.68.2, 4 (see below, n.12), 2.66.5; Ovid *Fasti* 6.419–36.

19. Diomedes and Odysseus, or Odysseus alone: *PEG* i F25, cf. pp. 88–89; Eur. *Rhes.* 501–02, 516–17 (the *agalma*: statue); Antisthenes *Aias* 6; Ovid *Metam.* 13.335–56; Virg. *Aen.* 2.162–75; Serv. *Aen.* 2.166; schol. Lyk. *Alex.* 658 (Scheer, 1958).

20. Ovid *Fasti* 6.433–34.

21. Cassius Hemina F7 (*HRR I* pp. 100-101); *Aen.* 2.166, 2.296, 2.567 and Serv. Aen. on these lines; Sil. Ital. 13.51–78.

22. Dion. Hal. *Rom. Ant.* 1.68.2, 4 ('For so long as these sacred objects remain in your land, your city will endure forever without harm': see 1.68–69 in full, and also 2.65.2, 2.66.5-6); Ovid *Metam.* 5.730–31; Livy 26.27.13; Paus. 2.23.5; Sil. Ital. 13.36–50; cf. Prop. *El.* 4.4.69.

23. Figure 3.1: diameter: 19mm; *CNG* 851836; Crawford *RRC* 458/1; Sydenham *CRR* 1013.

24. Plaut. *Bacch.* 953–61 (writing *c.*205–184 BC); Dillon, 2017: 3, 46 n.15.

25. Ovid *Fasti* 6.429–32.

26. Dillon, 2018: 94, 230 n.51.

27. Ovid *Fasti* 6.437–54; Hdn 1.14.4.

28. Ovid *Fasti* 6.437–54 (also 3.346, 3.354, 6.365, 3.422; Pliny *Nat. Hist.* 7.45; see also Val. Max. 1.4.

29. Dercylus *Foundations of Cities* F7 (Plutarch *Parallel Stories*, 'Ilus and Anytus' 17; *FHG* iv, p.387).

30. Serv. *Aen.* 7.188: *acus matris deum, quadriga fictilis Veientanorum, cineres Orestis, sceptrum Priami, velum Ilionae, palladium, ancilia.* For the *pignora*, see Herbert-Brown, 1994: 76–77; Ando, 2001: 394–95; Ando, 2008: 182–83; Littlewood, 2006: 132–35; Praet, 2016. The Palladion as one of the *pignora*: Ovid *Fasti* 6.445; the shields as *pignora*: Ovid *Fasti* 3.346, with Littlewood, 2007: 186–87; Praet, 2016: 186–87. Only Servius refers to Orestes' ashes, the veil and the sceptre (see Praet, 2016: 285–86).
31. Livy 10.47.7, Summary of Book 11, 29.11.1; Ovid *Metam.* 15.622–744; Strabo 12.5.3; Val. Max. 1.8.2; Festus 268L. See Edelstein & Edelstein, 1945: i.431–51, ii.252–53; Dillon & Garland, 2015: 138–39; Dillon, 2020.
32. *IG* iv^2 1 122.33 (Halieis); *IG* ii^2 4960a (Athens).
33. Livy 29.10.5; trans. Dillon & Garland, 2015: 139.
34. Livy 29.11.1; cf. Strabo 12.5.3 who compares the two occasions.
35. Cic. *Har. Resp.* 2.25; Livy *History of Rome* 29.10–14; Ovid *Fasti* 4.179–372; Dion. Hal. *Rom. Ant.* 2.19.4–5; Pliny *Nat. Hist.* 7.120; Val. Max. 1.8.11; Festus 268L; Gruen, 1990: 5–33; Beard, North & Price, 1998: 1.164–65, 2.43–46; Dillon & Garland, 2015: 139–40, 316–17.
36. See Gustafsson, 2000: 43 with Latin text, his translation. Discussed by Gustafsson, 2000: 43.
37. Pliny *Nat. Hist.* 28.18–19; see also *Nat. Hist.* 3.65; Plut. *Mor.* 278f–279a (*Rom. Quest.* 61); Solinus *Coll. Mem.* 1.4–6; John of Lydus *Mens.* 4.73; Serv. *Aen.* 1.277, 2.351.
38. Serv. *Aen.* 2.351: *et iure pontificum cautum est, ne suis nominibus dii Romani appellarentur, ne exaugurari possint.*
39. Serv. *Aen.* 1.277; Pliny *Nat. Hist.* 3.65 (and adds that the statue of the goddess Angerona has a bandage over her mouth to remind Romans of the secret); Plut. *Mor.* 278f–279a (*Rom. Quest.* 61); Solinus *Coll. Mem.* 1.4–6. For the 'secret' name: Stanley, 1963: 238; Gustafson, 2000: 44–45; Ando, 2008: 190; Ferri, 2010: 101–28.
40. The sources for the Veii *evocatio* are Livy 5.19–23; Dion. Hal. *Rom. Ant.* 12.14–15, 13.3 (possibly drawing on the same source as Livy); Plut. *Cam.* 5–7; Pliny *Nat. Hist.* 28.418.
41. For Veii as an *evocatio*, see especially Gustafsson, 2000: 46–55, 102–05; Ferri, 2010: 129–60; Orlin, 2010: 36–39; also Dumézil, 1970: 426–27; Hickson, 1993: 37, 167 no. 113.
42. Livy 5.21.1–4.
43. Plut. *Cam.* 6.3.

44. Formula: *Sat.* 3.9.8; temple of Juno Regina: see Platner & Ashby, 1929: 290; Richardson, 1992: 215–16; Orlin, 1997: 15, 53, 62, 144.
45. Plut. *Cam.* 6.3 notes that the story is credible because there were many accounts – including in written histories – of statues sweating, making noises, turning their head aside and closing their eyes.
46. Livy 5.22.4–5.
47. Plut. *Cam.* 6.1–2.
48. Dion. Hal. *Rom. Ant.* 13.3.
49. For the *evocatio* at Carthage, see: Basanoff, 1947: 63–66; Rawson, 1973: 168–72; Berti, 1990: 70–75; Blomart, 1997: 106; Gustafsson, 2010: 59–60; Orlin, 2010: 38; Champion, 2017: 210–13.
50. Macrob. *Sat.* 3.9.7; Serv. *Aen.* 12.841; see Gustafsson, 2010: 45.
51. As noted by Orlin, 2010: 38; Champion, 2017: 210.
52. Macrob. *Sat.* 3.9.5. This fragment of Furius: *IAR* 6 F1.
53. Rawson, 1973: 170; Champion, 2017: 210.
54. Macrob. *Sat.* 3.9.7–8. The authenticity of the text is assured by the archaic nature of the Latin: see Courtney, 1999: 107–12.
55. Serv. *Aen.* 2.244; see Gustafsson, 2000: 44.
56. Serv. *Aen.* 2.351; see Dumézil, 1970: 424.
57. See Rawson, 1973: 171–72.
58. Ser. *Aen.* 12.841.
59. Gustafsson, 2010: 59 notes the scholarly opinions on the *evocatio* at Carthage.
60. Wissowa, 1912: 374; cf. Gustafsson, 2010: 59.
61. Rawson, 1973: 169.
62. Macrob. *Sat.* 3.14–15, quoting Virg. *Aen.* 2.350–51.
63. Sall. *Hist.* 2 F87.
64. The inscription: Hall, 1972 (ed. pr.); *L'Année épigraphique*, 1977: 237 no. 816; discussions: Hall, 1972; Gall, 1976; Rüpke, 1990: 164; Beard, North & Price, 1998: 1.133, 2.248 no. 10.3b; Gustafsson, 2000: 60–62.
65. Hall, 1972: 570 (who discovered and published the inscription).
66. Gall, 1976; Beard, North & Price, 1998: 1.133; cf. Rüpke, 1990: 164. Gustafsson, 2000: 60–62 surveys and discusses the modern opinions.
67. Hall, 1972: 572; Gall, 1976: 520; Alvar, 1985: 247; Beard, North & Price, 1998: 2.248 no. 10.3b n.1; Gustafsson, 2000: 60–61; Kloppenborg, 2005: 439–40.
68. For the *evocatio* of Vertumnus, see Basanoff, 1945: 56–60; Suits, 1969: 484–86; Marquis, 1974; Scullard, 1981: 130–31, 174; Gustafsson, 2010: 55–56.

69. Prop. *El.* 4.3–8.
70. For the sack, see Zon. 8.7.
71. Varro 5.74 (Titus Tatius); 5.46 (principal god of the Etruscans, spelling it as Vortumnus).
72. Varro 5.46. Pliny *Nat. Hist.* 34.16 actually has the Romans looting 2,000 statues from Volsinii.
73. *InscrIt* xiii.1: p. 547; *InscrIt* xiii.2: p.495; *CIL* i² 4.2836; Festus 228L (209).
74. Hicks, 2013, argues that Tacitus' (Latin) account of the transfer of the statue of Serapis to Alexandria follows the lines of a Roman *evocatio* ritual, while Plutarch's (Greek) account of the same incident does not (Tac. *Hist.* 4.83–84; Plut. *Mor.* 361f).
75. Kloppenborg, 2005; cf. Magness, 2008: 209; and Schmidt, 2010: 6–8.
76. Tac. *Hist.* 13.1; see esp. Kloppenberg, 2005: 445–47; also discussing Josephus *Bell. Jud.* 6.290–300; 300: the priests in the temple heard a voice like a host saying, 'We are leaving.'
77. Cf. Dumézil, 1970: 2.427. He points at 2.427 to relevant passages in Tert. *Nat.* 2.17, *The Digest* 11.7.36, Plaut. *Amph.* 258 and Livy 1.38.1–2, discussed below.
78. Livy 26.34.12.
79. Livy 5.40.1–3; cf. Plut. *Marc.* 21.5.
80. Pliny *Nat. Hist.* 34.40. For these examples, of Marcellus and Fabius Maximus, and other cases of Roman looting of statues, and their display in triumphs of Roman generals, see esp. Pollitt, 1978: 156–58.
81. Tert. *Apol.* 25.14–16, *Nat.* 2.17.16, cf. *Apol.* 10.5 ('captive gods' occurs in a long list of all the different types of gods which the Romans worshipped). For Virgil's *Aeneid*, see Matthew Dillon in chapter 1.
82. See Rutledge, 2007.
83. Arr. *Anab.* 1.10; Plut. *Alex.* 11.6.
84. Minucius Felix *Octavius* 25.5–6, see also 7.
85. Livy 1.38.1–2.
86. Livy 28.34.7.
87. Plaut. *Amph.* 257.
88. *The Digest* 11.7.36 (the sixth-century AD codification of Roman law) seems to err when it states that when a place is captured by an enemy, things cease to be religious or sacred. The Romans of the Republic would not have agreed.
89. Pliny *Nat. Hist.* 34.16.
90. Paus. 8.46.1–5.

91. Plut. *Sull.* 12.4–7.
92. Diod. 40.4: Dillon & Garland, 2015: doc. 12.30, p.494; cf. Pliny *Nat. Hist.* 7.97, and App. *Mith.* 7.117.
93. Mice in Lanuvium: Cic. *Div.* 1.99 (citing the historian Sisenna *HRR* 1 F5 [p.277], and *Div.* 2.59 [*portentum*]; Sisenna, 120–67 BC, was a contemporary historian of the Social War); 1.199: other omens in 90 BC were that the statues of the gods sweated, rivers ran with blood, the heavens opened up and voices were heard – of unknown provenance – predicting dangerous wars (*Div.* 1.99, see also 98). In the well-known list at Livy 21.52.1–8 of omens and prodigies that occurred in 218 BC, two were at Lanuvium: one included a victim which had been sacrificially killed for her, as stirring back to life, and a crow flying into the temple of Juno Sospita and alighting on the goddess' couch (21.52.4); crows again in 214 BC: 24.10.6. Prodigies were frequently reported from Lanuvium, many involving Juno Sospita: see Kragelund, 2001: 65; Schultz, 2006: 210.
94. Cicero mentions the dream: Cic. *Div.* 1.4, 1.99, 2.136; while Obseq. 55 (drawing on Livy's lost account) provides the details.
95. Obseq. 55; cf. Schultz, 2006: 208.
96. Cic. *Nat. Deor.* 1.82.
97. Cic. *Nat. Deor.* 1.82.
98. Figure 3.2: *CNG* 735602; diameter: 19mm; Crawford *RRC* 379/2; Sydenham *CRR* 772. For Juno Sospita armed on coins, see Kragelund, 2001: 66–67; Schultz, 2006: 213, with fig. 9.1.
99. Schultz, 2006: 225–26 figs 9.3a–b, but with a different interpretation than that advanced here.
100. That it was this temple at Rome is incorrectly argued by Richardson, 1992: 217; cf. Schultz, 2006: 210–11.
101. Livy 32.30.10, 34.53.3 with Richardson, 1992: 216.
102. Hom. *Il.* 22.213.
103. Aeschylus *Seven Against Thebes* 217–18.
104. Apollo: Diod. 17.41.8; Curt. 4.3.21; Herakles: Arr. *Anab.* 2.18.1; Plut. *Alex.* 24.5; Curt. 4.2.17.
105. Virg. *Aen.* 2.351–52, cf. 2.602-603, 3.1. At *Aen.* 12.285–86, Latinus, defeated in battle, flees, taking with him his defeated gods.
106. Phocaea: Hdt. 1.164.3; Myous: Paus. 7.2.11.
107. Plut. *Ant.* 75.4–6 (trans.: Dillon & Garland 2015, 651–52: doc. 14.53), for which see Scott, 1929: 134–37; Hekster, 2010: 610–11. Cf. *Ant.* 24.3–4, where Antony is assimilated with Dionysus. Hekster, 2010,

discusses the cases of Roman emperors, such as Nero and Domitian, deserted by gods. For example, Minerva departed from her temple and deserted Domitian: Suet. *Dom.* 15.3.

108. Virg. *Aen.* 8.698–706.
109. Bellona, according to Varro, derives from *bellum*, war: *Ling. Lat.* 5.73. See John Serrati in this volume.
110. Figure 3.3: *CNG* 782914; diameter: 18mm; Crawford *RRC* 296/1c; Sydenham *CRR* 561b.
111. Virg. *Aen.* 8.714–22.
112. Serv. *Aen.* 8.698.
113. Orlin, 2008.
114. Prop. *El.* 3.11.41, for which see Gurval, 1995: 198–203. For Roman versus Egyptian gods at Actium, see Wyke, 1992: 100–05; Gurval, 1995: 230–35; Ando, 2008: 122; Orlin, 2008: 244, see also 234, 236.
115. Prop. *El.* 4.6.25–70.
116. Macrob. *Sat.* 3.9.9–10; Versnel, 1976: 377–83.
117. Livy 8.9–10; for the *devotio* of the Roman general: Versnel, 1976: 394–405; Hickson, 1993: 96–97. Decius' son performed a *devotio* in 295 BC at Sentinum (Livy 10.28), as did his grandson at Ausculum in 279 BC (Cic. *Tusc.* 1.89, *Fin.* 2.61).
118. For the cinctus Gabinus, see Serv. *Aen.* 7.612; Isid. *Etym.* 19.24.7.
119. Virg. *Aen.* 7.611, with Serv. *Aen.* 6.112.
120. Oakley, 1998: 6–10.
121. Livy 8.11.1.
122. Livy 1.455.1–2; for the temple, see Platner & Ashby, 1929: 297–302; Richardson, 1992: 221–24.
123. The standard treatment of temples vowed and built by Roman generals while on campaign is Orlin, 1997: 45–66, and see 199–202 for temples dedicated in the Republic and the reasons for this – plague or war, with war being the most common reason; see also Hekster & Rich, 2006: 152–55.
124. Cic. *Leg. Agr.* 2.61, cf. 60, 62.
125. Flor. *Epit.* 1.14.2; Richardson, 1992: 378–79.
126. Tac. *Ann.* 2.49; Richardson, 1992: 206–07.
127. Tac. *Ann.* 2.49; also Cic. *Laws* 2.28; Richardson, 1992: 365.
128. Commemorated by the inscription *ILS* 3; Ovid *Fasti* 6.193–94; Richardson, 1992: 378.
129. Livy 22.9.11, 22.20.10; discussed below.
130. Vow of 200 BC: Livy 31.21.13 (17: 200 wagons of war-booty), 34.53.7. Vow of 198 BC: Livy 35.41.8 (temple dedicated to Jupiter but by this he

means Jove as in Ved-*iov*-is, but is incorrect in placing both temples on the Capitoline). Vediovis was also spelled as Veiovis: Father Dis, Veiovis and Manes are the three gods named at the beginning of Macrobius' formula for the *devotio* of Carthage in 146 BC (see above). For these temples, see Richardson, 1992: 406; Orlin, 1997: 184–85.

131. Livy 36.36.5–7; Richardson, 1992: 228.
132. Livy 40.34.4; Richardson, 1992: 408.
133. Livy 40.34.4–6; Val. Max. 2.5.1; Richardson, 1992: 290; Orlin, 1997: 146.
134. See the table in Orlin, 1997: 200–02, see also 127, 194–95.
135. See chart at Orlin, 1997: 201–02. Of the three listed, one, that of 146 BC, to Jupiter Stator by the praetor Q. Metellus Macedonicus was in fact a portico around the temple of Jupiter Stator (Richardson, 1992: 225).
136. Plut. *Mar.* 26.2; Richardson, 1992: 156.
137. Gell. *Noct. Att.* 10.1.7; Pliny *Nat. Hist.* 8.20; Tert. *Spect.* 10; Suet. *Claud.* 21.1; Richardson, 1992: 384, 411.
138. Plin. *Nat. Hist.* 7.97 (Dillon & Garland, 2015: doc. 12.29, p.493).
139. Aug. *Res Gest.* 20.4 (see Brunt & Moore, 1967: 62; Cooley, 2009: 194–95); App. *Civ.* 2.68.281; Dio 43.22.2, 45.6.4; Richardson, 1992: 166.
140. Aug. *Res Gest.* 21.1 ('from the spoils of war': *ex manibiis*; see Brunt & Moore, 1967: 62; Cooley, 2009: 199); vow: Suet. *Aug.* 29.2; Ovid *Fasti* 5.569–78; the temple: Ovid *Fasti* 5 455.1–2; for the temple, see Platner & Ashby, 1929; Richardson, 1992: 330.
141. Figure 3.4: diameter 19mm; American Numismatic Society, 1937: 158.235; Sydenham *CRR* 1147.
142. For the temple of Jupiter Feretrius, see Platner & Ashby, 1929: 293–94.
143. See, for example, *CNG* 163516.
144. Plut. *Marc.* 6.6–7.4. An inscription commemorates his spolia and names the king (which Plutarch does not): *InscrIt* xiii.1 79 & 550. See also Flower, 2000: 35–41. For the temple, see the references at Flower 35 n.2.
145. Orlin, 1997: 69 lists several examples.
146. So Orlin, 1997: 70 argues.
147. Livy 35.1.9–10 (*si fudisset cecidissetque hostes*), 36.36.2; Orlin, 1997: 55–56.
148. Livy 22.9.7.
149. Livy 22.9.7–22.10.10; Dumézil, 1970: 2.475–76.
150. Livy 22.9.10, 22.10.2–6, 23.30.13–14 (here Livy presents the vow as having been made by Fabius as Dictator, but in Book 22 it is a senatorial vow), 23.31.10 (on Capitoline); for these, see Richardson, 1992: 251, 408.

151. Livy 33.44.1–3 (195 BC), 34.44.1–3, 6 (194 BC). For the Sacred Spring, see: Dumézil, 1970: 2.475–76 (also discussing the other religious arrangements decreed by the Senate in 217 BC).
152. Livy 10.23.
153. Livy 26.9.7–9; in 463 BC, when Rome was decimated by a plague, the Senate ordered a *supplicatio*, and the women swept the temple floors with their hair: Livy 3.7.8. For women's tears and hair in *supplicationes*, with these two examples from Livy, see Erker, 2009: 152–53.
154. Livy 30.17.3–6.
155. Polyb. 21.3.
156. Sabines: Livy 3.63.6; Gauls: Livy 31.22.1; Antiochus: Polyb. 21.3; Myonnesus: Livy 37.47.4; 189 BC *supplicatio* and sacrifice: Livy 37.52.2.
157. Metellus: Sall. *Jug*. 55; Cicero, in Cilicia: Cic. *Fam*. 15.4; for Catiline: Cic. *Catil*. 3.6.15, *Sull*. 30.85; Julius Caesar: Cic. *Prov*. 11.
158. For the *lectisternium* in the Republic, see Warde Fowler, 1911: 261–65; Ogilvie, 1965: 655–57; Dumézil, 1970: 476–77, 567–68; Berg, 2008: 242–48. Leigh, 2002, discusses how Ov. *Met*. 8.651–60 approximates to a *lectisternium* ritual (for Jupiter and Mercury).
159. Livy 22.1.20. Jupiter's couch at his Capitoline temple: 5.52.6, but this is for the different rite, the Iovis *epulo*.
160. Livy 29.14.14.
161. Livy 5.13.5–8; Dion. Hal. *Ant. Rom*. 12.9; for which see Ogilvie, 1965: 655–57; Leigh, 2002: 625–26.
162. First *lectisternum*: 399 BC, plague; second: not actually reported by Livy (392? BC); third: 7.2.2, plague (364 BC); fourth: 7.27.1 (348 BC); fifth: 8.25.1, war (326 BC). See also Livy 22.1, cf. 21.62.4.
163. Livy 42.30.8–9. See also Livy 36.1 (191 BC: *lectisternium*, for war against King Antiochus III of Seleucia, 241–187 BC).
164. Aug. *Res Gest*. 13 (Brunt & Moore, 1967: 54–55; Cooley, 2009: 158–61); and Suet. *Aug*. 22.

Bibliography

Alvar, J., 1985, 'Matériaux pour l'étude de la formule *sive deus, sive dea*', *Numen* 32: 236–73.
Ando, C., 2001, 'The Palladium and the Pentateuch: Towards a Sacred Topography of the Later Roman Empire', *Phoenix* 55: 369–410.
Ando, C., 2008, *The Matter of the Gods. Religion and the Roman Empire*, Berkeley.

Basanoff, V., 1947, *Evocatio: étude d'un rituel militaire romain*, Paris.

Beard, M., North, J. and Price, S., 1998, *Religions of Rome*, vols 1–2, Cambridge.

Berg, C. van den, 2008, 'The "Pulvinar" in Roman Culture', *TAPhA* 138: 239–73.

Berti, N., 1990, 'Scipione Emiliano, Caio Gracco e l' "evocatio" di "Guinone da Cartagine"', *Aevum* 64.1: 169–75.

Blomart, A., 1997, 'Die *evocatio* und der Transfer "fremder" Götter von der Peripherie nach Rome', in Cancik, H. & Rüpke, J. (eds), *Römische Reichsreligion und Provinzialreligion*, Tubingen: 99–111.

Brunt, P.A. & Moore, J.M., 1967, *Res Gestae Divi Augusti. With an Introduction and Commentary*, London.

Champion, C.B., 2017, *The Peace of the Gods: Elite Religious Practices in the Middle Roman Republic*, Princeton.

Cooley, A.E., 2009, *Res Gestae Divi Augusti: Text, Translation, and Commentary*, Cambridge.

Courtney, E., 1999, *Archaic Latin Prose*, Atlanta.

Dillon, M.P.J., 2017, *Omens and Oracles. Divination in Ancient Greece. Knowledge of All Things That Were, and That Were To Be, and That Had Been Before*, Oxford.

Dillon, M.P.J., 2019, 'Militarising the Divine: the Bellicosity of the Greek gods', in Dillon, M.P.J., Matthew, C. & Schmitz, M. (eds), *Religion and Classical Warfare I: Ancient Greece*, Barnsley: 86–119, 228–34, 274–76.

Dillon, M.P.J., 2020, *Asklepios. His Healing Hands: Faith and Miracles*, Oxford.

Dillon, M.P.J. & Garland, L., 2015, *Ancient Rome: Social and Historical Documents from the Early Republic to the Death of Julius Caesar*, 2nd edition, London.

Dumézil, G., 1970, *Archaic Roman Religion*, vols 1–2, Chicago.

Erker, D.Š., 2009, 'Women's Tears in Ancient Roman Ritual', in Fögen, T. (ed.), *Tears in the Graeco-Roman world*, Berlin: 135–60.

Ferri, G., 2006, 'L'*evocatio* romana – I problemi', *Studi e materiali di Storia delle Religioni* 30.2: 205–44.

Ferri, G., 2010, *Tutela segreta ed evocatio nel politeismo romano*, Rome.

Ferri, G. 2010a, 'Una testimonianza epigrafica dell'evocatio? Su un'iscrizione da Isaura Vetus', *Giornata di studi in onore di Lidio Gasperini*, Roma: 183–94.

Figueira, T., 1985, 'Herodotus on the Early Hostilities Between Aegina and Athens', *AJPh* 106.1: 49–74.

Finn, J., 2017, *Much Ado About Marduk: Questioning Discourses of Royalty in First Millennium Mesopotamian Literature*, Boston.

Fleming, D.E., 2003, 'Ur: After the Gods Abandoned Us', *CW* 97.1: 5–18.

Flower, H.I., 2000, 'The Tradition of the Spolia Opima: M. Claudius Marcellus and Augustus', *ClAnt* 19.1: 37–64.

Gall, J. le, 1976, 'Evocatio', in *Mélanges offerts à J. Heurgon. L'Italie préromaine et La Rome républicaine*, Rome: 519–24.

Gantz, M., 1993, *Early Greek Myth. A Guide to the Literary and Artistic Sources*, Baltimore.

Gilan, A., 2014, 'The End of God-Napping and the Religious Foundations of the New Hittite Empire', *Zeitschrift für Assyriologie* 104.2: 195–205.

Gruen, E., 1990, *Studies in Greek Culture and Roman Policy*, Leiden.

Gurval, R.A., 1995, *Actium and Augustus: The Politics and Emotions of Civil War*, Ann Arbor.

Gustafsson, G., 2000, *Evocatio Deorum: Historical and Mythical Interpretations of Ritualised Conquests in the Expansion of Ancient Rome (Acta Universitatis Upsaliensis Historia Religionum* 16), Upsala.

Hall, A., 1972, 'New Light on the Capture of Isaura Vetus by P. Servilius Vatia', in *Vestigia 17, Akten des VI. Internationalen Kongresses für Griechische und Lateinische Epigraphik München 1972*, Munich: 568–71.

Hekster, O., 2010, 'Reversed Epiphanies: Roman Emperors Deserted by Gods', *Mnemosyne* 63: 601–15.

Herbert-Brown, G., 1994, *Ovid and the Fasti: An Historical Study*, Oxford.

Hickson, F.V., 1993, *Roman Prayer Language. Livy and the Aeneid of Vergil*, Stuttgart.

Hundley, M.B., 2013, *Gods in Dwellings: Temples and Divine Presence in the Ancient Near East*, Atlanta.

Johnson, E.D., 2013, 'Time and Again: Marduk's Travels', in Feliu, L., Llop, J., Mille Albà & Sanmartín, J. (eds), *Time and History in the Ancient Near East*, Winona Lake.

Kloppenborg, J.S., 2005, '*Evocatio deorum* and the Date of Mark', *JBL* 124.3: 419–50.

Kragelund, P., 2001, 'Dreams, Religion and Politics in Republican Rome', *Historia* 50: 53–95.

Leigh, M., 2002, 'Ovid and the Lectisternium (*Metamorphoses* 8. 651–60)', *CQ* 52: 625–27.

Littlewood, R.J., 2006, *A Commentary on Ovid Fasti Book VI*, Oxford.

Littlewood, R.J., 2007, 'Imperii Pignora Certa: The Role of Numa in Ovid's *Fasti*', in Herbert-Brown, G. (ed.), *Ovid's Fasti: Historical Readings at Its Bimillenium*, Oxford: 175–98.

Luckenbill, D.D., 1968, *Ancient Records of Assyria and Babylon vol. II*, Chicago.

Magness, J., 2008, 'The Arch of Titus and the Fate of the God of Israel', *Journal of Jewish Studies* 69: 201–17.

Marquis, E.C., 1974, 'Vertumnus in Propertius 4, 2', *Hermes* 102: 491–500.

Oakley, S.P., 1998, *A Commentary on Livy 6–10*, vol. 2, Oxford.

Ogilvie, R.M., 1965, *A Commentary on Livy Books 1–5*, Oxford.

Orlin, E.M., 1997, *Temples, Religion and Politics in the Roman Republic*, Leiden.

Orlin, E.M., 2008, 'Octavian and Egyptian Cults: Redrawing the Boundaries of Romanness', *AJPh* 129: 231–53.

Orlin, E., 2010, *Foreign Cults in Rome: Creating a Roman Empire*, Oxford.

Platner, S.B. & Ashby, T. 1929, *A Topographical Dictionary of Ancient Rome*, London.

Pollitt, J.J., 1978, 'The Impact of Greek Art on Rome', *TAPhA* 108: 155–74.

Praet, R., 2016, 'Re-anchoring Rome's Protection in Constantinople: The Pignora Imperii in Late Antiquity and Byzantium', *Sacris Eruditi* 55: 277–319.

Rawson, E., 1973, 'Scipio, Laelius, Furius and the Ancestral Religion', *JRS* 63: 161–74 (= Rawson, E. [ed.], 1991, *Roman Culture and Society*, Oxford: 80–101).

Richardson, A., 1992, *A New Topographical Dictionary of Ancient Rome*, Baltimore.

Robertson, N., 1996, 'Athena and Early Greek Society: Palladium Shrines and Promontory Shrines', in Dillon, M.P.J. (ed.), *Religion in the Ancient World: New Themes and Approaches*, Amsterdam: 383–475.

Rüpke, J., 1990, *Domi militiae. Die religiöse Konstruktion des Krieges in Rom*, Stuttgart.

Rutledge, S.H., 2007, 'The Roman Destruction of Sacred Sites', *Historia* 56: 179–95.

Schmidt, E.A., 2010, 'The Flavian Triumph and the Arch of Titus: The Jewish God in Flavian Rome', in *Beyond Borders: Selected Proceedings of the 2010 Ancient Borderlands International Graduate Student Conference*, Santa Barbara: 1–12.

Scott, K., 1929, 'Octavian's Propaganda and Antony's *De sua ebrietate*', *CPh* 24: 133–41.

Scullard, H.H., 1981, *Festivals and Ceremonies of the Roman Republic*, London.

Schultz, C.E., 2006, 'Juno Sospita and Roman Insecurity in the Social War', in Schultz, C.E. & Harvey, P.B. (eds), *Religion in Republican Italy*, Cambridge: 207–27.

Stanley, K., 1963, 'Rome, Ἔρως, and the Versus Romae', *GRBS* 4: 237–49.

Suits, T.A., 1969, 'The Vertumnus Elegy of Propertius', *TAPhA* 100: 475–86.

Trundle, M., 2019, 'The Role of Religion in Declarations of War in Archaic and Classical Greece', in Dillon, M., Matthew, C. & Schmitz, M. (eds), *Religion and Classical Warfare I: Ancient Greece*, Barnsley: 24–33, 212–14, 265–67.

Turcan, R., 2000, *The Gods of Ancient Rome*, Edinburgh.

Versnel, H.S., 1976, 'Two types of Roman devotio', *Mnemosyne* 29: 365–410.

Warde Fowler, W., 1911, *The Religious Experience of the Roman People From the Earliest Times to the Age of Augustus*, London.

Wissowa, G., 1912, *Religion und Kultus der Römer*, 2nd edn, Munich.

Wyke, M., 1992, 'Augustan Cleopatras: Female Power and Poetic Authority', in Powell, A. (ed.), *Roman Poetry and Propaganda in the Age of Augustus*, London: 98–140.

Ziolkowski, A., 1992, *The Temples of Mid-Republican Rome and their Historical and Topographical Context*, Rome.

Chapter 4

The Religious Functions of Roman Arms and Armament

Brandon R. Olson

Since its inception as a professional force with the Marian reforms during the last decade of the second century BC, the Roman Army has remained a source of scholarly fascination. In antiquity, scholars such as Frontinus in the first century AD and Vegetius in the late fourth century AD saw the military as worthy of study.[1] Furthermore, Napoleon's use of the legionary standard in the late eighteenth and early nineteenth centuries and Hitler's use of Roman iconography in the twentieth century demonstrates an enduring interest in the Roman Army. The formal academic study of the Roman military in the English-speaking world began in the middle of the nineteenth century, and yet, by the early twentieth century a dominant academic paradigm did not exist.

During the 1930s, Birley created the Durham school, which became the dominant intellectual paradigm in Britain dedicated to the academic study of the Roman Army.[2] Birley envisioned a 'methodological study' that was firmly based in epigraphic and archaeological evidence.[3] The Durham school promoted a limited interdisciplinary approach at the confluence of history, archaeology, epigraphy and prosopography and advocated a thorough grounding in archaeology and textual sources, which, prior to 1930, did not exist in academia.

Due to many factors including geographic isolation, poor public transport between the English intellectuals in the north and south, and the loyalty the Durham scholars possessed, they often times found themselves 'in conflict with others within Durham, and also in the context of "North versus South"'.[4] The conflict between the southern schools of Cambridge, Oxford, and London and the northern schools of Durham, Newcastle and those in Scotland caused a divergence between Roman civil studies and Roman military studies in Britain. The south housed the broad civil studies of Roman culture, while the north held the narrow studies of the Roman

Army. Southern scholars sought intellectual insight from universities within the Anglo-Saxon world, while the Durham school looked to Europe for scholarly support. Ultimately the Durham school came to adopt a German approach of peer departments, as scholars between northern universities and those in Germany collaborated on a regular basis. James argued that as early as the 1960s this continental divergence caused northern military studies to become 'isolated, theoretically stagnant and increasingly marginalized'.[5]

The primary weakness of the Durham school was its narrow focus. It failed to contextualize the Roman Army in terms of economic, social, religious and cultural aspects. Birley noted that 'the study of the Roman army really involves an exercise in Military Intelligence ... The principle task of Military Intelligence is to discover and assess the strength, Order of Battle, organisation, equipment and value for war of an enemy's army.'[6] Birley's characterization of his own scholarly approach was about the army as a fighting machine and, above all, as a monolithic system.[7] The school also failed to adapt to the broader theoretical shifts within the disciplines of history and archaeology from the 1950s through to the early 1970s.[8]

Since the 1980s, several scholars have taken an active role in dispelling the traditional interpretations of the Roman Army as a single machine-like entity. The leading advocate of this approach was James.[9] James stated, 'The idea that "the Roman army" can be conceptualized as a monolithic machine ... is a modern construct bearing no relation to the ways in which Romans thought and wrote about their own armed forces.'[10] James argued that modern presentism within Britain had, up to that point, dictated how historians and archaeologists have interpreted the Roman Army.[11] He concluded that 'Our tradition has been to see them [Roman soldiers] from the top downwards, as a single organisation ... as cogs in the machine.'[12] These views were woven into the politics of Early Modern Britain where individuals were seen as subjects rather than citizens, from the top down. Moreover, the view of a monolithic Roman Army is not just a British interpretation but is 'equally embedded in German and French literatures'.[13] Notions of modern European and British armies as organized cohesive bodies capable of reducing free citizens to subjects were projected onto ancient Greece and Rome.

The Romans never perceived their military as a single entity, which is evident throughout the Classical literature, as the ancient literary sources regularly used terms such as *miles*, *legio*, *cohors*, *numerus* and *exercitus* when referring to the military.[14] These authors thus frequently referred to groups of soldiers, not a collective whole.[15] For example, Vegetius noted, 'By an army is meant a number of troops, legions and auxiliaries, cavalry and infantry, assembled to make war.'[16] In fact James stated 'To speak of "the Army", singular, is a serious misrepresentation of the nature of Roman thinking and institutions.'[17] Therefore, according to James, 'there was no such thing as "The Roman Army" because there was no such concept.'[18]

With this perception of the Roman Army discounted, James suggested that 'the reality of "the Army", insofar as it existed at all, lay in the soldiers themselves, as a social grouping and a real, self-aware force in Roman society.'[19] MacMullen noted, 'The closeness of their community enabled them to fulfil their individual potential as soldiers.'[20] Additionally, there are numerous funerary monuments where soldiers refer to each other as *fratres* (brothers) and *commilitones* (comrades).[21] This framework encouraged scholars to examine the social institutions that soldiers brought to and developed within the Army and investigate their roles and functions within the organization, rather than producing the narrow military narratives that focus on military strategy and function. The present work contributes to this historiographic development by examining how Roman soldiers used their equipment to devise and ultimately practise religious rituals.

The innovation and subsequent deployment of the Roman panoply and that of its auxiliaries played a central role in the Army's ultimate success. The mobile yet rigid formation of the Roman legion and its constituent parts marked a technological advantage over the Greek world, while the development of the *corvus* single-handedly neutralized what was, at the time, the key to Carthaginian dominance prior to the First Punic War. The technological benefits of Roman military equipment cannot be understated, but one could argue that their non-utilitarian functions were no less important. Weapons, armour and the various trappings harnessed by the Roman Army had obvious functional roles for the soldier and unit, but over time as the Army became a professional force and notions of camaraderie, an aura of belonging and a sense of duty and honour became commonplace, this same gear became a medium for religious praxis. The purpose of this investigation is to examine such religious expression by exploring two unique behaviours attributed to certain gear: votive deposition in the form of dedications made to propitiate a deity in sacred spaces and the commemoration of posthumous memory as a form of ancestor worship. It is through careful attention to the archaeological, epigraphic and literary records of these items that it is possible to begin to identify certain facets of the religious behaviour of Roman soldiers and appreciate the non-utilitarian functions of their equipment.

Votive Deposition: The Adoption and Adaptation of a Celtic Tradition

The various religious belief systems and affiliated practices of the Romans greatly changed over time. From an ill-defined animistic tradition whereby adherents believed spirits inhabited everything around them, to the Greek-inspired Roman pantheon of gods, and later the development of emperor worship and adoption of Christianity, Roman religion was never a static construct. As Rome expanded from Latium and came into contact with other cultures, it would, on occasion, adopt foreign religious beliefs and practices.[22] Throughout the second and first centuries BC, Rome had regular interactions with various Celtic tribes comprising Gaul. It was through this contact that Roman soldiers were first fully exposed to Celtic religious belief systems and began repurposing them for their own needs.

The act of ritually depositing valuable arms and armour into a sacred space (e.g. temple, sanctuary or venerated natural space) as a religious rite is not a Roman development. The dedication of militaria as a form of religious ritual to propitiate or thank a deity has origins antedating the existence of Rome. Archaeologists have discovered numerous forms of Celtic weaponry and helmets in rivers and streams throughout Gaul and Britain.[23] The Celtic tradition of tossing objects into water as a religious rite originates in the Bronze Age (Hallstatt culture: *c.* 800–500 BC) and lasts through the Roman periods (Le Tene Culture: *c.* 500 BC to first century BC). The archeological evidence for this practice is abundant and extensively studied, with Wait and Roymans publishing a comprehensive account of Celtic weapons discovered in various contexts including rivers, though other terrestrial and aquatic locales are considered, in Britain and Gaul.[24] Wait examined Celtic swords, helmets and shields in his study of ritual and religion in Britain, while Roymans adopted a similar approach in his study of Gaul. Both scholars identified and plotted all known Celtic swords and helmets from Britain and Belgic Gaul (see Figures 4.1 and 4.2). Both studies note the propensity of the Celts in offering valuable arms and armour into a water source.

Several pieces of intact, fully functional Roman weapons and armour have been recovered from similar aquatic contexts. Some scholars explain

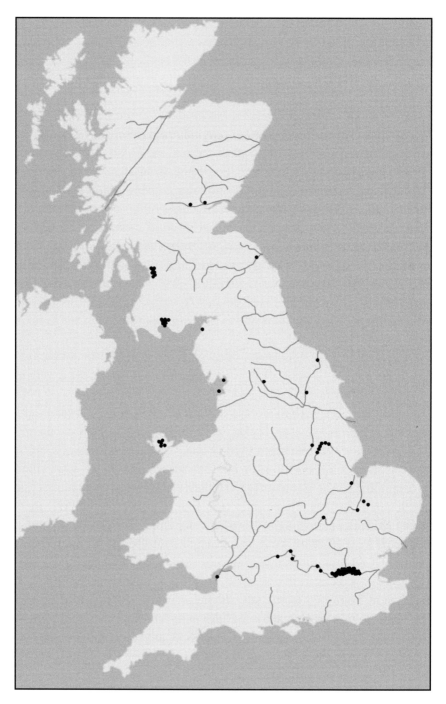

Figure 4.1:   Distribution of Celtic arms and armour discovered in aquatic contexts in Britain, after Wait, 1985.

the phenomenon as a series of accidental losses, while others allude to intentional deposition in springs, rivers and lakes.[25] Although one cannot disregard accidental loss, the facts that Roman arms and armour were expensive and heavily regulated, and that the veneration of water played an important role in Roman religion,[26] suggest that gear found in water was a result of intentional votive deposition. The dedication of objects to gods took two forms in Roman religious praxis: votive offerings, items dedicated to appease or offer thanks to a deity; and vows, objects dedicated to fulfill a contract with a deity.[27] The religious rites, votive offerings and vows were requisite for the relationship between gods and mortals because it provided a means through which humans and the divine could interact. Roman religious practice prescribed a strong tradition of dedicating objects and a veneration of water, demonstrating that military equipment recovered from aquatic contexts, especially in the western provinces, represented a religious practice among soldiers that emulated a widespread Celtic religious practice.[28]

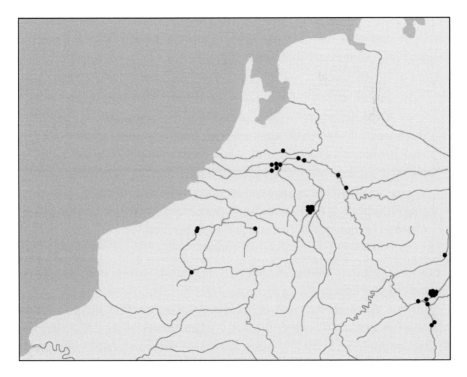

Figure 4.2:   Distribution of Celtic arms and armour discovered in aquatic contexts in Belgic Gaul, after Roymans, 1996.

Celtic Evidence

Celtic religion was deeply rooted in a veneration of water, as streams, rivers, lakes, wells and bogs were sacred places for Celtic worship. Aquatic locations represented life, curative qualities, fertility and well-being.[29] Rivers, lakes and streams became places centred around votive behaviour, whereas in bogs individuals made both offerings and sacrifice. It is through the classical sources, the presence of Celtic water deities and the archaeology that Celtic water veneration that the various ideological practices associated with it emerge.

A number of Roman and Roman era authors make mention of water veneration by numerous Celtic tribes. Strabo and Justinus note how the Celts ritually deposited valuables in sacred lakes in their descriptions of the destruction of Tolosa by Quintus Servilius Caepio.[30] In 105 BC, the Roman proconsul Caepio went to southern Gaul and fought against the Tectosagi. At the siege of Tolosa, he, according to Strabo and Justinus, committed a sacrilegious act by draining a sacred lake to retrieve a great treasure, identified as the booty pillaged from Delphi by the Gauls in 279 BC. Following his acquisition of the Delphic treasure, Caepio continued his campaign and marched to Arausio, where he suffered a disastrous defeat, which Orosius chronicles in detail:

> 'The enemy, after gaining possession of both [Roman] camps and great booty, by a certain strange and unusual bitterness completely destroyed all that they had captured; clothing was cut to pieces and thrown about, gold and silver were thrown into the river, corselets of men were cut up, trappings of horses were destroyed, the horses themselves drowned in whirlpools, and men with fetters tied around their necks were hung from trees, so that the victor laid claim to no booty, and the conquered to no mercy.'[31]

Upon his return to Rome in defeat, Caepio was stripped of his Roman citizenship and exiled.

Further classical accounts of Celtic water veneration include Caesar, who alludes to a deep respect for water when he describes the subjugation of Uxellodunum in 51 BC.[32] Caesar notes that the inhabitants continued to resist his advance until troops fully blocked a spring running through the settlement. The inhabitants interpreted the dry stream as an inauspicious omen and quickly surrendered.

Roman contact with Celtic groups initiated ideological reforms for both cultures. Prior to the Roman conquests of Gaul and Britain, the Celts did not wholly identify the divine physically, but Green noted that Roman contact provided a catalyst for Celtic concepts of the divine to be reified in a physical sense.[33] As a result of this contact, Celtic deities began appearing in literary and epigraphic contexts and took on names, behaviours and in some cases specialized roles. The following Celtic water deities can be pulled from the literary sources: Verbia (goddess of the Wharfe River), Sequana (goddess of the Seine River), Souconna (goddess of the Saone River), Sulis (goddess of the springs at Bath among other things), Coventina (goddess of a spring at Carrawburgh) and Condantis (a goddess worshipped in Britain, whose name means 'watersmeet').[34]

Based on classical accounts, the presence of several water deities and the studies of Wait and Roymans, the Celts had a strong and long-lasting tradition of dedicating military equipment in water. This tradition both predates and continues well after the Roman conquests of Gaul and Britain. Upon the arrival of Roman soldiers in what later became the western provinces, they encountered a well-established religious ritual, one that they then incorporated into their religious system.

Roman Evidence

In discussing the importance of water in Roman religion during the Republican period, Edlund-Berry argues that, although the use of water figured greatly in religious practices, it was an unofficial, private affair.[35] The veneration of water and its associated deities was not an official state-sponsored ritual. The sites of several Roman bridges show evidence of religious activity. Archaeologists excavating areas near river crossings discovered several coins and other artefacts, demonstrating that offerings of valuable property into water were made by the Romans.[36] Returning to Roymans and his study of Romanization in Belgic Gaul, he categorized and investigated the Roman evidence in the same manner as the Celtic material and noted a plethora of Roman military gear recovered from aquatic contexts (Figure 4.3).[37]

Based on the practice of water veneration in certain contexts and similarities in the spatial configuration of Celtic and Roman military gear found in water, it is evident that Roman culture adopted and adapted deities and religious practices from other groups. Mithraism, an Imperial adoption, had a strong following among the Roman Army. Many reliefs from Britain and Gaul survive depicting Mithras slaying the primeval bull, with a serpent and scorpion trying to prevent the blood from reaching the fertile ground. At least three Roman deities were subjected to substantial Celtic influence while retaining a Roman identity.[38] The combining of the Celtic goddess Sulis and the Roman goddess Minerva demonstrate a Romano-Celtic deity, while other hybrid deities include a Celtic Mars and a Romano-Celtic sky god from Britain. A statuette from Martlesham in England depicts a mounted warrior with an inscription dedicating it to Mars Cocidius, while an altar from Chester possesses a dedicatory inscription to Jupiter Optimus Maximus Tanarus, who was a Celtic thunder deity from Gaul and Germany.[39] When Rome expanded into new territories, cultural exchange occurred on both sides and it certainly appears that Celtic culture left an indelible mark on Roman religion in the western provinces.

Classical literary accounts, the presence of specific water deities and the archaeology of Celtic groups in Britain and Gaul suggest that soldiers stationed in Gaul witnessed and eventually adopted an established

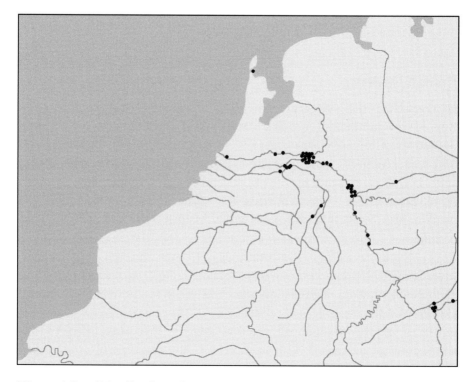

Figure 4.3:   Distribution of Roman arms and armour discovered in aquatic contexts in Belgic Gaul, after Roymans, 1996.

religious tradition of water veneration where individuals dedicated valuable military gear in water (Figure 4.3). There are precedents for Celtic influence on Roman religion, and the adopted practice of water veneration and votive deposition of valuable and heavily regulated gear fits this mould. The practice has its origins as early as the second century BC and had considerable staying power among the soldiers as it continued well into the Imperial period. Despite subtle differences in preferred material types and depositional locales, the archaeology demonstrates a great degree of cultural exchange and continuity in the religious realms of the Celts and Romans. The purpose and belief systems behind such a tradition varied across time and space. Although generally, in practice, the Roman and Celtic traditions concerning water appear similar, different cultural and ideological backgrounds gave the ritual a distinctively different meaning.

Commemoration: Safeguarding Posthumous Memory

The intellectual origins of the scholarly study of memory are complex and difficult to define. The ways in which conceptions and uses of memory changed over time, however, contributed to the construction of a coherent theoretical framework. In order to understand the crucial role that memory plays in this investigation of soldierly commemoration as a facet of ancestor worship, a historiographic analysis of memory is necessary as Roman commemoration practices are best examined through a theoretical framework of memory.

From Michelet in the nineteenth century to Collingwood in the early twentieth century, historians employed memory in a similar way.[40] According to these historians, memory, as the living imagination of past peoples, was one of the subject matters of historical understanding.[41] They studied history to recreate the past in the present as it was originally seen. In this respect, the relationship between history and memory was fluid and incorruptible.[42] Today's historians have a different perception of memory, as the distortions of memory have been analyzed more critically; whereas previous historians found 'spontaneous heroism, they [current historians of memory] find calculating power'.[43] Academic studies arise as a result of its potential as a 'calculating power'. The study of memory within historical discourse emerged during the mid-1960s at a time of transformation in history, initiated by Yates and White, who first introduced memory as a tool for the historian.[44] Subsequent work, such as that of Nora and the adoption of Halbwachs to the English-speaking world, further refined the use of memory in history, which developed divergent branches of memory study within history today.[45]

Historical studies utilizing memory after Collingwood took shape in the 1960s and were influenced by such differing approaches as the history of collective mentalities, the 'linguistic turn' and the Annales School generally. Collective mentalities were seen as the way that people in the past perceived their world. An awareness of the revolutions in the technologies of communication through time led historians back to memory as a source of culture through orality.[46] The crossing of 'the threshold of literacy in antiquity made humans self-conscious about the traits of memory, and so raised doubts in their minds about their hold on the past'.[47] Here, according to Yates in 1966, the invention of the art of memory took place.[48]

During the late 1970s and early 1980s, scholars of memory adopted the framework constructed by Halbwachs, a French sociologist.[49] Halbwachs took the term 'collective memory' and argued that it evokes the presence of the past. He placed memory into the social realm rather than the psychological.[50] This form of memory is always reshaped by its social contexts. According to Halbwachs, 'there is no point in seeking where … [memories] are preserved in my brain or in some nook in my mind to which I alone have access: for they are recalled by me externally, and the groups of which I am a part at any time give me the means to reconstruct them.'[51] Within this model, commemoration is a means to preserve collective memories, which in any other case are provisional. He separated history and memory and contended that memory is defined by its present use. Halbwachs stressed that memory is susceptible to corruption by its social context, evoked the presence of the past and recognized that historians can couple it with politics.

From these historiographic shifts, memory became a popular mode of historical investigation. Kline argued that 'the emergence of memory promises to rework history's boundaries'.[52] In Lendon's 2005 work he examined the role of the past in ancient warfare by studying the link between ancient cultures, primarily the Greeks and Romans, and their past. For Lendon, to understand the Roman concepts of warfare and military change one must comprehend the relationship of the Greeks and Romans to their past.[53] Although Lendon occasionally referred to the Roman military as 'monolithic' and at times interpreted Roman military behaviour in terms of the 'standards of modern armies', he did offer a pioneering approach to memory and ancient military studies.[54] He recognized that previous scholars studied the ways the Roman military fought from two perspectives: discipline and cohesion. Lendon argued that each perspective partially contributes to the field, but to fully understand the military one must examine the 'society's unique habits of sociability, its way of forming links between men, in its culture'.[55] In order to study this culture, scholars must examine how the Romans perceived and utilized their past because 'the Roman past, real or imagined, combined with the admiration of later men for that past, is a powerful tool for explaining how the Romans fought changed over time'.[56] Therefore, the way Roman soldiers fought was, in part, a result of their admiration of past soldiers.

Carroll discussed the methods Romans devised to commemorate themselves after death.[57] Carroll's investigation of Roman funerary monuments focuses on memory and commemoration and the real fear of memory loss. The Romans used monumental inscriptions to give a longer life to a man's name and his memory, and, she argues, they believed that immortalizing their names ensured their memory would survive.[58] Through a treatment of archaeological, primary and secondary sources, Carroll demonstrated that the perpetuation of memory of the deceased occurred through mnemonic and visual means in the public sphere. Moreover, she proved that memory loss was not a phenomenon reserved for the upper echelons of Roman society, but rather it was a real fear for anyone attempting to preserve their memory through inscriptions, sculpture or portraits.

It is at the junction of Lendon's assertion that an admiration of past soldiers played a key role in Roman warfare and Carroll's focus on the importance of posthumous memory in Roman society, that the present investigation argues that Roman soldiers used their gear as commemorative devices as part of a unique form of ancestor worship within the Army. The practice began following the Marian reforms and continued into the Imperial period.

Posthumous memory and the commemorative devices utilized to maintain it differed greatly in antiquity.[59] The belief that an individual, soldier or otherwise, enjoyed an afterlife through the perpetuation of their memory after death via an array of commemorative practices was central to Roman religion, as evidenced by Carroll's exhaustive study and ancient literary sources such as Cicero, who states, 'The life of the dead is set in the memory of the living.'[60] Posthumous memory was important in life and death, as the concept encompassed reproducing or recalling an individual and their character and virtues. Recent studies within the civilian realm explore the material manifestations of Roman commemorative practices (i.e. sculpture, funerary monuments, inscriptions, monumental structures and portraiture) and demonstrate that these pervaded all realms of the visual landscape in projecting the name and at times image of the deceased in order to secure and perpetuate memory in life and death.[61] The same type of behaviour is also found within the military realm. Roman soldiers, as individuals in a profession that took them far from their natal homes, for whom premature death was an imminent threat, engaged in commemorative practices through inscribing military gear.[62] Beginning in the Republic, and continuing into the third century AD, soldiers throughout the Roman world inscribed an array of implements, including swords, spearheads, lead sling-bullets, shields and helmets. The inscriptions served many functions, ranging from simply denoting personal property to other more religiously charged purposes, such as commemorating individuals. The personalization of certain Roman gear served a dual purpose. The inscriptions differentiated personal property among a well-populated and highly organized system comprised of uniformly equipped members. They also, over time, became a means through which soldiers could safeguard their, as well as their predecessors', posthumous memory. Commemorative practices perpetuating memory in the ancient world were never static. Rowlands argues that in inscribed practices, memory is manifested in commemorative monuments that are repetitive and materially visible. Roman infantry helmets, as repetitive in the ranks and materially visible during combat and parade, thus lend themselves to a commemorative practice.[63]

Commemoration and Memory in the Roman Army

Ancestor worship in the civilian realm is well attested, with the creation and display of wax death masks (*imagines*) in funeral processions and familial homes, the celebration of the *Paternalia* – a nine-day religious festival where family members honoured their ancestors through a series of sacrifices undertaken at family tombs – and the construction and display of commemorative monuments.[64] Commemorative practices focused on an individual's name, image and property to identify, preserve and perpetuate one's memory. Often commemorative inscriptions, whether funerary or monumental, included a *titulus*, whereby the deceased is identified by their name in connection to supplemental information, such as patronyms, tribal affiliations, geographic origins and military units. Images, although reserved for individuals who possessed the resources to commission them, played an important role in commemorative practices. Consuls, aristocrats and later emperors plastered civic, religious and domestic spaces with their name and image because society recognized the media as anthropomorphic representations of the individual.[65] Personal property also played a role in preserving memory. Hales argued that it is important to interpret personal property as the man because Roman society saw the two as inseparable.[66] The importance of memory and the display of the name, image and property in commemorative devices are further attested to by acts of memory censorship and erasure. A ban on one's memory was considered the most severe penalty imposed by the Roman legal system and sought to eradicate the culprit's memory by attacking and destroying objects perpetuating his name, image and property.[67]

The rise of unique soldierly commemoration practices was not possible without a supportive social environment. While separated from their homes, legionaries were surrounded by comrades who became a pseudo-family that provided a support network for its members. The camaraderie that developed fostered an environment where soldiers took care of each other in life as well as after death by providing a proper burial, when possible, and carrying out any requests outlined in a will.[68] These relationships strengthened camaraderie in the ranks through their unique commemorative practices, which at times included erecting funerary monuments,[69] but more often inscribing their most valuable personal property, their military gear.

Soldiers did not employ every piece of their equipment as commemorative monuments. The infantry helmet was the most conducive item in the legionary panoply for commemoration through inscriptions because it encompassed the three facets of posthumous commemoration: name, image and property. The helmet was a valuable piece of personal property that projected their image as a Roman legionnaire, and could have their personal name inscribed on it. Infantry helmets, coupled with nominal inscriptions, provided a form of commemoration that circulated throughout the army. New helmet owners recognized and respected the inscriptions of a former comrade.[70] Legionary soldiers were continually reminded of colleagues who came before and the soldiers fighting or celebrating with them in the present. Infantry helmets were, therefore, not only protective gear, but also commemorative monuments.

Epigraphic Evidence

The current corpus of intact infantry helmets available for academic study is merely a minute fraction of the total number of helmets issued during the Republican and Imperial periods. Surviving Imperial examples outnumber Republican types, most likely because far more were produced. Helmets were expensive and, as noted above, heavily regulated, making their survival into modernity a rather rare feat. The most insightful examples capable of reflecting intentional commemorative practices are those that bear multiple inscriptions.[71] Though the examples presented below date to the Imperial period, earlier helmets with nominal inscriptions do exist and demonstrate the commemorative tradition outlined above originated in the Republic.[72]

In discussing the supply of arms, MacMullen examined the tradition of inscribing arms and armour and identified three categories of inscribed equipment: those inscribed with the owner's name and unit, items inscribed with multiple names, and those that bear the name of a manufacturer. MacMullen argued that since soldiers did not keep their gear with them, as it was the responsibility of an overseer of arms who stored the equipment in a designated storeroom until needed, nominal inscriptions were meant to differentiate personal property.[73] Bishop and Coulston acknowledged

Figure 4.4:   The 'Thames Helmet' with multiple nominal inscriptions; copper alloy; length: 29.5cm; height: 13.5cm. © Trustees of the British Museum 1950, 0706.1.

the value of inscribed gear for dating individual pieces, but agree with MacMullen that nominal inscriptions primarily served to mark ownership. For MacMullen, and Bishop and Coulston, inscriptions on gear were, with very little question, meant to denote personal property and, in instances where items present multiple names, the evidence merely demonstrates that valuable gear was extensively circulated and recycled. Although multiple inscriptions do show a conscious act of marking personal property, they also indicate a unique commemorative practice.

The 'Thames Helmet', housed at the British Museum in London, is a Coolus-type helmet dating to the first century AD.[74] The British Museum purchased the helmet in 1950 from a private collector, who stated that the helmet was dredged from the Walbrook River, a tributary of the Thames River.[75] The neck guard bears several inscriptions, indicating at least four different owners (Figures 4.4 and 4.5).[76]

1. Ɔ · M · · VRS · L · DVLCI[77]

   C(enturia) M(arci) Val(erii) Urs(i) L(uci) Dulci

   '(Property) of Lucius Dulcius in the century of Marcus Valeris Ursus' The inscription follows a pattern: abbreviated century designation with a C in retrograde, abbreviated *tria nomina* of the centurion, and an abbreviated *praenomen* followed by an unabbreviated *nomen* in the genitive case indicating the owner. The centurion's *nomen* appears in ligature.

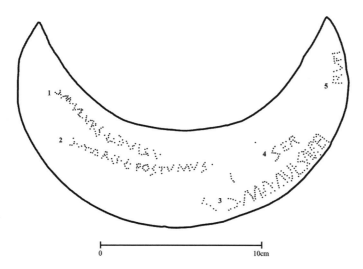

Figure 4.5:   The inscriptions on the Thames Helmet neck guard.

2.   Ɔ · MARCI · L · POSTVMVS
     C(enturia) Marci L(ucius) Postumus
     'Lucius Postumus in the century of Marcus'
     Like the first inscription, the century designation is abbreviated with a
     C in retrograde and the owner's *praenomen* is abbreviated. The centu-
     rion's *praenomen* is not abbreviated and in the genitive case, whilst his
     nomen is not given. The owner's *nomen*, however, is unabbreviated and
     in the nominative case.
3.   Ɔ · MA · AVL · SAVFEI[78]
     C(enturia) Ma(rtialis) A(uli) Aul(i) Saufei
     '(Property) of Aulus Saufeus in the century of Martialis'
     The inscription is similar to the first in that the century designa-
     tion is abbreviated with a C in retrograde and the centurion's *prae-
     nomen* is abbreviated. The owner's *praenomen* is abbreviated, and his
     nomen is unabbreviated in the genitive case. The centurion's name
     is problematic, as there appears to be a dot separating the 'M' and
     'A' following the century designation. If this is the case, the inscrip-
     tion would read: '(Property) of Aulus Aulus Saufeus in the century
     of Marcus.' Although Aulus can be abbreviated with a single letter 'A'
     and as 'AUL', the name is a well-attested *praenomen*, but not *nomen*.
     The owner's name, therefore, should be read as Aulus Saufeus and
     the 'A' is most likely associated with the centurion's praenominal
     abbreviation.
4.   SER
     Ser(vius)
     'Servius'
     The inscription is a standard *praenomen* abbreviation denoting the
     nominative case.
5.   RVFI
     Rufi
     '(Property) of Rufus'
     The inscription is a *praenomen* in the genitive case.

The Verulamium Museum in St Albans holds a Coolus-type helmet with
multiple inscriptions on the neck guard.[79] Archaeologists recovered the
helmet from Nijmegen, a Roman city in what is now the eastern part of
the Netherlands. The original fort, founded in the first century AD, is
situated on the bank of the Waal River. The helmet dates to the first century
AD and bears two nominal inscriptions on the neck guard:

1.   PP · . · PAPIRI
     (Centuria) p(rimi) p(ili) . Papiri
     '(Property) of . Papirius (in the century) of the first maniple.'
     The inscription is not well preserved. It is most likely that the PP
     is an abbreviation referring to a centurion. A letter representing the
     praenomen of the owner has been lost.

2.   Ɔ VICTORSI M · VS.R[----]
     C(enturia) Victoris M(arci)[----]
     '(Property) of Marcus [----] in the victorious century.'
     The inscription contains a century designation abbreviated with a
     C in retrograde and the centurion's *praenomen* is likely an errone-
     ous genitive. The owner's *praenomen* is abbreviated, and his *nomen*
     cannot be reconstructed with certainty.

The Bavarian State Archaeological Collection in Munich, Germany, houses
a Coolus-type helmet discovered in 1959 near the small Roman fortress of
Burlafingen.[80] Similar to the two previous examples, the helmet dates to the
first century AD and bears two nominal inscriptions and a specific legion
on the neck guard: 'Publius Aurelius', 'Marcus Munatius in the century of
Arabus', and *legio* 'XVI Gallia'. The name Publius Aurelius is not associated
with a century or *legio* XVI Gallia.

The previous examples indicate evidence of a soldierly tradition of
commemoration using an important piece of armour and provide insight
as to how the individuals sought to commemorate and identify themselves
to future soldiers. Some soldiers associated themselves along different
divisions within the army where a specific century, legion or maniple is
denoted. The forms of commemoration reflected through this gear also
demonstrate camaraderie at multiple levels, as soldiers understood and
appreciated the tradition by leaving the names of previous soldiers intact
and adding their own.

Conclusion

Infantry soldiers were as preoccupied with memory as other Romans, and
their unique lifestyle and position in society prevented them from adopting
traditional commemoration practices. To fulfil this need, legionaries
devised unique commemorative methods based on their name, image and
property. Few soldiers possessed elaborate tombstones and they knew, from
burying comrades on the battlefield, it was possible that they would not

have a lasting memory after death. To remedy this, they inscribed their names on their helmets to commemorate themselves and each other. Since Roman officials recycled gear, new legionary recruits gained possession of equipment bearing the names of those who served before them and they understood the importance of this custom and practised it, memorializing their names for themselves and future soldiers and veterans. While actively fighting an enemy or celebrating with comrades in a parade or triumph, these inscriptions were visible, and soldiers were constantly reminded of their comrades during times of stress, fear and celebration and thus continued a tradition of admiration of previous soldiers.

An examination of two specific behaviours attributed to Roman soldiers and their gear, commemoration and votive deposition, demonstrates a mere glimpse into the religious world of the Roman Army. These behaviours show a level of hybridity, specifically with Greek and Celtic practices. Roman equipment served a vital utilitarian function for its owner by protecting one's body and giving the individual the means to act offensively during an engagement, but this was far from their only function. Whether tasked as commemorative monuments or vows to appease a deity, Roman military equipment served as a conduit to fulfill the religious needs of a Roman social group that sought to participate in Roman religious and ideological behaviour far outside of its cultural nucleus.

Notes

1. See Veg. *Mil.*, and Front. *Strat.*
2. See Birley, 1952, 1953, 1958, 1961 & 1988: 3–11.
3. Birley, 1984: not paginated.
4. James, 2002: 15.
5. James, 2002: 1.
6. Birley, 1988: 3.
7. James, 2002: 21.
8. These theoretical changes include, but are not limited to, cultural historical approaches and Lewis Binford's processual archaeological paradigm. See, for example, Binford, 1972 & 1983.
9. Previous notable attempts include: Grant, 1974; Campbell, 1984; MacMullen, 1984; Goldsworthy, 1996.
10. James, 1999 & 2001.
11. See also Alston, 1995: 3–4; Luttwak, 1976: xi–xii.
12. James, 2001: 78.

13. James, 2002: 38.
14. *Miles*: a military man, soldier or warrior; *legio*: a body of soldiers consisting of 4,200–6,000 men; *cohors*: legions, auxiliary troops or allies; *numerus*: a division of the army, a troop or a band: *exercitus*: an exercised, disciplined body of men, an army. All definitions cited are from Lewis, 1879.
15. See for example Tac. *Ann.* 1.3, 4.5.
16. Veg. *Mil.* 3.1.
17. James, 2002: 39.
18. James, 2001: 78.
19. James, 2002: 39.
20. MacMullen, 1984: 455.
21. See *CIL* 13.6870, 6886, 6910; Carroll, 2006: 187.
22. Beard, North & Price, 1998: 114–66.
23. Wait, 1985; Roymans, 1996.
24. Wait, 1985; Roymans, 1996.
25. For accidental loss, see Klumbach, 1974; Robinson, 1975; Oldenstein, 1990. For the potential of votive deposition, see Bishop & Coulston, 2006: 26–34.
26. Ruegg, 1995; Roymans, 1996; Edlund-Berry, 2006; Olson, 2011.
27. Beard, North & Price, 1998.
28. Alcock, 1965; Olson, 2011.
29. Green, 1993: 51–52.
30. Strabo 4.1.13; Just. *Epit.* 32.3.
31. Oros. 5.16.
32. Caes. *Bell. Gall.* 8.43.4.
33. Green, 1983: 12.
34. For Celtic water deities, see Alcock, 1965; Green, 1993; Webster, 1986.
35. Edlund-Berry, 2006: 180
36. Ruegg, 1995; Smith, 1859; Rhodes, 1991.
37. Roymans, 1996.
38. Green, 1983: 43.
39. Green, 1983: 46.
40. Memory as a social construct, not a psychological one.
41. This work in no way implies that the numerous historians from this period are homogeneous but rather that they perceived memory within their works in a similar way.
42. In Collingwood, 1994, his interpretations of memory are very elusive because at times he opposes history and memory (238, 252, 293, 302 &

366), refuses to comment on the debate (252) and accepts the use of memory in certain types of history, namely in self-reflection (293 & 294).

43. Hutton, 2000: 535.
44. Yates, 1966; White, 1975; Hutton, 2000.
45. Nora, 1996; Halbwachs, 1992.
46. For the premier study of the reconfiguration of orality and literature, see Ong, 1982. See also Clanchy, 1979.
47. Hutton, 2000: 533.
48. Yates, 1966, and for a modern interpretation see Hutton, 1993, and Gordon, 1995.
49. Halbwachs, 1992.
50. See Hutton, 1994.
51. Halbwachs, 1992: 38.
52. Klein, 2000: 128.
53. Lendon, 2005: 13.
54. Lendon, 2005: 170.
55. Lendon, 2005: 171.
56. Lendon, 2005: 171.
57. Carroll, 2006.
58. See Pliny *Letters* 1.17.4 & 5.8.
59. Varner, 2000, 2001, 2004.
60. Carroll, 2006, and Cic. *Phil.* 9.4.10. All literary translations are the author's unless otherwise noted.
61. See Varner, 2001, 2004; Carroll, 2006; Hedrick, 2000.
62. Olson, 2011, 2013.
63. Rowlands, 1993; Bradley, 2000.
64. Ov. *Fasti* 2.537–39. See also Beard, North & Price, 1998: 291–96.
65. Varner, 2004: 9–10.
66. Hales, 2000: 44.
67. For memory erasure, see Mustakallio, 1994; Flower, 1998, 2000; Varner, 2004.
68. For wills, see Champlin, 1991.
69. Among many recent studies, see especially Saller & Shaw, 1984; Gilchrist, 2003; Hope, 2003; Mouritsen, 2005; Carroll, 2006.
70. The commentary presented in the *Roman Inscriptions of Britain* of the Thames Helmet (*RIB* 2425.2) suggests that a few inscriptions have been erased. Having inspected the helmet first-hand, there is no evidence of deliberate erasure. Seemingly partial inscriptions may just as well have been abbreviations.

71. MacMullen, 1960; Bishop & Coulston, 2006.
72. See, for example, the Montefortino helmet (third–second century BC) housed at the Valladolid Museum with the inscription: *N PAQVI.*
73. MacMullen, 1960: 23.
74. The helmet has been published in the *Roman Inscriptions of Britain* series (*RIB* 2425.2), MacMullen, 1960: 36 (n. 47); Wright, 1951: 142–43; Robinson, 1975: 32 (pl. 54).
75. I would like to thank Ralph Jackson and Richard Hobbs of the British Museum for permission to examine the Thames Helmet and for access to the museum acquisition records.
76. The following epigraphic commentary was first published by the present author in: Olson, 2013: 12–14.
77. The epigraphic conventions employed are selective and based on the systems of Bodel, 2001, and Keppie, 1991.
     [----] Four dashes within brackets represent missing letters, the exact number of which cannot be ascertained.
     Overlined characters represent letters joined in a ligature.
     (abc) Letters within parentheses represent missing letters that have been supplied by the editor.
     … Dots represent missing letters.
78. Wright, 1951: 142–43, also interprets the second and third letters as an abbreviation for Martialis.
79. The helmet has been published in the *Roman Inscriptions of Britain* (*RIB* 2425.3) and Robinson, 1975: 32–33 (pls 58–61).
80. The helmet, inventory number 1965/801, was published by Klein, 2003: 33 (abb. 7).

Bibliography

Alcock, A., 1965, 'Celtic Water Cults in Roman Britain', *Archaeological Journal* 122: 1–12.

Alston, R., 1995, *Soldier and Society in Roman Egypt: A Social History*, London.

Beard, M., North, J. & Price, S., 1998, *Religions of Rome: Volume 1: A History*, Cambridge.

Binford, L. 1972, *An Archaeological Perspective*, New York.

Binford, L., 1983, *Working at Archaeology*, New York.

Birley, E. (ed.), 1952, *The Congress of Roman Frontier Studies, 1949*, Durham.

Birley, E., 1953, *Roman Britain and the Roman Army: Collected Papers*, Kendal.

Birley, E., 1958, *Archaeology in the North of England: Inaugural Lecture of the Professor of Romano-British History and Archaeology Delivered in the Appleby Lecture on 6 May, 1958*, Durham.

Birley, E., 1961, *Research on Hadrian's Wall*, Kendal.

Birley, E., 1984, 'Forword' in Speidel, M. (ed.), *Roman Army Studies I*, Amsterdam: not paginated.

Birley, E. 1988, 'The Epigraphy of the Roman Army', in Speidel, M. (ed.) *The Roman Army: Papers 1929–1986*, Amsterdam: 3–11.

Bishop, M. & Coulston, J.C.N., 2006, *Roman Military Equipment: from the Punic Wars to the Fall of Rome*, Oxford.

Bodel, J., 2001, *Epigraphic Evidence: Ancient History from Inscriptions*, London.

Bradley, R., 2000, *An Archaeology of Natural Places*, New York.

Campbell, J., 1984, *The Emperor and the Roman Army, 31 BC–AD 235*, Oxford.

Carroll, M., 2006, *Spirits of the Dead: Roman Funerary Commemoration in Western Europe*, Oxford.

Champlin, E., 1991, *Final Judgments: Duty and Emotion in Roman Wills, 200 BC–AD 250*, Berkeley.

Clanchy, M., 1979, *From Memory to Written Record: England 1066–1307*, Cambridge, Massachusetts.

Collingwood, R.G., 1994, *The Idea of History*, Oxford.

Edlund-Berry, I., 2006, 'Hot, Cold, Smelly: The Power of Sacred Water in Roman Religion, 400–100 BCE', in Schultz, C. & Harvey Jr, P. (eds), *Religion in Republican Italy. Yale Classical Studies* 33, Cambridge: 162–80.

Flower, H., 1998, 'Rethinking "*Damnatio Memoriae*": the Case of Cn. Calpurnius Pater in AD 20', *ClAnt* 17, no. 2: 155–87.

Flower, H., 2000, '*Damnatio Memoriae* and Epigraphy', in Varner, E.R. (ed.), *From Caligula to Constantine: Tyranny and Transformation in Roman Portraiture*, Atlanta: 58–69.

Gilchrist, R., 2003, *The Social Commemoration of Warfare*, Abingdon.

Goldsworthy, A., 1996, *The Roman Army at War, 100 BC–AD 200*, Oxford.

Gordon, D., 1995, 'History as an Art of Memory', *History and Theory* 34: 340–54.

Grant, M., 1974, *The Army of the Caesars*, London.

Green, M., 1983, *The Gods of Roman Britain*, Oxford.

Green, M., 1993, *Celtic Myths*, Austin.

Halbwachs, M., 1992, *On Collective Memory*, Chicago.

Hales, S., 2000, 'At Home with Cicero', *G&R* 47: 44–55.

Hedrick, C.W., 2000, *History and Silence: Purge and Rehabilitation of Memory in Late Antiquity*, Austin.

Hope, V., 2003, 'Trophies and Tombstones: Commemorating the Roman Soldier', *World Archaeology* 35: 79–97.

Hutton, P., 1993, *History as an Art of Memory*, Hanover.

Hutton, P., 1994, 'Sigmund Freud and Maurice Halbwachs: The Problem of Memory in Historical Psychology', *History Teacher* 27: 145–58.

Hutton, P., 2000, 'Recent Scholarship on Memory and History', *History Teacher* 33: 533–48.

James, S., 1999, 'The Community of the Soldiers: A Major Identity and Centre of Power in the Roman Empire', in Baker, P. (ed.), *TRAC 98: Proceedings of the Eighth Annual Theoretical Roman Archaeology Conference Which Took Place at the University of Leicester, April 1998*, Oxford: 14–25.

James, S., 2001, 'Soldiers and Civilians: Identity and Interaction in Roman Britain', in James, S. & Millett, M. (eds), *Britons and Romans: Advancing the Archaeological Agenda*, York: 77–89.

James, S., 2002, 'Writing the Legions: The Developments and Future of Roman Military Studies in Britain', *Archaeological Journal* 159: 1–58.

Keppie, L., 1991, *Understanding Roman Inscriptions*, London.

Klein, K., 2000, 'On the Emergence of Memory in Historical Discourse', *Representations* 69: 127–50.

Klein, M., 2003, *Die Romer und ihr Erbe: Fortschritt durch Innovation und Integration*, Mainz.

Klumbach, H., 1974, *Romische Helme aus Niedermanien*, Koln.

Lendon, J.E., 2005, *Soldiers and Ghosts: A History of Battle in Classical Antiquity*, New Haven.

Lewis, C. (ed.), 1879, *A Latin Dictionary*, Oxford.

Luttwak, E., 1976, *The Grand Strategy of the Roman Empire*, Baltimore.

MacMullen, R., 1960, 'Inscriptions on Armor and the Supply of Arms in the Roman Empire', *AJA* 64: 23–40.

MacMullen, R., 1984, 'The Legion as a Society', *Historia*: 440–56.

Mouritsen, H., 2005, 'Freedmen and Decurions: Epitaphs and Social History in Imperial Italy', *JRS* 95: 38–63.

Mustakallio, K., 1994, *Death and Disgrace: Capital Penalties with Post Mortem Sanctions in Early Roman Historiography*, Helsinki.

Nora, P., 1996, *Realms of Memory: Rethinking the French Past*, Columbia.

Oldenstein, J., 1990, 'Two Roman Helmets from Eich, Alzey-Worms District', *JRMES* 1: 27–37.

Olson, B.R., 2011, 'The Dedication of Roman Weapons and Armor in Water as a Religious Ritual', *Popular Archaeology* 3.

Olson, B.R., 2013, 'Roman Infantry Helmets and Commemoration among Soldiers', *Vulcan* 1: 1–17.

Ong, W., 1982, *Orality and Literacy: The Technologizing of the Word*, London.

Rhodes, M., 1991, 'The Roman Coinage from London Bridge and the Development of the City of Southwark', *Britannia* 22: 179–90.

Robinson, H.R., 1975, *The Armour of Imperial Rome*, New York.

Rowlands, M., 1993, 'The Role of Memory in the Transmission of Culture', *World Archaeology* 25, no. 2: 141–51.

Roymans, N., 1996, 'The Sword or the Plough. Regional Dynamics in the Romanisation of Belgic Gaul and the Rhineland Area', in Roymans, N. (ed.), *From the Sword to the Plough: Three Studies on the Earliest Romanisation of Northern Gaul*, Amsterdam: 9–126.

Ruegg, S.D., 1995, *Underwater Investigations at Roman Minturnae*, Jonsered.

Saller, R. & Shaw, B., 1984, 'Tombstones and Roman Family Relations in the Principate: Civilians, Soldiers, and Slaves', *JRS* 84: 124–56.

Smith, C.R., 1859, *Illustrations of Roman London*, London.

Varner, E.R., 2000, *From Caligula to Constantine: Tyranny and Transformation in Roman Portraiture*, Atlanta.

Varner, E.R., 2001, 'Portraits, Plots, and Politics: *Damnatio Memoriae* and the Images of Imperial Women', *MAAR* 46: 41–94.

Varmer, E.R., 2004, *Mutilation and Transformation: Damnatio Memoriae and Roman Imperial Portraiture*, Boston.

Wait, G.A., 1985, *Ritual and Religion in Iron Age Britain*, BAR British Series 149(i), Oxford.

Webster, G., 1986, *Celtic Religion in Roman Britain*, New Jersey.

White, H., 1973, *Metahistory: The Historical Imagination in Nineteenth-Century Europe*, Baltimore.

Wright, R.P., 1951, 'Roman Britain in 1950: I. Sites Explored: II. Inscriptions', *JRS* 41: 120–45.

Yates, F., 1966, *The Art of Memory*, Chicago.

Chapter 5

The Cult of the Eagles in the Roman Republic

Christopher Matthew

Nothing symbolized the might of Rome more than the eagle (*aquila*) – especially in its guise as a military standard. Across the Mediterranean world and beyond, wherever the wings of the legionary eagle cast their shadow, the soldiers of Rome were literally only paces behind. Yet for the members of Rome's legions and the people within the Empire's settlements, the eagle was far more than just an animalistic totem to be used to facilitate deployment and operations on the field of battle. Rather, the legionary eagle assumed a life of its own (quite physically in some accounts) and became a point of singular focus and devotion for the men who carved out Rome's empire. The veneration of the eagle became Rome's military 'cult'.

The Roman military seems to have used the image of the eagle as one of its military standards from very early in its history. Pliny the Elder states that in much earlier times Rome's army had employed five main animal motifs as their symbols: the eagle, the wolf, the horse, the Minotaur and the boar.[1] Keppie suggests that the animals depicted on the earlier standards were reflections of the religious beliefs of a primarily agricultural society.[2] This conclusion, however, seems unlikely when it is considered that at least two of the animals – the eagle and the Minotaur – do not have clear links to agriculture, and the wolf could only really be seen as an enemy of agriculture/pastoralism (from a shepherd's perspective). Webster, on the other hand, suggests that the creatures depicted on the earlier standards were representative of certain attributes and characteristics that an army may want to project – being swift like an eagle, for example, or as strong as a bull or as savage as a boar.[3] While this may possibly be the case, at least in part, it is also important to recognize that all of the creatures used as early Roman military standards have links to mythology and religion – the eagle was a symbol of the god Jupiter, the horse was associated with Neptune, the boar with Diana, the bull (through the form of the Minotaur) with Venus, and the wolf had ties to both the god Mars and Romulus and Remus, the mythical founders of the Roman state. As such, the early Roman standards, while possibly portraying certain martial attributes, also linked Rome and the units of its army to the divine and a certain amount of religiously sanctioned protection and authority of Roman conquest and expansion.

Pliny attributes the use of the eagle with the 'first rank' of the manipular legions of the Early Republic, while the remaining four were distributed one per *ordine*.[4] Polybius, on the other hand, writing in the second century BC, states that there were two standard bearers per *speira* of the early legion (by which he is assumed to be referring to the maniple).[5] Conversely Varro, writing around 47–45 BC, states that the maniple was the smallest tactical sub-unit of the legion and had only a single standard.[6] Regardless of their number, as symbols of the different classes of Rome's early legions, a desire to protect the standards associated with one's own contingent within the propertied, class-ranked structure of Rome's part-time militia fostered a fanatical devotion which bordered on the suicidal. This devotion could be used to spur troops, even allied troops, into action. For example, during a battle in 446 BC:

> 'The Romans experienced the most difficulty on the right wing; there Agrippa, young, active, and courageous, perceiving that the battle was everywhere going better than on his own front, grabbed the standards from the men who carried them, and began to take them forward himself, and even to cast some of them into the press of the enemy. The disgrace with which his soldiers were now threatened spurred them into the attack, and the victory was extended to every part of the line.'[7]

Similarly, Plutarch states that at the Battle of Pydna in 168 BC:

> 'The Romans, when they attacked the Macedonian phalanx, were unable to force a passage, and Salvius, the commander of the Pelignians, snatched the standard of his unit and hurled it amongst the enemy. Then the Pelignians, because it is an unnatural and scandalous thing amongst Italians to abandon a standard, rushed on towards the place where it was and dreadful casualties were inflicted on both sides.'[8]

Livy, Frontinus and other writers record several similar incidents during the Early Republic, including two where the standard-bearer himself was dragged into the ranks of the enemy by his commander and the rest of the troops of the unit were forced to follow.[9] The number of such references across the literary record would suggest that these are more than elements of poetic licence or literary embellishment, and are probably based upon actual occurrences. Such actions consequently demonstrate the high level of regard that the members of the early Roman Army had for their standards.

Then, at the end of the second century BC, a number of reforms took place which altered the nature of the Roman Army and elevated the veneration of the legionary eagle above all other military emblems. In 107 BC, the consul Gaius Marius opened enlistment in the Roman legions to members of the 'head count' (*capite censi*) – those in possession of so minimal an amount of wealth that they were entered onto Rome's census list by 'head' (i.e. by number) rather than by the value of their property.[10] This reform essentially removed the propertied and class-based structure of the earlier part-time legions, the members of which served out of a sense of duty and loyalty to the state, and replaced it with an open, egalitarian system where any member of the Roman state could now join the army as a vocation.[11]

In 104 BC, Marius (then in his second consulship) introduced another reform to alter the nature of the legions. Pliny states that he abolished the use of the other animal standards that had been used earlier, in favour of the exclusive use of the eagle standard as the identifying emblem of Rome's military.[12] This was part of a series of inter-related reforms which stemmed from the earlier opening up of service in the legions to volunteers. The 'head count' reform of 107 BC, the adoption of the cohort as the standard tactical unit of the legions (104 BC) and the uniform equipping of all legionaries in the guise of 'Marius' Mules' (104 BC) ended the class-ranked structure of the former manipular army and with it the end of the use of standards which were symbolic of that structure. The eagle, as the insignia of the legion as a whole and attached to the *primus pilus* (chief centurion of the first cohort of the legion), was retained while those standards which no longer held a place in the new military system installed by Marius were essentially removed.[13] Initially these eagles seem to have been made of silver and small in size – small enough to be hidden inside clothing.[14] Later the eagles carried golden thunderbolts in their talons and became larger.[15]

Other standards, such as the smaller banners attached to each century of the cohort, were still used for signalling, identification and for facilitating deployment on the field of battle. Additionally, numismatic and monumental evidence from well into the Empire demonstrates that some of the earlier manipular standards and titles were used, in conjunction with the legionary eagle, well after the Marian reforms. A number of coins from 82–49 BC depict the legionary eagle flanked by two standards from which small banners or plaques are suspended bearing the letters 'H' and 'P' respectively (Figure 5.1). These letters presumably refer to the *hastati* and the *principes* – two of the ranks of troops from the earlier, pre-Marian legions. If this is the case, it is interesting to note that these standards do not bear any of the other animal images that Pliny states were used by the early legions. Consequently, it must be assumed that only some of the titles of the earlier manipular army were retained after the Marian reforms, but not their respective iconography. There is considerable uncertainty as to the purpose of these former standards within the structure of the post-Marian legion but, with the merging of the earlier maniples into the cohort as part of Marius' reforms of 104 BC, these standards may have become representative of each cohort and century within a legion as there would be little other reason for their retention nor other tactical units for them to represent.

Figure 5.1: Silver denarius. Reverse side depicting the legionary eagle and earlier military standards. Date: 82 BC; mint: Massalia. Legionary eagle; on left, standard of *hastati*; on right, standard of *principes*. Line border, EX S·C C·VAL·FLA IMPERAT; weight: 3.82g; Crawford *RRC* 365.1a, Sydenham *CRR* 747a. Image courtesy of the American Numismatic Society (1896.7.72).

One of the main results of Marius' reforms was in the sense of loyalty possessed by the members of the legions. Those in the earlier propertied, class-ranked, manipular system had served out of a sense of duty to the state, the belief being that those who held a certain level of wealth in the state had an inherent inspiration to fight to defend it. With the opening of the legions to volunteers in 104 BC, however, this sense of duty and loyalty was replaced as many members of the legions had little or no personal stake in the protection of the state and only served as part of their chosen profession. A consequence of this was that the eagle, as a symbol of that new profession, became the single point of focus, identity and devotion for the members of Rome's new legions. Duty was now to the legion itself, and its commander, rather than to the state. Thus Marius, by fostering an indirect loyalty to Rome through a devotion to its legions, effectively replaced the sense of duty to the state that had been present in the earlier manipular armies but which had been removed by his own 'head count' reform of 107 BC.

Studies of modern military personnel have shown that a strong sense of identification with a particular unit or group is one of the keys to battlefield effectiveness. For example, a sense of belonging to a group can mitigate any sense of loneliness or isolation that a soldier might experience on the field of battle, where the threat of sudden death is all too present as the soldier's world 'myopically condenses' into the realm of the front line.[16] Loyalty to one's unit additionally revolves around a strong code of conduct which, in turn, is based upon a strong sense of group support and vital mutual survival within the group which can help mitigate feelings of stress, impotence and vulnerability – all of which can make the turmoils of combat more bearable.[17] As Marshall, in his ground-breaking (and controversial) study of men in combat, states:

> 'I hold it to be one of the simplest truths of war that the thing which enables an infantry soldier to keep going with his weapons is the near presence or presumed presence of a comrade … He is sustained by his fellows primarily and by his weapons secondarily.'[18]

Marshall also outlines how the military effectiveness of a group is dictated by unit cohesion and affiliation.[19] Additionally Grossman, in his examination of the psychology of killing, suggests that unit cohesion makes the act of killing easier for the individual soldier through a sense of group anonymity.[20] Furthermore, soldiers regularly identify with, and have a sense of pride in, the accomplishments of their unit as a whole and work more effectively within a unit with combat experience.[21] These characteristics of modern soldiers are also present in the Roman Army. Battle honours and unit decorations, in the form of crowns (*coronae*) or plates (*phalerae*), were regularly suspended from the pole upon which the legionary standards were mounted (see Figures 5.1 and 5.5). This is similar to many modern regimental 'colours' which have the name of campaigns in which the unit has fought embroidered onto the flag or banner.

For the Romans, if the very eagle under which they marched had a significant history, this too could add to the pride of the unit. During his revolt against Rome, for example, Catiline carried an eagle which had supposedly belonged to Gaius Marius himself and had seen service in his war against the Germanic Cimbri in 101 BC.[22] Again, this bears many similarities to modern military institutions where regimental 'colours' could have a long and prestigious history of their own. Such examples would suggest that many of the other attributes of unit bonding, identification and cohesion found in modern military units can also be attributed to Rome's legions.

While the eagle retained a position of prominence as a legionary standard into the time of the Empire, other emblems began to be employed as well. Units with Caesarean origins (such as the *VII* and *VIII Augusta*, *X Gemina*, *III Gallica* and *III Macedonica*) regularly carried an image of a bull, an animal associated with the goddess Venus from whom Caesar claimed descent, as an additional insignia of the unit. Later, units created or reformed by the Emperor Augustus (such as the *II Augusta*, *XIV Gemina*, *XXI Rapax* and possibly the *IIII Scythia*) similarly carried the image of a Capricorn – Augustus' birth sign. During the early Empire, the *imago* of the emperor was also carried as an additional military standard and served to identify the unit with its commander-in-chief. Other emblems were adopted in recognition of a particular battle that a unit had taken part in. Caesar's *V Alaudae*, for example, adopted the image of an elephant as one of its additional standards following the Battle of Thapsus in North Africa in 46 BC.[23]

Despite the use of these other military standards, one of the things that remained with the elevation of the eagle to a place of prominence within the legion was the desire of the legionaries to protect their standards at all costs. The very fate of the legion itself was seen to be intertwined with that of its standard. Caesar, for example, in an incident which bears many similarities to the actions of standard-bearers in the Early Republic, recounts how, during the invasion of Britain in 55 BC, the *aquilifer* (the standard-bearer tasked with carrying the legionary eagle) of *Legio X*, seeing that his comrades were reluctant to storm an enemy-held beach, jumped down from his ship and ran towards the enemy while still bearing the legionary eagle. The remainder of the legion, out of fear of losing their standard to the enemy, followed the standard-bearer ashore.[24] Caesar also records how when a Roman camp was attacked by the Gauls in the Meuse Valley during the winter of 54/53 BC, the *aquilifer* of *Legio XIV* threw his eagle over the rampart back into the camp in order to save it while he died fighting heroically outside the rampart.[25]

Many of these accounts bear parallels to similar actions fought around standards and regimental 'colours' up to the nineteenth century – after which time standards were rarely taken onto the actual field of battle. This shows that, in this capacity at least, some things did not change across two millennia of warfare. However, while the devotion of modern soldiers to their unit's 'colours' is in little doubt, the main difference between a modern military standard and a Roman legionary eagle is that the evidence from the Republican period and throughout the Empire shows that, for the legionaries of Rome, the veneration of the *aquila* took on an almost quasi-religious nature.

Webster states that for the Romans, 'the standards were the religious focus of the Army and could be said to embody the very "soul" of the unit.'[26] Such a sentiment is also found in the ancient literature. Appian, for example, says that the *aquila* 'is the standard held in the highest honour by the Romans'.[27] Similarly, Vegetius states that it was a duty of the first cohort of the legion to protect the eagle, which was 'always the most special and distinctive symbol in the Roman Army of a whole legion'.[28] Germanicus referred to eagles as 'the birds of Rome and the Roman Army's protecting spirits'.[29] This suggests that the eagle was seen to possess divine, or at least supernatural, powers. Later, the Christian writer Tertullian would write that he believed that Roman religion was totally martial in its character, with the Romans worshipping the legionary eagles and other standards, swearing oaths to the standards and paying more divine honours to the standards than to any other god.[30]

As if to confirm Tertullian's statement, the literary evidence from across Roman history shows the legionary standards being the focus of what can only be considered quasi-religious worship. While in a camp or fort, the eagle and other standards were kept in their own shrine (*sacellum*) within the command headquarters (*principia*). On special occasions, such as in celebration of victory or during religious events, the eagles were dressed with garlands of flowers and anointed with oils. Pliny the Elder, in his discussion of the use of unguents, found this practice somewhat disturbing: [31]

> 'But the most wondrous thing of all is that this kind of luxurious gratification should have made its way even into the camp: at all events, the eagles and the standards, dusty as they are, and bristling with their sharpened points, are anointed on festive days. I only wish it could, by any possibility, be stated who it was that first taught us this practice. It was, no doubt, under the corrupting influence of such temptations as these, that our eagles achieved the conquest of the world. Thus do we seek to acquire their patronage and sanction for our vices.'

Suetonius similarly describes how the eagles were anointed and wreathed when the ascension of a new emperor (or contender for the position, depending upon the viewpoint of the soldiers) was announced.[32] Thus, according to Pliny and Seutonius, the legionary eagles were dressed and anointed as a means of supplication so that they would support future military ventures and imperial expansion. In this manner, the *aquila* functioned in the same manner as any other cult statue within the construct of Roman religious practice which might similarly be dressed and anointed when the deity it represented was prayed to.

Oaths were also sworn before (or to) the eagle and other standards by both soldiers and commanders. In AD 62, during Rome's war against Parthia, the governor and legate of Cappadocia, Lucius Caesennius Paetus, swore before the standards that no Roman would enter Parthian-controlled Armenia until Emperor Nero had sent written instructions informing him as to whether a peace treaty had been accepted or not.[33] The Soldier's Oath (*sacramentum militare*) would have also been sworn before the legionary eagle and other standards.[34] Standards topped with an open hand (*manus*), possibly attached to each century of the legion, were indicative of the gesture made when making the *sacramentum* and would have reminded each soldier of the solemn vow they had made.[35] On Trajan's Column (for example panels VIII, XL, LIV and LXI) these standards can be seen carried along with the legionary eagle and other insignia. It can only be assumed that something as important as the swearing of an oath of allegiance and loyalty would be made before all of the standards under which a soldier may march – in particular the legionary eagle.

The eagle was also associated with Jupiter, the main god of the Roman pantheon. This is evidenced by the thunderbolt, another symbol of Jupiter, which was clutched in the talons of the *aquila*. Webster claims that this association may have been the motive for Marius' retention of this insignia in 104 BC to the exclusion of all of the other animal motifs of the earlier legions.[36] One of Jupiter's roles was to act as an overseer (or guarantor) of oaths. Thus the soldier's *sacramentum* fulfilled a number of religious and military requirements: it created a sworn oath of loyalty to the legion by pledging a vow to its most honoured symbol, and it swore an oath to the main god of Roman religion through interaction with an animal motif readily associated with the deity. This, in effect, made the *sacramentum militare* both a military pledge and a divinely sanctioned and protected vow of obedience within the military institutions of the Roman state.

Another religious aspect of the veneration of the eagles was their involvement in sacrifices. The Jewish historian Josephus tells how, as Jerusalem fell to the army of Titus in AD 70, 'the Romans brought their standards into the Temple area and, erecting them opposite the East Gate, sacrificed to them there.'[37] This is a unique reference to the legionary standards being sacrificed to – although it does correlate with Pliny's description of the eagles being dressed with garlands and anointed with oils during celebrations, and Tertullian's later description of the Romans worshipping their standards. Unfortunately, Josephus does not go into any detail as to what the process of this sacrifice involved and what was actually given over to the standards. It is possible that what Josephus is referring to is the standards being present at a sacrifice, but not necessarily being sacrificed to. As previously noted, the legionary eagles were anointed and wreathed with garlands when a special event was being celebrated by the army – such as celebrating a victory. Josephus adds that following the 'sacrifice' to the standards, the troops enthusiastically hailed Titus as *Imperator*.[38] This would tie nicely with a celebration of victory, and the standards would have most likely been wreathed and perfumed for such an event. The details of this adornment of the standards may be what Josephus is describing as a 'sacrifice'. Interestingly, Josephus also states that the Sanctuary of the Temple, near to where the sacrifice was said to have taken place, was in flames while this was taking place. It would seem odd that the Roman troops would pick that particular, and potentially dangerous, spot to conduct some form of religious ritual in which a large body of troops was assembled, the standards were anointed and decked with garlands, a possible sacrifice of some kind was made and Titus hailed as *Imperator*. This leaves a number of possibilities for the interpretation of Josephus' passage: either it is conflated in its timeframe, the 'sacrifice' was only done quickly, the ceremony was held elsewhere – possibly near the temple gate but not necessarily inside the sacred precinct – the fire was not that large, or a combination of any or all of the above. Regardless of whether the standards were actually sacrificed to or not, the important point of note is that the standards were still present at an important military/religious rite and were dressed for the occasion.

There is other evidence for the standards being present at such rituals. When the Emperor Trajan commenced his invasion of Dacia in AD 101, a sacrifice of bulls and sheep was made outside the Roman camp. The depiction of this event on panel VIII of Trajan's Column clearly shows the presence of the legionary eagle, the *manus* standards and other military insignia (Figure 5.2). An event similar to this may be what Josephus misinterpreted as a sacrifice being made to the standards in Jerusalem in AD 70.

Similarly, epigraphic evidence from Mainz, attributed to *Legio XXII Primagenia*, describes dedications that were made 'for the honour of the eagles'.[39] What these dedications were comprised of is not clear, nor is what they were made for. However, such inscriptions would also suggest that

Figure 5.2: Detail of Panel VIII from Trajan's Column in Rome showing the presence of the legionary standards at a sacrifice. Author's photo.

either offerings of some kind had been made before the eagles (or at least on behalf of them) or that these standards were simply present at an event or rite without being the primary focus of the ritual. It thus seems clear that whatever their role and/or function within these rituals, the military standards of the Roman Army were an integral part of the religious rites of the legions.

Other accounts in the ancient literature ascribe to the standards prophetic and animate characteristics – suggesting that they were seen as more than simple military emblems and to possess semi-divine qualities. In 58 BC, when the army of Marcus Licinius Crassus was preparing to attempt a crossing of the Euphrates in Syria, the standards (so we are told) 'refused' to be pulled from the ground in a prophetic demonstration against the future massacre at the Battle of Carrhae.[40] In AD 41, when Scribonianus, the governor of Dalmatia, broke out in open revolt against the Emperor Claudius, the rebellion quickly collapsed because Scribonianus' standards likewise 'refused' to be pulled from the ground.[41] In more general terms, the order for a legion to strike camp was *signa tollere* ('raise the standards'). Webster suggests that, similar to the descriptions of the prophetic standards of Crassus and Scribonianus, if the standards 'refused' to be pulled from the ground when a camp was struck, the soldiers would have seen it as an omen for them to stay where they were.[42] Whether these reports can be taken at face-value, or should be seen as a form of literary embellishment to account for the failure of the respective ventures, is not important. What is important for understanding the place of the military standards within the belief systems of the Romans, on the other hand, is that such descriptions of the standards possessing a quasi-divine nature were seen as both acceptable and believable to the soldiers of the Roman Army, the citizen body in general who would have heard such reports and to the historians who wrote them down.

The eagle also held a special place in the mind of the Roman state as well as with the soldiers who fought to create and protect it. The eagle, as a symbol of Rome's military might, became the sign of Rome's *imperium*. Josephus states that wherever the eagle was marched, it was seen as an emblem of empire and a portent for victory.[43] When a legion was on the march, the *aquila* was placed at the head of the legionary infantry – behind the scouts, vanguard and the command group.[44] Thus, while not at the very head of the marching column, the *aquila* 'led' the troops it represented into enemy territory, in triumphal parades or wherever else the legion chose or was ordered to go. A consequence of this was that the eagle, and the legions that carried it, became the physical representations of Rome's foreign, military and diplomatic policy. Through its connection with the god Jupiter, both the legions and their eagles became the embodiment of the Roman belief in their divinely sanctioned right to conquer 'lesser peoples' and to spread Roman culture throughout the world. This sentiment was epitomized in the early Empire by the poet Virgil in his *Aeneid* when he stated that Rome's preordained destiny was to 'become illustrious, and extend her authority to the breadth of the earth and her spirit to the height of Olympus'.[45]

As far back as the end of the Republic, the success or failure of a military venture was tabulated in eagles and standards won or lost. During the Slave War against Spartacus in 71 BC, a Roman victory near Mt Cantenna was quantified by the recapture of five Roman eagles and twenty-six other standards from the rebel slaves.[46] This is only a generation after the reforms of Marius had elevated the eagle to the dominant position amongst Roman military standards, and demonstrates just how revered and widely used this insignia had become. Later, Servius Sulpicius Galba summed up his account of the Battle of Mutina between the forces of Mark Antony and those of Hirtius and Pansa in 43 BC by stating that, 'two eagles and sixty standards of Antony's have been brought in. It is a great victory!'[47] Even if an enemy was not Roman, and therefore did not carry legionary eagles as part of their insignia, victories were still tabulated in terms of 'standards captured'. Caesar, for example, quantified his victory against the Gauls at Alesia in 52 BC via the capture of seventy-four enemy standards.[48] As well as a simple means of describing the extent of a victory by providing a number of enemy units defeated, such accounts additionally show that the Romans not only recognized the symbolic importance of their own military standards, but also how other cultures may have similarly viewed theirs.

In a further display of Roman power, and the eagle's place as a representative of it, subjugated enemies could be made to swear oaths of surrender or fealty, not to Rome, but to the eagles of the legions which had conquered them. Seutonius states that when the Emperor Caligula fell ill, Artabanus, the king of the Parthians, 'paid homage to the Roman eagles and standards, and to the statues of the Caesars'.[49] An inscription from the late first century AD recording the accomplishments of Tiberius Plautus Silvanus Aelianus, the *legatus Augusti pro praetor* of a province bordering the Danube, similarly states:

> 'In this position he brought over more than 100,000 of the people who live on the other side of the Danube to pay tribute to Rome, along

with their wives and children, leaders and kings. He suppressed a revolt among the Sarmatians ... he compelled kings who had been previously unknown to, or hostile to, the Roman people to worship the Roman standards on the riverbank he was protecting.'[50]

Some foreign rulers used the image of the eagle as a symbol of their loyalty to Rome – even if it apparently contravened local religious or political tradition. In Judea, for example, Herod installed a golden eagle over the Great Gate to the Temple in Jerusalem.[51] This was quite a controversial move by Herod, who had been installed in his position as ruler by Rome. Jewish tradition prohibited the use of the images of living beings in their art – in part based upon the First Commandment, which stated that, 'I am the Lord your god ... you shall have no other gods before Me', and the Second Commandment, 'you shall not make for yourself a carved image – any likeness of anything that is in heaven above, or that is in the earth beneath, or that is in the sea under the earth'.[52] Over time, the Second Commandment was interpreted as meaning that no 'graven images' (i.e. those to be worshipped) would be tolerated, whereas animal motifs for purely decorative purposes were acceptable. Yet according to Josephus, the presence of the gilded eagle on the Temple gate raised the ire of two local rabbis, who encouraged their followers to tear down the image as they took the Second Commandment literally to mean that no images of any kind were allowed. It is also possible that these two religious leaders recognized the eagle as an image that was worshipped by the Romans – a 'graven image', contrary to the later interpretation of the Second Commandment. The followers of the rabbis were arrested and taken before Herod, who accused them of being temple-robbers, had those who had removed the eagle burnt alive and the others involved in the plot handed over for execution.[53]

While the removal of the eagle may have been based upon religious grounds using an interpretation of the Second Commandment, as Josephus seems to firmly believe in his account, there may also be other reasons behind the Jewish actions. Firstly, as a venerated symbol, the Roman eagle would clearly be in breach of the First Commandment as well as the Second. Additionally, it is possible that the reason why the presence of the eagle on the Temple gate had aroused such a response by some in the Jewish community was that it was the enduring emblem of those who had installed the unpopular Herod on the throne of Judea to begin with – Rome. Thus Herod, through his installation of the eagle, was symbolically stating that the power of Roman *imperium*, through which he had been placed on the throne, transcended the religious and symbolic significance of the Temple itself. In other words, everything in a Roman province – land, people, property and even religious beliefs – were secondary to the power symbolized by the Roman *aquila* and the legions who carried it into foreign lands.[54]

The loss of a legionary eagle to an enemy while on campaign, especially a foreign enemy, was the ultimate disgrace – both for the Roman state and for the defeated legion which lost it. Again, this bears many parallels to the 'colours' of modern military units. During the Iraq War in 2003, a supply truck belonging to the US 1st Marine Recon Division broke down during an advance into enemy territory and was subsequently blown up to avoid the vehicle and the supplies it carried from falling into enemy hands. Unbeknownst to the marines at the time, the truck contained First Recon's 'colours' – a flag reportedly carried by the unit since the Vietnam War. One of the marines remarked that 'the colors should never leave the commander's side. Losing them is a reflection on his leadership and on all of us.'[55] The Romans similarly saw the loss of an eagle as a reflection of their own actions and suffered almost any trial to preserve the honour of the unit. Caesar's *aquilifer* who cast his eagle over the rampart at Dyrrachium in order to protect it is said to have declared as he did so:

> 'I have faithfully guarded this eagle for many years in my life and now, dying, I restore it to Caesar, with equal faithfulness. I beseech you, do not allow our military honour to be disgraced, something which has never happened in Caesar's army before, and carry the eagle to him safely.'[56]

Although some legions did survive the loss of their eagle, such an outcome in battle generally equated with the loss of the legion itself.[57] Seen as an affront to Roman prestige and a challenge to Roman power, the recovery of eagles and other standards lost to a foreign enemy became a paramount concern for the Roman state – particularly during the Empire. During the last years of the Republic and the early years of the Empire, the Roman Army suffered several defeats which resulted in the loss of their prized eagles. In 53 BC the eagles of Marcus Licinius Crassus were lost, along with his son and most of his men, fighting against the Parthians at the Battle of Carrhae.[58] Roman standards were also lost in Dalmatia – most likely in 48 BC.[59] Other standards had been lost in Spain and Gaul.[60]

Yet more standards were lost to the Parthians when Decidius Saxa was defeated in Syria in 40 BC.[61] Mark Antony lost yet more standards to the Parthians a few years later in 36 BC.[62] Then, in AD 9, the largest catastrophe hit the Roman Army since the Battle of Carrhae. In that year three legions were massacred in the Teutoburg Forest in Germania, with estimated losses of 20,000 men.[63] Some of the bodies of the fallen were left unburied. Others, such as the body of the Roman commander Varus, were partially burned and dismembered.[64] Captured officers were said to have been sacrificed, cooked in pots or burned on altars in religious rituals.[65] Other captives were cast into pits, and spoils were distributed amongst the victorious Germans.[66] The captured eagles of the lost legions were erected in sacred groves as offerings in honour of the Germanic gods.[67] Tacitus concludes his description of the horrors of the massacre by stating that, in his exultation of victory, the German leader, Arminius, had openly insulted the military standards and legionary eagles.[68] The placement of this description of the insult to the eagles at the end of a long list of other atrocities emphasizes, through the literary constructions that contain it, that out of all that happened, this was seen as the worst offence against Rome of all.

News of the disaster struck Rome, and Emperor Augustus, hard. Emergency measures were put in place to raise more troops against an expected German advance on Rome, no festivals were celebrated, Germans and Gauls living in Rome were expelled, and the event was examined retrospectively through the accounts of several bad omens and portents which seem to have foretold of some disaster to come but which were, for some reason, ignored.[69] Augustus is said to have remained unshaven and unkempt – crying out in lamentation and anguish over his lost troops.[70]

The loss of these eagles (and not just the ones lost in Germany) seems to have weighed heavily on the mind of the new emperor. In order to restore lost Roman *imperium*, numerous military and diplomatic campaigns were undertaken to try to get these symbols of Rome's majesty back. The eagles lost in Gaul, Spain and Dalmatia were reclaimed in the decade between 35 BC and 25 BC.[71] Those which had been lost to the Parthians at the end of the Republic were recovered via diplomatic means a few years later in 20 BC.[72] Augustus' massive propaganda machine instantly swung into action to portray this event as a military victory, and by the following year a series of silver commemorative coins had been issued showing a Parthian, kneeling in submission and returning one of the lost standards, bearing the inscription *CAESAR AVGVSTVS SIGN(IS)*

Figure 5.3: Silver denarius. Reverse side depicting the recovery of Crassus' legionary standards from the Parthians by Augustus. Date: 19 BC; mint: Rome; reverse: kneeling Parthian presenting standard to right. CAESAR AVGVSTVS SIGN RECE; weight: 3.93g; Reference: BMC.58, *RIC* I (second edition) Augustus 315. Courtesy of the American Numismatic Society (1944.100.38324).

RECE(PTIS) ('Caesar Augustus, the standards restored') (Figure 5.3). The reclamation of these standards would also work its way into other areas of Roman art – with a depiction of a Parthian returning a standard taking centre place on the breastplate worn by Augustus on the Prima Porta statue (Figure 5.4). Augustus also took special care to detail these events in his *Res Gestae*. The recovered standards were housed in a temple to Mars Ultor (Mars the Avenger), which Augustus had built at his own expense, and a series of games were held to mark their return.[73] This act was commemorated on another series of silver coins issued in 19/18 BC (Figure 5.5).

The poet Ovid would twice recount the reclamation of the lost eagles in his *Fasti*. In one poem he outlines the intertwining role of the divine in their recapture, the affront to Roman authority that their loss had initially caused and how the actions of Augustus (again playing it up as a military

Figure 5.4: Detail of the breastplate on the Prima Porta statue of Augustus showing a Parthian returning one of Crassus' lost eagles. Photo courtesy of Patrick Tuffy.

victory) had restored Roman honour, brought home Rome's most potent symbol of *imperium* and were a cause for celebration:

'It is not enough that Mars earned the name just once;
He hunts the standards held by Parthia's hand.
This was a race protected by horses, arrows, plains,
And fenced off by its circle of rivers.
The deaths of the Crassi gave spirit to the race,
When troops, standards and leader died as one.
Parthia held Rome's standards, the glory of war,
An enemy held aloft the Roman eagle.
This disgrace would have lasted, had Caesar's potent arms
Not defeated Ausonia's wealth.
He peeled back old scars, the decades of shame;
Recaptured standards recognised their own.
What benefit are your arrows now, fired as you fled,
Your terrain, your swift horses, Parthian?
You return the eagles and offer defeated bows;
You now possess no proof of our dishonour.

Figure 5.5: Silver denarius. Reverse side depicting one of the eagles recovered by Augustus housed in the temple of Mars Ultor. Date: 18 BC; mint: Colonia Patricia. Domed hexastyle temple of Mars Ultor; within, an *aquila* between two standards, MAR VLT; weight: 3.82g; Reference: BMC.373, *RIC* I (second edition) Augustus 105A. Courtesy of the American Numismatic Society (1937.158.417).

> The twice vengeful god received a shrine and title;
> The merited honours discharge the oath.
> Hold the commemorative games in the Circus, Quirites,
> The stage seems not sufficient for the manly god.'[74]

In another poem, Ovid depicts the recapture of the eagles as a divinely sanctioned act of revenge (hence their housing in a temple to Mars the Avenger) against the killing of Crassus and his troops back in 53 BC:

> 'Clearly sadness is sometimes mingled with pleasure;
> Lest feast-days bring people unrestricted bliss.
> Crassus today at the Euphrates lost his eagles,
> And son, and men, and was finally Death's prize.
> "Why gloat, Parthian?" the goddess asked.
> "The standards return. An avenger will punish Crassus' death."'[75]

Succeeding emperors would follow this tradition of recovering lost legionary eagles. Shortly after the death of Augustus and the rise of Tiberius as the new emperor, his nephew Germanicus campaigned extensively in Germania. In AD 14, one of the eagles lost in the Teutoburg Forest was recovered from one of the Germanic tribes involved in the massacre, the Marsi.[76] The following year, the eagle of another of Varus' lost legions (the 19th) was recovered from a wood guarded by the Bructeri.[77] A triumphal arch was erected in Rome to commemorate the return of these eagles.[78] Later still, during the reign of the Emperor Claudius in AD 41, the third of Varus' lost eagles was recovered during a campaign against the Chauci.[79] As if to bring the whole affair of the Teutoburg massacre to a close, Tacitus also records how, in AD 50, a victorious campaign against the invading Chatti liberated a number of Roman prisoners – among them men from Varus' legions who had been held captive for more than forty years.[80]

These commemorative tools – the poems, the festivals, the monuments and written histories – for all of their propaganda value in embellishing the accomplishments of emperors from Augustus (who was Ovid's patron) to Claudius, clearly show how much reverence the eagles of the legions were held in by the people of the Roman state; whether simply because they were a symbol of Roman might, they had become interwoven with the religious beliefs and ideals of the state, or a combination of both. The eagles were not just a means of identity for the legions. Rather, they had also become the focus of awe and reverence, almost to the point of religious devotion, to the general populace of the Roman state.

The symbolism of the legionary eagle is one of the most lasting legacies of ancient Rome, an icon that was adopted by later cultures and empires – from Napoleonic France to Nazi Germany and modern America – who wished to portray a similar level of *imperium* to that of the Roman Empire in their own attempts to consolidate power and prestige. In the eyes of the Romans, following the reforms of Gaius Marius at the end of the second century BC, the eagle came to not only symbolize the individual legions to which these standards were attached, but the might of the Empire as a whole, and required almost fanatical devotion from soldiers, civilians and emperors alike. Whether the Roman devotion to the legionary eagles can be seen as a true 'cult', in the strictest sense of the term, is a matter of semantics. The veneration of the legionary standard carried with it many of the hallmarks of other religious practices. The eagles were protected and recovered, they were worshipped and honoured, and in some instances they were assigned semi-animate characteristics. All of these elements are found in the practices of other religious cults in the Roman world. But more than this, the eagle became the very symbol of Rome itself. Thus Tacitus is entirely correct when he describes the eagles as 'the birds of Rome and the Roman Army's protecting spirits', for the two (the state and the army) were inexorably intertwined. For the Romans, even though they may not individually participate in the military or other area of government policy where the *aquila* played a dominant role and held an esteemed position, everyone – man, woman or child, patrician or plebeian – were devotees of the 'cult of the eagles'.

Notes

1. Pliny *Nat. Hist.* 10.16; some modern works, possibly due to typographical errors, have a bear as one of the standards rather than a boar as Pliny states (for example, see Warry, 1980: 136).
2. Keppie, 1984: 67.
3. Webster, 1998: 134.
4. Pliny *Nat. Hist.* 10.16; the interpretation of this passage, and subsequently the position and function of the main manipular standards of Rome's early military, has been a controversial topic amongst scholars (for example, see Warry, 1980: 136; Webster, 1998: 133; Sekunda, Northwood & Simkins, 2003: 26–27; Rawlings, 2007: 59). Additionally, Pliny's language is somewhat vague and open to interpretation (hence part of the controversy). For example, by 'first rank', is Pliny suggesting that it was placed in/beside the first rank of the legion when it formed up for battle? Is he suggesting that it belonged to/was indicative of the highest-ranking soldiers? Or is he suggesting that the standard itself was ranked first ahead of the others in terms of its importance? An answer to such questions is unlikely to be ever found with any certainty. However, it does seem that the eagle was symbolic of the legion as a whole, while the other four emblems were indicative of the four different contingents which made up the early legion: the *velites*, *principes*, *hastati* and *triarii*. See Matthew, 2010: 51–53.
5. Polyb. 6.24.
6. Varro *Ling. Lat.* 5.88.
7. Livy 3.70.10: *in dextro plurimum laboris fuit. ibi Agrippa, aetate viribusque ferox, cum omni parte pugnae melius rem geri quam apud se*

videret, arrepta signa ab signiferis ipse inferre, quaedam iacere etiam in confertos hostes coepit. See also Front. *Strat.* 2.8.2. It is possible that Livy is here retrojecting a concern that seems more common in the soldiery of the first century back onto those of the fifth for the sake of literary style. As such, this passage needs to be viewed with an element of caution in regards to its validity for the military of early Rome.

8. Plut. *Aem.* 20.
9. For example, see: Livy 4.29.3, 6.8.3–5; Front. *Strat.* 2.8.1, 2.8.3–5; see also: Val. Max. 3.2.20; Flor. *Epit.* 1.11.2.
10. For the status of the *capite censi* and accounts of the Marian reform, see Polyb. 6.19; Sall. *Jug.* 86.1–3; Plut. *Mar.* 9; Julius Exuperantius *History* 12–13.
11. For discussions of the Marian reforms, see: Rich, 1983: 290–91; Evans, 1994: 74–76; Matthew, 2010: 9–28.
12. Pliny *Nat. Hist.* 10.4.
13. For the eagle being associated with the *primus pilus*, see: Pliny *Nat. Hist.* 33.19.58. Keppie, 1984: 67 suggests that the early *aquilifer* was part of the senior century of the first maniple of the *triarii*. If this was the case, then the eagle was associated with the most senior unit in the legion both before and after the time of Marius. Thus Marius did not actually invent the use of the eagle as the symbol of the legion, but merely raised its position by removing the use of the others while the eagle retained its original position within the formation. Connolly, 1980: 218 conversely states that Marius introduced the use of the eagle, but this goes against Pliny. The later writer Vegetius (*Epit.* 2.7) lists the position of a standard-bearer as a *principale* – a promotion to a higher position within the unit with increased pay.
14. For the eagles being made of silver: App. *Civ.* 4.101; for them being hidden under clothing: Flor. *Epit.* 4.12.
15. For the thunderbolts: Dio 43.35; for heavier standards (at least for praetorian units) carried on pack animals: Suet. *Calig.* 43. Webster, 1998: 137 also suggests that the legionary eagles became gilded silver while those of the praetorian units were solid gold. Connolly, 1980: 218–19 alternatively suggests that in the time of Caesar the *aquila* was silver and gold, and by the time of the Empire they were all made entirely of gold.
16. Stouffer, Lumsdaine, Lumsdaine, Williams, Smith, Janis, Star & Cotttrell, 1949: 99.
17. Stouffer *et al.*, 1949: 135–37, 143–49.

18. Marshall, 1947: 42–43.
19. Marshall, 1947: 124–28; for discussions of similar characteristics from a Roman perspective, see: MacMullan, 1984: 446–51; Lee, 1996: 207–09.
20. Grossman, 1986: 150–53.
21. Stouffer *et al.*, 1949: 137–39, 257–59.
22. Sall. *Cat.* 59.3.
23. App. *Civ.* 2.96.
24. Caes. *Bell. Gall.* 4.25.
25. Caes. *Bell. Gall.* 5.37; see also: App. *Civ.* 2.61 for a similar event that occurred at the Battle of Dyrrachium during the Civil War. Caesar (*Bell. Civ.* 3.64), on the other hand, reports that a dying *aquilifer* passed his standard to a troop of cavalry and begged them to not allow it to be captured but to return it to Caesar. In an account of a somewhat extreme use of a standard as a rallying point, Tacitus (*Hist.* 3.17) records how at the Battle of Bedriacum in AD 69, Antonius killed the fleeing standard-bearer of one of his cavalry units and personally carried the standard back into the fray – around which more than 100 troopers made a valiant stand.
26. Webster, 1998: 133.
27. App. *Civ.* 2.61.
28. Veg. *Mil.* 2.6: *Haec enim suscipit aquilam, quod praecipuum signum in Romano est semper exercitu et totius legionis insigne.*
29. Tac. *Ann.* 2.17: *Romanas avis, propria legionum numina.*
30. Tert. *Apol.* 16.8: *Religio Romanorum tota castrensis signa veneratur, signa iurat, signa omnibus deis praeponit.*
31. Pliny *Nat. Hist.* 13.3.23: *maxime tamen mirum est hanc gratiam penetrasse et in castra; aquilae certe ac signa, pulverulenta illa et cuspidibus horrida, unguuntur festis diebus, utinamque dicere possemus quis primus instituisset! ita est nimirum: hac mercede corruptae orbem terrarum devicere aquilae. ista patrocinia quaerimus vitiis.*
32. Suet. *Claud.* 13.
33. Tac. *Ann.* 15.16.
34. In Roman legal and religious tradition any form of *sacramentum* (military or other form of sacred oath) rendered those who swore it *sacer*, or 'beholden to the gods', if they violated the vow. Livy (22.38.1–5) states that for the legions, such a pledge of loyalty did not occur in Rome's history until 216 BC, and that within this oath that was administered by the tribunes, the soldiers declared that they would not

flee in fear and would not leave their ranks except to obtain a weapon, attack an enemy or save a fellow Roman. Gellius (*Noct. Att.* 16.4.2–5) also describes a military oath where the swearer vowed not to steal and to report anything that they had seized with malicious intent to their superiors. When a levy was raised, those enlisted also swore to muster on the appointed day. Polybius (6.21) states that one man from the levy was selected to come forward and swear that he would obey his officers and orders to the best of his ability. The rest of the levy then came forward and swore the same oath following the first man's example. According to Tacitus (*Hist.* 2.79), the first step in transferring imperial power to Vespasian in AD 69 was taken by the regional Prefect, Tiberius Alexander, who had the troops stationed in Egypt swear loyalty to him. By the second century AD, soldiers swore an oath of allegiance and loyalty to the emperor (for example, see: Pliny *Letters* 10.52–53; see also: Veg. *Mil.* 2.5).

35. For a brief discussion of oaths taken before the standards, see: Webster, 1998: 137. See also Taylor's chapter on the *sacramentum* and other military oaths in *Religion and Classical Warfare*.

36. Webster, 1998: 135. However, it is more likely that it was simply more expedient for Marius, as part of his reforms, to retain the use of the standard that was already associated with the legion as a whole and abandon the use of the other four standards.

37. Joseph. *Bell. Jud.* 6.326.

38. Joseph. *Bell. Jud.* 6.326.

39. *CIL* 13.6679, 13.6690.

40. Plut. *Crass.* 23; Dio 3.40.18.

41. Suet. *Claud.* 13.

42. Webster 1998: 133.

43. Joseph. *Bell. Jud.* 3.134.

44. Joseph. *Bell. Jud.* 3.111.

45. Virg. *Aen.* 6.780–82; later (6.792–805) Virgil discusses how Augustus was destined to march Roman *imperium* beyond India and 'the path of the sun' into realms and areas even Hercules and Bacchus had not traversed.

46. Front. *Strat.* 2.5.34; for an account of the battle, which does not mention the recaptured standards, see Plut. *Crass.* 11.

47. Cic. *Ad Fam.* 10.30.

48. Caes. *Bell. Gall.* 7.88.

49. Suet. *Calig.* 14.

50. *ILS* 986: ...*in qua plura centum mill.* | *ex numero Transdanuvianor.* | *ad praestanda tributa cum coniugib* | *ac liberis et principibus aut regibus suis* | *transduxit; motum orientem Sarmatar.* |... | *ignotos ante aut infensos p.R. reges signa* | *Romana adoraturos in ripam, quam tuebatur, perduxit* | ...

51. Joseph. *Bell. Jud.* 1.646.

52. Exodus 20.2-4.

53. Joseph. *Bell. Jud.* 1.646–58.

54. The Jewish reluctance to pay homage, by way of taxes and tribute, to the Roman emperors – for which they again cited religious principles as the reason – was one of the things that also caused great tension between the Romans and the Jews. A poll tax imposed on the Jews in conjunction with a regional census in AD 6 led to a short-lived revolt against Roman authority in Judea (Acts 5.37) and tensions between the Jews and Romans would run high for decades to come. It is possible that the Jewish Zealot movement began as a protest against this tax (see: Smith, 1971: 1–19). The Jewish sentiment against Roman taxation due to religious principles was epitomized in a passage of the Gospel of Matthew (22.21) which reads, 'Render unto Caesar the things that are Caesar's, and unto God the things that are God's.' For similar Biblical passages and their contexts, see Mark 12.13–17; Luke 20.20–26.

55. Wright, 2004: 187.

56. Caes. *Bell. Civ.* 3.64; for another example of the Roman Army seeing the loss of an eagle as a disgrace, see Joseph. *Bell. Jud.* 6.230.

57. See Watson, 1969: 128–29.

58. Plut. *Crass.* 23–27; Flor. *Epit.* 1.46.8–10; App. *Civ.* 2.18; Ovid *Fasti* 5.579–86, 6.465–68; Pliny *Nat. Hist.* 6.47.

59. *Res. Ges.* 29; see also Brunt & Moore, 1967: 73 for their notes on this passage.

60. *Res. Ges.* 29; see also Brunt & Moore, 1967: 73 for their notes on this passage.

61. Plut. *Ant.* 28; App. *Civ.* 5.10; Dio 48.24.3–48.26.1.

62. Plut. *Ant.* 38; Dio 49.25.4–49.26.2; Flor. *Epit.* 2.20.

63. For ancient accounts of the battle, see: Vell. Pat. 2.119; Suet. *Aug.* 23; for the estimated losses, see: Wells, 2003: 187.

64. Vell. Pat. 2.119.

65. Tac. *Ann.* 1.61.

66. Tac. *Ann.* 1.57, 1.61.

67. Tac. *Ann.* 1.60, 2.25.

68. Tac. *Ann.* 1.61.
69. Dio 56.23.
70. Suet. *Aug.* 23.
71. *Res. Gest.* 29; the campaigns to recapture these standards would have most likely been carried out by commanders appointed by Augustus rather than the emperor leading them personally.
72. *Res Ges.* 29; Suet. *Aug.* 21.
73. For the temple of Mars Ultor, see *Res Gest.* 21.
74. Ov. *Fasti* 5.579–98.
75. Ov. *Fasti* 6.463–68.
76. Tac. *Ann.* 1.60–61; Dio 56.23.
77. Tac. *Ann.* 2.25.
78. Tac. *Ann.* 2.41.
79. Dio 60.8.
80. Tac. *Ann.* 12.27.

Bibliography

Brunt, P.A. & Moore, J.M., 1967, *Res Gestae Divi Augusti*, London.

Connolly, P., 1980, *Greece and Rome at War*, London.

Dessau, H. (ed.), 1892, *Inscriptiones Latinae Selectae*, Berlin.

Erdkamp, P. (ed.), 2007, *A Companion to the Roman Army*, Oxford.

Evans, R.J., 1994, *Gaius Marius: A Political Biography*, Pretoria.

Grossman, D., 1986, *On Killing: The Psychological Cost of Learning to Kill in War and Society*, New York.

Keppie, L., 1984, *The Making of the Roman Army*, London.

Lee, A.D., 1996, 'Morale and the Roman Experience of Battle', in Lloyd, A.B. (ed.), *Battle in Antiquity*, London: 199–218.

MacMullan, R., 1984, 'The Legion as Society' *Historia* 33: 446–51.

Marshall, S.L.A., 1947, *Men Against Fire: The Problem of Battle Command*, New York.

Matthew, C.A., 2010, *On the Wings of Eagles: The Reforms of Gaius Marius and the Creation of Rome's First Professional Soldiers*, Newcastle upon Tyne.

Rawlings, L., 2007, 'Army and Battle During the Conquest of Italy (350–264 BC)', in Erdkamp, P. (ed.), *A Companion to the Roman Army*, Oxford: 45–62.

Rich, J.W., 1983, 'The Supposed Roman Manpower Shortage of the Later Second Century BC', *Historia* 32: 287–331.

154 Religion and Classical Warfare

Sekunda, N.V., Northwood, S. & Simkins, M., 2003, *Caesar's Legions: The Roman Soldier 753 BC to AD 117*, Oxford.

Smith, M., 1971, 'Zealots and Sicarii: Their Origins and Relation', *HThR* 64: 1–19.

Stouffer, S.A., Lumsdaine, A.A., Lumsdaine, M.H., Williams, R.M., Smith, M.B., Janis, I.L., Star, S.A. & Cotttrell, L.S., 1949, *The American Soldier Vol. II: Combat and its Aftermath*, Princeton.

Warry, J., 1980, *Warfare in the Classical World*, Norman.

Watson, G.R., 1969, *The Roman Soldier*, London.

Webster, G., 1998, *The Roman Imperial Army of the First and Second Centuries AD*, Norman.

Wells, P.S., 2003, *The Battle that Stopped Rome*, New York.

Wright, E., 2004, *Generation Kill: Devil Dogs, Iceman, Captain America and the New Face of American War*, New York.

Zangemeister, C. (ed.), 1905, *Corpus, Inscriptionum Latinarum XIII: Inscriptiones trium Galliarum et Germaniarum Latinae – pars II, fasc. I: Inscriptiones Germaniae superioris*, Berlin.

Chapter 6

Women, Warfare and Religion in the Roman Republic

Lora Holland Goldthwaite

W arfare is traditionally assigned to the male sphere in the ancient world. But warfare, as this volume confirms, involves more than just the fighting on a battlefield: it encompasses military life as a whole, from combat to the religious, social, economic and political aspects of war. Religion is also foundational for warfare, since the outcome, whether victory or defeat, is often attributed to divine favour or will. Other chapters in this volume focus on religious aspects of war such as *evocatio*, rites and ceremonies, omens and divination, triumphs and even medical practices. Here we will consider the role of the female in the intersection of religion and warfare during the Roman Republic. This topic has largely been subsumed either in studies of women generally, or in studies of Roman warfare or of Roman religion as a whole.

Before turning to the specific interplay of women, warfare and religion, it is important to note that an evolving understanding of female roles in Roman society through the production of new scholarship directly correlates to the rise of new disciplines such as women and gender studies and to new analyses by (primarily) female scholars who have looked at this topic without the assumption, *apropos* male-dominated/text-dominated scholarship of the nineteenth to mid-twentieth century, that women are by nature excluded from those public spheres of activity.[1] A critical source for some of the new scholarship has been material evidence from archaeological excavations; for instance, examination of remains of leather footwear from the military encampments at Vindolanda and other sites in Britain during the Roman Empire has shown that some belonged to women and children.[2] Their presence at what was traditionally assumed to be an all-male fort significantly changes our perception of the role of women in day-to-day activities, which would include everyday religious activities, of Roman military life during the Empire. Epigraphical and other material sources of evidence have also played key roles in the new scholarship.

In addition to considering a wider array of sources, new approaches inform recent scholarship on gender and warfare in the ancient world, including comparative anthropological studies that seek to understand the ancient experience in modern terms.[3] Most studies of this type, however, focus on ancient Greece.[4] A recent exception is Nathan Rosenstein's examination of the role of women and other family members in Italy during the frequent wars of the Mid-Republic, in which he uses comparative evidence from the ante-bellum American South and other modern cultures where women engaged in manual labour, especially agricultural work, either in place of or alongside men.[5] Other approaches take gender and sexuality as a starting point that sometimes concerns warfare, but these, too, usually focus on Greece and on the female experience as victim of male violence in martial contexts.[6] A recent wide-ranging collection of essays includes three articles dealing with the late Roman Republic.[7] Alison Keith's analysis of the elegiac *puella*'s double role as spoils and a beneficiary of conquest, Judith Hallett's incisive study of Fulvia, and Alison Sharrock's analysis of warrior women in Roman epic, especially Virgil's Camilla, add eye-opening perspectives on these topics. The first two focus both on poetic evidence, which is intrinsically biased to some degree since it was written by an elite male, and on material evidence, which adds a completely new dimension to our understanding of the literature. Even in the case of Camilla, critical analysis of a text written by men about women and warfare can offer interesting new insights even if it sheds little light on the lived experience of women in Republican Rome. Still other recent volumes use women and religion as the starting point, but again, focus on Greece, Imperial Rome and other parts of the Mediterranean.[8]

In the face of all this ground-breaking and important work that mostly excludes the women of the Roman Republic, nevertheless there has been a small but steady progression towards bringing to light significant intersections between women, religion and warfare during the Republic in the scholarship over the past two decades.[9] The emerging picture that is the focus of this chapter suggests that the Romans of the Republic considered the female to be as essential a force for the protection of Rome, both in the state religion and in the domestic sphere, as the males who managed and fought the wars against its enemies. By working in tandem, both sexes did their part, each having a mostly separate, but complementary, role. The evidence for the importance of the female in religion and warfare has been undervalued in the scholarship because the female role is often quite different from that of the male and the lived experience of these ancient women is not available to us in the male-authored texts. But the evidence leads to the inescapable conclusion that the protection of the Roman state and the preservation of the *pax deorum* required males and females working together. With the rise of women's studies, scholarship about the Vestals – from Mary Beard to Meghan DiLuzio – highlights their role as preservers and protectors of the Roman state through the many duties they performed both by themselves and with other priests and priestesses; earlier scholarship had often relegated their duties to women's concerns or had sought to pinpoint their origins as daughters or wives of the kings.[10]

A broader picture of female officiants in cults is now available after many decades of study concentrated almost exclusively on the Vestals. In the expansionist period following a probable calendrical reform of the late fourth century BC (see below), an increase in Roman warfare rendered the need to protect Rome and the *pax deorum* increasingly important. The continuing importance of the male-female spheres working in tandem is apparent in the role of married women in religious aspects of warfare during this time. M.-L. Hänninen argued for a 'network' of Roman matrons working together in the Republican cult of Juno Regina during the Second Punic War, a topic Celia Schultz picked up and expanded on. Both of these scholars also offered new insights into Caecilia Metella, who in 90 BC acted upon a dream sent from Juno Sospita, a goddess with martial aspects.[11] Schultz's discussion is part of a larger argument that Republican matrons, priestesses and other women participated in a wider range of religious activities than had previously been recognized in the scholarship: not only in rites and rituals of 'women's concerns' such as childbirth, the home and fertility, but also in political and financial concerns and expiatory rites – sometimes in concert with virgins or with men – for the maintenance and preservation of the state, particularly during wartime. Schultz's conclusions speak of the female role in wartime as separate but equally as important as the fighting done by the men.

Beard's seminal article on the sexual status of the Vestals, Amy Richlin's epigraphical study of non-elite priestesses during the Roman Empire and new research into sources such as Festus by (mostly) female scholars, such as Fay Glinister, are three examples among many that paved the way for larger studies such as Celia Schultz, Sarolta Takács, Robin Wildfang and Meghan DiLuzio's recent monograph on Republican state priestesses.[12] Of course the Vestals are featured prominently in many of these books; but the contextualisation of the Vestals in a larger picture of female officiants and participants sets some apart. DiLuzio especially paints a coherent picture of the main priesthoods of the pontifical college as married pairs working together to preserve the *pax deorum* (the virginal priestesses are exceptional in this). The agency of the state married priestesses and various support personnel, working alongside their husbands or other male priests, derives from admittedly sparse and difficult evidence; yet its inclusion is crucial for understanding that some important priesthoods operated fully only as cooperative units.

DiLuzio assessed all the available evidence for the married pairs of priests and priestesses that conducted the main business of the pontifical college, namely the *rex* and *regina sacrorum*, the *flamen* and *flaminica Dialis*, and other major flaminates (and perhaps the lesser ones as well), the Vestal Virgins and scores of auxiliary personnel from various social groups who worked together for the proper conduct of rituals, festivals and rites.[13] Sometimes husbands and wives, brothers and sisters, and other familial pairings or groupings outside of the priesthoods were also required to act together for the proper completion of a rite or ritual. This concept is in line with Roman ideas about the familial relationships and cooperative behaviours of the human sphere mirroring that of the divine, for instance, when Cicero points to the familial relationship of Ceres with her children Liber and Libera, from which he says the word for human children, *liberi*, derives.[14] Likewise, he affirms that the marriages and family relationships of the gods mirrors that of humans.[15]

It is worth noting that there is likely to be an Etruscan connection to a religious and cultural system that required male and female to work together during the early centuries of the Roman Republic. In a significant study, Giovanna Bagnasco Gianni has argued that Etruscan society featured this very type of complementary gendered system during the period of the Tarquin rule in Rome, noting that 'Etruscan women had formal authority outside the domestic sphere' that included religious matters.[16] The relationship of the Etruscans and Romans of the regal period and the early centuries of the Republic is complex, but it certainly is not irrelevant and there is fertile ground for future study as our knowledge of Etruscan society continues to deepen and expand.

The complementary arrangement of male and female working together pervades the Roman religion of the Republic. Schultz has gathered the inscriptional evidence for non-elite male/female religious cooperation in a monograph that makes a persuasive argument for a greater role for females than previous scholars had detected.[17] DiLuzio likewise has gathered and assessed a wide range of evidence for priestly couples of non-elite status performing together for the public rites of the *curiae* and possibly *flamines montanorum*, priestly couples associated with rites on the hills of Rome, possibly including the Septimontium Day described by Varro.[18] Although these do not concern warfare specifically, they do reinforce the idea of additional gendered pairs working together to maintain the *pax deorum* in Roman Republican religion.

Other priesthoods seem to have started as a male-female cooperative effort. Mars and the month of March were associated with the *Salii*, a public priesthood of men and women who processed together, performing a dance. There is only a notice in Festus for the feminine form of *Salii*, that is, *Saliae*, who are described as *virgines*; both Cincius and Aelius Stilo agreed, according to the notice in Festus, that they danced in military-style dress along with their male counterparts.[19] Scholars have offered non-military interpretations for the rituals that included these women, but the ancient sources on Salian ritual and its timing during the year suggest that its primary function was martial. The fact that the *Saliae* became obsolete may also derive from the reforms of the calendar cited above: Jörg Rüpke makes the point that these reforms isolated the Roman elite from neighbouring communities who continued to use the old lunar calendar.[20] A much-contested word in Festus that refers to the *Saliae* as *conducticiae* ('hired') may, in fact, simply reflect an old interconnectivity of religious ritual and reciprocity with neighbouring communities, in which their own Salian maidens performed with Roman priests before the calendrical reforms had weakened those connections.[21] Ritual participation between communities was commonplace during this early period, as Roman participation in rites with other Latins, such as the *feriae Latinae* at the Alban Mount, suggests. At any rate, in Rome the Salian priesthood, previously a male-female cooperative effort, had apparently become an all-male institution by the Augustan era.

As excellent as DiLuzio's interpretation of the admittedly difficult evidence for married pairs is, her arguments overall could benefit from positing chronological developments more clearly. In this way her work is complemented by Rüpke's study of the religion of the Republican period. Most useful is his argument that a reform from strictly a lunar to a luni-solar calendar in the late fourth century BC fixed the lengths of the months so that the Kalends and Nones of the month could be determined 'without human interference'.[22] This, he argued, resulted in a reduced need in the pontifical college for the priesthoods that previously had been concerned with announcing the special days. From a religious point of view, then, this is a watershed moment since the reforms of the calendar led to a decrease in the importance of the office of *rex* and *regina sacrorum* and eventually rendered it obsolete.

The requirement of male/female cooperation in martial and religious aspects of Roman culture probably predated the fourth century BC. If Rüpke's analysis of the calendar reforms is correct, the joint priesthood of the *rex* and *regina sacrorum* and other personnel associated with the public declaration of the dates for the Kalends and Nones became less important after the reforms of the luni-solar calendar. Though not directly related to the conduct of war, the calendar and its maintenance is not without its martial aspects, especially in assigning the proper time for propitiations, rites and festivals. Other rites on special days continued to be performed by men and women in concert well into the Imperial era and even later.

One such festival is the Matronalia, as it is commonly referred to in the scholarship. Fanny Dolansky has argued that this festival of the first day of March, known during the Republic as the *femineae kalendae* or *Martiae kalendae*, was centred on the affairs of the home, especially on legitimate childbirth, the husband-wife relationship and the relationships between *matronae* and the household as a whole, although modern scholars have tended to emphasize its public rites. These were performed at the temple of Juno Lucina, the goddess of childbirth, on the Esquiline.[23] Both the domestic and the public aspects of the festival, however, are located in the double aspects of Mars as god of war and agricultural god concerned with fertility, both of which must be properly maintained for the preservation of the state. Ovid, in fact, refers to childbirth as female military service: *tempora rite colunt Latiae fecunda parentes, / quarum militiam votaque partus habet.*[24] Moreover, both the domestic and the public rites required the participation of both men and women. Republican-era inscriptions made by men to Juno Lucina are suggestive of male participation in the rites of the *femineae kalendae*, and Livy records an important role for women in expiating prodigies, especially during wartime, among other types of evidence Schultz adduces for the Republic.[25] The *Martiae kalendae* also marked the day on which the Salian priesthood processed through the streets of Rome carrying the *ancilia*, the sacred shields that were part of the *pignora* ensuring the safety of the Roman state. During the Republic, these rites also were carried out by men and women together, *Salii* and *Saliae*. Two fragments of Lucilian satire that discuss the rites and public processions of the *Salii* are set in the month of March.[26] We can only imagine the crowded streets and temples and the pervasive goodwill, feasting and gift-giving in homes (*domus*) on this day, the day on which the Roman state was fortified by prayers, sacrifices, songs and dances to Mars and Juno Lucina, the perfect union of military might and domestic success that together preserved and strengthened the Roman state. Ovid cites as one possible origin of this festival the story of how the Sabine women stopped the war between their Roman husbands and Sabine kin, restoring both peace and, presumably, domestic tranquillity. Though its origins are shrouded in myth, this festival's timing at the beginning of the month named for the god of war suggests a linkage, perhaps to strengthen the domestic front as the men prepared for the start of the season for war.

Rome's Vestals, however, had the most consistent and long-lived religious role in protecting Rome during wartime and from other dangers to the state. As stated previously, our understanding of the role of the Vestals in Roman society has become much richer and nuanced over the past century of modern study. The Roman understanding of this ancient priesthood was that it predated all other priesthoods, if they believed the myth of Ilia, daughter of Aeneas who bore the twins Romulus and Remus.[27] The chastity requirements were already in place, but under whose authority Ilia was charged is not clear in the surviving fragments of Ennius. Livy states that the Vestals originated at Alba Longa, and in fact pre-Roman Vestals were known both there and at Lavinium.[28] When Numa Pompilius established the male priesthoods in Rome, the Vestals became part of the pontifical college and were subject to the *pontifex maximus*. Their main charge was to guard the eternal flame in the temple of Vesta. Many of the daily tasks of the Vestals were similar to those of ordinary women in the domestic sphere: they ground grain, carried water and tended the hearth. They also performed rites and rituals by themselves and in concert with others across the city and throughout the year. Of the greatest importance was their purity when carrying out these actions, and their selection at the age of 6 was an important aspect of the state's ability to ensure their chastity. Their chaste state was subject to intense scrutiny and speculation, especially during wartime or other periods of crisis.

Varro records the names of the first 'official' Vestals at Rome. The most famous of these was Tarpeia, a legendary figure of early Rome. There are contrasting accounts of her in the literary tradition. Livy tells how the Sabine king Titus Tatius, Rome's enemy at the time, corrupted her with

Figure 6.1: Silver denarius. Reverse: Tarpeia between two soldiers who are about to cast their shields upon her. L. Titurius L.f. Sabinus, moneyer, 89 BC. Obverse: bust of the Sabine king Tatius.

gold so that she betrayed Rome, and the Sabines crushed her to death, since she had demanded 'what they bore on their left arms' – not with their gold rings as per the original agreement, but their shields after Tarpeia changed her demand and asked for their weapons.[29] In Roman art, Tarpeia is depicted buried to her waist in shields with arms upraised – a composition that resembles a *tropaeum* – and surrounded by soldiers (Figures 6.1 and 6.2).[30] Dionysius of Halicarnassus, however, follows the early historian Calpurnius Piso, who claims her as a heroine who saved Rome by acting as a double agent against the Sabines. In fact, Piso claims, though Dionysius seems a bit sceptical, that Tarpeia was honoured with a burial monument where she fell and annual libations on the Capitoline arx. Significantly, with the death of Tarpeia – for whatever reason she was doomed to die – the Roman state stood firm and the Sabines were unable to capture the Roman Forum.

We can compare the lust for gold that Livy cites as a possible reason for Tarpeia to betray Rome to a similar desire for this metal that Virgil attributes to the downfall of Camilla, the warrior maiden, in the *Aeneid*. The poet makes explicit, if obscure, references to Tarpeia in his characterization of this maiden.[31] Camilla's own name suggests that she is a servant of Diana, the goddess to whom her father dedicated (*vovit*) her.[32] She is twice described as a general of an army of Volscians, as well as an Amazon.[33] Alison Sharrock, however, points out that Virgil does minimal 'othering' of Camilla despite

Figure 6.2: Silver denarius. Reverse: Tarpeia standing, wearing a tunic, raising both hands, buried to her waist under ten shields. Mint at Rome, struck under Augustus; P. Petronius Turpilianus, moneyer, 19–18 BC. Obverse: bust of Caesar Augustus.

calling her an Amazon: she is also a soldier, a hero deserving of respect and honour.[34] Among her army are specially chosen female *ministrae*, one of whom is named Tarpeia, a warrior brandishing a bronze axe.[35] We could dismiss the name as coincidence but for the fact that Camilla dies in the fighting because of her lust for gold.[36] When she sees the Trojan priest Chloreus decked out in his golden finery, she hunts him down. Virgil offers two possible reasons for this: either to affix the Trojan arms to temples, much as hunters often attached the horns, antlers and other hunting trophies to temples of Diana, or to display herself in captured gold.[37] This alternative resonates with Livy's story of Tarpeia cited above. A third small detail additionally connects the two: burial in their fatherland. We saw above that Calpurnius Piso claimed that Tarpeia was buried and honoured with annual rites of libation where she fell, that is, on the Capitoline Hill; Diana tells her nymph Opis that Camilla's body will not be despoiled, but she will have a burial mound in her fatherland.[38] Virgil twice makes reference to Tarpeia's *arx* and *sedes* on what will become the 'golden' Capitoline during Aeneas' tour of Evander's city in *Aeneid* 8,[39] thus neatly linking the theme of maidenly lust for gold with both Tarpeia the Vestal and Camilla the warrior.

Throughout the rest of Roman history, Vestals paid for *incestum* by being buried alive – not by shields, but in an underground chamber. Plutarch asserts that Rhea Silvia,[40] the legendary mother of Romulus and Remus, avoided this punishment because her sister interceded for her, and she was simply put in chains and confined. Under the Etruscan king Tarquinius Priscus, the Vestal Pinaria suffered this fate, according to Dionysius of Halicarnassus.[41] The earliest such incident that Livy reports is the punishment of the Vestal Oppia in 483 BC, but he does not state how or where the penalty was carried out.[42] This happened during a time of great instability and wars with neighbouring peoples. The *vates* who charged her cited the appearance of various portents and signs that they interpreted as a warning from the gods that she was ritually impure. Livy does not record precisely how she was punished, but Dionysius of Halicarnassus,[43] who gives her name as Opimia, specifies that she was led through the Roman Forum and buried alive inside the city walls.

The site of the burial in the fifth century BC was probably the same, or near the same, underground chamber where prisoners of war would later be buried alive during the third century BC in the area of the Forum Boarium. This market was located along the line of the original *pomerium* of Rome; this means that the burial site was bounded by the original wall of the city, which in Roman legend was built over the foundation sacrifice of Remus at the inauguration of the city. Subsequent offerings there would strengthen it for the protection of Rome. Elsewhere in this volume (chapter 7), Paul Erdkamp argues persuasively for a linkage between the burial alive of Vestals and subsequent human sacrifice of Greek and Gallic couples, prisoners of war, as acts of propitiation to atone for the dead priestesses.[44] The burial area in the Forum Boarium continued in use for Gallic and Greek victims who were buried alive, but not for Vestals.

After the fourth century BC, condemned Vestals were buried alive inside the Colline Gate, which was part of the new *pomerium* of Rome, the so-called Servian Wall. The Colline Gate was the northernmost and farthest away from the heart of the Roman city; it was also perhaps one of the most vulnerable to attack.[45] Whatever the reason for its choice, this was where condemned Vestals were led, stripped of their priestly accoutrements and wearing funeral garb. Mourning friends and family joined the long procession from the area of the Roman Forum to this gate, where an underground chamber had been prepared, containing food and a lamp. The underground chamber was located inside the protective wall, 'on the right side of the Via Strata in the Campus Sceleratus'.[46] The death of a Vestal was, like blood itself, both a purifier and a polluter. Each death made the Roman state safer and stronger; each death required an enormous *piaculum*. From a religious point of view, a Vestal's chastity when performing rituals and rites was needed to keep the *pax deorum* because of the demands of the Roman gods for pure and unblemished offerings. In terms of the political, social and military concerns of the Roman state, attention had to be paid to the possibility that an unchaste Vestal had violated this peace when the state was threatened. Since she was unable to regain her purity, her death provided the only way to restore the *pax deorum*. As DiLuzio succinctly puts it, 'Vestals served as a convenient mechanism for restoring stability in times of panic and crisis.'[47]

Augustus, in his autobiography, prided himself on restoring the religious institutions of the Republic; but the priesthoods he himself took were not part of the married pairs of old. It can be understood why he would not want the title of *rex sacrorum*, and the flaminate of Jupiter was in disuse at this time (though we may imagine that Augustus, like Julius Caesar before him, would have resisted taking on the restrictions of that office). Instead, he took the offices of *pontifex maximus, augur, quindecimvir, epulo, frater arvalis, sodalis Titius* and *fetialis*. Likewise, Livia is not portrayed as performing rituals in tandem with her husband; in fact, she is not mentioned in the *Res Gestae* at all. Instead, the Vestals, the only female religious personnel cited therein, are twice ordered to sacrifice annually for the safe return of Augustus to Rome from various expeditions abroad, and are presumably included in the prayers for Augustus' health conducted by the four major colleges.[48]

In addition, the Vestals, in their role as members of the pontifical college, had probably been performing the duties of the *flaminicae*. Tacitus states that pontiffs often had performed the sacred duties of the *flamen Dialis* during the vacancy of that office in the first century BC, and that the *religio* had not suffered as a result.[49] With the advent of the *pax Augusta*, the role of the Vestals seems to have turned to a more specialized role that emphasized the protection of the emperor.

The flaminate was also apparently altered to accommodate the new imperial family. In 40 BC, the same year he married Augustus' sister Octavia, Mark Antony was appointed *flamen* for the cult of Divus Iulius – and presumably Octavia became the *flaminica*. After Augustus' death, Livia served as *flaminica* of the deified Augustus, just as Agrippina would later serve in the same role for the deified Claudius.[50] Germanicus, who had married Augustus' granddaughter Agrippina the Elder, became a *flamen Augustalis*, with Agrippina presumably a *flaminica Augustalis*. But the case of Livia, and later Agrippina the Younger, is a clear example of the changes to the old married pairs that were in place by the Augustan era: these widows were not married to a *flamen divi Augusti*, but each as a widow was a *flaminica* alone. The family ties were important. Tacitus reports that when Germanicus died, it was decreed that only a Julian family member could assume the priesthood he vacated.[51] In summary, the priesthoods of the Republic were irrevocably altered by the advent of Augustus; once the province of the priestly colleges working in tandem, the welfare of the state, including its safety and victory in war, had now become centred on – and dependent on – the imperial family.

Non-elite women also had a role in the intersection of religion and warfare. Slave-women seem to have participated to some degree in the public rites of the Matralia in honour of Mater Matuta. Whereas Ovid indicates that female slaves were excluded, Plutarch specifies that there was, in fact, one slave woman in attendance who was ritually beaten.[52] Votive dedications at her temples indicate that she too, like Juno, was worshipped by men and women alike, and that weapons were dedicated to her.[53]

A festival was celebrated on 7 July, the so-called *Nonae Caprotinae*, on which *liberae pariter ancillaeque sacrificant* (women, both free and slave, sacrifice).[54] This day was sacred to Juno Caprotina, a Roman military and fertility goddess whose epithet may refer to the goat, whose skin and horns the Latin goddess Juno Sospita also wore; or perhaps to the wild fig, *caprificus*, a tree that plays a role in a myth surrounding this festival; or the *Palus Capreae*, the marsh where Romulus was taken up from Earth to the heavens. Plutarch gives two possible origins for the festival: the state crisis provoked by the death of Romulus, and the Gallic siege of Rome in the fourth century BC.[55] Carin Green has argued for the archaic origin for the festival, with the fourth-century BC modification reflecting a change in social values.

More to the point, however, is the central role of women in times of state crisis. When the enemy demanded women, a servant-woman (*ancilla*) named Tutela offered to dress in elite garb with a retinue of other women similarly dressed, and by this trickery they gained access to the enemy camp, made the men drunk, then signalled to the waiting Romans, who invaded the camp at night and saved the women and Rome. The protective function of the female is alluded to in the name of the slave-woman Tutela, whose status as a serving-woman, as Green argues, is probably best understood as 'a female servant or minister of a god'.[56] I agree with Green that Tutela and her retinue were more likely public slaves serving as temple officiants than women owned privately.[57] Their religious status gave them both credence and influence in a matter so crucial for the state, a perfect fusion of women, warfare and religion. Macrobius records that they were manumitted, rewarded with a dowry from public funds and the right to wear 'the customary dress of that time'.[58] Significantly, in this story of the *feriae ancillarum*, men and women fight together to save Rome. In fact, they feast together and engage in mutual jesting either at the same time or after the women have dressed in armour, taken up weapons and engaged in a mock battle with each other.[59] This festival, like the Matronalia, required male and female cooperation and was sacred to the goddess Juno and, by extension, given the nature of the activities associated with it, to Mars the god of war. It also required deception on the part of the women.

Legendary history and Roman mythology provide additional exempla of the female role in warfare that sometimes intersects with religion, such as the stories about two young women, Cloelia and Horatia. Matthew Roller has recently examined the Cloelia episode in terms of exemplarity in Roman culture, which in his scheme has four major components: an action, an audience, a monument and imitation. He juxtaposes the stories of Horatius Cocles and Cloelia, showing how each served as an exemplum in Roman culture. Livy's account of the Cloelia episode emphasizes her status as a female warrior and *virgo*, indeed a *dux agminis virginum*, and her desire for public honour.[60] The gist of the story is that when she (and/or perhaps another girl named Valeria) was given to the Etruscan king Porsenna as a hostage, she took advantage of an opportunity to lead a group of her fellow female hostages to freedom and safety by jumping into the Tiber and swimming across to Rome even as enemy javelins fell around them. For her actions, she was awarded an equestrian statue on the *via Sacra*, an honour normally reserved for men, and was revered through the ages for her 'manly' courage.

It is worth noting that ancient writers extolled Fulvia as being more male than female, much as Velleius Paterculus characterized her as female only in body, *nihil muliebre praeter corpus gerens* ('not at all a woman except for her body').[61] But as Roller also notes, the archaic setting for the story and the dating of Roman equestrian bronze statuary do not coincide; he speculates that the original statue may have been that of a goddess, 'say Venus Equestris or Venus Cloacina or Vica Pota', and that only later was an actual bronze equestrian statue of the maiden realized.[62] It seems unlikely, however, that the maiden Cloelia was connected with the worship of Venus, and we know too little about Vica Pota to make a clear connection. There was a cult of Fortuna Equestris in the second century BC,[63] but again there is no clear evidence for a connection to an earlier period. Although there are no overtly religious aspects to Cloelia's story in the sources, the location of her statue on the *via Sacra* may suggest that its origins do coincide with religion, perhaps as *Virtus* or *Fides* personified.

The story of Horatia, on the other hand, provides an aetiology for the cult of Juno Sororia. During the Roman war with Alba in the seventh century BC, two sets of triplet brothers, the Horatii and the Curiatii, the former Romans and the latter Sabines in most accounts, were chosen to face each other in mortal combat in order to determine the final outcome of the war. Two of the Horatii were killed, but the final Roman brother killed all three Curiatii and took from each the spoils of battle. From Livy is known what happened when Horatius returned victorious to Rome:

'Horatius leading the way came bearing before him the triple spoils. His sister, the virgin, who had been betrothed to one of the Curiatii, met him in front of the Capena Gate. When she recognised upon her brother's shoulders the embroidered military cloak of her fiancé, which she herself had woven, she dishevelled her hair and weeping called out her dead fiancé's name. His sister's cry of mourning in the midst of his own victory and such public jubilation roused the martial spirit of the youth. And so, he drew his sword and ran it through the girl at the same time berating her with words: "Go away from here to your fiancé with your badly-timed love," he said, "you who are forgetful of your dead brothers and your living one, and forgetful of your fatherland. So may things go for any Roman woman who will mourn an enemy."'[64]

Horatius' murder of his sister could not go unpunished, but his father begged for his son's life on the grounds that the sister was justly killed and he would be childless now, since his other sons had given their lives in service to Rome. The people acquitted Horatius but required the father to conduct expiatory rites:

'After certain rites of atonement were done, which in turn were handed down in the Horatian clan, he sent the young man, with his head covered, under a wooden beam that had been set across a road, as if under a military yoke. It remains there today and is always repaired at public expense: they call it the sisterly beam. A tomb for Horatia was constructed of squared stone on the spot where she was struck and fell.'[65]

From the longer version of the story as told by Dionysius of Halicarnassus and from the anonymous scholiast's note to Cicero,[66] the religious significance of the sisterly beam (*sororium tigillum*) is clear from the cult attached to it: two altars were erected on either side of the street over which the beam stretched, one to Janus Curiatius and the other to Juno Sororia. Unfortunately, the worship of these two deities is known only from this story. While the details are not known, the cults seem to have been conducted by the Horatian clan, despite the use of state funds. Like Tarpeia, Horatia was buried where she fell, yet another example of a maiden who, although the male-authored literature cannot resist maintaining the suspicion of treachery in her actions, was honoured with burial and associated rites.

Stories of women taking an active role in combat warfare are widespread in the ancient world: when their homes and towns are threatened, women are often moved to defend them. A story from Greek history features Telesilla of Argos, poet and warrior. When the Spartans attacked her town, she staged a successful defence since the Argive warriors themselves were fighting elsewhere at the time. Male scholars typically have dismissed the evidence.[67] Jane MacIntosh Snyder has led the way in reversing the trend to scepticism, at least in terms of the story as a reflection of some historical reality.[68] Conversely, most of the evidence from Latin authors does not concern individual women, but a group of women, usually in a besieged town. Livy reports how women of the Roman Republic and other non-combatants such as slaves engaged with their enemies by hurling broken roof tiles and other missiles from the roofs of buildings and city walls, for instance, at the fall of Veii. On the Roman side after that battle, Livy reports that even before the Senate could decree it, the Roman mothers filled all the temples and gave thanks to the gods.[69] Other authors record many details of barbarian women fighting just as fiercely as their men, for instance, Plutarch's account of the battle at Aquae Sextiae in 102 BC during the Cimbrian War.[70] Women could also help in other ways. When the Gauls attacked Rome in 390 BC, the Roman women aided the war effort by giving gold – and their hair, for bowstrings and catapult cords.[71] Appian relates how Carthaginian women donated their hair for use as cords for artillery weapons when the Romans were besieging their city.[72] Fictional accounts also depict women as combatants: for instance, in the postscript to Camilla's story in the *Aeneid* the Rutulian women, after they see the example that Camilla has set by her death, begin to fight from the walls. Virgil characterizes them as heroic: *primaeque mori pro moenibus ardent*, 'and they are eager to be the first to die for their city'.[73] This suggests that a writer of the Late Republic could conceive of such actions as more than desperation: women could be warriors vying for glory in battle.

Now that scholars have begun to treat in detail the relationship of women and wartime – both fictional and historical women – during the Late Republic, we begin to have an important new perspective to topics that have long been a focus of study in other respects. An important contribution in the volume mentioned above is Alison Keith's study of women in Latin elegiac poetry. By assessing epigraphical evidence along-side the literature, Keith has given us a new way to look at the elegiac *puella*, arguing that she 'illustrates the Roman elegy's intimate correlation with Roman imperialism in its celebration of the sexual spoils of military conquest'.[74] Keith confines this study to Tibullus, Propertius and Ovid, noting especially Propertius' debt to Gallus. Especially interesting is the correspondence she notes between inscriptional evidence for slave and libertine women's names of the Late Republic and Empire and the names of the elegiac mistresses, including Nemesis, Corinna and even Cynthia.

Religious aspects of the elegiac *puella* are beyond the scope of Keith's analysis, but there is fruitful fodder to be found there. Keith does not include Catullus in her study, though we can see some parallels in his poetry, for instance, *Carmen* 10, in which his friend Varus introduces him to an unnamed girlfriend, a *scortillum* (a bitch), who catches the poet off guard, much to his chagrin.[75] In boasting about money he made during his military service in Bithynia and the fancy litter he acquired, the girl asks Catullus to take her in the litter to the temple of Serapis, thereby emphasizing her foreignness and venality, as well as her religiosity.

Propertius offers examples even more germane to the elegiac *puella*. His Cynthia appears to be very interested in religion – or, as the poet jeal-ously imagines, at least pretends to be religious in order to have an excuse to meet other lovers. He sees Cynthia's ghost in a dream, and he remarks on its appearance that it was wearing on its finger the usual beryl ring: *solitum digito beryllon*.[76] Though the bejewelled ring could simply be a sign of the wealth she has acquired through gifts and a general fondness for jewellery, the beryl was so commonly used in divination that the practice has its own name: beryllomancy. In Book 2, his mistress had asked Propertius for a crystal, a stone not only admired for its value, but for its use in crystallomancy, and for ivory dice, items also used in divination. That these objects were not simply a woman's playthings, but had a 'divine' purpose, so to speak, gains further support from other references to religious activities. This same woman elsewhere seeks knowledge about her dreams from Vesta and consults the Praenestine *sortes*. The latter is in a context of consulting various divinities outside of Rome, including a night-time rite lit with torches at Diana's famous grove at Lake Nemi.[77] Unlike the *scortillum* in Catullus 10 who wished to be carried to the temple of Serapis, Cynthia, whose name is also an epithet of Diana, seems quite Romanized in her religious activities. It is also worth pointing out that Diana's cult was very attractive to freed people, which Keith's study showed to be a common status for women holding 'elegiac' names.[78]

Judith Hallett's analysis of the elite Roman Fulvia represents another significant advance in the scholarship. Fulvia is probably best known as the wife of Cicero's foe Clodius, and later of Mark Antony, whom she aided in matters both political and military. It seems likely that Antony used her features on coinage he struck at Lugdunum in Gallia Cisalpina (Figure 6.3). By combining literary evidence with the material evidence on sling bullets, inscriptions and coins, Hallett has revealed a woman subject to a social narrative that seems sadly modern: an elite woman who asserts influence and power is both exalted and insulted, is both praised and reviled, especially regarding her unattractiveness as a potential sexual partner. Paradoxically, Fulvia, like the legendary Cloelia, as mentioned earlier, is often characterized as more male than female, in part because of her martial courage and excellence, and in part as a way to deny her femininity.

Figure 6.3: Silver quinarius, of Mark Antony, depicting a bust of winged Victory with the features of his wife Fulvia, 43–42 BC, Gallia Cisalpina mint. Cetamura del Chianti, Inv. C-2015-678. Photo courtesy of N.T. de Grummond.

Conclusion

The nexus of women, religion and warfare in the Republic involved all ages and social classes, with participation ranging from actual combat to rites for the safety of Rome. As is still true for women even in the modern world, the primary narrative of the female role devalues it and insists that it be primarily domestic and subordinate to the public role of the male. It is the task of modern scholars to find the overlooked and the undervalued, to consider both literary and material evidence, to discover why and where the evidence is different from or even contradictory to the normative male-authored narratives of antiquity. The realization that ancient women of talent and ability faced many of the same misogynistic hurdles as their modern counterparts in realizing their goals and ambitions, that ancient women of necessity engaged in fighting and other activities that belie the eternal narrative of the 'weak female', that among ancient women are 'hidden figures' who made important contributions to their societies – these will all, it is to be hoped, continue to inform twenty-first-century approaches to the scholarship on female participation in Roman religion and warfare.

Notes

1. An early exception is the Marxist historian Mary R. Beard, who in 1946 wrote a short history of women that included a survey of ancient women in warfare. My contribution is dedicated to the memory of four dear friends, colleagues and mentors: Edwin Brown, Carin M.C. Green (especially for her work on the nexus of women, religion and warfare), Eleanor Leach and Georgia Machemer. I am grateful to Amy Richlin for her generous encouragement of my endeavours and to the editors for their patience. Latin translations are mine unless otherwise stated.
2. See Douglas, 2015, for bibliography and current state of the research on leather artifacts from Roman Britain.
3. E.g. Foxhall, 2013. For an overview of new approaches to women in Roman religion, see Holland, 2012: 204–06.
4. See Fabre-Serris Keith, 2015, for bibliography and current state of the research on the intersections of women and war in antiquity. The articles on the Late Republic in that volume will be dealt with in more detail later in this paper.

5. Rosenstein, 2005.
6. For recent work, see Masterson, Rabinowitz & Robson, 2015.
7. In Fabre-Serris & Keith, 2015.
8. See, for instance, the 2017 volume edited by Dillon, Eidenow & Maurizio, 2017.
9. For brief remarks on earlier important work, such as Brouwer's 1989 study of the Bona Dea cult, see Holland, 2012: 207.
10. Beard, 1980, and DiLuzio, 2016, with bibliography of recent work on the topic.
11. Hänninen, 1999a: 29–38, and 1999b: 39–52; Schultz, 2006. Badian, 2015, identifies her as a 'noble virgin' and rejects the widely held view that she was the mother of the infamous Publius Clodius, enemy of Cicero, and his sister, Clodia.
12. Beard, 1980; Richlin, 1997, reprinted, linked and annotated in Richlin, 2014: 197–240; Glinister, 2011; Schultz, 2006; Wildfang, 2006; Takács, 2018; DiLuzio, 2016.
13. DiLuzio, 2016, *passim*.
14. Cic. *de nat. deorum* 2.24: *Liber etiam (hunc dico Liberum Semela natum, non eum quem nostri maiores auguste sancteque Liberum cum Cerere et Libera consecraverunt, quod quale sit ex mysteriis intellegi potest; sed quod ex nobis natos liberos appellamus, idcirco Cerere nati nominati sunt Liber et Libera, quod in Libera servant, in Libero non item).*
15. Cic. *de nat. deorum* 2.28: *et formae enim nobis deorum et aetates et vestitus ornatusque noti sunt, genera praeterea coniugia cognationes, omniaque traducta ad similitudinem inbecillitatis humanae.* See also Holland, 2012, for familial relationships among the gods of Roman myth and religion that did not derive from Greek counterparts.
16. Bagnasco Gianni, Cataldi & Facchetti, 2017: 279.
17. Schultz, 2006: 72–73.
18. DiLuzio, 2016: 68–78; see also Holland, 1953.
19. Festus 439L. See also Glinister, 2011, and Chapter 3 of DiLuzio, 2016. Habinek, 2005: 20, also notes the existence of the Saliae 'at some point' but denies them a role in warfare, following a theory that they were part of an initiation ceremony.
20. Rüpke, 2012: 101.
21. For *Salii* in other communities, see the testimonia of Serv. *ad Aen.* 8.285 and Macr. *Sat.* 3.12, 1–9, and John Serrati in this volume.
22. Rüpke, 2012: 101.
23. Dolansky, 2011.

24. Ovid *Fasti* 3.243–44.
25. Schultz, 2006: 33–37, 55–57.
26. Lucilius 9.347–48 (*ROL*).
27. Enn. *Ann.* 32–48; cf. Ovid *Am.* 3.6.73–78. For discussion of Ovid's treatment of this myth, see Armstrong, 2005: 106–09.
28. Livy 1.20; Wissowa, 1912: 520–21. See also the discussion by Beard, North & Price, 1998, 1: 51–58.
29. Livy 1.11.6–9. Another early theme of female betrayal and Vesta cult is alluded to in reference to Caca, sister of the Etruscan seer Cacus, who betrayed her brother to Hercules and was afterwards worshipped by the Vestals (Serv. *ad Aen.* 8.190). Lactantius refers to her as an early hearth goddess (*Inst.* 1.20.36). In Etruscan art, she may be portrayed in a series of urn sculptures in an attitude of sadness or possibly guilt standing near her brother who is surrounded by soldiers. For the images, see de Grummond, 2006: 29, 176.
30. Dion. Halic. *Rom. Ant.* 2.40.
31. Sharrock, 2015: 164 calls the use of the name Tarpeia 'problematic'.
32. Virg. *Aen.* 11.557–60.
33. Virg. *Aen.* 7.803–05, 11.432–33, 11.648–49.
34. Sharrock, 2015: 162–67.
35. Virg. *Aen.* 11.655–58.
36. The names of Tarpeia the Roman and Tarpeia the Italian are only one among many such naming doublets in the *Aeneid*, a phenomenon that scholars have long noted.
37. Virg. *Aen.* 11.778–79: *sive ut templis praefigeret arma / Troia, captivo sive ut se ferret in auro.*
38. Virg. *Aen.* 593–94. A further small point is that in the *Aeneid*, burial mounds are often accompanied by liquid libation, e.g. that of Anchises at *Aen.* 5.90–93 and that of Polydorus, who was betrayed for gold, at *Aen.* 3.62–67.
39. Virg. *Aen.* 8.347 and 652.
40. Plut. *Rom.* 3.2.
41. Dion. Halic. *Rom. Ant.* 3.67.3.
42. Livy 2.42.
43. Dion. Halic. *Rom. Ant.* 8.89.4–5.
44. See Paul Erdkamp in this volume, who argues against an Etruscan origin for the practice; however, it could have been prompted by cross-cultural fertilization since excavations at Tarquinia in recent decades and subsequent analysis of human remains buried in sacred areas have

revealed secure evidence of human sacrifice, including foundation sacrifice under a wall and one adult male buried with a sherd of Euboean pottery on his chest. For the evidence and conclusions of the scientific analysis, see de Grummond, 2016. Ottini *et al.*, 2003, discuss skeletal evidence of human sacrifice from eighth-century BC Rome at the site of the later Carcer/Tullianum.

45. Two of the most serious threats to Rome's sovereignty during the Republic occurred in the vicinity of this gate. Hannibal camped near it during his attempt to conquer Rome and the Samnites attacked this gate in 82 BC during the Sullan period of unrest; but the gate withstood even these threats.

46. Livy 8.15.8.

47. DiLuzio, 2016: 151.

48. Aug. *Res Gest.* 7, 9, 11–12.

49. Tac. *Ann.* 3.58.

50. Tac. *Ann.* 13.2.6.

51. Tac. *Ann.* 2.83.

52. Ovid *Fasti* 6.481–82 (*famulae*), 551 (*ancillae*); Plut. *Rom. Quest.* 16.

53. Smith, 2000: 138–39.

54. Macrob. *Sat.* 1.11.36.

55. Plut. *Rom.* 29, *Cam.* 33.

56. Green, 2010: 288. Bremer, 1987: 76–88, accounts for the oddity that women of slave status would be credited with saving Rome by arguing that the rite was a type of 'reversal' festival like the Saturnalia.

57. Public slaves during the Republic were often temple attendants. We can also adduce the practice from an inscription of unknown provenance, but attributed to Capua, in which a freedwoman of the goddess Diana made a dedication on behalf of herself and her husband: *M Orfio M f Fal | Rufa Dianes | l sibi et coiiuci suuo fecit* (*CIL* i². 1597 = *CIL* x.4263, dating to the late second to early first century BC). A former temple slave, she married a man with filiation and tribe, to whom she referred as a legally married spouse, *coniunx*.

58. Macr. *Sat.* 1.11.40: *memor beneficii senatus omnes ancillas manu iussit emitti dotemque his ex publico fecit et ornatum quo tunc erant usae gestare concessit.*

59. Varro *LL* 6.3. Panaite, 2013: 135–36, records temples in Germany dedicated during the Roman Empire to a goddess Tutela, associated with the protection of roads and crossroads.

60. Livy 2.13.4–11.

61. Vell. Pat. *Hist. Rom.* 2.74. See the discussion of Fulvia below.
62. Roller, 2004: 95.
63. Livy 40.40.
64. Livy 1.26. 2–3.
65. Livy 1.26. 13–14.
66. Dion. Hal. *Rom. Ant.* 3.21–22; schol. Cic. *Pro Mil.* 7.
67. For example, Graf, 1984: 254, who analyzes three accounts of women fighting and dismisses them as mere *aitia*, including the Telesilla episode: 'the paradoxical narrative content refers to a paradoxical strangeness in a ritual, a statue, not a reflection of historical reality.'
68. Snyder, 1989: 60–62. Goff, 2004: 241, has suggested that it was the ritual nature of Telesilla's 'skills as *choregos*, or chorus-leader, that seemed appropriate for transfer to the military sphere'.
69. Livy 5.21, 5.23.
70. E.g. Livy 5.21; Plut. *Vit. Mar.* 19.
71. *SHA Maximilian* 33.2; Serv. *ad Aen.* 1.720; Lact. *Inst.* 1.20.27.
72. App. *Lib.* 93.
73. Virg. *Aen.* 11.891–95.
74. Keith, 2015: 140.
75. The pejorative term *scortillum*, 'little piece of skin' (Cat. *Carmen* 10.3), marks the woman's social status.
76. Prop. *El.* 4.7.9.
77. Prop. *El.* 2.29b.27–28, 2.32.3, 2.32.9–10.
78. For discussion of freedwomen and the cult of Diana, see Holland, 2008.

Bibliography

Armstrong, R., 2005, *Ovid and His Love Poetry*, London and New York.

Badian, E., 'Caecilia Metella (2)', *Oxford Classical Dictionary* (third edition). DOI:10.1093/acrefore/9780199381135.013.1212

Bagnasco Gianni, G., M. Cataldi, and G. M. Faccetti, "Inscribed Objects Associated with Textile Production: News From Tarquinia", in Gleba, M. & Laurito, R. (eds), *Contextualising Textile Production in Italy in the 1st Millennium BC, Origini* XL, Rome: 277–92.

Beard, M., 1946, *Woman as a Force in History. A Study in Traditions and Realities*, New York.

Beard, M., 1980, 'The Sexual Status of Vestal Virgins', *JRS* 70: 12–27.

Beard, M., North, J. & Price, S., 1998, *Religions of Rome. Vol. 1: A History*, Cambridge.

Bremmer, J., 1987, 'Myth and Ritual in Ancient Rome: The Nonae Capra-tinae', in Bremmer, J. & Horsfall, N. (eds), *Roman Myth and Mythography*, London: 76–88.

de Grummond, N., 2006, *Etruscan Myth, Sacred History, and Legend*, Philadelphia.

de Grummond, N., 2016, 'Etruscan Human Sacrifice: The Case of Tarquinia', in Murray, C. (ed.), *Diversity of Sacrifice: Form and Function of Sacrificial Practices in the Ancient World and Beyond*, Albany, *IEMA Proceedings* 5:145–68.

Dillon, M., Eidenow, E. & Maurizio, L. (eds), 2017, *Women's Ritual Competence in the Greco-Roman Mediterranean*, Oxford.

DiLuzio, M., 2016, *A Place at the Altar: Priestesses in Republican Rome*, Princeton.

Dolansky, F., 2011, 'Reconsidering the Matronalia and Women's Rites', *CW* 104.2: 191–209.

Douglas, C., 2015, *A Comparative Study of Roman-Period Leather from Northern Britain*, Glascow, MPhil. thesis.

Fabre-Serris, J. & Keith, A. (eds), *Women and War in Antiquity*, Baltimore.

Foxhall, L., 2013, *Studying Gender in Classical Antiquity*, Cambridge.

Glinister, F., 2011, 'Bring on the Dancing Girls', in Richardson, L. & Santangelo, F. (eds), *Priests and State in the Roman World*, Stuttgart: 107–36.

Goff, B., 2004, *Citizen Bacchae: Women's Ritual Practice in Ancient Greece*, Berkeley.

Graf, F., 1984, 'Women, War, and Warlike Divinities', *ZPE* 55: 245–54.

Green, C., 2009, 'The Gods in the Circus', in Bell, S. & Nagy, H. (eds), *New Perspectives on Etruria and Early Rome: In Honor of Richard Daniel De Puma*, Madison: 65–78.

Green, C., 2010, 'Holding the Line: Women, Ritual, and the Protection of Rome', in Ahearne-Kroll, S., Holloway, P. & Klhoffer, J. (eds), *Women and Gender in Ancient Religions: Interdisciplinary Approaches*, Tübingen: 279–95.

Habinek, T., 2005, *The World of Roman Song: From Ritualized Speech to Social Order*, Baltimore and London.

Hallett, J., 2015, 'Fulvia: The Representation of an Elite Roman Woman Warrior', in Fabre-Serris, J. & Keith, A. (eds), *Women and War in Antiquity*, Baltimore: 247–65.

Hänninen, M.-L., 1999a, 'The Dream of Caecilia Metella', in Setälä, P. Savunen, L. (eds), *Female Networks and the Public Sphere in Roman Society*, Rome: 29–38.

Hänninen, M.-L., 1999b, 'Juno Regina and the Roman Matrons', in Setälä, P. & Savunen, L. (eds), *Female Networks and the Public Sphere in Roman Society*, Rome: 39–52.

Holland, L., 2008, '*Diana Feminarum Tutela?* The Case of *Noutrix Paperia*', in *Collection Latomus, Studies in Latin Literature and Roman History* 14: 95–115.

Holland, L., 2011, 'Family Nomenclature and Same-Name Divinities in Roman Religion and Mythology', *CW* 104.2: 211–26.

Holland, L., 2012, 'Women and Roman Religion', in James, S. & Dillon, S. (eds), *A Companion to Women in the Ancient Mediterranean*, Malden MA and Oxford: 104–14.

Holland, L.A., 1953, '*Septimontium* or *Saeptimontium?*', *TAPhA* 84: 16–34.

Keith, A., 2015, 'Elegaic Women and Roman Warfare', in Fabre-Serris, J. & Keith A. (eds), *Women and War in Antiquity*, Baltimore: 138–56.

Masterson, M., Rabinowitz, N. & Robson, J. (eds), 2015, *Sex in Antiquity: Exploring Gender and Sexuality in the Ancient World. Rewriting Antiquity*, London and New York.

Ottini, L. *et al.*, 2003, 'Possible Human Sacrifice at the Origins of Rome: Novel Skeletal Evidences', *Medicina Nei Secoli, Arte e Scienza* 15.3: 459–68.

Panaite, A., 2013, 'Protective Deities of Roman Roads', in Alexandrescu, C.-G. (ed.), *Jupiter on Your Side: Gods and Humans in Antiquity in the Lower Danube Area*, Bucharest: 133–42.

Richlin, A., 1997, 'Carrying Water in a Sieve: Class and the Body in Roman Women's Religion', in King, K. (ed.), *Women and Goddess Traditions in Antiquity and Today*, Minneapolis: 330–74.

Richlin, A., 2014, *Arguments with Silence: Writing the History of Roman Women*, Ann Arbor.

Roller, M., 2004, 'Exemplarity in Roman Culture: The Cases of Horatius Cocles and Cloelia', *CPh* 99.1: 1–56.

Rosenstein, N., 2005, *Rome at War: Farms, Families, and Death in the Middle Republic*, Chapel Hill and London.

Rüpke, J., 2012, *Religion in Republican Rome: Rationalization and Ritual Change*, Philadelphia.

Schultz, C., 2006, *Women's Religious Activity in the Roman Republic*, Chapel Hill.

Sharrock, A., 2015, 'Warrior Women in Roman Epic', in Fabre-Serris, J. & Keith, A. (eds), *Women and War in Antiquity*, Baltimore: 157–78.

Smith, C.J., 2000, 'Worshipping Mater Matuta: Ritual and Context', in Smith, C.J. & Bispham, E. (eds), *Religion in Archaic and Republican Rome: Evidence and Experience*, Edinburgh: 136–55.

Snyder, J., 1989, *The Woman and the Lyre: Women Writers in Classical Greece and Rome*, Carbondale.

Takács, S., 2008, *Vestal Virgins, Sibyls, and Matrons: Women in Roman Religion*, Austin.

Warmington, E., 1938, *Remains of Old Latin III: Lucilius. The XII Tables*, London and Cambridge MA.

Welch, T., 2015, *Tarpeia: Workings of a Roman Myth*, Ohio State University Press.

Wildfang, R., 2006, *Rome's Vestal Virgins. A Study of Rome's Vestal Priestesses in the Late Republic and Early Empire*, London and New York.

Wissowa, G., 1912, *Religion und Cultus der Römer*, 2nd edn, Munich.

Chapter 7

War, Vestal Virgins and Live Burials in the Roman Republic

Paul Erdkamp

'In essence, the Romans were at the time still barbarians.'
C. Cichorius, 1922[1]

On three occasions during the Republic – in 228, 216 and 113 BC – a Greek man and woman and a Gallic man and woman were buried alive in an underground chamber on the Forum Boarium. As far as is known, these were the only cases of ritual killings (as defined by the repetition of ceremony and the direct killing of the individuals involved rather than fighting leading to death) of foreign peoples performed in this way in Rome. Few ancient authors inform about them, and an attitude of bafflement or rejection is to be found in most writers that do. Modern handbooks on Roman religion generally pass cursorily over these events. For example, the recent companion to Roman religion edited by Jörg Rüpke dedicates only a few lines of its many pages to these remarkable events.[2] The reason might be that these rituals, usually seen as human sacrifices,[3] appear alien to Roman religion. Despite all the killings of individuals in a ritualistic manner in ancient Rome, human sacrifice does not seem to fit with what is known of Roman religion. Hence, puzzled by the terrible events that the Roman Senate had ordered, the German scholar Conrad Cichorius pointed to the general religious nervousness, depression and fear, even mass psychosis, that struck Roman society in these years and made the rulers of Rome powerless against the base and terrible demands by the Roman masses. Thereby he at least absolved Rome's ruling classes from the guilt of such barbaric action.[4]

What considerations drove the Roman Senate to decide on the burial alive of Greek and Gallic individuals will probably never fully be understood, as the sources are short, sparse and fragmentary, largely consisting of brief fragments from lost sources. But the fact that all writers of the extant texts lived long after the events they mention is just as detrimental to our ability to understand the rationale behind the decisions. Attitudes and mentalities had changed so much that our Roman sources also seem puzzled and taken aback by these ritual killings. When Livy mentions them in Book 22 (that is, the only passage covering these events in the surviving books of the *ab urbe condita*), he adds the statement that the ritual was 'un-Roman'.[5] Christian authors use them to attack pagan religion and denounce its demonic nature.[6] In other words, caution needs to be exercised when relying on the interpretations found in the ancient sources, which may reflect apologetic or hostile – in any case, anachronistic – readings by much later authors.

The difficult nature of our sources has resulted in widely differing explanations. At least since Cichorius' study mentioned above, the live burials are strongly linked to scandals involving Vestal Virgins, who were killed in a ritual that closely resembles that of the live burials of the Greeks and Gauls. On several occasions Vestal Virgins who were condemned for losing their virginity were buried alive in an underground chamber within the *pomerium*, the sacred border of Rome. Cichorius pointed out that all three live burials of Greeks and Gauls were preceded by live burials of one or more Vestal Virgins. Conversely, there were no live burials of Vestal Virgins between 228 and 113 BC that did not go hand-in-hand with live burials of Greeks and Gauls subsequently being carried out.[7] It surely is impossible to see the resemblance and temporal coincidence of both kinds of ritual killings as the result of mere chance and to deny a close link.

Modern scholars, however, often stress the link with particular military threats, probably because the victims were foreigners and in particular the Gauls were seen as arch-enemies of Rome throughout the Republic. All cases, moreover, can be connected to military events that posed danger to Rome, such as the fear of a Gallic invasion in 228 BC, the catastrophe of Cannae in 216 BC and the defeat by the Scordisci in 113 BC.[8] Most recently, both Várhelyi and Eckstein have argued against the link with the trials of Vestal Virgins and in favour of the close connection to immediate military threats. Várhelyi argues that the connection is most dubious for 228 BC, the first and most critical occurrence.[9] Moreover, she argues, the link is problematic because of the different locations of the live burials, while the Vestal parallel neither explains the choice of the victims, nor the inclusion of both men and women.[10] As will be argued below, neither does the theory that the live burials were the response to immediate military threats. Eckstein sees the scandals involving unchaste Vestals as merely one among many prodigies.[11] Therefore, he argues, there should not be too much focus on these events. In his view, a story preserved in the works of Zonaras, a Byzantine writer of the twelfth century who followed closely the history of Cassius Dio, offers the closest parallel to the live burials and explains their rationale.[12] According to his account, the Romans were informed of an oracle that said that men from Praeneste would possess the *aerarium* in Rome. In order to fulfil the prophecy, men were taken from Praeneste and incarcerated in the walls of the *aerarium*. Eckstein sees the military context of this story – the implied threat that men from Praeneste would conquer Rome – as proving that military threats were the main cause of the live burials.[13] Apart from a superficial similarity, the connection is weak and unsubstantiated in our sources. For one, this supposed parallel does not explain why the live burials consisted of both men and women. It ignores, moreover, the direct links explicitly made in our sources between the live burials of condemned Vestals and that of Greek and Gallic victims.

Hence, this chapter will argue in favour of a strong link between the live burials of Vestal Virgins and that of Greek and Gallic couples. This is not to deny an important element of fear of military threat in these rituals, but in my view this is of a more general nature than the immediate response to current events on the battlefield assumed by modern authors. In order to make this point, I will examine the sources on both the three cases of live burial of Greeks and Gauls in 228, 216 and 113 BC, and the trials and live burials of Vestal Virgins in the Mid-Republic. This will not answer all our questions, but will shed light on the nature of the link between these Roman religious acts and military threat.[14]

The Case of 228 BC

A few basic elements can be taken from the sources on the first instance of the live burial of Greeks and Gauls: the ritual originated in the consultation of the Sibylline Books and took place in the Forum Boarium. According to a fragment from Cassius Dio,[15] the Romans buried a Greek and a Gallic couple, a man and woman in each case, during the consulate of Fabius Maximus Verrucossus, which dates the event to 228 BC. It can never be completely certain that this was the first case of such a ceremony, but the silence in our sources is confirmed by the remark of Plutarch that this was a first. Plutarch explicitly links the ritual to the threat of a Gallic invasion and the panic this caused in Rome: 'Their alarm was also shown by their preparations for the war ... and by the extraordinary sacrifices which they made to the gods.' After stressing the foreign nature of the ritual to Roman religion, he continues:

> 'At the time when this war burst upon them they were constrained to obey certain oracular commands from the Sibylline Books, and to bury alive two Greeks, a man and a woman, and likewise two Gauls, in the place called the Forum Boarium. And in memory of these victims, they still to this day, in the month of November, perform mysterious and secret ceremonies.'[16]

Apparently, despite the supposedly foreign nature of the ritual, there was a religious tradition related to it at the site, which was continued at least until Plutarch's day. Plutarch's emphasis on the un-Roman nature of the ritual says more about his response than about Roman religion, which is confirmed by the fact that the ritual was indeed repeated in 216 and 113 BC.[17]

Following Plutarch, Eckstein argues that the extraordinary ritual was brought about directly by the threat of a Gallic invasion that had paralyzed Rome since 232 BC.[18] He interprets all four sources as saying that the purpose of the ritual 'was to ward off a potential occupation of the city by foreign elements and in particular the Gauls'.[19] Indeed, Plutarch is very explicit about the immediate threat of the Gauls causing the ritual, but the other sources are very much less clear on this matter.

The oracle in Zonaras 8.19 is often related to Cassius Dio Fragment 50, where reference is made to 'an oracle of the Sibyl which told them that they must beware of the Gauls when a thunderbolt should fall upon the Capitol near the temple of Apollo'. However, there is no mention of Greeks here, as there is in the oracle in Zonaras:

> 'In as much as an oracle had once come to the Romans, that Greeks and Gauls should occupy the city, two Gauls and likewise two Greeks, male and female, were buried alive in the forum, in order that in this way destiny might seem to have fulfilled itself, and these foreigners, thus buried there, might be regarded as possessing a part of the city.'[20]

While this passage does not contradict Plutarch's narrative, it does not provide confirmation either. There is as little evidence here of an immediate Gallic threat as there is of an impending Greek invasion. Zonaras, who is probably adhering to Cassius Dio here, merely points to a general fear of foreign foes, nothing more.[21]

The Christian writer Orosius, whose account, written in the early fourth century, derives from Livy's lost books, has the following brief note:

'Two years later, the pontifices who were powerful, but wicked, brought death to the city through their sacrilegious rites. For the *decemviri*, following the demands of an ancient[22] superstition, buried alive a Gallic man and woman at the same time as a Greek woman in the cattle market. But straightaway this occult ritual brought about the reverse of what was intended, for they atoned for the terrible death they had worked on these foreigners through having their own people horribly slaughtered.'[23]

Orosius does not mention any direct military threat either, let alone providing a causal link between such a threat and the subsequent ritual. The desired effect, it is implied, is the opposite of the massacre of Romans, consisting of success on the battlefield, but that does not imply any particular imminent danger. The fact that Gauls are buried might point to fear of a Gallic opponent, but the same logic points to a Greek enemy. The only explicit causal link is that between the ungodly ritual and the subsequent Roman defeats, but that says nothing about the reason for the Romans to conduct this ritual in the first place. Moreover, the Gallic invasion of 225 BC ended with a sound victory at Telamon, so Orosius may actually have had the disastrous first years of the Second Punic War in mind.[24]

In short, there is only one source – Plutarch's *Life of Marcellus* – that offers a particular wartime threat as motive for the Romans to consult the Sibylline Books and subsequently bury alive two Greeks and two Gauls. It can never be certain as to whether this narrative reflects the events of 228 BC, or if Plutarch – or the source(s) on which his account is based – created this link on the basis of the historiographic tradition of a long-time threat of a Gallic invasion at the time. The other sources also see fear of an outside threat as background to the Senate's decision, but in a much more general way. This shows at least that there were different traditions and interpretations concerning the live burial of 228 BC, and it is not easy for us to determine which of these readings, all of which were written down centuries after the events, has a stronger claim to authenticity.

Intermezzo: The Threat of a Gallic Invasion

An additional reason for rejecting the idea that the threat of a Gallic invasion formed the background to the ritual killing of 228 BC is that at the time there was no such threat. I have argued so in a previous publication and it would go too far for the purpose of this article to repeat all my arguments here. Let me just summarise its main points.[25]

In Book 2, Polybius, who is largely adhering to Fabius Pictor, his main Roman source, tells us that in 232 BC the Romans discovered plans for a grand coalition of Cisalpine and Transalpine Gauls to invade Italy. Fear of this invasion caused panic in Rome for the next seven years and paralyzed their actions overseas, in particular against the rising power of the Barcids in Spain. In 225 BC the Gauls finally invaded, but were beaten in a resounding Roman victory at Telamon. In my view, the account of the Gallic invasion is deliberately distorted by Fabius Pictor, who as a Roman senator was closely involved. Moreover, Fabius Pictor wrote his historic account (the first ever by a Roman writer) in Greek and primarily for a Greek public, after he had led a Roman embassy to Greece, whose mission was to seek Greek allies in the war against Hannibal and in particular against the latter's ally Macedon. Pictor had every reason to depict Rome as a natural ally of the Greeks, while at the same time exonerating Roman failure against Carthage. He did so by adding the supposed seven-year threat of the Gallic invasion from 232 BC onwards, which did not actually make that much difference for the rest of the narrative found in Polybius Book 2. Despite the supposed paralyzing threat, Rome successfully waged war in Illyria in 229 and 228 BC. Note that in the latter year the Romans are supposed to be so much panicked that they resorted to human sacrifice! Two years later Rome had started a more aggressive policy towards Carthage, so Polybius tells us, which is confirmed by the location of the Roman legions in the south of Italy and on Sicily at the start of 225 BC. Hence, the Gallic invasion came as a surprise to Rome at a time that was most inopportune. Rome had to take a step back when confronted with an unexpectedly large-scale war in the north. The result was the Ebro treaty and the abandonment of Saguntum.

Fabius Pictor made good use of the fact that ever since the Gallic invasions of Greece and Asia Minor in the early third century BC, the Greeks saw the Gauls as their arch-enemies and as a barbaric threat to prosperity and civilization. The Greek victory over the Gauls at Delphi in 279 BC was a hugely celebrated event afterward, as Pictor undoubtedly witnessed during his embassy to Delphi. Hence, Fabius Pictor used the Gallic invasion of Italy for propagandistic purposes by stressing that the Gauls were the natural enemies of the Romans and by stressing the paralyzing impact of the pending invasion on Roman policy. Telamon was made into the counterpart of the victory over the Galatians at Delphi in 279 BC. Pictor exploited a common theme of Hellenistic propaganda, where kings legitimized their power by saving Greek prosperity and civilization from the barbaric Gauls. It is difficult to say which elements are Fabius' and which Polybius'. However, despite criticism on certain points, the latter generally adhered to Fabius' account concerning the Gallic wars because he had no reason to doubt his veracity in this case and the propagandistic content suited his own purposes. Fabius Pictor's version of events influenced all later historiographic traditions, and thus it is not surprising that it also determined the narrative of Plutarch's life of Marcellus, a contemporary of Rome's first historian.[26]

The Cases of 216 and 113 BC

In 216 BC, twelve years after the first case, the Sibylline Books were again consulted, resulting in the decision of the Roman Senate to repeat the live burial of a Greek and a Gallic couple. This happened after the disastrous defeat of the Romans at Cannae, and a causal link between the two is regularly stressed or cursorily assumed.[27] Livy's account, however, throws a different light on the chain of events:

> 'These terrible disasters aside, the Romans were also alarmed by a number of prodigies, especially the conviction that year of two Vestals, Opimia and Floronia, on charges of sexual misconduct. Of these one had been buried alive, as the custom is, near the Porta Collina, and the other had committed suicide. ... Occurring as it did along with all the other misfortunes, this piece of sacrilege was naturally interpreted as a portent, and the decemvirs were therefore instructed to consult the Books. Quintus Fabius Pictor was also sent to the oracle at Delphi to ask what prayers and acts of supplication they could employ to appease the gods, and further enquire when the Romans would see an end to their great diasasters. Meanwhile, a number of outlandish sacrifices were conducted on instructions from the Books of Fate. These included a Gallic man and woman, and a Greek man and woman, being interred alive in the Forum

Boarium, in a spot enclosed with stones which had already been the scene of this very un-Roman practice of human sacrifice.'[28]

According to Livy's account, fear may be seen as background of the live burial, but two causes for the general terror among the people are identified: the defeats they had suffered and a string of portents, amongst which one particular event is emphasized, namely the trial and death of two Vestal Virgins, one of whom was buried alive. I will discuss the live burials of Vestal Virgins later. The main point to be made here is that under the circumstances of so many misfortunes this event was seen as a pollution (*nefas*) that needed to be propitiated in order to put an end to these calamities. The Senate attempted to find out how to propitiate the pollution in two ways: by sending Fabius Pictor to the oracle at Delphi and by ordering the *decemviri* to consult the Sibylline Books. The purpose of both actions is implied by the motivation that Livy gives for sending Fabius Pictor to the oracle at Delphi, i.e. lifting the curse and ending the string of catastrophies. The prayers and supplications that Fabius Pictor is to seek in Delphi, by the way, offer a contrast to the un-Roman rite that subsequently follows in Rome, and the same contrast is found in the response he brings back from Delphi, which includes sending gifts to the Pythian Apollo. Meanwhile, the Sibylline Books order some unusual sacrifices, amongst which are the live burial of a Gallic man and woman and a Greek man and woman. In short, while the disasters befalling Rome on the battlefield are a crucial circumstance in the chain of events, it is in particular the live burial of the one Vestal Virgin and suicide of the other that Livy emphasizes as the direct cause of the live burial of the Gauls and Greeks.

Plutarch does not mention the live burial of Greeks and Gauls in 216 BC, which in itself is interesting, although it is difficult to draw conclusions from this absence. The main point is that also according to Plutarch, Fabius Pictor was sent to Delphi in order to appease the gods and placate the *prodigia*:

'All the rites which the augurs advocated for the propitiation of the gods, or to avert inauspicious omens, were duly performed. And besides, Pictor, a kinsman of Fabius, was sent to consult the oracle at Delphi. And when two of the Vestal Virgins were found to have been corrupted, one of them was buried alive, according to the custom, and the other slew herself.'[29]

The order of events in Plutarch's narrative seems to suggest that the issue of the Vestal Virgins arose only after Fabius Pictor was sent to Delphi. This may correspond with the separation implied in Livy's narrative between the sending of Fabius Pictor on a mission to Delphi and the consultation of the Sibylline Books, and may therefore imply that the consultation of the Sibylline Books followed in particular the death of the Vestal Virgins, but it is unclear to what extent both accounts can be combined into one narrative. In any case, Livy clearly links the repetition of the live burial of a Greek and Gallic couple in 216 BC to the death of the Vestal Virgins, and our other sources say nothing to contradict this reading.[30]

The last time a live burial of Vestal Virgins occurred followed by that of Greek and Gallic couples was in 114 and 113 BC, but the few sources there are pay much more attention to the trials and killing of the Vestals in these years than to the death of the Greek and Gallic victims. It is only Plutarch who mentions both rituals and in addition offers a clear connection between them. All other sources – the summary of Livy's Book 63, Asconius in his commentary on Cicero's *Pro Milone*, Cassius Dio, Obsequens and Orosius – only refer to the trial and death of the Vestals without mentioning the ritual killing of Greeks and Gauls.[31] Plutarch starts his brief narration of the ritual killings of these years with the observation that Roman rulers forbade its allies to conduct human sacrifices, while they themselves had not long before performed such a ritual. He starts his narration with the virgin daughter of a Roman knight named Helvia being struck by lightning. Due to the particular circumstances of her death, this is seen as a portent:

> 'The soothsayers declared that it was a terrible disgrace for the Vestal Virgins, that it would be bruited far and wide, and that some wanton outrage would be found touching the knights also. Thereupon a barbarian slave of a certain knight gave information against three Vestal Virgins, Aemilia, Licinia, and Marcia, that they had all been corrupted at about the same time, and that they had long entertained lovers, one of whom was Vetutius Barrus, the informer's master. The Vestals, accordingly, were convicted and punished; but, since the deed was plainly atrocious, it was resolved that the priests should consult the Sibylline Books. They say that oracles were found foretelling that these events would come to pass for the bane of the Romans, and enjoining on them that, to avert the impending disaster, they should offer as a sacrifice to certain

strange and alien spirits two Greeks and two Gauls, buried alive on the spot.'[32]

Plutarch's narration of events leading up to the trial and death of the Vestals agrees with what is found in the other sources. However, it is what follows that is most interesting from our point of view, as he writes that the circumstances of the death of the Vestals were so dreadful that the authorities authorized the consultation of the Sibylline Books. The priests confirm that the events – it remains unclear whether they mean the unchastity of the Vestals, the trial and/or their deaths – resulted in a curse that, if not propitiated, would lead to disaster. Plutarch is explicit: the live burial of the Greek and Gallic man and woman was intended to lift the curse that arose from the events surrounding the death of the Vestal Virgins.[33] Insofar as there is a threat to Rome, it is itself a result of the ritual killing of the Vestals, not the cause of either live burial.

Interestingly, Eckstein acknowledges the apotropaic purpose of the ritual in Plutarch, but despite the clear wording of our Greek author, he links this to the danger of a military threat, not to the scandal of the Vestals.[34] While modern scholars often point to the Roman defeat by the Celtic Scordisci in 114 BC as explanation for the ritual, there is actually no mention in our main ancient source of any immediate military threat triggering the ritual killing of the Greeks or Gauls. The direct link between these two events is a modern invention,[35] while Clark also notes the absence of serious military troubles at the time, observing that a connection between the live burial of Greeks and Gauls and a military threat could only have been made in retrospect, 'when the repeated successes of the Cimbri validated the internal pressures of public fear and political strife that motivated the Vestals' trials'.[36] Florus likens the defeat to an omen, but that is no link to the ritual killing.[37] Cichorius observes that at the time there was only one war, so if one assumes a direct link between the live burial of Greeks and Gauls and an immediate military threat, this campaign is the only one that could provide a context for it. The defeat of the Romans by the Scordisci in faraway Thrace can hardly have caused widespread panic in Rome.

In short, the most detailed and explicit source reveals that in 216 BC the live burial of Greeks and Gauls was intended to lift the curse that was revealed by a series of *prodigia*, the most important of which was the trial and death of two Vestal Virgins. In 113 BC, the curse that is to be placated by the ritual killing of the Greeks and Gauls is directly attributed to the events surrounding the deaths of the Vestal Virgins.

Gauls and Greeks

As Schultz notes: 'No satisfactory explanation of the choice of Gauls and Greeks has yet been proposed.'[38] The identity of the victims of the live burials in 228, 216 and 113 BC, in particular that of the Gauls, seems quite naturally to point to a military context for the ritual's motivation, as Rome waged war with the Gauls on many occasions throughout the Republic. However, as has been seen, this link is only implied – and that in completely different ways – in the accounts of Plutarch and Cassius Dio of the events in 228 BC. Plutarch links it to the Gallic invasion, Cassius Dio to a more general threat by Greeks and Gauls. There is one other source that interprets the victims as representatives of enemy peoples. The elder Pliny writes: 'Our own age even has seen a man and a woman buried live in the Ox Market, Greeks by birth, or else natives of some other country with which we were at war at the time.'[39] Interestingly, it is not the Gauls that are mentioned, in contrast to the general modern focus on them, while Pliny appears not very certain about the other peoples involved, only knowing that they were from some hostile peoples.[40] As has been noted, Rome did not fight Greeks in any of these years, which sheds doubt on Pliny's reading. It is quite possible that the interpretation by Pliny the Elder, Plutarch and Cassius Dio, all of whom wrote centuries after the rituals they describe, of the victims as representing Rome's enemies is no more than an assumption based on the ritual's apparent logic.

Várhelyi rejects the idea that the victims represent prospective adversaries, because this would imply that, 'in addition to the actual combat on the battlefield, there would have been a more abstract understanding of a parallel war, on a symbolic, religious level, between Rome and its enemies', arguing that the Romans did not perceive actual warfare as parallel to a divine conflict in the way that the Mexica (Aztecs) did. Her argument is not fully convincing, however, for the supposed prerequisite is not established, nor does the absence of Aztec-style beliefs of a divine conflict rule out similar beliefs of a different kind. After all, the Romans did see divine support as fundamental to their success and did regularly try to bring the gods of their enemies on their own side. In principle, it cannot be ruled out that the Romans killed victims in order to appease the gods and ensure their continued support. This argument will be elaborated below.[41]

Problematic for the reading of the live burial of Gauls and Greeks as intended to ward off an immediate military danger is that Rome never fought Gauls and Greeks at the same time, while an explanation for the victims should hold for both peoples. The cases of 216 and 113 may be regarded as repetitions of 228, and so the focus should be on the first instance of the ritual. Based on the assumption that the Greek and Gallic identity of the victims must reflect wartime opponents, it is a widely accepted idea that this points to an Etruscan origin of the ritual, as the Etruscans did indeed fight both Greeks and Gauls before they were subjected by Rome at the end of the fourth and beginning of the third centuries BC.[42] In other words, it is assumed that this ritual, including the involvement of Gallic and Greek victims, originated in Etruscan society at least several generations before it was held for the first time in Rome.

Such a theory does seem to fit some traits of early Etruscan society, as presented in our sources. Gladiatorial combat, which was supposedly adopted by the Romans in 264 BC, is ascribed to the Etruscans too.[43] Moreover, the interpretation of scenes on Etruscan sarcophagi as human sacrifices has given rise to a hypothetical Etruscan ritual that was similar to Roman *devotio*. According to this theory, there was a widespread practice of *devotio hostium* in the Italian peninsula in the fourth and third centuries BC, in which war captives were sacrificed by their enemies. Apart from the dubious connection between *devotio* in the Roman tradition and the live burials in Rome,[44] there are some severe weaknesses in this theory. The idea of *devotio* in Roman beliefs has been put forward as a comparison and related practice to the live burial of Greeks and Gauls, but the grounds for this assumed connection are very weak. Several sources tell us about Roman generals who dedicated themselves and the soldiers of the enemy to the gods of the dead and to the Earth and subsequently sought their death in battle. The first case, according to Livy, occurred in 340 BC in the person of Decius Mus, and the Roman historiographic tradition has his son and grandson follow his example.

According to Livy, life-size images were buried in the earth of the general, who did not die in order to fulfil the vow by proxy.[45] Although the general devotes himself and the enemies to the gods in a way that the Greek and Gallic victims might have been (although no source says so), the similarities are weak. The general and enemy soldiers are supposed to die in battle, while only the substitution is buried underground. Moreover, burying an image underground does not correspond to the live internment of victims in an underground chamber. Várhelyi has pointed out that there is no further evidence of the widespread practice of *devotio hostium* in Italy and that the bloody sacrifices depicted on the sarcophagi do not fit the nature of the ritual in Rome.[46] One may add that the prominent involvement of women in the live burials in Rome does not fit the hypothetical sacrifice of war captives by the Etruscans either. In short, the sarcophagi offer no support for the theory of an Etruscan origin for the ritual in Rome.

There are other problems with the theory of an Etruscan origin. All our sources say that the ritual was introduced after consultation of the Sibylline Books by Roman priests. The Sibylline Books were generally consulted after grave prodigies, and repeatedly caused foreign cults and rites to be introduced in Rome.[47] Regarding the live burials of 228 BC, there are two possibilities: either the Sibylline Books prescribed the ritual as performed, including the Greek and Gallic identity of the victims, or they merely prescribed such a ritual in general terms, without specifying the ethnic identity of the victims. In the latter case, the theory of an Etruscan origin does not really help, as it still leaves the problem of why Gauls and Greeks were chosen in 228 BC, when only the Gauls, but not the Greeks, can be regarded as enemies of Rome. In the first case there is also a problem, as the Sibylline Books consisted of oracular verses in Greek, which are generally related to increasing influence from the Greeks in southern Italy, and in particular to the Sibyl of Cumae.[48] The introduction of many Greek cults in third-century Rome at the instigation of the Sibylline Books reflects such Greek influence.[49] Now, why would the Sibylline Books, written in Greek and originating in a Greek community (possibly Cumae), contain an Etruscan ritual?

Hence, it is argued that in the Greek context in which the Sibylline Books were created, the Greeks and Gauls were perceived as Rome's most threatening enemies.[50] Again, this seems far from obvious. Why would a Greek oracle, stemming from a Greek colony in Italy, portray Greeks as Rome's enemies on equal footing with the Gauls? Greekness as an ethnic and cultural unity that bound together Greeks from all over the Mediterranean world had already emerged, as the implied mention of 'Greeks' in the Sibylline Books itself would indicate. It seems unlikely that a member of a Greek community seeking to represent two arch-enemies of Rome would pick Gauls – despised as barbaric and uncivilized – and Greeks, i.e. people of his own cultural background and ethnicity. Why not an Italic people such as the Samnites, who waged war on the Greeks of Campania as much as on Rome, or the Etruscans?

It is unlikely that this issue will ever be solved with certainty, but I would like to suggest that the supposed logic that the two pairs of victims represented enemies of Rome may have to be abandoned. Why have two pairs from different peoples in the first place? Why not the most dangerous foe? Why include women, if the idea is to represent military opponents? I would like to put forward the hypothesis that a Greek man and woman were included in the ritual because they represented their own – Greek – community when the Sibylline oracles were created. So, if the ritual killing conducted in Rome in 228 BC was indeed prescribed by the Sibylline Books, it is possible that the Greeks were included because they originally represented the Greek community itself, while the Gauls were the arch-enemies of the Greeks. In other words, the couples represent enemies of each other, not common foes of a third party.

The Live Burial of Unchaste Vestal Virgins

In the mid- and late-Republic, Vestal Virgins were chosen among young girls from prominent families who had a living father and mother. Their service lasted at least thirty years, but many served their entire life.[51] The Vestal Virgins tended the sacred fire, which symbolized the hearth of the entire community, but their services included many public rites, at the heart of which was purification from pollution.[52] They were released from their father's authority, but unlike other unmarried women in Roman society, they did not have a guardian.[53] They were, however, subjected to the authority of the *pontifex maximus*, the head of the priestly college of *pontifices*, who had the right to physically punish Vestals when they failed in their obligations. When a Vestal was charged with severe misconduct, including loss of virginity (*incestum*), the *pontifex maximus* presided over the trial before the college of *pontifices*, which could condemn her to death if found guilty.[54] Her execution took the form of a live burial, and unlike the case of the Greeks and Gauls, there was no prior consultation of the Sibylline Books. Already in the earliest cases in our sources, it seems established practice that an unchaste Vestal was buried alive.

The live burial of the convicted Vestal can be constructed from the descriptions offered by Dionysius of Halicarnassus, Plutarch and Pliny the Younger, who was an eyewitness of the live burial of the senior Vestal Cornelia during the reign of Domitian. Most notably, Dionysius likens the ceremony to a funeral:

'While they are yet alive they are carried upon a bier with all the formality of a funeral, their friends and relations attending them with lamentations, and after being brought as far as the Colline Gate, they are placed in an underground cell prepared within the

walls, clad in their funeral attire; but they are not given a monument
or funeral rites or any other customary solemnities.'[55]

The Vestal is to go down a ladder into the underground chamber by herself,
finding there oil, water, milk, bread, a bed and a burning lamp, 'as though,'
Plutarch remarks, 'they would thereby absolve themselves from the charge
of destroying by hunger a life which had been consecrated to the highest
services of religion'.[56] After the Vestal had entered the chamber, the opening
was hidden under great quantities of earth. Plutarch emphasizes the
impact of the ritual on the populace of Rome: 'No other spectacle is more
appalling, nor does any other day bring more gloom to the city than this.'[57]
In another work, Plutarch refers again to the impact that these events
had on the city: 'And yet not even by this manner of avoiding the guilt
have they escaped their superstitious fear, but even to this day the priests
proceed to this place and make offerings to the dead.'[58]

According to our sources, Vestals were convicted and put to death as
far back as under the Tarquins. Dionysius of Halicarnassus narrates the live
burial of the Vestal Pinaria under Tarquinius Priscus.[59] In 483 BC, according
to Livy, the Vestal Oppia was 'condemned for *incestum* and executed'.[60]
The tradition regarding this case must have been uncertain, because
Dionysius of Halicarnassus mentions for the same year the death of the
Vestal Opimia, while Orosius names her Popilia and Eusebius Pompilia.[61]
In 472 BC, so Dionysius claims,[62] the burial alive of the Vestal Urbina
lifted the curse that induced sterility and miscarriages among women
in Rome. In 420 BC, the Vestal Postumia was accused and subsequently
acquitted for dressing too well and being too clever.[63] For the year 337
BC, Livy relates that the Vestal Minucia also came under suspicion for
dressing too smartly.[64] Accused on the allegations of a slave, she was tried,
convicted and buried alive next to the Porta Collina.[65] In 274/273 BC, the
Vestal Sextilia was buried alive for *incestum*.[66] Orosius is the only source that
mentions an unchaste Vestal named Capparonia being hanged in 266 BC.[67]
Hanging would have been exceptional, so one wonders whether Orosius
misunderstood or misrepresented his source. Some of these stories seem
quite unbelievable and it can never be quite certain whether the trials
and executions of Vestal Virgins in the Early Republic are historic or later
inventions. The story of Tuccia shows that such stories of convicted Vestal
Virgins were grateful subjects for elaboration and drama. The summary
of Livy's Book 20 simply states that the Vestal Tuccia was condemned for
incestum, but our other sources tell the story of her miraculous salvation

by the intervention of the gods. According to this story, she proved her innocence by filling a sieve of water from the Tiber and carrying it to the temple of Vesta without spilling any.[68] While the bare fact of the conviction of a Vestal Virgin may well have been preserved in the priestly chronicles, it is very unlikely that the narrative details and motives are all historic.[69]

It is a pity that Livy's full account of the trial of Tuccia is lost and that the other sources tell us little besides the supposed miracle, as this trial preceded the live burial of a Greek and Gallic couple in 228 BC. Eckstein denies any link between the two events, because he regards the time between them as too long.[70] Cichorius argued that the position in the summary of events as presented in *Periochae* 20 indicates either 231–229 BC or one of the years of the Illyrian War, i.e. 229 or 228 BC. The latter dating would bring it close to the ritual killing of the Greeks and Gauls. Even assuming that Eckstein is right and that the trial of Tuccia must have occurred between the summer of 231 and the spring of 229, the argument against a connection is rather thin. This is probably the first case of the live burial of Greeks and Gauls and there is no indication of what considerations and debates led to it. Hence, it is impossible for us to say that a link is possible with a gap of one year, but not of two.

The next case has already been mentioned above, but again the sources are extremely concise. In 216 BC, the Vestals Opimia and Floronia were convicted of unchastity. One of them killed herself, the other was buried alive, while the man who had had sex with the Vestal Floronia was flogged to death. In particular the deaths of these Vestals induced the Senate to order the priestly college of the *decemviri* to consult the Sibylline Books, leading to the repetition of the ritual killing of a Greek and Gallic couple.[71]

Interestingly, the next calamity involving a Vestal occurred in 206 BC, when, so Livy narrates, the fire in the Temple of Vesta went out, causing great fear among the populace.[72] The unnamed Vestal who had been on duty that night was ordered by the *pontifex maximus* to be scourged for her negligence. What follows is significant: 'Although this was the result of human negligence, and was not a divinely sent portent, it was still decided that atonement should be made with full-grown victims and that public prayers should be offered at the temple of Vesta.'[73] While there had been fear among the populace, who saw the extinction of the fire as a grave prodigy, it was apparently decided that this was not the gods' doing, but just the very human fault of one particular Vestal.[74] Some form of expiation was still deemed necessary, however, but as there was no reason to assume a severe disruption of the *pax deorum*, this could be limited to quite regular processions and sacrifices. To what extent this is the possibly anachronistic interpretation of Livy (or his sources) or a true account of the considerations at the time is unfortunately impossible to say. In 178 BC, there occurred again a miracle, when the fire that had gone out started burning again, which was regarded as proving that the Vestal Aemilia was innocent of the sacred fire going out.[75]

The next case leading to the death of the Vestals involved occurred in 114 and 113 BC. As seen above, the death by lightning of the daughter of a Roman equestrian was interpreted as a bad omen involving the Vestals and Roman equestrians, which led to the enquiry into the conduct of the Vestals. Several of our sources tell us that the Vestals were condemned and killed, but Asconius and Macrobius mention political unrest stemming from the fact that, in December 114, three Vestals were tried on the charge of *incestum*, but two of them were acquitted, while the third was not immediately killed. The popular assembly carried a bill that overthrew the earlier judgement of the priestly college and condemned all three Vestals to death: they were subsequently buried alive.[76] The fragments from Cassius Dio's Book 26 provide details of the sexual escapades of the Vestals and also mention the unrest in Rome the trial led to. Plutarch, who does not mention the political strife and the intervention of the tribune of the plebs, does however add that the unrest and fear after the deaths of the Vestals caused the Senate to have the Sibylline Books consulted, resulting in the ritual killing of the Greek and Gallic couple.[77]

Notably, this was the last case of the ritual killing of a Greek and Gallic couple, but also the last case of the live burial of unchaste Vestals until Domitian (in his position of *pontifex maximus* and under very dubious circumstances) had the chief Vestal Cornelia convicted of *incestum* and killed in the traditional custom, while her lovers were beaten to death. At the same time, two other Vestals were allowed to choose their own manner of death. Unlike the Republican cases, there are contemporaries (or nearly so) in the person of Pliny the Younger and Suetonius providing details on these cases. Interestingly, Suetonius explicitly says that Domitian's predecessors, Vespasian and Titus, had condoned the *incestum* of the Vestals, which makes one wonder, first, whether that was common knowledge, and second, for how long such leniency had been policy. The main point, however, is that live burials, which had occurred almost simultaneously in about 228, 216 and 113 BC, and each time the killings of Vestals preceding that of Greek and Gallic couples, disappeared after the latter year, for good in the case of Greek and Gallic couples, and for two centuries in the case of Vestal Virgins. It is incredible that these ritual killings occurred in the same years and disappeared at the same time without any close causal link between them. It is more than likely that a change in religious attitude caused both rituals to be abandoned at the end of the Republic.[78]

Ancient Attitudes Towards the Live Burials

Although the ritual killing of unchaste Vestal Virgins surely is the closest parallel to the live burial of Greek and Gallic victims in Rome, and the two rituals are moreover closely linked in time and religious background, there is a fundamental difference in the way our sources treat the two rituals. Schultz rightly points out that the ritual killing of foreign victims is the only Roman rite that is called a human sacrifice in our sources. In his passage (discussed above) on the case of 216 BC, Livy includes the live burial among the *sacrificia extraordinaria* and says that the place of the ritual had been tainted before by *hostiis humanis*.[79] Livy here uses terminology specifically referring to sacrifice, not just any sacred rite. Also Plutarch, when mentioning the burial of 113 BC, places it in the category of human sacrifice. This is implied by the context: while the Romans forbade their allies to conduct human sacrifices, they themselves were guilty of such a practice. It is not the live burial of unchaste Vestals he is referring to, but the ritual killing of the Greek and Gallic couples. No ancient writer ever refers to the ritual killing of the unchaste Vestals as a sacrifice, nor is the victim of this ritual ever likened to a sacrificial victim.[80]

However, do the views of Livy and Plutarch reflect the general attitude, in particular the attitude of the Romans conducting the rite? Owing to the absence of contemporary sources, the religious beliefs of the people involved in the ritual killings of 228, 216 or 113 BC are impossible to ascertain. Nevertheless, the disapproving views of the later pagan writers – let alone those of the Christian authors – cannot have been shared by the majority of the ruling families that were involved in the decision as senators and members of the priestly colleges.[81]

Greeks and Romans abhorred human sacrifice and regarded the custom as a sign of barbarism, cruelty and superstition rather than true religion.[82] Should the implied criticism of Plutarch be accepted, when he says that the Romans forbade the tribe of the Bletonesii to conduct human sacrifice and even at first intended to punish their leaders? 'And yet,' Plutarch observes, 'they themselves, not many years before, had buried alive two men and two women, two of them Greeks, two Gauls, in the place called the Forum Boarium. It certainly seems strange that they themselves should do this, and yet rebuke barbarians on the ground that they were acting with impiety.' Were the Romans hypocrites? Though the argument remains speculative, I would say 'no'. The essence of most sacrifices – whether of animals or of inanimate offerings – was sharing a meal with the gods.[83] Part of the animals offered to the gods was burnt and shared with the gods, while the rest was consumed by the human participants of the ritual, or even sold on the market as plain meat. Of course, there were exceptions to this, as offerings to the gods of the underworld were entirely burnt to ashes, and in some rare rites animals were offered that were not commonly food for men. Despite these exceptional cases, the main element in a sacrifice remains the sharing between gods and mortals, which surely made human sacrifice into the sinful and impious act, often linked to cannibalism, that it was in the eyes of Greeks and Romans. None of the elements of a normal sacrifice were, however, present in the burial alive of Greek and Gallic victims. There was no act in which the victim was killed, there was no immolation and there was no act of burning part of the victims' remains as an offering to the gods.[84] In this sense, the ritual killing of the Greek and Gallic couple was not a human sacrifice, and neither was the live burial of Vestals nor the ritual killings of hermaphrodites, parricides or other individuals in Roman religious rites.[85] Hence, it seems likely that the senators deciding on these rituals did not see them as human sacrifices, despite the disapproving views and reproachful terminology of Livy and Plutarch.

Several centuries later, the few pagan commentators whose texts have survived seem puzzled and embarrassed, either apologetic and rationalizing, or judgemental, while Christian authors gratefully refer to the rite to denounce pagan rituals as the vile work of demons. The same kind of rejection is not found in the case of the unchaste Vestals, neither with pagan nor with Christian writers. One wonders whether this is the reason why the ancient sources on the live burials of Greeks and Gauls in 228, 216 and 113 BC are so very sparse. Of course, much is lost and most of the relevant works survive only in summaries and fragments, but even in comparison with other events, the available evidence is extremely sparse. Only Plutarch preserved the detail that the death of the Vestals in 114 and 113 BC was followed by the ritual killing of Greeks and Gauls – none of the other sources on the trial and killing of the Vestals in that year mentions the latter event. To many writers, the rite of burying alive a Greek and Gallic couple may have seemed out of place in the glorious history of Rome's past.

There is no evidence that Fabius Pictor or Polybius ever mentioned the live burial of Greeks or Gauls in their works, but how significant is this, in view of the fact that only fragments and *testimonia* survive of the first Roman historian and most of Polybius' work is also lost? Nevertheless, Fabius Pictor is mentioned by Polybius as an important source on Roman issues in the 220s BC. Moreover, he is directly linked to the live burials of 216 by the fact that he was sent to Delphi in order to find out how to end the sequence of disasters. Even if the live burial of Greeks and Gauls occurred in his absence, it was very much entwined with his own mission. Would he have mentioned the events of 228 and 216 BC in his work – written in Greek, primarily for a Greek audience, and against the background of diplomatic attempts to find allies among the Greek states against Macedon? I do not think so, because Fabius Pictor tried to depict Rome as part of the civilized world and resembling Greece as much as possible, and this also influenced his description of Roman religion. Hence, when he comes back from his mission to Delphi after the Roman defeat at Cannae, the response of the oracle includes sending gifts to the Pythian Apollo. Moreover, after his return, Fabius Pictor brought a laurel to the altar of Apollo in Rome.[86]

When the Greek historian Dionysius of Halicarnassus, writing in Augustan times, offers his readers a description of a procession held at the occasion of the first *ludi Romani* in the fifth century BC, he cites Fabius Pictor as his source.[87] It is generally observed that Dionysius in this passage emphasizes the similarity of this Roman procession to Greek ones in order to make the point that Rome was essentially a Greek city. That is undoubtedly true and it is difficult for us to separate Fabius Pictor from Dionysius of Halicarnassus in this passage, but the point is that the latter would have found the work of Fabius Pictor an ideal source because the first Roman historian wanted to give precisely that same message. Dionysius regularly emphasizes the resemblance between Greek and Roman ritual, as can be seen for example in the following passage: 'At the very end of the procession came the statues of all the gods, carried on men's shoulders – with much the same appearance as statues made by the Greeks, with the same costume, the same symbols and the same gifts.'[88]

In short, since the point of Fabius Pictor was to depict the Romans as very much like the Greeks in order to present the Roman Senate as suitable allies to the Greek states, he would not have mentioned that in the very recent past, the Senate of Rome had buried alive in their city a Greek and a Gallic couple in a ritual that was very close to being a human sacrifice. So it is unlikely that Fabius Pictor mentioned this ritual killing in his narrative of 228 or 216 BC.

Neither is there any reason to assume that Polybius in his work referred to these events. Significantly, he does not mention it in his account of the supposed Gallic threat from 232–225 BC, despite his emphasis on the panic arising in Rome. Unfortunately, his narrative of Roman events after Hannibal's victory at Cannae is not preserved fully, so certainty regarding the case of 216 is not possible. It is sometimes assumed that when he writes that 'in seasons of danger the Romans are much given to propitiating both gods and men, and there is nothing at such times in rites of the kind that they regard as unbecoming or beneath their dignity', he is referring to the live burials.[89] However, Polybius offers this observation when describing the anxiety in Rome on the eve of the Battle of Cannae: 'All the oracles that had ever been delivered to them were in men's mouths, every temple and every house was full of signs and prodigies, so that vows, sacrifices, supplicatory processions and litanies pervaded the town.'[90] So, there is no reason to interpret his statement as referring to the ritual killings of Greeks and Gauls after the battle rather than the rites he mentions. In his famous Book 6 on the Roman constitution, he stresses the pomp and circumstance with which religious ceremonies in Rome were conducted, adding that the Roman rulers – unlike their Greek counterparts – were wise to use superstition to control and manipulate the common people.[91] Whether this also applied to the live burials of Greeks, Gauls and Vestals will unfortunately never be known.

Prodigy, Pollution and War

The concise and often fragmentary nature of our sources, the generally long time separating the authors from the events they narrate – even stronger: the uncertainty whether the stories they tell have any resemblance with historic events – hamper our understanding of the beliefs and mentalities underlying the trials and ritual killing of the Vestals.[92] Not all aspects of these rituals can be considered, as that would require a much longer study, but hopefully I will be able to provide some answers that assist in an understanding of the link between the two different rites of live burials.

Eckstein not only denies any link between the trial of a Vestal and the ritual killing of 228 BC, he also diminishes the possible connections in 216 and 113 BC. Too much focus should not be placed on the Vestals, he argues, as the scandals and deaths of Vestals were merely one in whole series of terrible events that led the Senate to consult the Sibylline Books.[93] Moreover, he argues that the burial alive of a Vestal was the punishment for a crime committed, whereas the burial alive of the Greek and Gallic couples was a sacrifice.[94] As I argue below, the ritual killing of unchaste Vestals was not a mere punishment. However, the sources do not treat the scandals of the Vestals as no more than prodigies, like hermaphrodites or lightning striking temples. Prodigies implied that something in the relation to the gods had gone wrong.[95] The passages discussed above imply that the scandals of the Vestals were revealed by *prodigia* rather than being *prodigia* themselves.[96] Hence, I disagree with Stapels when he says that, 'The loss of a Vestal's virginity was a sign that all was not well with the state's relationship with its gods.'[97] It was not merely a sign – it was a fundamental cause of the disrupture.

In other words, the unchastity of the Vestals is not itself a prodigy, but a cause of the ruptured *pax deorum* that is disclosed by the *prodigia* and that needs to be restored by appropriate action. After all, the idea that the *pax deorum* is maintained by the minute execution of rites is at the heart of Roman religion,[98] and the Vestals were responsible for many rites that secured the wellbeing of the entire community. That is what Cicero writes, referring to the sister of Fonteius, a Vestal Virgin: '[S]he who has been, on behalf of you and of your children, occupied for so many years in propitiating the immortal gods.'[99] The crucial role of the Vestal Virgins may be illustrated by one example. Each year, Vestal Virgins gathered the first ears of grain from the new harvest. The first grain was ground and baked by them to provide the sacred salted meal (*mola salsa*) that was used to sanctify animal victims of a sacrifice.[100] Sacrifices accompanied every meaningful action undertaken by a Roman magistrate. In this sense, Vestal Virgins were involved in every single action undertaken by the *Res Publica*.

Unchaste Vestals performing these rituals were revealed by prodigies.[101] This is the logic behind the death of the maiden Helvia. Her death, struck by lightning, and in particular the way she was found, with her tunic up to her waist and her tongue sticking out, was treated as a portent, which was interpreted as signifying a terrible disgrace involving Vestal Virgins and Roman equestrians.[102] In other words, scandals involving unchaste Vestal Virgins were a pollution, rather than revealing one, and this pollution needed to be expiated by extraordinary measures. Hence, Dionysius of

Halicarnassus claims that once the Vestal Urbina was buried alive, the sterility and miscarriages that had struck the community of Rome ceased.[103]

The live burials of Vestal Virgins were in essence burial ceremonies.[104] Was that because the rite should be seen not as the execution of the Vestal, but as the burial of a Vestal who was presumed dead? Condemned Vestals were not stripped of their status of priestesses of Vesta, and executing them would therefore have been a terrible act.[105] As seen above, Plutarch stresses that a life was taken that had been consecrated to religious service.[106] Treating convicted Vestals as dead may therefore be seen as an attempt to take away the pollution in the least harmful way.

Admittedly, there are some problems with the analogy: for example the food and light left in the underground chamber. However, the food might be seen as that left for the dead. In my view, this reading agrees better with the sources than the theory of Staples, which assumes the 'fiction' that the Vestal was not really killed and that 'the tomb was not really a tomb'.[107] One argument was that thereby the prohibition against burial within the *pomerium* was not violated. However, there were several exceptions to this rule, including other Vestals, who were buried within the *pomerium*.[108] More seriously, one must assume that the buried Vestal was replaced. Hence, the fiction that she was not really killed could not last long. Parker likens it to a 'trial by ordeal'.[109] The theory of Takács that the unchaste Vestal 'was inserted into the crop-producing earth to symbolically incite agricultural growth'[110] lacks any basis in the ancient sources, and in particular misses the connection with warfare.[111]

This ritual killing of the Vestals and the circumstances surrounding their deaths caused widespread fear of a rupture in the *pax deorum*.[112] In 216 and 113, this fear triggered the live burial of a Gallic and a Greek couple, most explicitly so in the words of Plutarch regarding the latter case:

> 'Since the deed was plainly atrocious, it was resolved that the priests should consult the Sibylline Books. They say that oracles were found foretelling that these events would come to pass for the bane of the Romans, and enjoining on them that, to avert the impending disaster, they should offer as a sacrifice to certain strange and alien spirits two Greeks and two Gauls, buried alive on the spot.'[113]

Prominent in Roman accounts of their wars is the idea that Roman success on the battlefield was due to divine support; conversely, any imminent danger to the wellbeing of the *Res Publica* was caused by a rupture in the *pax deorum*. This was more than just a literary motif in Livy.[114] The gods were on the side of the Romans, which was even more fundamental to their success than discipline or strategy. This is most succinctly expressed by Fabius Maximus (at least in the words that Livy puts in his mouth), who was appointed dictator after the consul C. Flaminius had disastrously lost the Battle at Trasimene. In a speech held before the Senate, the dictator Fabius Maximus says that the defeat was caused by Flaminius' neglect of the proper rites and *prodigia*. Hence, he urges the Senate to ask the gods themselves how to expiate their wrath by consulting the Sibylline Books. The *decemviri* not only found the cause of the rupture of the *pax deorum* in a vow to Mars that had not been kept, but also the measures to be taken to remedy divine displeasure, including grand games, temples to Venus Erycina and Mens, and a *ver sacrum*, i.e. the offering of the first harvest to the gods.[115] (Interestingly, no live burial of Greeks and Gauls, as one would have expected if direct military threat was the main reason for deciding this ritual.) The general link between war, prodigies and the *pax deorum* is revealed in a brief statement in Livy: 'As a war with Macedon was daily expected, the senate resolved, that before it broke out, all prodigies should be expiated, and the favour of such gods, as should be found expressed in the books of the Fates, invoked by supplications.'[116] In other words, expiating was not merely a response, but could be decided upon as a precautionary measure to make sure that the Romans could count on the support of the gods when entering a grave war.

Roman *pietas* and divine support go hand-in-hand. Chaste Vestal Virgins guaranteed the support of the gods that the Romans regarded as essential for their success in the field of war. This was not just an idea projected onto the distant past. Pliny the Younger, who was a witness to the trial and death of the chief Vestal Cornelia, wrote that she exclaimed: 'How can Caesar think me guilty of *incestum*, when he has conquered and triumphed after my hands have performed the sacred rites?'[117] In other words, military success would not have been possible with an unchaste Vestal performing the required rituals.[118] This connection is also implied by Livy when he recounts the chain of events that led to the condemnation of a Vestal Virgin in 483 BC: the war with the Volsci and Veii did not go well and was being hampered by civil unrest at the time.[119] Hence, prodigies were interpreted as revealing that the sacred rites had not been performed correctly, leading to the trial, conviction and death of a Vestal Virgin. Even more explicit regarding the chain of causality in this case is Dionysius of Halicarnassus, who also notes the difficulties Rome experienced at home and on the battlefield:

'While these things were happening in the camp, in Rome itself many prodigies in the way of unusual voices and sights occurred as indications of divine wrath. And they all pointed to this conclusion, as the augurs and the interpreters of religious matters declared, after pooling their experiences, that some of the gods were angered because they were not receiving their customary honors, as their rites were not being performed in a pure and holy manner. Thereupon strict inquiry was made by everyone, and at last information was given to the pontiffs that one of the virgins who guarded the sacred fire, Opimia by name, had lost her virginity and was polluting the holy rites. The pontiffs, having by tortures and other proofs found that the information was true, took from her head the fillets, and solemnly conducting her through the Forum, buried her alive inside the city walls. As for the two men who were convicted of violating her, they ordered them to be scourged in public and then put to death at once. Thereupon the sacrifices and the auguries became favourable, as if the gods had given up their anger against them.'[120]

Conclusion

The purity of the Vestal Virgins was linked in complex ways with success on the battlefield. Impure Vestals endangered the support of the gods that was seen as fundamental for Rome's success at war; conversely, Roman defeats on the battlefield and enemies threatening the existence of Rome indicated something was fundamentally wrong, leading to trials of Vestals. However, while it was necessary to expunge unchaste Vestals, in themselves the trials and deaths of condemned Vestals caused a grave threat to the *pax deorum*, a pollution that needed to be atoned. On numerous occasions the Roman Senate ordered the Sibylline Books to be consulted in order to lift a pollution of the community of Rome. In 228, 216 and 113 BC, in the aftermath of the ritual killings of Vestal Virgins, the Sibylline Books ordered the live burial of a Greek man and woman and a Gallic man and woman.[121] Hence, the ritual killing of the Gallic and Greek couples was to expiate the ritual killing of the Vestals that preceded it. Questions remain regarding the origin of the live burial of the Greeks and Gauls and the considerations that led to its first implementation in 228 BC. If a Greek origin is likely, that might mean that the choice of victims should not be regarded as representing foes of Rome, but rather as representing the hostility between Greeks and Gauls. The involvement of both men and women was natural in a ritual that was intended to preserve the entire community and that had to placate the horrible and public deaths of Vestal Virgins. It seems possible that the resemblance between both ceremonies triggered the decision to placate the live burial of Vestal Virgins by the live burial of Greek and Gallic couples rather than by other means, such as the introduction of an external cult or new festival, as happened on other occasions. The live burial of the Greeks and Gauls was linked to military threat only indirectly. Even unchaste Vestals retained their position of priestess of Vesta, and the Romans feared that the circumstances of their deaths caused a disruption of the peace of the gods, which the Romans saw as a precondition for their continued success on the battlefield. After 113 BC, the ritual killings of Vestals ceased for two centuries, and when they re-emerged in the Flavian period, fear of divine anger had abated and the live burials of Greeks and Gauls no longer had a place in Roman religion.

Notes

1. Cichorius, 1922: 12, 'Im Kern waren die Römer damals eben immer noch Barbaren.'
2. Scheid, 2007: 269.
3. E.g. Gruen, 2011: 158, discussed in more detail below.
4. Cichorius, 1922: 12.
5. Livy 22.57.6. Cf. Schultz, 2010: 20; Várhelyi, 2007: 283–85.
6. Min. Fel. *Oct.* 30. Cf. Rives, 1995: 65, 74–75.
7. Cichorius, 1922: 18, followed by Erdkamp, 2009: 497–99; Schultz, 2010: 17.
8. Thus, e.g., Beard, North & Price, 1998: 81.
9. Várhelyi, 2007: 279, 288. Following Várhelyi, Clark, 2014: 79 n. 82, briefly suggests that the causality in 228 BC need not have been the same as in 216 and 114/3 BC, as Rome had been victorious in the 220s: 'The connection between the Vestals and the burials of Greeks and Gauls would thus be a product of their coincidence in 216, rather than an explanation thereof.'
10. Várhelyi, 2007: 295–301, proposes a sacral law from fourth-century BC Cyrene as the closest parallel, revealing that purification from

avenging gods was the purpose of the ritual. However, the similarities are limited and superficial: in Cyrene, figurines from wood or clay of a male and female figure were buried in soil. The ritual killings in Rome involved burials in underground chambers of living victims. It remains uncertain how closely the beliefs between both rituals were indeed related.

11. Eckstein, 1982: 69–96, already argued against a clear connection with the trials of Vestal Virgins in favour of a direct link with immediate military threats.

12. Zon. 8.19.9, based on Book 12 of Cassius Dio's Roman history. (To be found e.g. on p.41 of volume II of the Loeb edition of Cassius Dio.) Cf. n. 19.

13. Eckstein, 2012: 216–17. He does admit, though, that in 216 and 114/113 BC the sexual scandals among Vestal Virgins were crucial events on the road that led to the Senate's decisions. The connection between the prophecy of Praeneste and the live burials is also rejected by Várhelyi, 2007: 287, arguing that 'the similarities may also be seen as suggestive of some mistaken antiquarian work rather than a direct link'.

14. This chapter focuses on the sources, first, in order to make clear the complex and weak historiography on both forms of live burials, and secondly, because this is a discussion of the Vestal Virgins primarily in relation to the live burials of Greeks and Gauls. Much more detailed studies of the Vestal Virgins have appeared in the past decades, often employing concepts from anthropology to shed light on the beliefs and attitudes inherent in their role as priestesses and cult practices. Beard, 1980 & 1995, explored the possibilities and limitations of anthropology with regard to the Vestal Virgins. Cf. Schultz, 2016, offers a fundamental discussion of the epistemology of Roman religion. In any case, caution is needed with comparisons that are based on superficial and semantic similarities, which underlie some other studies. Less convincing is, for instance, Parker, 2004, who tends to project ideas from unrelated contexts onto ancient Rome. See Gallia, 2015: esp. 104–06.

15. Dio F50 = Tzetzes on Lycophron, *Alexandra* 603. (Cf. p.41 of Loeb edition of Cassius Dio.)

16. Plut. *Marc.* 3.3–4. Translation: *Plutarch's Lives*, transl. B. Perrin, Cambridge MA, 1955 (Loeb).

17. Rives, 1995: 80: Plutarch sees human sacrifice as a sign of bad religion; superstition rather than true religion. Hence, it needs to be borne in

mind that Plutarch's rendering of these events was influenced by his understanding of them.

18. Similarly, Beard, North & Price, 1998, 81: 'in the face of a Gallic invasion'.
19. Eckstein, 2012: 212.
20. Zon. 8.19. Cf. n. 14. Translation: *Dio's Roman History*, transl. E. Cary, Cambridge MA, 1989 (Loeb).
21. Contra Eckstein, 2012: 213.
22. 'Ancient' in the perspective of Orosius, not in that of the *decemviri*.
23. Oros. 4.13.3–4. Translation: *Seven Books of History against the Pagans*, transl. A.T. Fear, Liverpool, 2010.
24. Contra Eckstein, 2012: 213, who sees in Orosius' mention of a terrible massacre a reference to the Gallic invasion and thus supposes that Orosius implied a causal link between the Gallic invasion and the ritual killing. This is simply not what Orosius writes.
25. Erdkamp, 2009. The argument is rejected by Eckstein, 2012; see also Erdkamp, forthcoming.
26. Contra Eckstein, 2012: 212.
27. Implied in Beard, North & Price, 1998: 81, 'after the battle of Cannae', where also the live burials of 228 and 113 BC are linked to the danger of a Gallic war. Cf. n.15 above.
28. Livy 22.57.2–6. Translation: *Livy's Hannibal's War. Books 21–30*, transl. J.C. Yardley, Oxford, 2006 (with adaptation).
29. Plut. *Fab.* 18.3. Translation: *Plutarch's Lives*, transl. B. Perrin, London, 1958.
30. See also Levene, 1993: 49–51.
31. Livy *Per.* 63; Asconius, *Commentary on Cicero Pro Mil.* 46; Dio F87.1–5, Obsequens 37; Orosius, *History against the Pagans* 5.15.20–22. Obsequens wrote the *liber prodigiorum* in the fourth century CE on the basis of Livy.
32. Plut. *Rom. Quest.* 83. Translation: *Plutarch's Moralia*, transl. F.C. Babbitt, Cambridge MA, 1962 (Loeb). Dio Cassius discussed the trial in his lost Book 26. Dio F 87 also mentions the unrest resulting from it in Rome. Cf. Rawson, 1974: 200; Rives, 1995: 78, 84.
33. Likewise, Schultz, 2010: 19. Cichorius, 1922: 7–11, argues that Posidonius was Plutarch's source here. This may be true, but is not really relevant for our interpretation of the passage.
34. Eckstein, 2012: 215.
35. Nevertheless, a link is assumed by Cornell, 1981: 28; Eckstein, 2012; Beard, North & Price, 1998: 81. Flower, 2010: 169, sees fear of the

Cimbri and Teutones as the trigger behind both ritual killings in these years.

36. Clark, 2014: 185.
37. Flor. *Epit.* 1.39.4. Florus wrote in the first half of the second century CE. His only known work is an epitome of Livy's work.
38. Shultz, 2010: 17.
39. Plin. *Nat. Hist.* 28.3. Translation: *The Natural History of Pliny*, transl. J. Bostock & H.T. Riley, London, 1893.
40. Pliny's statement that this occurred in 'our own age' is a bit odd, as there is no indication that the ritual was repeated in the first century AD. It has been suggested that Pliny copied these words inadvertently from a source that was indeed contemporary to the event, but in view of the vagueness with which he refers to the victims of the killing, it does seem unlikely that he is copying from another source. It might be that he means 'in our own age' in a very broad sense.
41. Várhelyi, 2007: 281–83.
42. Várhelyi, 2007: 291. Cichorius, 1922: 19, observed that Greeks and Gauls would only make sense as enemies of the Etruscans.
43. Várhelyi, 2007: 291, points out that the first gladiatorial games in Rome were held at the Forum Boarium too, but so were many other ceremonies.
44. On *devotio*, cf. Versnel, 1976: 365–410; Beard, North & Price, 1998: 35. Shultz, 2010: 2 n.1; Dillon in this volume; Schultz, 2016: 70–71, points out that devotion was not seen in antiquity as a form of (human) sacrifice.
45. Livy 8.10.12.
46. Várhelyi, 2007: 292–93.
47. Beard, North & Price, 1998: 27.
48. Several authors from the Augustan period assume the Sibylline Books came from Cumae. For a Greek origin, see also Forsythe, 2005: 121 (cf. Orlin, 1997: 76–115; 2010); this is also accepted by Várhelyi, 2007: 295.
49. Beard, North & Price, 1998: 71. While there is debate on when the Sibylline Books were created, there is good reason to doubt a sixth-century origin. While Livy and Dionysius of Halicarnassus mention consultations of the Books in early Rome, it cannot be certain that these are authentic. Buitenwerf, 2003: 101, suggests that the reference to the Sibylline Books mainly had the purpose to strengthen the claim to authority.

50. Beard, North & Price, 1998: 81.
51. Gell. *Noct. Att.* 1.12.1; Dion. Hal. *Rom. Ant.* 1.76.3, 2.67.2.
52. See Wildfang, 2006, for a critical and succinct overview of the evidence for the ceremonies in which the Vestal Virgins engaged. On purification, see also Schultz, 2012.
53. On this matter, see in particular Gallia, 2015.
54. Beard, North & Price, 1998: 57.
55. Dion. Hal. *Rom. Ant.* 2.67.4. Translation: *The Roman Antiquities of Dionysius of Halicarnassus*, transl. E. Cary, London, 2015 (on the basis of the Loeb edition). Cf. Várhelyi, 2007: 289, 'in essence distorted, yet legitimate funerals'.
56. Plut. *Num.* 10.5.
57. Plut. *Num.* 10.6. Translation: *Plutarch's Lives*, transl. B. Perrin, Cambridge MA, 1914.
58. Plut. *Rom. Quest.* 96. Translation: *Plutarch's Moralia*, transl. F.C. Babbitt, Cambridge MA, 1962 (Loeb). Plutarch states that a ceremony also continued to be held at the site of the live burial of a Greek and a Gallic couple.
59. Dion. Hal. *Rom. Ant.* 3.67.3.
60. Livy 2.42.11.
61. Oros. 2.8.13; Eus. *Chron.* 2.101.
62. Dion. Hal. *Rom. Ant.* 9.40.1–3.
63. Livy 4.44.11–12; Plut. *Mor.* 89f.
64. Livy 8.15.7.
65. Oros. 3.9.5 adds that she was convicted after confessing to her crimes and that the location in which she was buried was subsequently called 'polluted'. See also Hier. *Ad Iov.* 1.41.
66. Livy *Per.* 14; Oros. 4.2.2.
67. Oros. 4.5.9.
68. Plin. *Nat. Hist.* 28.12; Val. Max. 8.1.5; August. *Civ.* 10.16. Cornell, 1981: 31 n.21, suggests Tuccia's condemnation was a mistake of the *epitomator*, but it is unclear how the *epitomator* could have mistaken the miraculous acquittal of Tuccia for a guilty verdict.
69. Similarly, Beard, North & Price, 1998: 9–10; Wildfang, 2006: 79.
70. Eckstein, 2012: 215–16.
71. Livy 22.57.2–3; Plut. *Fab.* 18.3. See above.
72. Livy 28.11.6.
73. Livy 28.11.7. Translation: *Hannibal's War. Books 21–30*, transl. J.C. Yardley, Oxford, 2006.

74. This is not unlike the rejection of certain events reported to the authorities as false prodigies in 169 BC: Livy 43.13.

75. Dion. Hal. *Rom. Ant.* 2.68.3–5; Val. Max. 1.1.7; Livy *Per.* 41; Obsequens 8.

76. Asconius *Commentary on Cicero Pro Milone* 32 (edition A.C. Clark, Oxford Classical Text, Oxford, 1907). The dates of the trial are given by Macrob. *Sat.* 1.10.5. The sources, Livy *Per.* 63; Plut. *Rom. Quest.* 83; Obsequens 37; Oros. 5.15.20–22, do not mention the political unrest and plebiscite, only the conviction and execution of the Vestals on the charge of *incestum*. Cf. Beard, North & Price, 1998, 137; Wildfang, 2006, 92–93; Gallia, 2015, 80–82.

77. Plut. *Rom. Quest.* 83.

78. In 73 BC, two Vestals were accused of *incestum*, but acquitted. See Wildfang, 2006: 96–97, for sources and historical context.

79. Livy 22.57.2–6.

80. Schultz, 2010: 18–19; 2012: 124–28; 2016: 68–70. I disagree with Parker, 2004: 575, who sees the ritual killing of Vestals as clear cases of human sacrifice.

81. Most priests in this period came from the leading families of Rome, who also provided the leading magistrates; Beard, North and Price, 1998: 103–04; Orlin, 2007: 60.

82. Rives, 1995; Schultz, 2010: 5–12; Gruen, 2011: 144–45, 157–58.

83. Scheid, 2007: 270: 'Roman sacrifice was, to ancient eyes, first and foremost, a banquet.' On the offering of inanimate edibles, see Schultz, 2016: 64.

84. Beard, North & Price, 1998: 81.

85. Schultz, 2010: 15: hermaphroditic children are always described as prodigies, never as sacrificial victims.

86. Livy 23.11.1–6.

87. Dionysius writes that he not simply describes processions as they were performed in his day, 'lest anyone should hold this to be weak evidence, according to that improbable assumption that after the Romans had conquered the whole Greek world they would gladly have scorned their own customs and adopted the better ones in their stead, I shall adduce my evidence from the time when they did not as yet possess the supremacy over Greece or dominion over any other country beyond the sea; and I shall cite Quintus Fabius as my authority, without requiring any further confirmation. For he is the most ancient of all the Roman historians and offers proof of what he asserts, not

only from the information of others, but also from his own knowledge.'
Dion. Hal. *Rom. Ant.* 7.71.1. Translation: *The Roman Antiquities of Dionysius of Halicarnassus*, transl. E. Cary, London, 2015 (on the basis of the Loeb edition).

88. Dion. Hal. *Rom. Ant.* 7.71.13. Translation: *The Roman Antiquities of Dionysius of Halicarnassus*, transl. E. Cary, London, 2015 (on the basis of the Loeb edition). Cf. Bernstein, 2007: 228–29.

89. Polyb. 3.112.9. Translation: *The Histories*, transl. W.R. Paton, Cambridge MA, 1922 (Loeb).

90. Polyb. 3.112.8. Translation: *The Histories*, transl. W.R. Paton, Cambridge MA, 1922 (Loeb).

91. Polyb. 6.56.

92. Likewise, Wildfang, 2006: 76, regarding Vestals in early Roman history. In general, see Feeney, 2007, in particular 139, 'larger thematic meaning is conveyed through narrative as in a novel'. Regarding prodigies in Roman historiography, especially Livy, see Rosenberger, 2007: 293–94.

93. Eckstein, 2012: 214.

94. Cf. Cornell, 1981: 28, who notes that there was no legal punishment for religious crimes.

95. Beard, North & Price, 1998: 37; Schultz, 2010: 15.

96. Likewise, Cornell, 1981: 31–32, who notes that Livy's terminology in 22.57 is, 'technically not exact'. Cf. Beard, North & Price, 1998: 19; Wildfang, 2006: 56. Schultz, 2012: 130–31 compares unchaste Vestals to hermaphrodites, as she sees both as contaminations of sexual categories.

97. Staples, 1998: 129.

98. Thus Orlin, 2007: 58.

99. Cic. *Font.* 46. Translation: *The Orations of Marcus Tullius Cicero*, transl. C.D. Yonge, London, 1856.

100. Wildfang, 2006: 16–17.

101. I disagree with the reading of the ritual by Parker, 2004: 584, that the sacrifice of the Vestal Virgin was the sacrifice of a scapegoat (p.575). For the same reason, I disagree with his statement that, 'The accused Vestal shared with other *prodigia* the essential feature of pollution.'

102. Thus also Beard, North & Price, 1998: 53: the unchastity of Vestals occasioned public prodigies that required measures of expiation.

103. Dion. Hal. *Rom. Ant.* 9.40.1–3.

212 Religion and Classical Warfare

104. Várhelyi, 2007: 289, 'The Vestal burials … appear as in essence distorted, yet legitimate, funerals.' Cf. Schultz, 2012: 123.
105. Cornell, 1981: 35–37, notes that the actions of other priests and magistrates also caused a breach in the *pax deorum* and that, hence, the *crimen incesti* is in itself insufficient to explain the live burial of the unchaste Vestal. In his view, the difference lies in the voluntary nature of the *crimen incesti*. However, in the case of priests and magistrates, it was their action that was *nefas*, not their person. As Cornell himself points out, in the case of unchaste Vestals, there was no expiation possible that allowed her to continue in her role.
106. Plut. *Num.* 10.5.
107. Staples, 1998: 137.
108. Serv. *Aen.* 11.206.
109. Parker, 2004: 586.
110. Takács, 2008: 88.
111. For a rejection of theories linking the Vestal Virgins to fertility, see Wildfang, 2006: 8–10. Instead, Wildfang explains the live burial of the Vestals by the position of Vesta as an earth goddess. Schultz, 2012: 133, compares it to the burial of defunct cult materials.
112. As a parallel, one may point to the widespread fear after the killing of Tiberius Gracchus, which required the Senate to consult the Sibylline Books, which ordered the magistrates to 'appease ancient Ceres' (Cic. *Verr.* 2.4.108). The *sanctitas* of a Vestal Virgin was not unlike the *sacrosanctitas* of a tribune of the plebs. Cf. Rawson, 1974: 195–96; Wildfang, 2006: 92; Gallia, 2015: 110.
113. Plut. *Rom. Quest.* 83. Translation: *Plutarch's Moralia*, transl. F.C. Babbitt, Cambridge MA, 1962 (Loeb). According to Staples, 1998: 137, the events of 114 and 113 BC show a determination to find all three Vestals guilty, which has to be explained by the general fear in Roman society. She writes, 'The ritual burial of the guilty Vestal, as described by Plutarch … would have been a powerful antidote to feelings of impending catastrophe.' That is not, however, what is to be read in Plutarch's narrative, who emphasizes the general fear and anxiety in Rome in response to the burial. Either the Senate's policy backfired terribly, or Staples' reading is wrong.
114. On *pax deum* as 'dramatic expression for a dramatic moment' in Livy, see Satterfield, 2016.
115. Livy 22.9.7–11. Cf. Satterfield, 2016: 173–74. On the *ver sacrum*, see for example de Cazanove, 2007: 47; Dillon in this volume. One may

also point to the similar decision to introduce games in Rome after the consultation of the Sibylline Books in 249 BC, after the disastrous expedition of M. Atilius Regulus and the loss of the entire Roman fleet in a storm.

116. Livy 42.2.3. Translation: *The History of Rome*, transl. William A. McDevitte, Berkeley, 1890.

117. Pliny *Letters* 4.11.7. Translation: *The Letters of the Younger Pliny*, transl. J.B. Firth, London, 1900.

118. Thus also Staples, 1998: 137.

119. Livy 2.42.9–11.

120. Dion. Hal. *Rom. Ant.* 8.89.3–5 Translation: *The Roman Antiquities of Dionysius of Halicarnassus*, transl. E. Cary, London, 2015 (on the basis of the Loeb edition). Cf. Levene, 1993: 158, on the differences between Livy's and Dionysius' accounts.

121. Cornell, 1981: 31, does note this link, which is missed in most publications on the Vestal Virgins; for example, Staples, 1998; Wildfang, 2006; Gallia, 2015.

Bibliography

Beard, M., 1980, 'The Sexual Status of Vestal Virgins', *JRS* 70: 12–27.

Beard, M., 1995, 'Re-reading (Vestal) Virginity', in Hawley, R. & Levick, B. (eds), *Women in Antiquity*, London: 166–77.

Beard, M., North, J. & Price, S., 1998, *Religions of Rome. Vol. 1. A History*, Cambridge.

Bernstein, F., 2007, 'Complex Rituals: Games and Processions in Republican Rome', in Rüpke, J. (ed.), *A Companion to Roman Religion*, Malden: 222–34.

Buitenwerf, R., 2003, *Book III of the Sibylline Oracles and its Social Setting*, Leiden.

Cichorius, C., 1922, *Römische Studien. Historisches, Epigrafisches, Literaturgeschichtliches aus vier Jahrzehnten Roms*, Leipzig.

Clark, J.H., 2014, *Triumph in Defeat. Military Loss and the Roman Republic*, Oxford.

Cornell, T., 1981, 'Some observations on the *crimen incesti*', *Publications de l'École française de Rome* 48.1: 27–37.

De Cazanove, O., 2007, 'Pre-Roman Italy, Before and Under the Romans', in Rüpke, J. (ed.), *A Companion to Roman Religion*, Malden: 43–57.

Eckstein, A.M., 1982, 'Human Sacrifice and Fear of Military Disaster in Republican Rome', *AJAH* 7: 69–96.

Eckstein, A.M., 2012, 'Polybius, the Gallic Crisis, and the Ebro Treaty', *CPh* 107: 206–29.

Erdkamp, P., 2009, 'Polybius, the Ebro Treaty, and the Gallic invasion of 225 BCE', *CPh* 104: 495–510.

Erdkamp, P., 'Polybius and the Gallic Crisis of 225 BC. A Response to Arthur Eckstein', forthcoming.

Feeney, D., 2007, 'Roman Historiography and Epic', in Rüpke, J. (ed.), *A Companion to Roman Religion*, Malden: 129–42.

Flower, H., 2010, *Roman Republics*, Princeton.

Forsythe, G., 2005, *A Critical History of Early Rome. From Prehistory to the First Punic War*, Berkeley.

Gallia, A.B., 2015, 'Vestal Virgins and their Families', *ClAnt* 34: 74–120.

Gruen, E., 2011, *Rethinking the Other in Antiquity*, Princeton.

Levene, D.S., 1993, *Religion in Livy*, Leiden.

Orlin, E., 1997, *Temples, Religion and Politics in the Roman Republic*, Leiden.

Orlin, E., 2007, 'Urban Religion in the Middle and Late Republic', in Rüpke, J. (ed.), *A Companion to Roman Religion*, Malden: 58–70.

Orlin, E., 2010, *Foreign Cults in Rome. Creating a Roman Empire*, Oxford.

Parker, H.N., 2004, 'Why were the Vestals Virgins? Or the Chastity of Women and the Safety of the Roman State', *AJPh* 125: 563–601.

Rawson, E., 1974, 'Religion and Politics in the Late Second Century BC at Rome', *Phoenix* 28: 193–212.

Rives, J., 1995, 'Human Sacrifice among Pagans and Christians', *JRS* 85: 65–85.

Rosenberger, V., 2007, 'Republican Nobiles. Controlling the Res Publica', in Rüpke, J. (ed.), *A Companion to Roman Religion*, Malden: 292–303.

Satterfield, S., 2016, 'Livy and the *Pax Deum*', *CPh* 111: 165–76.

Scheid, J., 2007, 'Sacrifices for Gods and Ancestors', in Rüpke, J. (ed.), *A Companion to Roman Religion*, Malden: 263–71.

Schultz, C.E., 2010, 'The Romans and Ritual Murder', *JAAR* 8: 1–26.

Schultz, C.E., 2012, 'On the Burial of Unchaste Vestal Virginis', in Bradley, M. & Stowe, K. (eds), *Rome, Pollution and Propriety. Dirt, Disease and Hygiene in the Eternal City from Antiquity to Modernity*, Cambridge: 122–35.

Schultz, C.E., 2016, 'Roman Sacrifice, Inside and Out', *JRS* 106: 58–76.

Staples, A., 1998, *From Good Goddess to Vestal Virgins. Sex and Category in Roman Religion*, New York.

Takács, S.A., 2008, *Vestal Virgins, Sibyls and Matrons. Women in Roman Religion*, Austin.

Várhelyi, Z., 2007, 'The Specters of Roman Imperialism. The Live Burials of Gauls and Greeks at Rome', *ClAnt* 26: 277–304.

Versnel, H.S., 1976, 'Two Types of Roman Devotio', *Mnemosyne* 29: 365–410.

Wildfang, R.L., 2006, *Rome's Vestal Virgins. A Study of Rome's Vestal Priestesses in the Late Republic and Early Empire*, London.

Chapter 8

With the Gods on their Side: Divination and Warfare in the Roman Republic

Kim Beerden

Although there is a considerable bibliography about divination in the Roman Republic[1] – including its interaction with politics – a systematic exploration of divination and its relation to warfare seems to be an underdeveloped topic in the literature.[2] The two fields of study rarely intersect: take for example current handbooks in the field of ancient warfare. These are mainly concerned with motives, tactics, equipment and so on.[3] Recent handbooks on religion that include discussions of divination mostly discuss the phenomenon in general or in terms of its political aspects, and not especially in a military context.[4] The roles of divination in Republican warfare are, then, mostly discussed in passing. There is no apparent reason why this should be the case. Indeed, its neglect is all the more striking for the reason that scholars of Greek warfare have convincingly argued that divination is certainly a very important topic when modern scholars wish to understand practices of warfare.[5]

Divination is a crucial phenomenon within the study of ancient religions – both Greek and Roman – because within the spectrum of religious practices, divination takes up a special position. Divination was perceived to be one of the few ways in which the supernatural directly communicated with humans. The supernatural was seen to provide information, and humans could use this to diminish the uncertainties that are always part and parcel of decision-making. The most important function of divination is its role in the process of decision-making – essentially a psychological process in which the person taking the decision aims to select the best of the available options. Divination can support a particular decision – signifying the support of the supernatural for this decision. It is easy to imagine how important the role of divination was in the context of warfare: support from the supernatural enabled the commander to legitimize his decisions, and this supernatural legitimization must have benefited the soldiers' morale.[6]

At the same time the supernatural could show that it did not agree with recent actions or plans. Religion, and divination specifically, defined the permissible and impermissible.[7] This is true for any area of daily life: divination was important for personal matters – think of decisions about marriage or where to live – but also for public matters. Political appointments, for example, needed to be validated by means of divination. But the sources also reveal that many divinatory signs pertain to issues related to warfare. As such, the study of Republican divination aids our understanding of the process of decision-making in warfare. This article, then, provides a much-needed exploration of divination and its relation to Republican warfare. This includes battles against 'foreign' enemies, as well as civil wars.

Questions that will be asked in what follows are: what kinds of divination were employed? Did generals attempt to manipulate signs, or their interpretation? How did soldiers respond to decisions that were validated by the supernatural? How did divination contribute to legitimization of commanders? What happened when divinatory signs were disregarded? And what effect does all of this have on the soldiers' morale?

Sources

The most important primary sources for divination and warfare in the Republic are Livy (first century BC–first century AD) and Julius Obsequens (thought to have lived in the fourth century AD). These two authors claim to report *prodigia*[8] from the supernatural. Livy introduces these in his narrative of the history of Rome, while Obsequens simply lists the signs that had been observed in particular years on the basis of Livy's work.[9] Apart from these two, an author such as Cicero (first century BC) has much to contribute to our investigation: in his work *De divinatione*, he provides ideas and arguments concerned with questions regarding how divination worked and could be used or misused.[10] Cicero's attitude toward the validity and truthfulness of divination has been much discussed. *De divinatione* is a dialogue in which the two speakers, Cicero and his brother, provide arguments *pro* and *contra* belief in divination and the validity of supernatural signs. But what did Cicero himself think of the matter? We cannot know. A thoughtful argument has, however, been made by M. Schofield – which has been accepted by such commentaries as that of D. Wardle – that Cicero was indeed inclined towards scepticism on the subject.[11] Although these works above (which are, it should be noted, to be dated to the Late Republic) are pivotal to any study of Republican divination, there are many more sources. The likes of Plutarch, Cassius Dio, Dionysius of Halicarnassus and Appian refer to Republican divination, but do not take it as their main theme and their works will be referred to where useful.[12]

Source criticism is key: the main concern when using these sources is that it should be kept in mind that the modern reader is always presented with a particular narrative of the use of divination in warfare. Ancient authors – from Livy to Cicero – have used divination as a rhetorical tool with which normativity may be expressed: for example, they may present a particular commander as 'good' or 'bad' because of his regard, or disregard, for supernatural signs – and therefore, for the supernatural itself. What we read in the sources, including the more historical ones, are normative attestations of the use of divination in the Republic. These norms are of great interest here because they show ideas about what divination was and how it should function.

A Definition of Divination[13]

Divination is part of the broader ancient religious spectrum, at times overlapping with such phenomena as prayer and sacrifice.[14] However, as mentioned above, divination is remarkable in the sense that while other religious phenomena are concerned with communication *towards* the supernatural, divination was believed to be coming *from* the supernatural. Divination revolves around the idea that the supernatural could provide signs – in many shapes and forms – which humans could then see, hear or even feel in the world around them.

An important distinction is the one between solicited and unsolicited signs. It was possible to ask for these signs at any time when a decision needed to be made. For example, when a commander needed to make a decision about a battle he could consult the birds, as Livy relates that Camillus did in 385 BC when the Volsci and their allies had to be fought:

'On the morning after he had made his camp, the dictator [Camillus] took the auspices, and coming forth from his tent offered up a victim and besought the favour of Heaven. He then with great cheerfulness presented himself before the soldiers, who were already arming by the first rays of light, as they had been warned to do when the signal for battle should be displayed. "Ours is the victory, soldiers," he exclaimed.'[15]

Another possibility was to travel to an oracle site, such as the one at Praeneste, around 35km east of Rome. This was a lot oracle, where the client would ask a question and a lot (*sors*) would be drawn: it seems that a child took a pre-written tablet or lot out of a box on which the answer to the question was written.[16] However, asking for signs was not always necessary: the supernatural was also thought to provide signs on its own accord. It could indicate its displeasure by sending lightning or by the birth of a hermaphrodite, as in 186 BC:

> 'At the same time, it was reported too from Umbria that a hermaphrodite about twelve years old had been discovered. In their fear and awe of this portent they ordered the prodigy to be removed from Roman soil and killed as soon as possible.'[17]

Humans then interpreted these perceived signs – solicited or not – and imbued them with meaning, resulting in information which they believed to be coming from the supernatural. In other words: 'Divination is the human action of production – by means of evocation or observation and recognition – and subsequent interpretation of signs attributed to the supernatural.'[18] It is important to note that the signs do not have meaning in themselves, but are given meaning by the person(s) interpreting them. Divination is, then, very much a culturally specific phenomenon.

Individuals could take up the interpretation of a sign themselves, but they could also make use of an expert: for example, the first-century BC commander Sulla saw a snake at his headquarters when he was waging war against the Samnites. His divinatory expert (in this case the *haruspex*) advised him to march against the Samnites right away. It was said that, as a result, Sulla was then victorious.[19] Experts professed to have authority on the subject either because they were part of a *collegium* entrusted with the task of interpretation of signs, claimed to have received inspiration from the supernatural, or possessed an authoritative text. Naturally, these options do not exclude one another.

Whether the sign was solicited or not, whichever way meaning was given to the sign and whoever provided this meaning, it always stands that interpretation is at the core of the divinatory process: the result of the interpretative process is perceived to provide information about past, present and future – it is therefore certainly not necessarily predictive. In public divination during the Republic, this information was most often related to the *pax deorum* – the idea that the supernatural and men existed in harmony – and support from the supernatural: was the supernatural pleased or displeased? Did it support the decision that was about to be made? This information could then be used in a process of decision-making.

Inspirational and Inductive; Public and Private

As indicated above, a sign from the supernatural could come in many shapes and forms: for example, in the shape of a bird flying by; the birth of a hermaphrodite; the entrails of an animal that had been sacrificed; or an inspired person making an oral statement, for example at an oracle site. In addition to the difference between solicited and unsolicited signs, the Romans distinguished between two categories: 'inspirational' signs and 'inductive' ones. Of the four examples provided above, only the latter is an inspirational sign: this category of signs is based on the idea that the gods would provide someone with inspiration (e.g., at an oracle or in a dream). Inductive divination, on the other hand, involved – according to the Romans – the kind of signs which required interpretation on the basis of learning. The bird flying by and the interpretation of the entrails are both examples of this kind of divination because the Romans argued that interpretation of these types of signs was based on skills and knowledge.[20]

It has often been stated that inspirational divination was not deemed as relevant or important to public matters (including warfare and battle). This is not to say that inspirational divination was not popular: on the contrary, it was probably very popular for private purposes.[21] Although the Republican sources pay little attention to these private divinatory practices, it is generally assumed that when people were ill, had worries or were unsure what to do, they would consult a lot oracle (*sortes*), consult an interpreter of dreams, go to an astrologer or use any other means of divination available to gain information with the aim to resolve their personal problem.[22] This could be a lot oracle such as the one at Praeneste that was mentioned above. It could also mean that an astrologer would be consulted, and although little is known about these practices, astrologers did work in Rome – among other reasons because they were sometimes expelled from the city.[23] Ennius, an author from the third–second century BC cited in Cicero, reveals a lively market place of various individuals claiming expertise who were working for private persons.[24] Still, the division into inductive and inspirational divination and their respective uses is not completely clear cut: there are also attestations of dreams and visits to oracles related to the public matter of warfare and battle – at least from the first century BC onwards. These, too, could be decisive in the decision-making process.

However, where public matters were concerned, inductive signs were held in higher esteem and were used for purposes of public divination. Public divination concerned itself with matters of the Republic – and warfare was certainly an important communal issue. The supernatural was seen as having an active role in the welfare of the state, and it could approve or disapprove plans. In the context of warfare and battle it can even be stated that: 'Divine support combined with the prowess of the soldiers [functioned] to increase the power of Rome. It was axiomatic that the gods should be involved and approve.'[25]

Traditionally, the inductive forms of divination that were used for public divination are categorized into three categories. The first is the observation of the flight and feeding of the birds: *auspicia* (*impetrativa* and *oblativa*, meaning that they could be both solicited and unsolicited, with the first held in lower esteem). Second is the interpretation of *prodigia*; these are signs such as lightning which were generally unsolicited. Third is the solicited practice of extispicy. During extispicy, the entrails of sacrificial animals were inspected for divine signs. Here interpretation of dreams and oracles will be discussed as the fourth (inspirational) category. The methods were, at times, used to complement one another, and those working with one method of divination do not appear to have had an unhealthy competition with the other groups. As far as is known, all methods were used from archaic times to the Late Republic: however, over time, changes in importance and perceived reliability certainly took place (and are discussed below).[26]

Methods of Divination: Auspicia, Prodigia, Extispicy, Dreams and Oracles

Auspicia

When *auspicia impetrativa* were solicited, the supernatural was asked to make known whether or not it favoured a particular undertaking. Birds within a specific zone were observed by a magistrate who was standing in a demarcated sacred area, the *templum*.[27] Varro, an author from the first century BC, provides us with an idea of the way this area was demarcated, by means of a ritual formula:

> 'Temples and wild lands be mine in this manner, up to where I have named them with my tongue in proper fashion. ... Between these points, temples and wild lands be mine for direction, for viewing, and for interpreting, and just as I have felt assured that I have mentioned them in proper fashion.'[28]

For the purposes of this chapter, it is also useful to know that when the army was camped, a special tent/*auguraculum* was set up for the purpose of ascertaining the divine will. When a commander set out with his army auspices were also taken, while when a commander crossed a river the auspices would need to be taken again in order to 'extend' the original auspices – these were called the *auspicia peremnia* (although these were no longer taken in Cicero's time).[29] Auspices were also normally taken before each battle, normally followed by a sacrifice and reading of the entrails.

Whereas in archaic times the flight of the birds was the focus of observation, by the Late Republic the behaviour of chickens while they were feeding was observed. How was this supposed to work? For the behaviour to be considered as a positive sign, it appears that hungry chickens, while feeding and eating enthusiastically, dropped their food.[30] The dropping of food and especially the sound this produced were considered positive signs,[31] and the supernatural was deemed to support the action that the magistrate was about to undertake on that particular day (both in peace and in war) or the post or rank that he was about to accept:[32] 'Tarentines, the keeper of the chickens reports that the signs are favourable; the sacrifice too has been exceedingly auspicious; as you see, the gods are with us at our going into action.'[33] The 'keeper of the chickens', called a *pullarius*, probably had a formal position in the army.[34] The obverse of a bronze *aes* ingot depicts the sacred chickens eating propitiously (Figure 8.1).

It is also important to mention the *augures*, who ensured procedures were performed correctly.[35] Apart from this they also observed *auspicia oblativa* – the unsolicited signs, especially in the sky – on their own accord. The *augures* were members of the elite who were united in their *collegium augurum*, which was, although all decisions were in the end made by the Senate, a powerful player in matters of public decision-making in the Republic.[36] A silver denarius minted by Sulla in 84–83 BC (Figure 8.2) depicts symbols of an augur on the reverse: the augur's staff (*lituus*) and

Figure 8.1: Cast copper alloy ingot (*aes signatum*). Obverse: the sacred chickens eating; 280–250 BC. Courtesy BM 1867,0212.4.

jug (*capis*). Sulla was not yet an augur when the coin was minted, but would become one a few years after.[37]

Prodigia and the Sibylline Books

Prodigia were unsolicited signs.[38] Occurrences that were 'out of the ordinary' (in a very broad sense of the word[39]) could be observed and reported by individuals, and were normally considered as a sign that the supernatural was displeased or, more generally, that the *pax deorum* was threatened. When an individual reported an occurrence as a sign, it was the Senate that decided whether or not to accept and recognize it as such. It remains unclear why one sign would be accepted, while another would not be: it seems the sign had to take place on Roman territory and that there needed to be a precedent.[40] The Senate could then consult the *collegia* of the *pontifices* or *decemviri sacris faciundis* – priests who were involved in the explanation and guarding of the Sibylline Books – or the Etruscan *haruspices* about the meaning of the sign and, more importantly, how it should be dealt with.[41]

Figure 8.2: Silver denarius. Obverse: diademed head of Venus right, with Cupid standing before her on left, holding a long palm (a symbol of victory). Reverse: two symbols of an augur, the *capis* (centre left) and *lituus*, between two weapon trophies. Minted by Sulla 84–83 BC in Asia during his campaign against Mithridates VI. Courtesy *CNG* 64, Lot: 795.

The three groups of priests involved in the interpretation of *prodigia* need some more explanation. The *decemviri* were an important *collegium* guarding the Sibylline Books that grew over time: from two members to ten, and then to fifteen and even sixteen by the time of the Late Republic. Still, they are normally referred to as *decemviri* (ten members) or *quindecimviri* (fifteen members). The Senate would ask the *decemviri* to consult the books when this seemed necessary or appropriate.[42] The *pontifices* were at first a group of three, but at the end of the Republic there were sixteen men appointed to this *collegium* at any one time, with the *pontifex maximus* as their leader. Their main function was to oversee all religious matters of the Republic, and the expiation of *prodigia* was one of them. As for the Etruscan *haruspices*, it is important to mention that they specialized in the interpretation of lightning and were united in an *ordo* which was held in high esteem (although there are certainly sources portraying these individuals as manipulative).[43]

Before any war was started, expiation of prodigies would have taken place to establish (or re-establish) the *pax deorum*.[44] If necessary, the *decemviri/ quindecimviri* would – on request of the Senate – consult the Sibylline Books, of which there were three. Its contents were thought to be the frenzied utterances of a Sibyl, brought to Rome by an old woman and bought by King Tarquin.[45] The *decemviri* guarded the Books and their content, making sure the original text was not changed and the text remained a secret (although some parts of the text were 'leaked'[46]). It was so important to have the 'original' text that, when the Books burned in 83 BC, an Empire-wide search was ordered to collect all available fragments – a difficult endeavour which was, according to Dionysius of Halicarnassus, not totally successful.[47]

When ordered to do so by the Senate, the *decemviri* selected the line or lines from the Book that they considered relevant for expiation of the *prodigium*.[48] The text the *decemviri* selected would, as far as is known, normally consist of instructions by which expiation could take place. This would usually be a ritual act: for example, a sacrifice would need to be made as in the fragment below. The contents of the Sibylline Books were guarded and therefore not disclosed to the public, and although we know the gist of the contents of the text we have very few extracts. One such rare extract was reported by Phlegon of Thralles in his second-century AD *Memorabilia*. He reports a publicized,[49] but very incomplete, extract from the second century BC in which a hermaphrodite is born; sacrifices to Demeter and Persephone should be made, among others:

'I declare that one day a woman will bear
A hermaphrodite having all the male parts
And all the parts that infant female women manifest
I shall no longer conceal but declare to you straightforwardly
Sacrifices to Demeter and holy Persephone.'[50]

The Sibylline Books could also be interpreted so as to prescribe new or out-of-the-ordinary rituals: on one occasion fear about impending war led to a consultation of the Sibylline Books because it was thought that the *pax deorum* was disturbed, and it was decided that human sacrifice would pacify the supernatural.[51] New gods were introduced on account of the Sibylline Books: the books instructed the Romans to import the Magna Mater from the East.[52]

Prodigia could occur anywhere within the sphere of Roman power, including in the army or among soldiers.[53] For example, Livy – and other sources based on Livy – mentions that many *prodigia* occurred during the Second Punic War in 217 BC. Among others, in Sicily the javelins of several soldiers had taken fire, and in Sardinia, as a horseman was making the round of the night-watch, the truncheon which he held in his hand caught fire. Many fires had flared up on the shore and two shields had sweated blood, while certain soldiers had been struck by lightning.[54]

When these signs were reported to the Senate and accepted as *prodigia*, the Senate ordered particular expiation rituals, mostly sacrifices, and also ordered the *decemviri* to consult the Sibylline Books. As a result, more expiations were ordered.[55]

The meaning of certain *prodigia* could also be related to warfare. Rosenberger discusses a number of *prodigia* announcing impending wars. Sounds of weapons, the spear of Mars moving on its own accord and non-domesticated animals coming into the city were seen as a sign of coming wars, especially bees and wolves.[56] The first two can, in our eyes, easily be connected to war. As for the animals, Rosenberger argues that the idea about bees (and other animals living in swarms) was that they could not live without their King. Wolves were connected to death.[57] Monstrous births were reported by Pliny in this context, and Cassius Dio provided *prodigia* signifying an uprising.[58] A comet in the western sky was seen during battles between Pompey and Caesar, and between Augustus and Antony in 43 BC – the comet was thought to mean civil war was at hand.[59] *Prodigia* announcing defeat may be identified as well, for example when lightning struck the *praetorium* (defensive constructions of the city) or Roman soldiers, or when it was raining stones or blood.[60]

Extispicy

Commanders employed a *haruspex* specialized in extispicy to join them during their campaign in times of war.[61] It is important to note that the *haruspices* active in the field of extispicy were not the same group as the Etruscan *haruspices* involved in the interpretation of *prodigia*. There were still other *haruspices* who were involved in private divination, but this third group does not seem to have enjoyed much prestige. So although the term *haruspex* was used for three groups of experts, the three groups had distinctly separate roles in the divinatory process.

Extispicy took place after sacrifice, when the *haruspices* interpreted the way the intestines (*exta*) looked – this happened on many occasions, among others before going into battle. The extispicy was normally preceded by the taking of the auspices. This example from Livy can be dated to 208 BC:[62]

> 'Some have related that the consul Marcellus offered a sacrifice that day, and that when the first victim was slain, the liver was found headless; that in the second everything usually found was present; that the head seemed even enlarged; also that the soothsayer had

not been at all pleased that, after organs defective and deformed, others had appeared which were more than promising.'[63]

There are two aspects worth commenting on in this example: the headless liver and the fact that the entrails of two animals were inspected. Regarding the liver, we do not know that much about the mechanics of extispicy, and what we know is normally deduced from papyri or uncertain interpretations of the bronze liver of Piacenza, an Etruscan divinatory 'liver model'.[64] From the example above it certainly becomes clear that if (part of) the entrails – in this case the liver – was missing, this was seen as a negative sign.[65] Also, the head of the second liver was enlarged – this was normally interpreted as a positive sign (but in this case the experts regarded it as negative).[66] As for the fact that a second animal was sacrificed when the signs from this first liver were negative, this was a perfectly normal practice.[67]

Dreams and Oracles

It has just been stated that 'inspirational divination', and this includes dreams and oracles, did not play such an important role in public matters. This still holds, but as has been mentioned, there was a first-century BC development where more commanders started to receive dreams, and in this way personal communication, from the supernatural.

Oracles were used as a way to 'double check' other signs. During the siege of Veii in 298 BC, the Romans heard about an old prophecy regarding the conditions which would lead to their victory. They double-checked the prophecy at Delphi and set out to fulfil the conditions.[68] Another example can be dated to 216 BC, when the oracle at Delphi was consulted by the Romans to ask what needed to be done to please the gods. The oracle answered that the Romans would win in battle if sacrifices would be made to Apollo.[69] An oracle could also be consulted in order to receive additional information from the supernatural when the situation was very grave: for example, in Livy the Roman consul was recalled from the war after terrible prodigies, in particular the unchastity of the Vestal Virgins.[70] It was unclear what should be done to appease the gods, and this led to the fact that both the Sibylline Books and the oracle at Delphi were consulted.[71] Pierre Bonnechere argues that such a 'second opinion' – a confirmation of another sign by means of an oracle – should not be seen as impious or distrustful towards the supernatural, but as a way for the individual to receive more certainty. It provided more authority to the decision.[72]

Diachronic Changes

It is hard to provide detail about diachronic changes because they are hard to discern: most sources are from the Late Republic.[73] Still, they certainly took place. In archaic and Early Republican Rome the auspices were taken when armies crossed rivers and just before battle was waged. This example – and it is interesting to note that first the auspices were taken, after which a sacrifice (and inspection of the entrails) took place – from 385 BC shows a favourable outcome:

> 'On the morning after he had made his camp, the dictator [Camillus] took the auspices, and coming forth from his tent offered up a victim and besought the favour of Heaven. He then with great cheerfulness presented himself before the soldiers, who were already arming by the first rays of light, as they had been warned to do when the signal for battle should be displayed. "Ours is the victory, soldiers," he exclaimed.'[74]

The frequency with which the auspices were taken seems to have diminished over time. That the *auspicia peremnia* were no longer taken in Cicero's times has already been mentioned above, but as Cicero argues, there is a general tendency: there is 'no taking of omens when crossing rivers, none when lights flash from the points of the javelins, none when men are called to arms'.[75] Rich argues the following – and he notes that this is a controversial, but in his opinion the best interpretation of the sources:[76] commanders had the auspices and extispicy at their disposal if they needed to make a military decision, including those on the battlefield. However, the auspices could only be taken by magistrates in charge of the army. Then a change occurred: from the Middle Republic onwards, often promagistrates were in charge of the army. This meant that the auspices were no longer taken in the field, as promagistrates could not do so. They could, however, perform extispicy, and therefore extispicy became the prime method that was used in a military context. According to Rich, then, the expanding role of the promagistrates in the context of warfare is the reason that auspices were not used on the battlefield in the Late Republic.[77] Instead, for practical reasons, extispicy was primarily relied upon.[78]

The frequency with which divination played a role in daily life seems to have increased in times of warfare. Many have noted that the frequency of the occurrence of *prodigia* (and consultation of the Sibylline Books) increased during the Second Punic War.[79] It has also been argued that there is a steep decline in *prodigia* after 133 BC – or at the latest 90 BC. This is striking: as the Late Republic is a time of unrest, this may have led us to expect another increase in divinatory practices. However, the likes of D. Engels and B. MacBain explain that with the rise of the strong politicians and commanders, allegiances shifted from the *res publica* to parties, individuals and one's class. In this argument, *prodigia* were less useful or necessary in the new political context.[80] Also, divinatory signs might have posed a threat if they were not according to politicians' or commanders' plans – and there may also have been increasing scepticism about the workings of divination. Or what if commanders or politicians manipulated the occurrence of signs or their interpretations?[81] Others argue that while the first century BC saw the decline established above, other divinatory methods (such as extispicy, but also the use of horoscopes, dreams and astronomy) grew in importance.[82] With these diachronic changes in mind, we may now turn to the various functions of divination in a discussion that will be largely synchronic.

Function: decision-making

The most important function of divination is its role in the process of decision-making. The signs thought to come from the supernatural, and their interpretation, could show supernatural support for this decision (or against it). It could reassure the leader of an army, it could legitimize him and boost the morale of the soldiers – or all at the same time. When a commander was reassured by divinatory signs, the outside world may have seen him as the legitimate leader of the army, and this in itself could be a way to increase morale among the solders. One divinatory sign may thus have several effects.

Reassurance

In the context of warfare these decisions took place on two levels: that of the Senate and that of the leader of the army. With the aid of divination, the Senate would decide whether or not war would be waged, and under whose command. Although the political decision-making process is not the main focus of this paper, one example can be provided. It relates to a battle in 191 BC that was fought against the Seleucids:

> 'All these sacrifices were favourable and good omens were obtained from the first victims, and the interpretation of the haruspices was this, that in this war the boundaries of the Roman people were being enlarged and that victory and a triumph were foreshadowed. When this had been reported, the Fathers, their minds freed of religious scruples, directed that the question be proposed to the assembly, whether they wished and ordered war to be entered with King Antiochus and those who had followed his path.'[83]

The commander was the one who would consult the supernatural on decisions concerned with any aspect of his campaign (including when battle should be waged). For example, when moving his army in 209 BC Fabius Maximus was warned by the auspices that he should not go in the direction of Metapontum (where Hannibal had laid an ambush).[84] A commander such as Sulla was provided with oracles that he would fight another battle in the region where he had fought his first, and would win again.[85] In a further example:

> 'The consul [Gnaeus Manlius Vulso, 189 BC] spent two days in exploring for himself the character of the mountain, that nothing might be unfamiliar to him; on the third day, after giving his attention to the auspices and then offering sacrifice, he divided his army into four columns and led them out, planning to lead two up the central part of the mountain and to send two from the sides to oppose the flanks of the Gauls.'[86]

In such cases, divination provided reassurance to those involved in the campaign or battle – this includes its commander, who could now believe that his decisions were supported by the supernatural.

Legitimization

According to the sources, commanders certainly used divination to enhance the image they projected of their person: in the eyes of their soldiers, their charisma would benefit when they received positive signs from the supernatural.[87] As P. Ripat argues, the worthiest members of society would receive divinatory signs, the interpretation of the most powerful man was the right one, and this meant that the best commanders were in communication with the supernatural – which provided him with knowledge.[88] Such personal legitimization may certainly be achieved by means of inductive divination: just before the Battle of Pharsalus in 48 BC, Caesar is reported to have seen a *prodigium* in the shape of a light above his camp, a torch rising from it and proceeding towards Pompey's camp.[89] To give another example, during the Second Punic War morale was low and after a defeat the commander Lucius Marcius made a speech. A flame shone from his head; the soldiers were emboldened by this and captured two Punic camps.[90]

In this part of the argument the dreams received by commanders were important: they were a powerful illustration of how commanders used divination to solidify their personal legitimacy, especially in the Late Republic.[91] According to the narrative, soldiers generally did not receive such dreams. Dreams thus stressed the contrast between commander and soldiers.

For example, one of the ways in which Sulla legitimized his march to the East was by means of a dream of the goddess Ma-Bellona that he received in 88 BC, at the time when he and Marius were in conflict about who should lead the Roman army against King Mithridates. Although Sulla received other dreams, this is his most famous one and even one of the most famous dreams known to us from the Republic. Our source is Plutarch, from the second century AD, but it is reasonably sure that it was publicized shortly after Sulla's death:[92]

> 'This goddess, as Sulla fancied, stood by his side and put into his hand a thunder-bolt, and naming his enemies one by one, bade him smite them with it; and they were all smitten, and fell, and vanished away. Encouraged by the vision, he told it to his colleague, and at break of day led on towards Rome.'[93]

Such dreams, whether they were 'real' or not,[94] were worth recording on coins decades later – signifying its enduring importance for the way Sulla wished to legitimize his power. This dream was depicted on coins and remained a well-know incident decades later (see Figure 8.3).

According to the narratives, dreams could foretell defeat: Cicero's *De divinatione* states that Hamilcar supposedly heard a voice in a dream, saying that he would be dining in Syracuse tonight.[95] That day, the

Figure 8.3: Silver denarius. Obverse: the goddess Venus. Reverse: Sulla's dream. Sulla (left) leans against a rock, sleeping, with a winged Nike (Victory) over him. The goddess Luna Lucifera (right) descends, holding a flaming torch in her right hand. Minted at Rome by the moneyer L. Aemilius Buca, January 44 BC. Courtesy *CNG* Triton XXI, Lot: 653.

Syracusans attacked his camp by surprise and carried off Hamilcar.[96] Roman commanders also had such dreams: Sulla, of course, but Pompey too was supposed to have seen an ambiguous image in a dream during one of the nights leading up to his defeat.[97] Even though the events were negative, the commanders were warned because of their personal connection to the supernatural. These narratives tie in to expectations of the supernatural as well as Roman commanders.[98]

Apart from announcement and warnings, the supernatural also conveyed its wishes to commanders by means of dreams. Decius Mus dreamt he would win fame by dying amongst the enemy – by sacrificing himself.[99] Again, even when the dreams foretold death or defeat, this still rendered the commander as special – at least as conveyed in the literary sources – because the supernatural communicated directly with the commander.

Claims to leadership could be enhanced even more when inductive and inspired divinatory methods were combined. See, for example, Scipio Africanus who reiterated the claim that his leadership was legitimized by the supernatural through signs of the birds as well as dreams (210 BC):

'Now the immortal gods, who are protectors of the Roman empire, who inspired all the centuries of the people to order that the command be bestowed upon me, by auguries, auspices and even visions in the night are likewise forecasting only joy and success.'[100]

In Livy, already briefly referred to above, two consuls dream that one of them should sacrifice himself in order for their army to be victorious; this dream is validated by means of extispicy.[101]

All in all, the idea that a commander had a particular god behind him, backing him in his endeavour, must have been very attractive to many as 'it helped to inspire confidence and loyalty and made the beneficiary seem personally auspicious'.[102]

Morale

Polybius attests the following about Scipio Africanus in an early example (209 BC) of a commander receiving a dream: 'finally he [Scipio] told them [his men] that it was Neptune who had first suggested this plan to him, appearing to him in his sleep ... [which] created great enthusiasm and ardour among the soldiers'.[103] Some of the examples provided above mentioned the effect positive signs had on the soldiers. The morale of the soldiers is a crucial aspect of all wars, including those of antiquity.[104] It has been argued that the psychological dimension to the study of morale, and its perceived subjectivity, has kept ancient historians from including morale in discussions of warfare.[105] However, it should certainly be included explicitly in this chapter.

The hazards of engaging in warfare are clear, and all kinds of personal and communal stress (e.g. heat, dust clouds, experience of violence and bloodshed, fear of the outcome or lack of faith in the commander or fellow-soldiers) could influence the outcome of a battle.[106] A.D. Lee considers a number of factors influencing morale: he argues that the important notion of honour, fear of punishment and of shame were crucial ideological factors in preventing desertion and cowardice. Furthermore, a unit of soldiers would be part of a group with its own identity, forming strong bonds of cohesion through time.[107] A. Goldsworthy argues that group dynamics were enhanced through training, rewards of service which encouraged a display of courage, and possibly through drink.[108] Their leader is another factor influencing morale, as devotion to his men and the strength of his leadership would stimulate the morale of his soldiers.[109] His perceived personal connection to the supernatural should be added to this list.

Religion is not explicitly taken into account in the study of morale by Lee, and receives little attention from Goldsworthy.[110] However, it is very important, as divination could work (among other factors) to alleviate fears of the masses (not only in warfare, but more generally). It may be argued that times of warfare are times of extreme uncertainty, and that people as well as soldiers are therefore more willing to perceive signs as coming from the supernatural.[111] It has, at the same time, been argued that the divinatory aspect to discipline should not be overestimated in comparison to all the other aspects above.[112] However, there are quite a few examples in which our authors consider divination to be important.

Turning to the sources, they make clear that divination could influence morale in a number of ways: Frontinus' *Strategemata*, dated to the end of the first century AD (so rather late for our purposes, although he discusses examples from the Republic), explicitly devotes a chapter to the idea that signs from the supernatural should either be interpreted positively by the commander, or otherwise he should be able to explain the occurrences as natural occurrences to his men.[113] An example of the former occurred during the Second Punic War in 204 BC:

> 'Scipio, having transported his army from Italy to Africa, stumbled as he was disembarking. When he saw the soldiers struck aghast at this, by his steadiness and loftiness of spirit he converted their cause of concern into one of encouragement, by saying: "Congratulate me, my men! I have hit Africa hard."'[114]

An example of the latter concerned the military tribune Gallus in 168 BC:

> 'Gaius Sulpicius Gallus not only announced an approaching eclipse of the moon [before the battle of Pydna], in order to prevent the soldiers from taking it as a prodigy, but also gave the reasons and causes of the eclipse.'[115]

Livy adds that this boosted morale of the soldiers. The Macedonians, on the other hand, panicked when the eclipse took place. Although Frontinus takes the commanders' perspective, both examples also indicate that soldiers were on the lookout for signs – they were in what has been called a state of 'omen-mindedness'.[116] As a consequence the commander needed to provide some kind of explanation, interpretation or expiation.[117]

Even more strikingly, Frontinus not only provides examples of how commanders could explain signs in a positive way, but also devotes a chapter to morale and how it can be improved. The commander should be using all kinds of psychological tricks and ways of pressuring his men into a courageous performance on the battlefield:

> 'Lucius Sulla, in order to make his soldiers readier for combat, pretended that the future was foretold him by the gods. His last act, before engaging in battle, was to pray, in the sight of his army, to a small image which he had taken from Delphi, entreating it to speed the promised recovery.'[118]

This example also shows that Frontinus suspected that Sulla used divination in order to boost morale, and did not necessarily believe that the future was foretold to him. Apart from this issue, the passage also demonstrates the way morale of the soldiers could be boosted by means of divination.[119] Perhaps the strongest example showing this is a speech made by the commander of the Roman army in Livy:

> 'When they have discharged their missiles without effect, and come thronging upon you where you stand, then let your blades flash out, and let every man of you bethink him that the gods are the Romans' helpers, that the gods have with positive omens sent him into battle.'[120]

Divination could stimulate (or deflate) morale. Even though they were not in a position to make independent decisions and their opinion generally did not influence the decision-making process of their commander, the soldiers did now know that things would turn out well: they knew the gods were on their side.

Deviant uses of Divination: Disregard?

A pious (and therefore 'good') commander would take the signs from the supernatural seriously. He would really take them into account, even if this meant that battle had to be postponed and this was inconvenient: 'The dictator [Appius Claudius, 362 BC] had been unable to give the battle-signal before noon, having failed for a long time to obtain favourable omens, for which reason the struggle had been protracted until night.'[121] Aemilius Paulus is another example of a pious commander: on the night before battle, an eclipse of the moon took place. Aemilius provided eleven heifers as a sacrifice to the moon. When he wanted to start a battle on the next day, he ordered for a sacrifice (and extispicy) to take place. It took twenty-one oxen to be sacrificed to Hercules – only from the twenty-first ox did Aemilius Paulus receive favourable outcomes and only then did he lead his army into battle.[122] However, according to the sources, there were many commanders who did not follow these shining examples and showed impiety in this way. They either disregarded the signs or did not even bother about obtaining them, or about doing so in the right manner.

Some commanders disregarded unfavourable signs if they did not support their plans. It was, however, thought that when signs were disregarded the supernatural would not be pleased, and the disregard could lead to defeat in battle. Very famously, according to Cicero, during the First Punic War Claudius Pulcher said of the chickens used for the *auspicia* which did not perform like they should that they could drink if they did not choose to eat – and proceeded to have them thrown into the sea. He attacked and then lost the battle.[123] There are more attestations of commanders disregarding such signs, mostly with dire consequences.

In 217 BC, when preparing for the Battle of Trasimene, Gaius Flaminius fell off his horse, and at the same time the standard-bearer had difficulties keeping the standard up. The officers were dismayed by these *prodigia*, but Flaminius disregarded the signs so proudly that the soldiers were actually encouraged. When he fell off his horse, he did not interpret this as a bad sign. When the auspices were negative, he disregarded them and he still continued into battle – and lost.[124] The consul Postumius offered sacrifice in 154 BC, but the head of the liver was missing in many victims. He set out despite this negative sign, but he had to return to Rome because of an illness only seven days later (and died soon after).[125] A final example comes from 126 BC:

'Some have related that the consul Marcellus offered a sacrifice that day, and that when the first victim was slain, the liver was found headless; that in the second everything usually found was present; that the head seemed even enlarged; also that the soothsayer had not been at all pleased that, after organs defective and deformed, others had appeared which were more than promising.'[126]

Even though the signs were negative, the army engaged in battle (and was defeated).[127] All in all, there are plenty of sources that suggest defeat or a bad end if negative signs were disregarded by the commander.

However, this idea should still be approached with caution. At times a victory might be won despite disregard for the signs. Cicero gives examples of commanders who disregarded the auspices and other signs, but still were victorious. He argues, as part of the wider argument of Book II of *De divinatione*, that common sense and experience are, in warfare, important as guidance.[128] However, it is then also argued that the auspices should be respected – and that commanders deserve punishment by the state if they do not – because the auspices are, after all, part of state religion and therefore part of official procedures.[129] An interesting case, in this sense, is that of the consul Flaminius: while he was already on campaign in the last quarter of the third century BC, the signs in Rome were negative and he was called back. However, he did not open the letter which ordered him back and won victories. When he, in the end, returned to Rome, the people were not pleased with him, as Plutarch relates.[130] Although, then, there are exceptional cases where a victory is achieved despite negative signs, these victories are not achieved in the 'right' way – whether it was against state religion or perhaps more emotional considerations.

There were commanders who did not follow the ritual procedures and signs which were not evoked when they should have. For example, it appears that the auspices were not taken, nor was extispicy practised, before the Gauls attacked Rome in 390 and gained a victory:

> 'There the tribunes of the soldiers, without having selected a place for a camp or fortified a position to which they might retreat, and, forgetting even the gods, to say nothing of men, without auspices or sacrificial omens, drew up their line with the wings extended to prevent being outflanked by the numbers of the enemy; yet could not stretch their front as wide as his, though they thinned it till the centre was weak and scarce held together.'[131]

The consequences of such disregard for the opinion of the supernatural seems clear: the defeat was crushing.

There was also the possibility of faulty procedures. If the commander knew what had happened but still continued to proceed, this did not bode well. For example, Livy relates an occasion in 176 BC where lots were cast. However, this did not occur in accordance with the auspices or in the right area; there was also a flaw in the auspices, of which the consul was aware, and soon afterwards he died in battle.[132] Cicero relates the second-century BC case where Tiberius Gracchus, when he was consul and organizing the election of his successors, made a procedural mistake without knowing it. When he remembered, after the new consuls had taken office, he immediately let the Senate know. The consuls stepped down because the procedures needed to be respected. All three men were considered particularly pious for taking the procedures this seriously.[133] Creative solutions, however, could also be found: in 293 BC the auspices were taken before a battle against the Samnites, but while they were in fact negative, the person responsible had told his commander Papirius Cursor that they were positive. Papirius heard of this deceit, but proceeded to lead his army into battle anyway, putting the deceitful man in the front line in case the gods wanted to vent their anger. The man was killed and Papirius was victorious.[134]

In all three cases the supernatural signs needed to be taken into account. It was necessary to do so because the supernatural needed to have its say in the decision. If the signs were not taken seriously, if the rituals were not followed or if the procedures had been faulty, a real problem seems to have appeared. The examples provided in the sources relate strong norms about what was considered pious behaviour – and impious behaviour was clearly punished. In the context of warfare, this normally meant defeat.

Deviant Uses of Divination: Manipulation?

The use and misuse of divination for political or military gain is an important subject in the sources. Sulla had oracles to support him, as we have discussed, and some have argued that the way Marius employed Martha, a prophetess from Syria, in the first century BC was to boost his claim to power and leadership.[135] However, these examples can be seen as ambiguous – it is not quite clear whether this is straightforward manipulation of divinatory signs. Other sources express, more or less explicitly, the idea that manipulation of divinatory signs and their interpretation took place: chickens could be starved before they had to eat, making them peck with more vigour. A report of a *prodigium* could be unreliable: in 55 BC, when the chances were that Cato would be elected to office, 'on a sudden Pompey lyingly declared that he heard thunder, and most shamefully dissolved the assembly, since it was customary to regard such things as inauspicious, and not to ratify anything after a sign from heaven had been given'.[136]

Sources such as these and the important role of divination in Roman decision-making (both in a general context but also in that of warfare) has led to a scholarly debate about the issue of possible manipulation of divinatory signs. If someone were able to manipulate the occurrence of supernatural signs or their interpretation, this would have been a powerful tool indeed. The debate is as follows: some argue that public divination in Republican Rome, over time, became a tool for the unbelieving elite to manipulate the gullible masses;[137] others are of the opinion that nobody – neither elite nor people – believed in divination anyway, and it was practised and accepted as such just because it had always been that way. In this way it simply alleviated fears, soothing the people. Some willingly deceived and others were willingly deceived – as long as the ritual requirements surrounding divinatory practices were respected, no questions were asked. The sources provide arguments for both opinions. Some members of the elite, Cicero being the most famous example, expressed doubts about the workings of divination, but still acknowledged its importance for Roman public religion.[138] Polybius, too, may be considered. He does not give much attention to divination (or religion more generally[139]) and mentions *prodigia* as incredible.[140] However, he argues that divination is used by Romans to calm their fears in times of war, implying that the people believed in it, or chose to do so.[141] In this last passage divination was, according to Polybius at least, used as a kind of 'opium for the people' in order to diminish hysterical tendencies in the masses.[142]

Seemingly, two intertwined issues were at stake. The first was concerned with belief: did the Romans – the people and the elite – believe in their gods, and therefore in divinatory practices? The second was whether the elite consciously used divination in order to take advantage of particular situations – and if so, for which purposes? Were the masses manipulated or soothed by means of divination?

Both issues will turn out to be a non-issue: the argument is that the elite did not believe in either the supernatural or in divination, and that they could and would therefore manipulate the signs. There are two aspects of this argument that need clarification. First, belief. It has been argued that the absence of ritual books – and other aspects of religion expected on the basis of Christian notions – shows that the Romans did not 'believe', but only 'practised' their religion.[143] However, the dichotomy between 'ritual' and 'belief' should not be drawn in this 'Christian' way. Furthermore, it is a *contradictio in terminis* to first argue that the Greeks (and I include the Romans here) performed their rituals, and then to claim they did this while thinking there was no recipient for, or aim to, their actions: '[One] would be hard put to show that the performers of ritual do not care about the results of their actions. One would rather expect the opposite.'[144] The question regarding belief, then, is incorrect.[145] Second, the therefore-aspect is problematic. It may as well be argued that because the elite believed in the supernatural and in divination, they could use it for their own purposes. The more one believes in something, the more smoothly and convincingly one can tweak it in a way that is suitable at a particular moment – whether consciously or subconsciously.[146] Whatever the answer to the question of belief (if one needs to be given at all), divination could always be manipulated. The first issue is, then, irrelevant.

As for the second issue: is it necessary to choose between the various purposes ('manipulation' or relief of 'stress';[147] 'genuine' or 'political'[148]) of divination? The concept of 'inconsistency' helps us here because it shows that the options need not be seen as mutually exclusive, but as inclusive. H.S. Versnel explains how ancient individuals can both believe and not believe at the same time; and that they may choose to ignore facts that are not convenient at a particular time, and not experience problems at all. They simply switch between different registers:

'[Adaptation is] part of the game. While one aspect [of a story] is dominant, others lose their relevance and become part of the background noise. It is all a matter of focus, of perception, of marked or unmarked positions. Evoking an undesired aspect at the wrong moment spoils the story and renders the message a mess: chaos. The good reader or perceiver applies the correct category.'[149]

Or in other words:

'Two visions do not even seem to be differentiated in terms of sharp boundaries or explicit intellectually satisfying reconciliations. In other words, the "logical" tension between the two different views does not seem to have been consistently experienced as tension.'[150]

As modern historians, 'it is our late-modern craving to remove the inconsistency as quickly and radically as possible'.[151] This is, however, beside the point when the aim is to understand divinatory practices because 'it is precisely the inconsistencies and contradictions in … beliefs which allow them to serve as a flexible means for the explanation of events'.[152] In short, choosing is unnecessary. If the aim is to gain a better understanding of the function of divination in the decision-making process, every source needs to be judged independently (especially taking into account that it portrays a particular narrative of divinatory practice) and it is likely that inconsistencies will be encountered, which do not need to be smoothed over.

Conclusion

The sources show divination as having functioned as a powerful tool in decision-making processes in the context of warfare. The different methods that have been discussed – *auspicia*, *prodigia*, extispicy, dreams and oracles – are different means to the same end: divination helped to establish the boundaries of what is and is not permissible,[153] and who and what is legitimate. It has also been shown how divination boosted morale. All three aspects make divination, especially in times of the uncertainty of ancient warfare, an influential instrument. The narratives show that reassurance about the validity of decisions was needed. Morale was boosted and the commander legitimized. Because of its great influence in these important matters, motivations ('genuine' or 'political') or aims ('stress reduction' or 'manipulation') behind the use of divination may all have had their place – whether they only existed in the divinatory narrative or also in reality. There is no need to choose between the different motivations or aims: this is even counterproductive as it would constrain and limit our understanding of divination as used in the decision-making process. Divination has been shown to be of crucial importance to both the minds and physical realities of those engaging in ancient warfare. The Roman army and its commander needed to engage in battle with the gods on their side.

Notes

1. The most notable contributions from recent years are: Rosenberger, 1997; Rüpke, 2005; Orlin, 1997; Rasmussen, 2003; Santangelo, 2013; Engels, 2007 (*RVW*). *RVW* will be extensively used in what follows: it incorporates the sources and current literature regarding divinatory occurrences.
2. For exceptions, see Rüpke 1990; Rosenberger, 1997.
3. Rich, 2013: 543–68, is an exception. Still, not more than two pages of this article on religion are devoted to divination. The same is true of Dawson, 1996: 115. In Stoll, 2007: 451–76, religion (let alone

divination) does not receive much attention at all; the same applies to the recent Sabin, van Wees & Whitby, 2007.

4. Rosenberger, 2007: 292–303, discusses war very briefly on 302. Beard, North & Price, 1998: 324–28, devote some pages to a discussion of religion of the Army, but only briefly touch upon divination; Scheid, 2003, mentions Republican divination in relation to warfare in passing on pp.113–14; Rives, 2004: 558–61, provides one source related to war; as does Gordon, 2004: 387–90. The various authors of the chapter 'Divination Romaine' *ThesCRA* 2005: 79–89, do not explicitly discuss divination in the context of warfare either.

5. Pritchett, 1979, is still the standard work on religion and war in ancient Greece, showing that much is to be gained by studying the two in combination. For his discussions of divination and war in the Greek world see 47–153, 296–323. See more recently the chapter on the Greek *mantis* in war in Flower, 2008: 153–87; or the chapter on Greek sacrifice before and during battles, incorporating much information about divination as well: Jameson, 1993: 197–227. For divination in Greek warfare, see Nevin, 2019, vol. 1 in this series.

6. This dual function combines the 'stress' hypotheses and the 'manipulation' – which are certainly not mutually exclusive – as referred to in Rasmussen, 2003: 25. Both hypotheses will be introduced in more detail below.

7. Parker, 2016: 130.

8. A particular kind of divinatory sign (see below, 'Three methods of inductive divination').

9. See MacBain, 1982: 8–19, on reliability of Obsequens and Livy. The *prodigia* reports are seen as relatively historical, especially when compared to sources regarding *exta* and *auspicia*: Rasmussen, 2003: 16–24; and especially for source criticism (also for the other authors dealing with Republican divination): Engels, 2007: 93–258.

10. Note that the work is, in the first place, a philosophical treatise which we should treat carefully when looking for historical information. For commentaries, see Pease, 1920–23; Wardle, 2006; Schultz, 2015.

11. But it should be clear that we do not know what Cicero actually believed or thought: Schofield, 1986: 47–65; Wardle, 2006: 10–14. For other ideas on the matter of scepticism, see Beard, 1986: *passim*.

12. See for brief source criticism concerned with these authors: Rasmussen, 2003: 23–24.

13. This paragraph is based on the following pages of my book, which can also be consulted for a more extensive definition: Beerden, 2013: 19–42.

14. Beerden, 2013: 32–34. Pliny *Nat. Hist.* 28.10–11; Livy 30.25.12, 42.20.4–6.

15. Livy 6.12.7–8. Trans.: Foster, 1924: 235.

16. Cf. Champeaux, 1982–87; Santangelo, 2013: 73–80.

17. Livy 39.22.5. Trans.: Sage, 1936: 283; whether they were really killed has been questioned by Rosenberger, 1997: 132 n.15.

18. Beerden, 2013: 20.

19. Cic. *Div.* 1.72. Cf. Val. Max. 1.6.4; on the *haruspex*, see Haack, 2006: no. 75.

20. Cic. *Div.* 1.132.

21. North 1990: 56–61.

22. North 1990: 56–61.

23. Barton, 1994: 31–37. Only from Augustus onwards was astrology used for public purposes: Santangelo, 2013: 246–58.

24. Cic. *Div.* 1.132. Cf. Wardle, 2006: 420–25.

25. Beard & Crawford, 1985: 31.

26. E.g., that auspices became less important: Cic. *Div.* 1.28–29.

27. The practice of taking the auspices was already established in the time of Tarquinius Superbus, last king of Rome: Livy 1.36.6 (*RVW* 36).

28. Varro *Ling. Lat.* 7.8. Trans.: Kent, 1938: 275.

29. Rüpke, 1990: 147; Cic. *Nat. Deor.* 2.3.9; Cic. *Div.* 2.36.

30. Cic. *Div.* 1.27

31. See the explanation in Wardle, 2006: 174–75, commenting on Cic. *Div.* 1.27.

32. North, 1990: 53–54.

33. Livy 9.14.4 (320 BC). Trans.: Foster, 1926: 213.

34. Wheeler, 2008: *passim*. Figure 7.1: Crawford *RRC* 12.1. There is a similar example in the British Museum: 1867,0212.4.

35. The procedures themselves are unclear, but see the authoritative article by Linderski, 1986.

36. Cf. Cic. *Leg.* 2.2.1.

37. See for more detail on the coin, Fears, 1975: 29–37

38. See for related and subcategories, Engels, 2007: 259–82.

39. For our purposes, the discussion about whether these occurrences are physically possible and whether there are then 'false' and 'true' signs is not relevant. Cf. Rasmussen, 2003: 37–41.

40. Rasmussen, 2003: 53–116, on developments regarding the acceptance of particular signs.
41. Orlin, 1997: 76–115, is the best short introduction to the Sibylline Books.
42. There is much literature on the subject, see for more information the references given in North, 2012.
43. MacBain, 1982: 43–59. Here one may also find a discussion about their number and about the year they were officially introduced in Rome – MacBain argues 278 BC. On Etruscan roots of Roman extispicy, cf. Rasmussen, 2003: 117–48, esp. 135–40.
44. Livy 42.2.3–7 (*RVW* 182). Cf. Livy 42.20 (*RVW* 183/184).
45. Dion. Hal. *Rom. Ant.* 4.62.1–3.
46. Satterfield, 2011: 117–18.
47. Dion. Hal. *Rom. Ant.* 4.62.6
48. Dion. Hal. *Rom. Ant.* 4.62.4–5; Cic. *Div.* 2.110 (*RVW* 340). For a clear introduction to the origins of, and procedures concerning, the Books see Orlin, 1997: 76–85.
49. See Satterfield, 2011, for an historical explanation about why exactly this part of the Books was made public.
50. As in Phlegon *Mir.* 10.3–7. Trans.: Hansen, 1996: 40. The text is very problematic, as is the translation. An edition can be found in Diels, 111–24.
51. Plut. *Marc.* 3.5–7 (*RVW* 90).
52. Livy 29.10.4–6 (*RVW* 132). See also Fontenrose, 1978: Q237 for ensuing involvement of the Delphic oracle.
53. The geographical spread of where *prodigia* occurred (and what that may have been *ager romanus*, which is the geographical area under the influence of Rome) and what this means for our knowledge of the spread of Roman influence in Italy has been extensively discussed in the literature, first by Mommsen: see for a recent overview Rasmussen, 2003: 219–40.
54. Livy 22.1.8 (cf. *RVW* 101).
55. Livy 22.1.14–20 (cf. *RVW* 101).
56. Rosenberger, 1997: 97–101, refers to the spear of Mars in Obs. 6 (*RVW* 169); 36 (*RVW* 236); 44 (*RVW* 250/253); 47 (*RVW* 258); 50 (*RVW* 261). Bees, wasps and so on in Livy 35.9.4 (*RVW* 152); wolves in Livy 3.29.9 and many more occasions.
57. Rosenberger, 1998: 98–99.
58. Plin. *Nat. Hist.* 7.34–35 (*RVW* 267); Dio 42.26 (*RVW* 331).

59. Plin. *Nat. Hist.* 92 (cf. *RVW* 280, 327.3); a foaling mule or plague may also indicate civil strife, cf. Obsequens 29 (*RVW* 227); 65 (*RVW* 322).

60. Rosenberger, 1997: 97–101.

61. To give examples: Herennius Siculus was part of G. Gracchus' entourage (Haack, 2006: no. 37); Spurinna was Caesar's *haruspex* (Haack, 2006: no. 88). Cf. on Caesar and his *haruspices*: Santangelo, 2013: 107–14.

62. This is a very brief and standard overview of the different signs and their interpreters, in this case drawn from Gordon, 2004: 387–90. For more extensive literature on the groups of experts, see North, 1990: 51–71.

63. Livy 27.26.13–14 (cf. *RVW* 126 for context). Trans.: Gardner Moore, 1940: 319.

64. Rasmussen, 2003: 126–48.

65. Cic. *Div.* 2.36.

66. See Engels, 2007: 469 (*RVW* 126); Rasmussen, 2003: 121–22.

67. Although Cicero argues against it in Cic. *Div.* 2.36–39. However, this only confirms the existence of such practices.

68. Plut. *Cam.* 4. Cf. Val. Max. 1.6.3; Dion. Hal. *Rom. Ant.* 12.13–18; Cic. *Div.* 1.100; 2.69; Livy 5.15.2, 5.51.6 (*RVW* 52); cf. Livy 5.21.8–9; Plut. *Cam.* 5.4–6 (*RVW* 53). See also Fontenrose, 1978: Q202.

69. Livy 23.11.1–3.

70. Livy 22.57.1–6 (*RVW* 107).

71. Cf. the time before the Battle of Cannae: Livy 23.11.1–6 (*RVW* 107.2).

72. Bonnechere, 2010: 133.

73. Beard & Crawford, 1985: 36–39, see more interaction between politics and religion in the Late Republic; diversification of cults resulting in religious choices for the individual; and the development of intellectualism on the topic of traditional religion. The first development is most important here.

74. Livy 6.12.7–8 (*RVW* 59). Trans.: Foster, 1924: 235.

75. Cic. *Nat. Deor.* 2.9. Trans.: Rackham, 1933: 131.

76. Cic. *Div.* 2.76, *Nat. Deor.* 2.9.

77. Rich, 2013: 547–48.

78. Cic. *Div.* 1.28.

79. Engels, 2007: 763–68, refers to scholars such as Bloch, Wülker, Latte, Gladigow and Cousin. See his treatment of this issue for many more references. See, however, for a more nuanced view Orlin, 1997: 85–86.

80. MacBain, 1982: 80–82. Consider also Rüpke, 1990: 148–50.

81. Engels, 2007: 778–79, 797.
82. Engels, 2007: 785; Rüpke, 1995: 577–78; cf. Rosenberger, 1997: 205–33.
83. Livy 36.1.3–5. Trans.: Sage, 1935: 155.
84. Livy 27.16.15–16 (*RVW* 123).
85. Plut. *Sull.* 17.1–2.
86. Livy 38.26.1–2. Trans.: Sage, 1936: 89.
87. Phang, 2008: 89.
88. Ripat, 2006: 166.
89. Plut. *Pomp.* 68.2 (*RVW* 327.4).
90. Val. Max. 1.6.2 (*RVW* 117).
91. Engels, 2007: 765, discerns a development from the importance of public to private divination in a military context because of an increase in dream divination (and perhaps the claim to a more personal relationship with the god). It is true that many – but not all – examples are from the Late Republic. See also Kragelund, 2007: *passim*.
92. Flower, 2013: 297–98.
93. Plut. *Sull.* 9 (*RVW* 272).
94. This question of source criticism remains a key issue (for all divinatory methods).
95. Cic. *Div.* 1.50.
96. And cf. Hannibal's dream just before the Second Punic War in Cic. *Div.* 1.49; Livy 21.22.6–9; Val Max. 1.7 ext.1 (RVW 96); and his dream in 205: Cic. *Div.* 1.48 (*RVW* 133).
97. Plut. *Pomp.* 68.2 (*RVW* 327.3).
98. I do not consider ambiguity to have played a very large role in actual divinatory practices – although it is very important as a rhetorical device in the sources: Naerebout & Beerden, 2012.
99. Cic. *Div.* 1.51: (*RVW* 66; Cf., among others, Flor. 1.14.2).
100. Livy 26.41.18 (*RVW* 121). Trans.: Gardner Moore, 1943: 163.
101. Livy 8.6.11 (*RVW* 66).
102. Wardman, 1982: 29.
103. Polyb. 10.11.7–8 (cf. *RVW* 124). Trans.: Paton, Walbank & Habicht, 2011: 143. Walbank adds in his commentary (Walbank, 1957: 213) that these passages do not give any reason to believe that Polybius believed in these dreams himself.
104. As has been argued by, among others, Goldsworthy, 1996: 249.
105. Lee, 1996: 199.
106. Lee, 1996: 200–02.
107. Cf. especially MacMullen, 1984: 440–56.

108. Goldsworthy, 1996: 250–64.

109. Lee, 1996: 203–12.

110. Goldsworthy, 1996: 250.

111. Livy 21.62.11 (*RVW* 97). Cf. the remarks above about the increase of *prodigia* during the Punic Wars, note 68 above. This thought can of course be found in other sources as well – most notably, Thucydides, e.g. 2.21.3, but also 2.54. Apart from lawlessness and carelessness towards the supernatural as a result of the plague, in this last passage Thucydides describes citizens clinging to possible interpretations of the oracle.

112. Phang, 2008: 89–92.

113. Front. *Strat.* 1.12.1–12.

114. Front. *Strat.* 1.12.1. Trans.: Bennett & McAlwain, 1925: 81 (*RVW* 135). Cf. Livy 22.3.9–14.

115. Front. *Strat.* 1.12.8. Trans.: Bennett & McAlwain, 1925: 83 (*RVW* 189). Cf. Livy 44.37.5–9 (*RVW* 189). Cf. Polyb. 29.16; Plut. *Aem.* 16.

116. Term by Freedman, 1998: 1

117. Eclipses of the moon, but of the sun too, were seen as very disturbing signs from the supernatural. See in 413 BC, e.g., Plut. *Nic.* 23.1, 23.4. Also, Ross, 2016: 99–120, discusses eclipses in the ancient Near East and Greece in the context of warfare.

118. Frontin. *Str.* 1.11.11 (*RVW* 281).

119. Frontin. *Str.* 1.11.11 (*RVW* 281). Cf. Val. Max. 1.2.3; Plut. *Sull.* 29.6–7. See for another example, Polyb. 10.11.7–8. Cf. on Scipio and auspices App. *Bell. Hisp.* 26 (*RVW* 128). Marius uses divination in a similar way, Front. *Strat.* 1.11.12 (*RVW* 251). Cf. Val. Max. 1.2.4; Plut. *Mar.* 17.1–3.

120. Livy 6.12.9–10. Trans.: Foster, 1924: 237 (*RVW* 59), slightly adapted.

121. Livy 7.9.5–6; Cf. Livy 32.9.1–5 (*RVW* 144), where an army is detained in Rome due to divinatory outcomes.

122. Plut. *Aem.* 17.7 (*RVW* 189).

123. Cic. *Nat. Deor.* 2.7; Cic. *Div.* 1.29, see also Wardle, 2006: 179. Cf. Livy *Per.* 19 (*RVW* 85).

124. Livy 22.3.9–14. Also on Flaminius, see Cic. *Div.* 1.77 (and Cic. *Nat. Deor.* 2.8; Val. Max. 1.6.6 [*RVW* 102]). A variation on this theme is Marcellus' horse turning wild during the battle in Plut. *Marc.* 6.5–6 (*RVW* 93).

125. Obsequens 17. Other examples: Mancinus: Liv. *Per.* 55; Obsequens 24. Cic. *Div.* 1.29 (*RVW* 314): Marcus Crassus was killed in the Parthian

War when he disregarded the divinatory signs. Other commanders lost their fleet; Cic. *Nat. Deor.* 2.7–8: Junius also lost his fleet; Val. Max. 5.1. ext. 4; Val. Max. 1.6.9; Dion. Hal. *Ant. Rom.* 16.1.1–4 (*RVW* 69); Obsequens 28.

126. Livy 27.26.13–14 (*RVW* 126). Trans.: Gardner Moore, 1943: 319. Cf. Plut. *Marc.* 29.4–5.

127. Another such example, this time with Crassus as commander, in: Plut. *Crass.* 19.4–8; 19.18–23 (*RVW* 318).

128. Cic. *Div.* 2.52 (*RVW* 332).

129. Cic. *Div.* 2.71 (*RVW* 85).

130. E.g. in Plut. *Marc.* 4.1–4.

131. Livy 5.38.1-2. Trans.: Foster, 1924: 129.

132. Livy 41.18.7–16 (*RVW* 177).

133. Cic. *Nat. Deor.* 2.10–12. Cf. Cic. *Div.* 1.33.

134. Val. Max. 7.2.5; Livy 10.40.4 (*RVW* 75).

135. Orlin, 2000: 197–99; Santangelo, 2013: 170.

136. Plut. *Cat.* 42.1.4–5. Trans.: Perrin, 1919: 337.

137. Cf. for a number of examples of those arguing for the decline of religion: Rasmussen, 2003: 31–32. On the 'cynical' and 'hysterical' dichotomy see MacBain, 1982: 7; Rasmussen, 2003, refers to the 'manipulation hypothesis' and 'stress hypothesis' and adds Rosenberger's 'liminal approach' which she finds convincing: 25–34.

138. Although *de divinatione* is first and foremost a philosophical treatise, written when he was retired from politics: Wardle, 2006: 27–28.

139. Although he praises the religious practices of the Romans in 6.56.7. Cf. e.g., Vaahtera, 2000: 251–64; Walbank, 1957: 11–12; Walbank, 1994: 28–42.

140. Polyb. 7.7.1, 12.24.5.

141. Polyb. 3.112.8–9. Walbank, 1957: 443, considers Polybius' reaction to Roman use of divination 'slightly contemptuous' and refers to 4.56.6–12 where Polybius reveals admiration for 'a statesmanship which [he believed] exploited and encourages such superstition for reasons of state'.

142. See the footnote above. This dual function combines the 'stress' hypotheses and the 'manipulation' – which are certainly not mutually exclusive.

143. Naerebout, 1997: 329–32; Versnel, 2011: 539–59.

144. Naerebout, 1997: 336.

145. Naerebout, 1997: 329–32; Versnel, 2011: 539–59.

146. F.G. Naerebout, lecture series 'Geloof aan de goden', Leiden University, 2015–16.
147. Rasmussen, 2003: 25
148. Versnel, 2011: 5, for a brief (historiographical) discussion of these terms in relation to belief.
149. Versnel, 2011: 7; citation: 148.
150. Versnel, 2011: 7.
151. Versnel, 2011: 86.
152. Harrison, 1997: 112.
153. Parker, 2016: 130.

Bibliography

Barton, T.S., 1994, *Ancient Astrology*, London.
Beard, M., 1986, 'Cicero and Divination: the Formation of a Latin Discourse', *JRS* 76: 33–46.
Beard, M. & Crawford, M., 1985, *Rome in the Late Republic*, London.
Beard, M., North, J. & Price, S., 1998 (eds), *Religions of Rome Volume I: a History*, Cambridge.
Beerden, K., 2013, *Worlds Full of Signs: Ancient Greek Divination in Context*, Leiden.
Bennett, C.E. & McElwain, M.B., 1925, *Frontinus. Stratagems. Aqueducts of Rome*, Cambridge MA.
Bonnechere, P., 2010, 'Oracles and Greek Mentalities: the Mantic Confirmations of Mantic Revelations', in Dijkstra, J., Kroesen, J. & Kuiper, Y. (eds), *Myths, Martyrs, and Modernity*, Leiden: 115–33.
Champeaux, J., 1982–87, *Fortuna: recherches sur le culte de la Fortune à Rome et dans le monde romain des origines à la mort de César* 2 vols, Rome.
Dawson, D., 2006, *The Origins of Western Warfare: Militarism and Morality in the Ancient World*, Oxford.
Engels, D., 2007, *Das römische Vorzeichenwesen (753–27 v. Chr.): Quellen, Terminologie, Kommentar, historische Entwicklung*, Stuttgart.
Fears, J.R., 1975, 'Sulla Or Endymion: A Reconsideration of a Denarius of L. Aemilius Buca', *American Numismatic Society Museum Notes* 20: 29–37.
Flower, H.I., 2013, 'Sulla's Memoirs as an Account of Individual Religious Experience', *Religion in the Roman Empire* 1: 297–320.
Flower, M.A., 2008, *The Seer in Ancient Greece*, Berkeley.
Fontenrose, J., 1978, *The Delphic Oracle. Its Responses and Operations, with a Catalogue of Responses*, Berkeley.

Foster, B.O., 1924, *Livy. History of Rome, Volume III: Books 5–7,* Cambridge MA.

Foster, B.O., 1926, *Livy. History of Rome, Volume IV: Books 8–10,* Cambridge MA.

Freedman, S.M., 1998–2006, *If a City is Set on a Height: The Akkadian Omen Series Šumma alu ina mēlê šakin* vol. 1, Philadelphia.

Gardner Moore, F., 1940, *Livy. History of Rome, Volume VI: Books 23–25,* Cambridge MA.

Gardner Moore, F., 1943, *Livy. History of Rome, Volume VII: Books 26–27,* Cambridge MA.Goldsworthy, A.K., 1996, *The Roman Army at War 100 BC–AD 200,* Oxford.

Gordon, R., 2004, 'Divination and Prophecy: Rome', in Johnston, S.I. (ed.), *Religions of the Ancient World: a Guide,* Cambridge MA: 387–90.

Haack, M.-L., 2006, *Prosopographie des haruspices romains,* Pisa.

Hansen, W., 1996, *Phlegon of Tralles' Book of Marvels,* Exeter.

Harrison, T., 1997, 'Herodotus and the Certainty of Divine Retribution', in Lloyd, A.B. (ed.), *What is a God? Studies in the Nature of Greek Divinity,* London: 101–22.

Jameson, M.H., 1993, 'Sacrifice before Battle', in Hanson, V.D. (ed.), *Hoplites: the Classical Greek Battle Experience,* London: 197–227.

Kent, R.G., 1938, *Varro. On the Latin Language, Volume I: Books 5–7,* Cambridge MA.

Kragelund, P., 2001, 'Dreams, Religion and Politics in Republican Rome', *Historia* 50: 53–59.

Lee, A.D., 1996, 'Morale and the Roman Experience of Battle', in Lloyd, A.B. (ed.), *Battle in Antiquity,* London: 199–218.

Linderski, J., 1986, 'The Augural Law', *Aufstieg und Niedergang der römischen Welt* II 16.3, Berlin/New York.

Linderski, J., 1995, 'Cicero and Roman Divination', *id., Roman Questions: Selected Papers,* Stuttgart: 458–84.

MacBain, B., 1982, *Prodigy and Expiation: a Study in Religion and Politics in Republican Rome,* Brussels.

MacMullen, R., 1984, 'The Legion as a Society', *Historia* 33: 440–56.

Naerebout, F.G., 1997, *Attractive Performances. Ancient Greek Dance: Three Preliminary Studies,* Amsterdam.

Naerebout, F.G. & Beerden, K., 2012, '"Gods Cannot Tell Lies": Riddling and Ancient Greek Divination', in Kwapisz, J., Petrain, D. & Szymanski, M. (eds), *The Muse at Play. Riddles and Wordplay in Greek and Latin Poetry,* Berlin: 121–47.

Nevin, S., 2019, 'Omens, Oracles, and Portents: Divine Guidance in Warfare', in Dillon, M.P.J., Matthew, C. & Schmitz, M. (eds), *Religion in Classical Warfare. Volume i: Ancient Greece*, Barnsley.

North, J., 1990, 'Diviners and Divination in Rome', in Beard, M. & North, J. (eds), *Pagan Priests: Religion and Power in the Ancient World*, London: 51–71.

North, J., 2012, 'Quindecimviri sacris faciundis', in Hornblower, S., Spawforth, A. & Eidinow, E. (ed.), *The Oxford Classical Dictionary*, fourth edition, Oxford.

Orlin, E.M., 1997, *Temples, Religion and Politics in the Roman Republic*, Leiden.

Orlin, E.M., 2000, *Foreign Cults in Rome: Creating a Roman Empire*, Oxford.

Parker, R., 2016, 'War and Religion in Ancient Greece', in Ulanowski, K. (ed.), *The Religious Aspects of War in the Ancient Near East, Greece, and Rome*, Leiden: 123–32.

Paton, F.W., Walbank, F.W. & Habicht, C., 2011, *Polybius. The Histories, Volume IV: Books 9–15*, Cambridge MA.

Pease, A.S., 1920–23, *M. Tulli Ciceronis de Divinatione*, 2 vols, Urbana.

Phang, S.E., 2008, *Roman Military Service: Ideologies of Discipline in the Late Republic and Early Principate*, Cambridge.

Pritchett, W.K., 1979, *The Greek State at War. Part III: Religion*, Los Angeles.

Rackham, H., 1933, *Cicero. On the Nature of the Gods*, Cambridge MA.

Rasmussen, S.W., 2003, *Public Portents in Republican Rome*, Rome.

Rich, J., 2013, 'Roman Rituals of War', in Campbell, B. & Trite, L.A. (eds), *The Oxford Handbook of Warfare in the Classical World*, Oxford: 543–68.

Ripat, P., 2006, 'Roman Omens, Roman Audiences, and Roman History', *G&R* 53: 155–74.

Rives, J., 2004, 'Religion and Politics: Rome', in Johnston, S.I. (ed.), *Religions of the Ancient World: A Guide*, Cambridge MA: 558–61.

Rosenberger, V., 1997, *Gezähmte Götter: das Prodigienwesen der römischen Republik*, Stuttgart.

Rosenberger, V., 2001, 'Zeichen göttlichen Zornes: eine mediengeschichtliche Untersuchung des römischen Prodigienwesens', in Brodersen, K. (ed.), *Gebet und Fluch, Zeichen und Traum: Aspekte religiöser Kommunikation in der Antike*, Münster: 69–88.

Rosenberger, V., 2007, 'Republican *Nobiles*: Controlling the *Res Publica*', in Rüpke, J. (ed.), *A Companion to Roman Religion*, Malden MA: 292–303.

Ross, M., 2016, 'Eclipses and the Precipitation of Conflict: Deciphering the Signal to Attack', in Ulanowski, K. (ed.), *The Religious Aspects of War in the Ancient Near East, Greece, and Rome*, Leiden: 99–120.

Rüpke, J., 1990, *Domi militia: die religiöse Konstruktion des Krieges in Rom*, Stuttgart.

Rüpke, J., 1995, *Kalender und Öffentlichkeit: Die Geschichte der Repräsentation und religiösen Qualifikation von Zeit in Rom*, Berlin.

Rüpke, J., 2005, 'Divination et décisions politiques dans la république romaine', *Cahiers du Centre Gustave Glotz* 16: 217–33.

Rüpke, J. *et al.*, 2005, 'Divination Romaine', in Boardman, J. *et al.* (eds), *Thesaurus Cultus et Rituum Antiquorum* (*ThesCRA*) III, Los Angeles: 79–89.

Sabin, P., van Wees, H. & Whitby, M. (eds), 2007, *The Cambridge History of Greek and Roman Warfare Volume 2: Rome from the Late Republic to the Late Empire*, Cambridge.

Sage, E.T., 1935, *Livy. History of Rome, Volume X: Books 35–37*, Cambridge MA.

Sage, E.T., 1936, *Livy. History of Rome, Volume XI: Books 38–39*, Cambridge MA.

Santangelo, F., 2013, *Divination, Prediction and the End of the Roman Republic*, Cambridge.

Satterfield, S., 2011, 'Notes on Phlegon's Hermaphrodite Oracle and the Publication of Oracles in Rome', *RMPh* 154: 117–24.

Scheid, J., 2003, *An Introduction to Roman Religion*, Edinburgh.

Schofield, M., 1986, 'Cicero For and Against Divination', *JRS* 76: 47–65.

Schultz, C.E., 2015, *A Commentary on Cicero, De Divinatione I*, Ann Arbor.

Stoll, O., 2007, 'Religions of the Armies' in Erdkamp, P. (ed.), *A Companion to the Roman Army*, Malden MA: 451–76.

Vaahtera, J.E., 2000, 'Roman Religion and the Polybian *Politeia*', in Bruun, C. (ed.), *The Roman Middle Republic: Politics, Religion, and Historiography c. 400–133 BC*, Rome: 251–64.

Versnel, H.S., 2011, *Coping with the Gods: Wayward Readings in Greek Theology*, Leiden.

Walbank, F.W., 1957, *A Historical Commentary on Polybius I*, Oxford.

Walbank, F.W., 1994, 'Supernatural Paraphernalia in Polybius' *Histories*', in Worthington, I. (ed.), *Ventures into Greek History*, Oxford: 28–42.

Wardle, D., 2006, *Cicero on Divination: De divinatione, Book 1. Translation with Introduction and Historical Commentary*, Oxford.

Wardman, A., 1982, *Religion and Statecraft among the Romans*, London.

Wheeler, E.L., 2008, '*Pullarii*, *Marsi*, *Haruspices*, and *Sacerdotes* in the Roman Imperial Army Roman', in Schellenburg, H.M., Hirschmann, V.E. & Krieckhous, A. (eds), *Miscellany. Essays in Honour of Anthony R. Birley on his Seventieth Birthday*, Gdansk: 85–201.

Chapter 9

Triumphal Transgressions

Jeremy Armstrong

'[Romulus] led his army home, carrying with him the spoils of those who had been slain in battle and the choicest part of the booty as an offering to the gods; and he offered many sacrifices besides. Romulus himself came last in the procession, clad in a purple robe and wearing a crown of laurel upon his head, and, that he might maintain the royal dignity, he rode in a chariot drawn by four horses. The rest of the army, both foot and horse, followed, ranged in their several divisions, praising the gods in songs of their country and extolling their general in improvised verses. They were met by the citizens with their wives and children, who, ranging themselves on each side of the road, congratulated them upon their victory and expressed their welcome in every other way. When the army entered the city, they found mixing bowls filled to the brim with wine and tables loaded down with all sorts of viands, which were placed before the most distinguished houses in order that all who pleased might take their fill. Such was the victorious procession, marked by the carrying of trophies and concluding with a sacrifice, which the Romans call a triumph, as it was first instituted by Romulus. But in our day the triumph has become a very costly and ostentatious pageant, being attended with a theatrical pomp that is designed rather as a display of wealth than as approbation of valour, and it has departed in every respect from its ancient simplicity. After the procession and the sacrifice Romulus built a small temple on the summit of the Capitoline hill to Jupiter whom the Romans call Feretrius; indeed, the ancient traces of it still remain, of which the longest sides are less than fifteen feet. In this temple he consecrated the spoils of the king of the Caeninenses, whom he had slain with his own hand.'

Dion. Hal. *Rom. Ant.* 2.34.1–4 (trans. Cary)

The Roman triumph was a fundamentally transgressive institution. At every level it tested boundaries and pushed against accepted norms as part of a complex negotiation of power, both amongst Rome's elite and between the elite and the community. On a ritual level, it involved crossing the sacred boundary of Rome, the *pomerium*, with a procession which moved from outside the city to the very heart of the archaic community – passing through virtually every important space within the city in the process. As part of the triumph, the doors of Rome's temples were thrown open, allowing symbolic access across those sacred boundaries too. Indeed, some scholars have argued that the ritual may have even transgressed the boundaries between the gods and men, with the *triumphator*, the triumphing general, perhaps occupying a liminal position between the two categories.[1] On a political level, it involved having an army and wielding military authority within the city of Rome – things which were explicitly prohibited at any other time – breaking down the fundamental boundary between *domi et militiae*.[2] It may have also blurred the boundaries of political offices, temporarily transforming republican magistrates into monarchic figures, equipped with the full regalia of the archaic Roman *rex* (king). On a broader level, the triumph also often sparked political (and even constitutional) crises, with lengthy debates over the granting of the triumph in the Senate and disputes over the fundamental power to control the triumph in the assembly.[3] On a social level, like the doors of the temples, the doors of Rome's great houses were also thrown open during the procession, allowing symbolic admittance – offering the *triumphator*, who may have represented a social and political rival, entrance into the private spaces of the city's powerful families. The triumph also saw a breakdown of the usual social and military order where, in a similar manner to the Saturnalia festival, both citizens and soldiers joked, bantered and sang rude songs (*carmina incondita*) about their leaders without fear of censure.[4] But more than that, the triumph was also an arena for ever-increasing aristocratic display and competition, where nobles actively sought to surpass the achievements of both their contemporaries and their predecessors. This is particularly notable during the Republic. In an environment where social and political parity, or at least equilibrium, seems to have represented the foundation of the *res publica*, the triumph was a notable exception. The triumph, therefore, broke all the rules.

And yet the triumph was also a point of stability within Rome's ever-changing social and political landscape – supposedly enduring the transitions from monarchy to republic, republic to empire, and arguably even outliving the empire itself.[5] Indeed, alongside *imperium* and the Senate, the triumph was one of the few Roman institutions which was maintained throughout Rome's long history. Additionally, despite its transgressive qualities – or indeed, perhaps, because of them – the triumph was also subject to countless rules, regulations and conventions. For instance, the *triumphator* had to hold *imperium*, warfare must have been conducted under the correct auspices, a certain number of combatants should have been killed and the war must have been fought against legitimate enemies (*hostes*), have extended Roman power and resulted in peace (or at least brought about a state where the army could be withdrawn). Finally, of course, the procession itself is usually thought to have followed a specific route and included a number of set actions. Although hotly contested, the triumph was therefore a highly choreographed and, quite literally, ritualized production by the Late Republic, from the debates which preceded it, to the procession itself and ultimately its aftermath. Its 'rule breaking' was therefore, somewhat paradoxically, tightly bound by rules. Indeed, like other transgressive rituals from other cultures, the entire institution represented a complex matrix of contraventions and reaffirmations of Rome's social order. Most importantly for the present context, however, the triumph was a ritual which helped the Romans delineate and define their relationship with warfare.

Status Quaestionis: **The present state of the investigation**

The triumph was – as has long been recognized – much more than a simple victory parade or celebration of a general and his army. Occupying a unique position in Roman culture, at the intersection of warfare, politics and religion, it has regularly been the subject of intense study. Although a range of traditions existed regarding its roots, like many other Roman rituals the triumph was understood to have originated in the murky days of the early regal period and so was intimately connected with the Roman community from its inception. The Romans, evidently, could not conceive of a time when they did not celebrate it.

As a ritual, the triumph was incredibly elaborate. By the Late Republic, after a triumph was granted – traditionally by the Senate, but occasionally through a direct vote of the people through the assembly[6] – a tribune of the plebs would put forward a *plebiscitum* (a resolution passed by the plebeian assembly) which would allow the general to retain his *imperium*, or command, within the *pomerium* of the city.[7] The city would also be

Figure 9.1: The emperor Titus, in a *quadriga*, in a triumphal procession depicted on the 'Arch of Titus' in the Forum Romanum, Rome. Photo by author.

prepared, with banquets laid out in the streets in front of the great houses. Temple doors would be opened, shrines covered in flowers and garlands, incense burnt on altars and the crowd would line the streets.[8] With all of this in place, the procession could begin. Outside the *Porta Triumphalis*,[9] in the *Campus Martius*, the general would address his army, hand out awards and distribute a portion of the plunder captured during the campaign to the soldiers. He would then step into his ceremonial *quadriga*, a four-horse chariot, and move towards the city gates where he would be greeted by the entire body of the Senate (see Figure 9.1). The Senate would then lead the procession inside the city followed by trumpeters, the spoils of war, musicians, sacrificial animals, the weapons and symbols of the enemy, the enemy leaders and then the lictors and the general himself. Behind the general were his sons, *legati* and other officers of the general, followed by the *equites* (cavalry) and finally the infantry. The procession would wind its way through the city (the exact route is still contested) to the *via Sacra* and into the Forum Romanum, and ultimately to the top of the Capitoline hill (see Figure 9.2). There the prisoners were executed and spoils and a laurel wreath were offered to Jupiter. The general would then feast with his friends in the great temple of Jupiter Optimus Maximus until he would finally return home, escorted by torches, musicians and the crowd. Although the procession itself usually took only a day, the implications lasted much longer. *Triumphatores* were often gifted land for houses by the state,[10] and their ashes were allowed to be buried within the city walls – something which was normally prohibited.[11]

Figure 9.2: The 'Arch of Titus', commemorating his triumph, on the *via Sacra* in the Forum Romanum, Rome; it is one of many monuments erected along the triumphal route. Photo by author.

Despite its supposed longevity and antiquity, however, it is clear this ritual of the triumph changed dramatically over time. The traditional, Late Republican, version of the triumph described above obviously does not match precisely with the description of Romulus' triumph given by Dionysius at the start of the chapter. Indeed, if the triumph did originate in the regal period, certain aspects of the Late Republican ritual would simply not have been possible for much of the archaic period. First and foremost, the archaeological evidence is fairly conclusive that the Forum valley was not drained, and the *Forum Romanum* was not constructed, until the second half of the seventh century BC. As a result, not only would the traditional route of the triumph through the Forum to the Capitoline not have been possible before this point, but there is little evidence to suggest the settlements on the various hills of Rome – including the Capitoline and Palatine – were unified in a way which would allow a truly 'Roman' triumph to exist until this date.[12] Additionally, even the most optimistic reconstructions of Rome's fortifications do not usually allow for full circuit walls, with a proper *Porta Triumphalis* ('triumphal gate'), until the mid-sixth century BC – and in fact it is highly likely circuit walls were only constructed in Rome in the fourth century BC (see Figure 9.3).[13] This does not mean that there was not a *pomerium* or sacred boundary which was symbolically crossed prior to this point, although the absence of walls and a gateway would obviously change the nature of this crossing. Likewise the temple of Jupiter Optimus Maximus on the Capitoline, which represented the end point of the procession, was traditionally not finished until 509 BC, although this does not mean that a sanctuary or sacred precinct to the god did not exist on the hill previously, as suggested by Dionysius.[14] But it is clear that the elaborate ritual described in our Late Republican sources, which was thought to go back to the time of Romulus, developed and evolved over time alongside the urban centre of Rome.

Even limiting ourselves to what might be considered the more 'historical' triumphs, beginning in the mid to late fourth century BC, it is likely that the triumph would have evolved significantly during the final centuries of the Republic.[15] As Rich has argued, Rome's rapidly growing power from *c.* 340 BC onward, coupled with the city's increasingly far-flung empire and conquests, resulted in the celebration of richer and more elaborate triumphs at more than double the rate of the early Republic. From 343 BC until the end of the Republic, triumphs were celebrated once every three years and – for a short period in the early third century BC – reached a peak of one almost every year.[16] It is usually thought (or at least expressed in our extant sources) that the increasing wealth of these Mid-Republican triumphs quickly led to spectacle becoming their central aspect.

The changes which these factors (and others) would have meant for the triumph notwithstanding, there are many aspects of the ritual which do seem quite ancient. The chant of '*io triumpe*', which forms a key aspect of the ritual and indeed gave its name to the triumph, is likely archaic in origin.[17] Additionally, as Bonfante, Versnel and others have argued, the triumph seems to feature strong Etruscan influences, further hinting at an archaic origin.[18] For instance, looking at the traditional dress and accoutrements of the *triumphator* – the chariot, the red *minium* painted on

Figure 9.3: Rome's fourth-century BC circuit walls, the so-called 'Servian Walls'. Photo by author.

the face, the *toga picta* (a purple and gold toga), the *tunica palmata* (a tunic embroidered with palm leaves), the *bulla* (a golden necklace), etc. – there are a number of strong parallels to be drawn from Etruscan contexts.[19] And taking things a step further, there have been suggestions that the myth of an archaic King of Caere named Mezentius, preserved in Virgil and Macrobius, may also hint at an 'Etruscan triumph'.[20] In this legend, the Etruscan leader Mezentius supposedly dedicated the first portion of the spoils (*prima spolia*) from his victory over either the Rutilians or the Latins to the god Jupiter in a ritual which closely mirrors the Roman triumph. This has led many scholars to suggest that the Roman triumph was perhaps part of a wider Central Italian set of rituals, also connected to the *ovatio* and the so-called 'triumph on the Alban Mount' (two alternative rituals used to celebrate victory which are usually thought of as 'lesser' forms of the triumph), which were concerned with the dedication of spoils and ritual cleansing or purification after war.

As a socio-political institution, the triumph was also very complex, particularly by the Late Republic. Given the glory which it conferred to the figure of the victorious general, the triumph was highly sought-after – and indeed the practice of 'triumph hunting' has been a regular focus of scholarship in recent years, from Harris' 1979 *War and Imperialism in Republican Rome* to more recent studies by Osgood and others.[21] Additionally, the awarding and authorization of triumphs also became the subject of intense competition amongst the elite, as seen in the myriad rules and requirements which were instituted over the years – although how rigid and 'official' these were is still hotly debated.[22] The first and most basic requirement was that the triumphing general had to hold *imperium* through holding the office of dictator, consul or praetor.[23] Indeed, the requirements around *imperium* were quite strict, as the general must not only have held it when the victory was achieved, but also when the triumph was celebrated, in addition to holding the correct auspices associated with the office.[24] According to Valerius Maximus, there was also a requirement imposed on the size/scale of the victory – at least 5,000 dead in a single battle.[25] The victory was also supposed to be against foreign enemies (*hostes*) and to result in both the expansion of the empire and the ending of hostilities.[26] Other rules and norms were variously noted and applied – and indeed the study of the *ius triumphandi*, or the rules surrounding the right to triumph, has become something of an 'industry' in its own right in modern scholarship.[27] As noted above, however, while various rules and conventions are recorded in our sources, it is also clear that the Senate, which traditionally claimed control over the granting of triumphs, did far more than apply a simple checklist in response to a general's request for the honour. The right of a general to triumph was almost always debated, and this debate formed an important part of the entire production in and of itself.[28]

Modern scholarly interest in the triumph arguably began with Gibbon in the mid-eighteenth century, and has continued largely unabated since then.[29] Although the work has obviously been diverse, scholars have traditionally focused on the religious and political aspects of the triumph, and a number of important works investigating these areas appeared between the mid-nineteenth century and the end of the twentieth century, including those by Goell (1854), Mommsen (1878), Laquer (1909), Pais (1920), Ehlers (1939), Payne (1962), Versnel (1970), Bonfante (1970) and Kunzl (1988). Following the 2007 publication of Mary Beard's *Roman Triumph*, however, the topic has experienced a massive increase in interest, with a large outpouring of works on a much wider spectrum of subjects ranging from its origins[30] and regulations[31] to its spectacle,[32] archaeology[33] and ultimately reception.[34] Despite this sudden diversification, the old traditional areas of religion and politics are still quite popular, and arguably for good reason – as they are both the best-attested in terms of evidence and seem to cut to the heart of what the ritual represented. The range of opinions, however, remains vast.

Looking first at religion, Laquer, followed more recently by Rüpke, suggested that the triumph could be seen as a rite designed to officially conclude a war.[35] Corresponding to the votive ritual performed by generals on the Capitoline hill before a campaign began, it is possible to see the triumph as a concluding counterpart to this rite, bringing the campaign to an end.[36] Alternatively Versnel, among others, argued the ritual was a vital part of the reintegration of the army into society following warfare,[37] while Bonfante, in a related argument, suggested the triumph was first and foremost a purifying rite associated with the expiation of blood guilt associated with warfare.[38] The figure of the *triumphator* himself has also come under scrutiny in the religious sphere. Was the triumphant general, in carrying out the various sacrifices and wearing the specific garb of the *triumphator*, acting as a *rex* or a priest during the triumph? Or, as Versnel suggested, was he perhaps personifying the god Jupiter himself? Most scholars these days would probably argue the former as opposed to the latter, but the matter is far from settled.

The political aspects of the triumph though have also, obviously, been explored in depth. The triumph was a hotly contested honour in the Republic, with the recipients' names recorded in the *Fasti Triumphales* – the inscribed list of generals who celebrated a triumph – giving glory to their family, both present and future. As a result, quite a few scholars have analyzed the competition for triumphs amongst Rome's elite, with some, like Pittenger,[39] pushing its importance, and others, like Itgenshorst, qualifying its influence.[40] The fascinating collection of rules and norms surrounding the right to triumph, the *ius triumphandi*, have also been explored, as has its role as a spectacle.[41] The triumph therefore has formed an important window into Middle and Late Republican politics, providing intriguing insights into how the elite interacted, both as individuals and in a corporate sense as the Senate. Moving into the Empire, the massive change which occurred under Augustus has also been investigated extensively. As the triumph became the preserve of the imperial family, it increasingly formed part of the wider image and propaganda of the emperor and, given its long history, it represents an interesting avenue to explore the manipulation of Republican practice during the Principate.

Broadly speaking though, modern scholarship has increasingly focused on how little we know about the triumph, rather than how much. As Östenberg noted in her recent monograph, following the works of Itgenshorst and Beard, the vast majority of our information on the triumph is not contemporary and the ritual was often utilized by ancient authors for particular literary purposes. The triumph was, as Claude Lévi-Strauss would say, 'good to think with' and could be readily deployed in a number of different contexts – for instance to critique elite ambition or greed, or to compare and contrast the character and achievements of individual generals. Indeed, as Beard suggested in her study, while the triumph was clearly used as a vehicle to attain glory, it was also the 'context … for some of the most critical thinking on the dangerous ambivalence of success and military glory'. [42] It is clear that the triumph was important to the Romans, although the how and the why remain elusive.

Transgressive Discourses

Given its long history, evidently adaptable character, as well as its literary functions, it is likely that a definitive statement of the triumph's purpose and meaning in Roman society will forever be beyond us. Returning to the transgressive character of the triumph though, some broad insights are perhaps possible. The triumph clearly fulfilled an important role in Roman society which allowed, and arguably necessitated, its transgressive nature. After all, why else would the Romans not only permit, but maintain and develop, such a contentious and disconcerting ritual for so many years? The triumph, in many ways by definition, upset the natural order of Roman society. The breaking down of conventional boundaries in all of the areas which the triumph transgressed is not something which would have been done lightly, or permitted without meaning. Although recent anthropological work has explored the 'futility' of establishing and maintaining strict, impermeable social boundaries, the way in which these boundaries are negotiated and transgressed is obviously still very important – particularly when they cover the spectrum contained within this ritual.[43]

Rituals of transgression help to define the very limits and boundaries they cross and, by their extraordinary nature, actually act to reaffirm the existing order. The Roman triumph in particular seems to have helped to moderate aspects of the Roman approach to warfare, religion, politics and community identity, and was generally deployed in this context. Unpicking the complexities of the boundaries transgressed by the triumph and the nature of the relationship and order which it underpinned is difficult though – as one might expect. Not only does it mean exploring a ritual and institution which seems to have occupied a central place in Roman society, thus making it hard for our sources to get a clear perspective on it, but its longevity, ritual nature and the general lack of contemporary evidence all introduce significant problems. The transgressive character of the triumph is also problematic in its own right. As an institution which intentionally broke down barriers and crossed boundaries, it seems to have actively interacted with and altered the social order by its very existence – in some ways 'moving the goal posts' on scholars, both ancient and modern, who wished to understand it. Finally, this transgressive aspect was not always as 'clean' and organized as one might hope. As with humour and other activities which push boundaries, sometimes the actor misses the mark and significantly oversteps the line they were meant to merely 'put their toe over'. The same is arguably true with the triumph, with some *triumphatores* perhaps pushing the boundaries a little too far or innovating 'too much'. However, despite the complexities of the triumph, a few basic unifying principles behind the ritual, as part of a transgressive discourse, are arguably visible.

First and foremost, rather than representing a side-effect, tension seems to have formed a core aspect of the Roman triumph. As noted above, all of our extant evidence suggests that the ritual walked the thin line between transgression and affirmation, balancing ritual proscriptions (e.g. the *ius triumphandi*, set sacrifices and practices, etc.) with social contraventions. This tension seems to have been an important part of the institution – a triumph was *supposed* to push and cross (albeit in a limited fashion) various limits. It was *supposed* to be an unusual and indeed a tense or unsettling environment. It was exciting, but also anything but comfortable – for both the general and the community. From the general's point of view, there was always the worry that the production would not go as planned – as seems to have happened with Pompey's 'triple triumph' in 61 BC when his elephants misbehaved and he was supposedly 'upstaged' by his prisoners.[44] And for the community, something which often goes ignored in the Late Republican accounts of Roman triumphs is the fact that the triumph involved the effective military occupation of the city by a general and his army – something which presumably would have made Romans, with the memory of the violent occupations of Rome by Marius, Sulla, Pompey, Caesar, Antony and even Octavian, at least slightly uneasy. This was an accepted, and indeed necessary, part of the triumph.

Second, the triumph was about negotiation and interaction. This began before the ritual ever occurred, as a general was never guaranteed a triumph. Despite the myriad 'regulations' recorded in our sources, it is clear that there was not a universally agreed 'checklist' for a triumph – this was not something which a general could necessarily 'earn'.[45] Instead, the right to triumph was always asked for and debated by the community before being granted, with the negotiation and debate around *ius triumphandi* arguably representing a vital part of the institution, at least as it existed during the Late Republic. Once the triumph was awarded, there seems to have been still further, albeit less formal, negotiation over what it involved. As our sources suggest, while the *triumphator* may have been able to improvise and innovate in his triumph, the final production was the subject of intense social scrutiny. Further, the triumph was focused around a sequence of exchanges. The general called and met with his soldiers, the general with his army then met with the Senate, the army and the Senate together then entered the community and met with the people, and finally the *triumphator* himself met with the gods. This was a ritual which was fundamentally interactive.

Third, the triumph was intimately intertwined with *imperium*. Very little about the triumph can be said for certain and, given the longevity of the ritual, trying to find any points of consistency and continuity across its history is tricky to say the least. However, at its very core, the ritual seems to have been intimately and inexorably connected to the grant of *imperium*. Wielding valid *imperium* during a victory represented the most basic requirement to celebrate the ritual, and maintaining this power seems to have been vital to its successful completion. This basic fact links the mythical triumphs of the *reges* ('kings') with the contentious triumphs of the Republic, and even the propagandistic iterations of the Empire (see below). Throughout Rome's history, the triumph was celebrated by, and limited to, men who wielded *imperium*. In some ways this last point is arguably the most obvious, given that both the triumph and *imperium* related to Roman activity in warfare – *imperium* being associated with military command and the triumph representing, in part, success in military ventures. However, just as the triumph was far more than a military parade, *imperium* represented far more than the simple right to command armies. Associated with the auspices, imbued with archaic connections and consistently defying straightforward interpretation – both in antiquity and today – *imperium*, as Beck suggested, was an 'overall structuring force on the Republican constitution'.[46] The relationship between *imperium* and the triumph is complex, but, like *imperium*, the Roman triumph seems, in many ways quite literally, to occupy the liminal space between the civic and military spheres in Rome. It was a key aspect of the dialogue which existed between these two facets of Roman society as far back as we can see in Roman history, managing and moderating the interaction which occurred across them.

I would therefore like to suggest that the Roman triumph represented a ritualized expression of the struggle and set of relationships which lay at the core of Rome's political system during the Republic. Rather than representing a corollary or consequence of Rome's elite competition during the Middle or Late Republic, the importance of the triumph in Roman society speaks to the basic nature of Roman politics and elite interaction with each other, and the community as a whole. Going back to the archaic age, when Central Italy's powerful *gentes* ('clans') began to settle in and around Rome, there was a negotiation which occurred between the *gentes* and Rome's *curiae* – the enigmatic divisions of archaic Roman society – through the medium of Rome's emerging urban centre, which crossed the same boundaries and featured the same aspects as Rome's triumph. Involving warfare, politics and religion, there was a regular discussion revolving around identity and power between the various actors and agents within the community which served to unify and define the population. This discussion took place in a wide range of formats and arenas, including votes and discussion within the assemblies and Senate house, sacrifices and rites at Rome's temples, and even in the domestic sphere. But it was almost always disjointed and piecemeal. It was only with the Roman triumph that the various facets were brought together in a single ritual, on a single day, embodying both the power and tension present in Rome's socio-political contract. The triumph, and the *ius triumphandi*, can therefore be located within the wider framework of the *mos maiorum* – Roman ancestral custom – and arguably form some of its most visible and contentious aspects.[47] This ritual represented a fundamentally Roman way of negotiating power within the community. But more specifically, the Roman triumph, like *imperium*, also relates to the two primary spheres of Roman society – the *domi et militiae* – and illustrates how they interacted and related.

Triumphal Tensions

As noted by Beard, Östenberg and others, our evidence for the Roman triumph is the first hurdle which must be overcome in any investigation of the ritual. Although there is a wide range of literary evidence available, the vast majority comes from a relatively narrow window of time in the Late Republic and Early Empire and rarely relates to contemporary events. This makes a *longue durée* analysis difficult and also forces us to view the triumph through a very particular social and political lens. It is impossible for us to know how archaic generals, who may have had a very different relationship with the community of Rome, would have engaged with this institution, or how the archaic community, which was likely still developing its corporate identity, would have felt about the ritual transgressions. We can only see how Rome's Late Republic and Early Imperial nobility interacted with the well-established community of Rome. By the time our sources were writing, the various actors and institutions were all well entrenched and knew the parts they had to play. However, those caveats aside, the inherent tension within the triumph is still visible in our evidence, and exploring how it is manipulated can help to reveal a little more about the relationship which underpinned the ritual.

The central aspect of the triumph was the movement of the general and his army across the *pomerium*, and virtually every other boundary within Rome, on their way to the centre of the ancient city. Managing this transgression (as the general and army were usually not to set foot inside the city of Rome itself) seems to have represented, quite naturally, a core concern and source of tension. If anything remains of the archaic institution in our Late Republican sources, it is likely around this most transgressive set of actions. Indeed, the procession was tightly controlled by the community and highly choreographed. Upon his return, the victorious general was required to wait outside the *pomerium* and politely ask to enter in order to perform the ritual. Thus, although the general obviously held the military power in the relationship, the community was given the official and ritual authority over the encounter. Once the triumph was granted, the route of the *triumphator* and his army was tightly scripted and bound by myriad ritual aspects and sacrifices. The overt tension of the triumph, as the transgression of the community by an 'outside' military force, was therefore mitigated by the ritualized character of the institution. It was all part of an accepted and standardized discourse in which each side gave the other power in a ritualized fashion.

But this overt transgression, and the tension which surrounded it, represents only one thread within the elaborate web of the tensions which existed within the triumph by the Late Republic. Although increasingly subtle and political, the triumph still seems to have operated along and across other transgressive lines within Rome's political system. Returning again to Dionysius of Halicarnassus' description of the first triumph, celebrated by Romulus after his victory over Caenina, Antemnae and Crustumerium, various tensions are visible. In his account, Dionysius emphasized the majestic character of Romulus as the *imperator* and *triumphator*, 'clad in a purple robe and wearing a crown of laurel upon his head, and, that he might maintain the royal dignity, he rode in a chariot drawn by four horses', and yet he also suggests that the procession featured an 'ancient simplicity'.[48] For Dionysius, the Roman triumph could, and should, involve both a lavish display of wealth as well as humble simplicity, existing in a delicate balance. But by the Late Republic, he laments, the more performative aspects of the triumph had increasingly taken centre stage. Somehow the balance between display and modesty which he argues existed in the glorious days of the archaic period had been lost. This worry over the increasingly ostentatious nature of the triumph in the Late Republic was not unique to Dionysius either. The central element of the triumph was a procession of the victorious general and his army through the streets of Rome, carrying the trophies of war, and as such one would expect wealth to be celebrated as a symbol of victory. However,

Rome's triumphal processions of the late third and early second century BC in particular were often decried for their overt displays of wealth. Marcellus' *ovatio* of 211 BC was heavily criticized for his display of Greek art – and particularly statues of the gods.[49] Livy famously discussed the 'moral decline' of the triumph in his narrative for the 180s BC, most notably the wealth displayed in the triumph of Cneius Manlius Vulso,[50] while Pliny criticized the wealth of Scipio Asiaticus' triumph of 189 BC.[51] While wealth and display were obviously central features of the triumph, our sources therefore suggest that they needed to be moderated somehow in this particular context. Once a *triumphator* and his army entered the community, the nature of the display was also a subject of tension.

But the tension in Dionysius' account is not only about the perceived transgression of this established norm or balance with regards to presentation. There was also a tension over its purpose. For Dionysius, the original emphasis of the triumph was on the gods and the community welcoming the army home. The procession began and culminated with sacrifices, and the entire production featured the elaborate regalia and chants which one might associate with archaic ceremonies. Although by no means solemn, this was still an important sacred event which featured strong parallels to other Roman rituals. His criticism of the triumphs of the Late Republic then was in many ways that the procession, and not the sacrifice, had increasingly become the highlight of the ritual, with the focus shifting from the gods and the community towards the wealth and importance of the *imperator*. There had been a shift in what the wealth represented and how it functioned in this context. In Dionysius' description of Romulus, his elaborate dress and decoration plays a part in his role as *rex* – both a military and religious leader – while the spoils formed a vital part of the sacrifices to the gods. By the Late Republic, however, our sources suggest that these spoils were a way to buy the loyalty of the army and gain the favour of the people, which would obviously have disastrous implications for the community.[52] As a result, there seems to have been a tension around intention and perhaps identity. Although the ritual ostensibly involved the limited transgression of the community's boundaries by an 'outsider', the 'outsider' was still expected to think like an 'insider'.

Given the nature of our evidence, it is impossible to know if Livy, Dionysius and our other literary sources were correct in either their description of the early triumph or their critiques of its changing focus by their own day. Indeed, given the relatively late development of Roman historical writing and the problematic nature of the material which existed previously, it is highly unlikely that Dionysius or his contemporaries would have been able to say *anything* about the early ritual with a degree of confidence even if they had wanted to. Their information about the early ritual, apart from perhaps the *Fasti Triumphales* or similar cryptic records like the consular *fasti* or *Annales Maximi* (yearly records kept by the *Pontifex Maximus*, or high priest of Rome), would presumably have been oral in nature. However, it is clear that there was a sense of tension surrounding the ritual during the Late Republic – that the triumph was seen as being pulled in various directions. Indeed, what is important for our study is that contemporary (or near contemporary) triumphs were never seen to exist without some sort of tension and criticism – although the type varied significantly. Lucius Mummius' triumph in 146 BC, following the sack of Corinth, was criticized for its use and display of captured artwork.[53] The triumphs of Sulla (81 BC), Murena (81 BC) and Lucullus (63 BC), all celebrated for victories over Mithridates VI of Pontus, were censured for not bringing the war to completion – something only done by Pompey.[54] However, there was also a certain amount of tension over Pompey's triumph, as he was thought to be overstepping by including his campaign against the pirates in a triumph initially voted for his victory over Mithridates.[55] It seems as if the Roman authors could not describe a triumph without criticizing it in some way. While the triumphs of the truly archaic and often idealized past could perhaps serve as a model, contemporary triumphs quite often feature at least some criticism.

This characteristic tension has been recognized by previous scholars, and indeed forms a core aspect of Beard's recent study.[56] For Beard and others, the triumph – as the pre-eminent vehicle for elite self-presentation or promotion in the Late Republic – would obviously be subject to the same critiques and criticisms as other forms of self-promotion in such a highly competitive environment. This type of criticism, it has been argued, was a way of controlling the impact and influence of triumphal self-promotion by other elites – and this is likely true to a certain extent, particularly in the Late Republic. However, to suggest that this criticism stems entirely from a desire to mitigate the self-promotion of one triumphant general by his political rivals may be overstating the point. It is also possible that the criticism and tension we see in our extant account stems not only from the elites but from the wider community, and formed an integral part of the triumph itself. The triumph was about controlling and circumscribing the power of the triumphing general as much as it was about granting him extraordinary authority and prestige. The two sides seem to have always existed in a balance. While the triumphant general was able to march his army through Rome, the community limited his route and access. While the generals of the Middle and Late Republic were able to display ever-increasing amounts of wealth, the community controlled this through subtle (and not so subtle) critiques and criticisms. The entire institution of the triumph, from initial request to the final dinner and sacrifices, was moderated and negotiated by both sides. Movement by one side required a response by the other.

Triumphal Negotiations

The tension within the triumph is closely connected to its other interactive aspects; it was not something which was done in isolation. It required multiple parties to agree and participate, and was meant to be seen and experienced. The triumph was about negotiation. The initial negotiation was traditionally with the Senate – although one could perhaps argue that negotiations began even before this point as the general needed the support of the army in the field, and their declaration of him as *imperator*. The general required this support in order to even lodge his request, although this was usually granted quickly as the army normally benefited from the triumph as well. With regards to the Senate, however, it is clear that a certain amount of discussion was expected – not just amongst the senators, but between the general and the Senate. Indeed, the general was evidently expected to use his personal influence to gain the support of individual senators, and Brennan has noted the regular use of *gratia* – effectively bribes – in Livy's accounts of these debates.[57] What the Senate represented in these negotiations is also important. With regards to the triumph, the Senate did not speak only for itself, but for the entire community. And as such, it seems it could be overruled by the wider voice of the community – represented by the Tribal Assembly – if the community of Rome felt the Senate was not expressing its desires appropriately.[58] Indeed, Livy makes his position on the matter quite clear when discussing the triumph of Postumius in 294 BC, noting the will of the people was the ultimate authority in this decision.[59] The triumphal procession itself also involved a series of interactions. The general engaged with the army outside the walls of Rome, then the Senate at the *Porta Triumphalis*, then the wider citizen body along the route of the triumphal way, and finally the gods at the culminating sacrifice. The triumph was effectively a sequence of meetings between the *triumphator* and the various representatives of the community where he, in a systemic manner, established his position and authority.

The religious negotiation was also an important one. The triumph traditionally involved the dedication of three (and sometimes four) types of spoils to different deities – the *spolia prima* (the 'first' or 'best' spoils) to Jupiter *Feretrius* on the Capitoline, the *secunda spolia* to Mars on the *Campus Martius* and the *spolia tertia* to Janus *Quirinus*.[60] To the *spolia prima* were sometimes added the *spolia opima* (spoils taken from the body of an opposing commander killed by the general in single combat), if these were acquired.[61] Picard argued that these three dedications related to three hierarchic divisions of the same lustrum, or purification ceremony, performed at various points in the city circling the Palatine.[62] Whether associated with purification or not, what is interesting in the present context is the list of deities involved. All three deities are associated with warfare, albeit in different ways. The epithet *Feretrius* is unclear, and may relate to either 'carrying' (*ferre*) the *spolia prima/opima*[63] or 'striking' (*ferire*),[64] or even an association with iron (*ferrus*). Additionally, there is an association between the god/temple and warfare, as the temple was where the sacred flint (*silex*) used in the declaration and conclusion of wars was kept.[65] The altar to Mars in the *Campus Martius* is known from only a few passages. Associated with Numa by Festus, it seems to have been located near the *Porta Fontinalis* – probably to the north-east of the Capitoline hill – and was rebuilt in the early second century BC.[66] Despite regular expansion and elaboration of the site, most notably by Aemilius Paullus, it is unlikely there was ever an actual temple associated with the altar, although this did not diminish its importance. Indeed, the altar of Mars on the *Campus Martius* may have given the name to the entire region and it seems to have maintained its position as the primary place for veneration of the god.[67] Finally, Janus *Quirinus* (or Janus *Geminus*) represented an entirely different association with warfare. The temple, located in the Forum, famously had two doors, which Virgil dubbed *geminae belli portae* ('the twin doors of war').[68] When Rome was at war, the doors were opened. When Rome was at peace, the doors were closed.[69] There is a clear link with Rome's military activities. The association with Quirinus is also intriguing. Although an extremely enigmatic deity, he was likely related to the *curiae* – the representation of the archaic, urban heart of Rome – and seems to have related to civic matters.[70] So although the temple seems to have had a military association, it was perhaps more liminal in nature. Taken as a whole then, the three key sacrifices of the triumphal procession seem to have marked a negotiation between the *triumphator* and three facets of Rome's pantheon associated with warfare – Mars, as the extramural war diety; Janus *Quirinus*, as a liminal, community-focused deity which seems to have controlled access to warfare; and Jupiter *Feretrius*, perhaps associated with the more personal and leadership-based qualities of generalship. Each facet required its own sacrifice and interaction.

This interactive element, between the general and Rome's various bodies (the Senate, the assemblies, the city's gods), is arguably even demonstrated by the most notable exception or aberration, the so-called 'Triumph on the Alban Mount'. In 231 BC, the consul C. Papirius Maso was refused a triumph in Rome by the Senate, and so celebrated the first version of the ritual to be held *in monte Albano*, the site of the *feriae Latinae* and the meeting place of the Latins.[71] This was seen as a lesser version of the ritual, although the reasons for this are complex. Livy suggests that the lesser prestige was due to the lack of community investment and involvement, which is likely true.[72] Not having the community support the performance of the ritual, either financially or physically, would have been a significant setback. However, this does not mean that the triumph on the Alban Mount lacked meaning or that its core interactive elements were invalidated. Indeed, Brennan has argued that the performance of the triumph on the Alban Mount was 'an act of protest against the arbitrary and uncertain process of receiving permission to triumph [in Rome]', meaning that it should still be seen within the wider, contested milieu of the 'regular' triumph in Rome.[73] We unfortunately know very little about the version of the ritual held on the Alban Mount, but it is intriguing that the location was seen as a viable venue for a triumphal procession at all – and one which should be recorded in Rome's *Fasti Triumphales*. Who would have witnessed Papirius' triumph is unknown, but given its date of 5 March given on the *Fasti*, it is possible that it was planned to coincide with the annual *feriae Latinae*.[74] Apart from giving Papirius an audience, this would have also had other ritual resonances. Just as the Roman triumph may have marked the culmination of a ritual which began with a votive rite performed on the Capitoline before a campaign, the consuls were also not allowed to take the field until they had celebrated the *Latinae*. Additionally, as far back as Niebuhr, scholars have argued that Papirius may have been triumphing not as a Roman consul, but as Latin military leader.[75] It is therefore possible that Papirius was engaging in a triumphal negotiation with the Latins, who at this time represented half of Rome's military force and an increasingly important voice in Roman society and politics. The Latins would perhaps have represented a less prestigious partner in the triumphal ritual, but one which still wielded power and which could be seen as valid participants in the wider social, political and religious context.

The Roman triumph was therefore interactive by nature and focused on the negotiation of a specific set of relationships: between the general and the army, the Senate, the citizen body and the community's gods. Although highly stylized, it illustrated the various relationships which the triumphant general maintained and which arguably shared in his victory. As part of the triumph, each actor in the pageant both gave and received. The general offered the army donatives outside the city wall and the gods the spoils of war, both arguably as payment for their help in winning the victory. Conversely, the community and Senate welcomed the general and his army with banquets and cheering, perhaps in exchange for the victory won on their behalf. This does not mean that these relationships and negotiations were always friendly, as the tension discussed above seems to have imbued all of them. However, the interactive and negotiated aspect of the triumph must also be acknowledged as central to its performance.

The Triumph and *Imperium*

This leads to the third core aspect visible in the Roman triumph, the importance of *imperium* to the ritual. Of all the countless rules and regulations associated with the triumph, wielding a valid grant of *imperium* seems to have been the most important.[76] Indeed, even in those instances where a general's *imperium* had lapsed before the celebration of the triumph, a special grant of *imperium* was conferred for the purpose of the triumph via a *plebiscitum*.[77] Without this power, the ritual seems to have been impossible. The reasons why this might be, though, are enigmatic. The nature of *imperium* is obviously hotly contested, even in a reasonably well-documented period such as the Late Republic, so exploring the origins of this type of institution in the archaic period or Middle Republic is likely an exercise in futility. If Roman nobles like Cicero and Appius Claudius, who both actually wielded *imperium*, could not decide what it was exactly, and why it was needed in the Late Republic, then we are unlikely to either.[78] However, this is not to say that we cannot say anything about it.

As the nature of the Roman government and its 'constitution' shifted, so did *imperium*. Clearly, the *imperium* wielded by the *reges*, ruling over the small collection of huts on the Tiber, was different from that wielded by the emperors governing Rome, at the centre of a vast empire. However, as noted previously, *imperium* seems to have represented a central principle of the 'Roman constitution'.[79] While Rome's governments changed, assemblies were created and fell into disuse and magistracies were introduced and discontinued, *imperium* remained an important principle which somehow linked the chief officials of the city to the wider population.

Imperium seems to have been initially granted by the *comitia curiata*, the archaic assembly of Rome during the regal period and Early Republic. The power of the *comitia curiata* was slowly leached away by the *comitia tributa* and *comitia centuriata* over the first two centuries of the Republic until, by the Second Punic War, it amounted to little more than the college of lictors. But initially the *comitia* seems to have been the main assembly in Rome and, even after it was relegated to a vestige, the Romans seem to have maintained the link between the *curiae* and *imperium* as the *comitia* continued to pass a *lex curiata de imperio* for each curule magistrate – although, as noted in Cicero, some first-century BC politicians increasingly saw this as being desirable (*opus*) as opposed to required (*nesse*).[80] The continued role of the *curiae* in the granting of *imperium* may have related in part to the auspices, as by the Late Republic the religious sphere was one of the only areas where the *curiae* seem to have had any duties remaining.[81] Many scholars have, however, taken this argument perhaps a bit too far and suggested the *curiae* and the *lex curiata* only related to the auspices – with *imperium* being granted by the vote of/election by the *comitia centuriata*.[82] Part of the support for this argument is that it is clear that some Romans, most notably Appius Claudius in the instance commented on by Cicero above, felt this to be the case. It is clear that at least some Late Republic Roman generals felt that their election in the *comitia centuriata* granted them sufficient authority to command Rome's armies. Additionally, and somewhat enigmatically, the fact that the tribal assembly could evidently grant a limited *imperium* valid within the community of Rome for the purposes of the triumph, suggests that this assembly could also be involved. But while the political powers of the *curiae* were largely distributed to other assemblies, and they clearly lost their ability to select magistrates themselves (if indeed they ever had this authority), there is little to suggest that they lost their connection to *imperium* during the Republic. It must not be forgotten, for instance, that the thirty lictors, which physically represented the *imperium* of a curule magistrate, were representatives of the *curiae* and presided over the *calata comitia curiata* – the curiate assembly.[83] This situation raises a number of important questions. Why did the *comitia curiata*, an archaic assembly which had lost many of its practical functions by the Late Republic, maintain such a close connection to the most important power in Rome's political system? Additionally, was there any difference between the *imperium* granted by the *comitia curiata* and that evidently governed by the *comitia tributa*?

Beginning with the former, although a firm answer is likely beyond us, the continued importance of the *comitia curiata* may be connected to the *curiae*'s traditional importance as an embodiment of the community. In the early city the *comitia curiata* seems to have been the dominant assembly and the democratic representation of the emerging archaic urban centre – in many ways existing in contrast to the more expanded citizen body represented by the twinned assemblies of the *comitia tributa* and *comitia centuriata*. The *curiae* elected the *reges*, likely passed the so-called *leges regiae* and even elected the first tribunes of the plebs, until their various powers were slowly leached away. But even when their official powers had gone, the *curiae* still seem to have symbolized the ancient, urban heart of the city. Many of the names of the *curiae* hint at their geographical nature and association with the centre of the city (e.g. Foriensis, Veliensis, Tifata) and, according to Tacitus, the shrine of the *Curiae Veteres* was one of the points by which the *pomerium* was defined. Finally, and as noted previously, the lictors were also connected to the *curiae*; *imperium*, therefore, seems to have represented a ritualized bond between a leader and the physical community of Rome.[84]

During the archaic period, the triumph seems to have marked an important aspect within the wider bond of *imperium* which connected the community, and by extension its army, to the war leader. In the regal and Early Republican periods, the Roman *rex*, Roman praetors/consuls and the Roman state did not have a monopoly on violence – indeed far from it. Although obviously problematic on a number of levels, all of the evidence we have from both the extant literature and archaeology seems to point toward a situation where clan-based warfare was common and the military forces of Rome (and other communities) represented but a part of a much wider and more diverse military picture. Local war leaders, often dubbed 'condottieri' by modern scholars, engaged in widespread, low-level raiding utilizing a host of different forces. At the most basic level, the clan or *gens* of a war leader likely represented the core of his army. This could then be expanded or supplemented through clients (if, indeed, these weren't already included within the *gens*), *sodales* or 'sword brothers', alliances with other clans (sometimes through regional associations like the enigmatic 'Latin League') and relationships with local communities.[85] Each of these relationships would have functioned differently. The relationship between *sodales* seems to have involved both military and religious aspects. The patron–client bond seems to have contained economic and legal aspects, although likely cemented by religion, while the clan-based alliances seem to have featured marriage connections as well as religious aspects.

The relationship between a war leader and a community is extremely hard to break down, given the anachronistic nature of the evidence, but is perhaps best embodied by the grant of *imperium*. This power seems to have given the general all of the traditional powers of a *paterfamilias* over members of the community, albeit bound by particular rules and conventions – being largely utilized outside of the *pomerium*, limited to those who took part in particular ritualized oaths (by both the soldiers and the general) and for a limited period of time. In this way, it seems to fit quite neatly within the wider spectrum of relationships which existed in archaic Central Italy. Bound by social and religious conventions, certain members of the community of Rome seem to have become, in effect, limited-term clients or members of the extended *gens* of the general, under his *patria potestas* for the duration of his *imperium*. The Roman triumph, in its archaic incarnation, seems to have represented a single – but important – stage in the wider negotiation of this relationship between a community and its chosen war leader(s). Although a *rex*, or in the Republic the praetor or consul, seemed to wield a tremendous amount of power within the community of Rome, this may not have directly related to their *imperium*. As Drogula has argued, the idea of *imperium domi*, or *imperium* within the *pomerium*, is problematic at best.[86] While it is certain that the *rex* and praetors/consuls would have wielded significant unofficial power due to their *auctoritas* and *gravitas*, the specific powers of *imperium* seem to have only applied outside of the *pomerium* in the military sphere. The power was granted by the *curiae* inside the community, but exercised by the magistrate outside of the community, and generally seems to mirror the power wielded by a paterfamilias.[87] Consequently, *imperium* may have represented a relationship where members of a community put themselves under the power and authority of a powerful war leader – in many ways, being temporarily adopted into their *gens* – in a military context outside of the *pomerium*. There was only one situation where a magistrate was allowed to wield *imperium* inside the community – during the celebration of a triumph.

The sacral aspects of the triumph, at least as they were preserved in the Late Republic, seem to hint that it could (and perhaps should) be seen as the culmination of a process which began before war was engaged. As noted previously, scholars have argued that the culmination of the triumph on the Capitoline does seem to mirror the votive rite performed on the same hill before a campaign. But more than that, the triumph represented one of the only times in which the full powers of the *rex* (or praetor/consul) were on full display and the full nature of his relationship with the community demonstrated. He was military leader, leader of the Senate, focus of the community, as well as acting as a priest and intermediary with the gods.

The changes which occurred in *imperium* during the course of the Republic, and particularly during the period *c.* 367 BC, would have had a massive impact on the nature of the triumph. As the bond which *imperium* represented evolved, so did the triumph. In the Early Republic, perhaps the biggest shift in *imperium* occurred between the 440s and 360s BC, when the nature of military leadership was transformed from the co-option of a gentilicial model to a more civic paradigm. This period also featured a new type of military leader, the so-called consular tribunes or *tribuni militum consulari potestate*. While there has been sustained debate on whether or not these magistrates wielded *imperium*, all the evidence suggests that they did not celebrate the triumph.[88] So while they clearly were able to command armies, there does seem to have been something fundamentally different about their power, something which precluded their participation in this ritual. As I have argued elsewhere, given that the consular tribunes were elected by a different assembly and seem to have represented part of a new, more community focused system of government in Rome in the 440s BC, it is possible that the specific grant of archaic *imperium* was no longer thought to be needed.[89] The *tribuni militum* had the *potestas* to accomplish what they needed to by virtue of their election in the *comitia centuriata*. It is possible that they did not also require *imperium* and all that that represented. As a result, there was no separation of *domi et militiae* – or at least not in quite the same way – and so the transgressive triumph was not required to moderate it.

Rome's experiment with the consular tribunes, however, was reasonably short-lived. Although supposedly utilized intermittently during the second half of the fifth century BC, and then exclusively following the Gallic sack of 390/387 BC – hinting that it was perhaps seen as the most effective way to mobilize the city's defences – it was abandoned in favour of the new consulship of 367 BC. Again there is, and has been, much debate about what this 'new' office represented. Livy suggested it was not new at all, but merely the old consulship, reintroduced with a few new features – most notably being open to plebeians.[90] Some have argued it was actually the old consular tribunate, again reintroduced with some new tweaks,[91] while others have suggested it was a wholly new magistracy, designed to combine the various types of military power and authority which existed in Rome.[92] Intriguingly, while the consular tribunes seem to have been favoured by Rome after the Gallic sack, Ridley has convincingly argued that this does not mean they were particularly effective in actual fact.[93] Indeed, their military record leaves quite a lot to be desired, suggesting that whatever type of authority they wielded was not as effective as the archaic *imperium* of the praetors. Additionally, there seems to have been a desire for the prestige associated with archaic *imperium*, including the presence of lictors and the right to triumph. The situation in 367 BC is therefore somewhat awkward, as the Romans seem to have wanted to marry the *potestas* of the consular tribunes with the prestige of the archaic praetors. As a result, when *imperium* was reintroduced in 367 BC, it was likely of a slightly different variety. No longer needed to bind an external warlord to the community, it was instead a symbolic granting of power within the community.

With this transition came a reinterpretation of the triumph. While it clearly retained many of its symbolic and religious aspects, it no longer carried the same meaning as before. Many of the ritual aspects, which had probably performed an important symbolic function in archaic Rome, became vestigial. Amongst these, perhaps the biggest aspect seems to have been the blurring of the boundary between *domi et militiae*. In the archaic period, this boundary seems to have been clearly defined. The *curiae*, as the embodiment of the community, granted *imperium* to a leader, but did not engage in warfare directly. Instead, the members of the *curiae* effectively relinquished their urban identity and subsumed themselves with the gentilicial identity of the *rex*/praetor when beyond the *pomerium* on the battlefield. The triumph, therefore, represented the merging of these two identities. In the fourth century BC, *imperium* evolved into a slightly different grant of authority. Although confirmed by the *comitia curiata*, it was now given to a magistrate elected by the *comitia centuriata* – an assembly which represented the army both extramurally and within the context of the city. The crossing of the *pomerium* still represented an important moment, but not quite in the same way as it had previously. By this period, it represented more of a limit on authority, not a limit on identity.

The triumph continued to evolve alongside *imperium* and the rest of Rome, although it still seems to have maintained its role moderating the division between *domi et militiae*. Throughout the Republic, the triumph continued to represent an overt and physical point of congruence and transgression for the general, the army, the community and the gods. Although the ritual changed with Rome's developing landscape, accommodating Rome's new walls in the fourth century BC and the construction of various roads, temples and arches, the principle underlying it remained the same. In many ways a physical manifestation of the relationship which *imperium* represented, the triumph was both an acknowledgement of this essential power as well as a celebration of its successful implementation, being only deployed after victories.

Triumphal Transitions

Although both the triumph and *imperium* revealed a, perhaps surprising, amount of adaptability during the course of the Republic, by the Late Republic the evolution of both institutions seems to have reached a pivotal point. As the relationship between Rome's armed forces and the community began to fundamentally alter, with a shift to more professional and increasingly separated armies, the relationship which both *imperium* and the triumph embodied began to erode and evolve. Rather than representing the power dynamic which underpinned a civic militia, Rome's relationship with warfare was increasingly one of delegation and entrustment. Rome's wars were being fought by forces distant from the urban and political heart of the community. This shift has obviously been documented in a myriad of other areas, with the rise of so-called client armies and the emergence of the Roman Army as a distinct society in its own right. However, the implications of this, for both *imperium* and the triumph, were also profound.

The triumph continued to perform an important function as a ritual celebration of the connection between the urban community and both the Army and the elite who commanded it. However, as this connection evolved, so did the ritual's meaning. As the community's relationship with warfare became less involved and more abstract, the triumph seems to have evolved accordingly. It became increasingly about spectacle and self-presentation by members of the elite to an urban audience which was increasingly disconnected from the realities of warfare, offering a mechanism for the elite to demonstrate their ability and wealth. In this way, the triumph seems to have taken on many of the associations of Rome's other elite, ritualized display mechanisms, most notably the *ludi*. Interestingly, the triumph fit quite easily into this new matrix, as many of its other attributes, most notably its inherent tension and negotiation, can also be seen in this sphere. Indeed, as Bispham has argued, by the Late Republic the *ludi* can be understood as a form of ritualized action and the locus for confrontation as well as negotiation amongst the elite and between this group and the community at large.[94] However, the community's relationship with warfare was increasingly lost during this period. The triumph was still a military parade and involved the transgression of a military force within the boundaries of the community, but this was in many ways an external force – not an aspect or true representation of the community.

As with many other rituals in the Late Republic, religion took a back seat to more practical, political concerns when it came to the triumph – particularly as the institution lost much of its community significance. However, this does not mean that we should ignore the ritual aspects entirely. Indeed, as the archaic triumph seems to have embodied a particular aspect of the relationship between the general and the community, the Late Republican iteration can also be seen through this lens. As seen in the debate between Cicero and Appius Claudius over its necessity, the official grant of *imperium* had increasingly lost its meaning during this period. Indeed, the increasingly complex relationship between *imperium* and the various Roman assemblies in the Late Republic probably only added to this confusion. While one might still be able to understand *imperium* as representing the official endorsement of a military leader by the community, how that endorsement was given and which assembly represented the community is increasingly muddled. In fact, during the Late Republic, the relationship between generals and the community was increasingly negotiated through spectacle. In this way, the triumph can be seen as evolving alongside Rome's relationship with warfare far more quickly than its other institutions. As with the archaic iteration, the triumph showcased the full nature of a magistrate's power and relationship. He was military leader, leader of the Senate and focus of the community, as well as acting as a priest and intermediary with the gods. Within this context, Rome's elite in the Late Republic regularly tried to apply their success and power within the military sphere to the domestic sphere. In this period, the general's most important features were his wealth and military strength, and the ability to deploy both of these within the community's social and political spheres. As a result, although resonances to the archaic triumph's meaning are visible, the fundamental relationship had changed irrevocably.

Conclusion

The evolution of the triumph continued during the Empire, when the ritual slowly fell out of favour for a number of reasons. The most important of these, however, is that the Imperial triumph seems to have lost the three core aspects which gave it its meaning during the Regal and Republican periods. Under the Empire, the triumph was no longer about tension, negotiation or indeed *imperium*. During this period, the triumph was more about affirming imperial power in a much more traditional, and much less transgressive, manner. The last recorded non-imperial triumph was celebrated in 19 BC by L. Cornelius Balbus, the proconsul for Africa, and even by this point the *ius triumphandi* was strictly controlled by Augustus. From this point on, the triumph became a strictly imperial prerogative and part of the imperial apparatus. Under the Empire, the strict lines that separated *domi et militiae* and marked off the various sections and areas of Rome and Roman society had already been broken down by the power of the emperor. His power already extended to every corner of Rome's socio-political framework. Indeed, while *imperium* was still nominally granted and triumphs celebrated, these were increasingly 'window dressings' on the real power systems; nods to Roman traditions, not expressions of real relationships. As such, their gradual evaporation would have meant little to the Romans, as their role in this new context could be taken over by any one of a number of different institutions which reinforced the emperor's military power.

The Roman triumph has long been recognized as an important but enigmatic window into Roman society. While the nuances of this importance will likely always be beyond us, as indeed they seem to have often eluded the Romans themselves, the fundamentally transgressive nature of the ritual can provide some clues. Most notably, the triumph seems to have been intimately connected to the network of relationships which underpinned the *res publica*, reflecting both their evolving nature and the inherent tension within and between them. In particular, the Roman triumph reflected the community's relationship with warfare – paralleling the Republican grant of *imperium*. Rome's Army, commanded by elite generals and based on a civic militia, required a complex set of interactions to bring the various entities together. These relationships transgressed many of Rome's core boundaries, just as warfare often transgressed social norms, and the ritualized performance of the triumph may have helped the Romans deal with and understand these tensions.

Notes

1. Versnel, 1970. See also Rüpke, 2006, where it is suggested that the figure of the *triumphator* may represent a temporary statue.
2. *Domi et militiae* was a Latin phrase which meant 'of the home and of the military', referring to the civic and military spheres. It was considered *nefas*, or contrary to divine law, to have an army within the boundaries of Rome: Gell. *Noct. Att.* 15.27.
3. See particularly Pittenger, 2008, for discussion.
4. Hahn, 2015: 153–54. See Livy 4.20, 53.11. This is most famously recorded by Seutonius for Caesar's triumph of 46 BC (Suet. *Jul.* 49).
5. The date of the last Roman triumph is often debated. Some have suggested Stilicho's triumph in AD 404 should be considered the last true triumph, as it was the last celebrated in Rome in antiquity. Others have argued it was Justinian's celebration of Belisarius' victory in AD 535 (McCormick, 1990: 125), while others have pushed it far later. For instance, Panvinio attempted to continue the fragmentary *Fasti Triumphales*, after it was discovered in the 1550s, by adding later 'triumphs' to the list, including Charles V's entrance to Rome in 1536.
6. The triumph of Flaminius and Furius in 223 BC was voted solely by the tribal assembly (Plut. *Marc.* 4.3). The power of the Senate in the authorization of triumphs may have related in part to their traditional control of the *aerarium*, which was used to finance them (Polyb. 6.15.7) – although Papirius' triumph on the Alban Mount hints that it may have related to control of the space as well.
7. Livy 45.35.
8. Livy 3.29; Plut. *Aem.* 32; Dio 74.1.
9. The location of this gate is still, frustratingly, unknown. However, many speculate that it is near the current modern church of S'Omobono. See Richardson, 1992: 301.
10. Plin. *Nat. Hist.* 36.24.
11. Plut. *Rom. Quest.* 79.
12. Hopkins, 2016: 20–39, for a detailed discussion.
13. Bernard, 2012.
14. Dion. Hal. *Rom. Ant.* 2.34.
15. Rich, 2014: 204–05, 214–15.
16. *Ibid.* 216.
17. Versnel, 1970: 38–48.
18. Bonfante, 1970; Versnel, 1970.
19. Bonfante, 1970: 57–62. *Minium* is a pigment made from ground cinnabar or red lead, which was a bright red colour. The *toga picta* was a toga which had been dyed purple and embroidered in gold. The *tunica palmata*

was worn under the *toga picta* and embroidered with palms. *Bullae* were hollow balls of metal, similar to an amulet, which were commonly covered in gold and worn around the neck as ornaments.

20. Versnel, 1970: 285–86.
21. Osgood, 2014.
22. See Pittenger, 2008, for discussion.
23. Livy 8.26, 39.45, 40.25.
24. The auspices, and specifically *auspicia maxima* ('the greatest auspices'), were traditionally conferred on the magistrates who wielded *imperium*.
25. Val. Max. 2.8.
26. Cic. *Deiot.* 5; Val. Max. 2.8; Livy 26.21.
27. Beard, 2007: 371; see Lundgreen, 2014: 19–20, for discussion.
28. Pittenger, 2008.
29. Gibbon, 1796.
30. See, for example, Armstrong, 2013.
31. Pittenger, 2008; Lundgreen, 2014.
32. Östenberg, 2009.
33. Popkin, 2016.
34. See, for instance, Čadková, 2017.
35. Laqueur, 1909: 220–30; Rüpke, 1990: 225–26.
36. See also Armstrong, 2013, for discussion.
37. Versnel, 1970: 388.
38. Bonfante, 1970: 52–57.
39. Pittenger, 2008.
40. Itgenshorst, 2005.
41. See particularly Beard, 2007.
42. Hickson, 1991; Beard, 2007, 295–305; Östenberg, 2009; quotation: Beard, 2007: 4.
43. Spierling & Halvorson, 2008, for comparative examples and recent discussion in the field of anthropology.
44. Plin. *Nat. Hist.* 8.20; Beard, 2007: 29.
45. See particularly Pittenger, 2008, for discussion.
46. Beck, 2011: 94.
47. Pittenger, 2008: 17.
48. Dion. Hal. *Ant. Rom.* 2.34.2.
49. Plut. *Marc.* 21.
50. Livy 39.6–7.
51. Plin. *Nat. Hist.* 33.148.
52. Livy 39.7.
53. Vell. Pat. 1.13.4; Plin. *Nat. Hist.* 34.36; Cic. *Off.* 2.76.
54. Cic. *Leg. Man.* 3.8; Plut. *Luc.* 37.

55. App. *Bell. Mithr.* 116. See Vervaet, 2014, for discussion.
56. Beard, 2007: 4.
57. Brennan, 1996: 317.
58. Livy 3.63; Dion. Hal. *Rom. Ant.* 11.50.
59. Livy 10.37.11: ... *sed iussu populi triumphasse diceret, adiciebat se quoque laturum fuisse ad populum, ni sciret mancipia nobilium tribunos plebis legem inpedituros; voluntatem sibi ac favorem consentientis populi pro omnibus iussis esse ac futura.*
60. Bonfante, 1970: 53.
61. The *spolia opima* were supposedly only acquired three times – twice in the regal period by Romulus and Aulus Cornelius Cossus, and in 222 BC by the consul Marcus Claudius Marcellus. There is also the disputed *spolia opima* of Drusus Germanicus, Augustus' son-in-law.
62. Picard, 1957: 130—33.
63. Festus 81L.
64. Prop. *El.* 4.10.
65. Livy 1.24.
66. Festus 189L; Livy 35.10.
67. Ovid *Fasti* 2.859–60.
68. Virg. *Aen.* 7.607.
69. Livy 1.19; Plin. *Nat. Hist.* 34.33.
70. See Grandazzi, 1997: 199–200, for discussion.
71. Livy 33.23.
72. *Ibid.*
73. Brennan, 1996: 320.
74. The date of the *feriae Latinae* shifted, but would have likely occurred in either April or March: Niebuhr, 1832: 2:34.
75. Niebuhr, 1832: 2:26–27.
76. It must be noted there is some debate over whether it was *imperium* or its associated *ausipicium* which really mattered. See, for example, Versnel, 1970: 174–75.
77. Livy 26.21; 45.35.
78. Cic. *Leg. agr.* 2.12, 30.
79. Beck 2011: 94.
80. Cic. *Leg. agr.* 2.12, 30.
81. See Richardson, 1992: 105–06, for an overview.
82. Brennan, 2000: 54–57; Smith, 2006: 220–23.
83. Gell. *Noct. Att.* 15.27.
84. Tac. *Ann.* 12.24. It is worth noting that in the Empire, as the *lex de imperio* of Vespasian shows, the granting of *imperium* seems to have shifted from the *comitia curiata* to the Senate. While this may simply represent an

administrative move, one could also argue that it demonstrates the evolution of who and what best represented the ancient, urban, heart of the city. Given the largely symbolic nature of *imperium* by AD 69, it is tempting to suggest that what we can see in that move is a shift in the understanding of Rome as a community.

85.　See Armstrong, 2016a: 74–128, for full discussion.
86.　See Drogula, 2007: 419–52, for full discussion
87.　Armstrong, 2016b: 101–19.
88.　For discussion, see Badian, 1990: 469; Richard, 1990: 783–85.
89.　Armstrong, 2017.
90.　See, for instance, Forsythe, 2005: 266; Holloway, 2014.
91.　Von Fritz, 1950; De Martino, 1972: 248–49; Brennan, 2000: 58–75.
92.　Richardson, 2008: 338–40; Wiseman, 1995: 106–07.
93.　Ridley, 1986: 444–65.
94.　Bispham, 2000: 14.

Bibliography

Armstrong, J., 2013, 'Claiming Victory: The Early Roman Triumph', in Armstrong, J. & Spalinger, J. (eds), *Rituals of Triumph in the Mediterranean World*, Leiden: 7–21.

Armstrong, J., 2016a, *War and Society in Early Rome: From Warlords to Generals*, Cambridge.

Armstrong, J., 2016b, 'The Ties that Bind: Military Cohesion in Archaic Rome', in Armstrong, J. (ed.), *Circum Mare: Themes in Ancient Warfare*, Leiden: 101–19.

Armstrong, J., 2017, 'The Consulship in 367 BC and the Evolution of Roman Military Command', *Antichthon* 51: 124–48.

Badian, E., 1990, 'Kommentar', in W. Eder (ed.), *Staat und Staatlichkeit in der frühen römischen Republik: Akten eines Symposiums, 12. –15. Juli 1988, Freie Universität Berlin*, Stuttgart: 458–72.

Beard, M., 2007, *The Roman Triumph*, Cambridge.

Beck, H., 2011, 'Consular Power and the Roman Constitution', in Beck, H., Duplá, A., Jehne, M. & Polo, F.P. (eds), *Consuls and Res Publica: Holding High Office in the Roman Republic*, Cambridge: 77–96.

Bernard, S., 2012, 'Continuing the Debate on Rome's Earliest Circuit Walls', *PBSR* 80: 1–44.

Bispham, E., 2000, 'Introduction', in Bispham, E. & Smith, C. (eds), *Religion in Archaic and Republican Rome and Italy: Evidence and Experience*, Edinburgh: 1–19.

Bonfante Warren, L., 1970, 'Roman Triumphs and Etruscan Kings: The Changing Face of the Triumph', *JRS* 60: 49–66.

Brennan, C., 1996, 'Triumphus in Monte Albano', in Wallace, R.W. & Harris, W.V. (eds), *Transition to Empire: Essays in Greco-Roman History 360–146 BC*, Norman: 315–37.

Brennan, C., 2000, *The Praetorship in the Roman Republic*, vols 1–2, Oxford.

Čadková, D., 2017, 'Czech Literature between the National Revival and the Avant-Garde', in Torlone, Z.M., Munteanu, D.L. & Dutsch, D. (eds), *A Handbook to Classical Reception in Eastern and Central Europe*, Hobeken: 121–32.

Charles-Picard, G., 1957, *Les trophées romains. Contributions à l'histoire de la religion et de l'art triomphal de Rome*, Paris.

De Martino, F., 1972, 'Intorno all'origine della repubblica romana e delle magistrature', *ANRW* I.1: 217–49.

Drogula, F., 2007, '*Imperium, potestas*, and the *pomerium* in the Roman Republic', *Historia* 56: 419–52.

Forsythe, G., 2005, *A Critical History of Early Rome: From Prehistory to the First Punic War*, Berkeley.

Gibbon, E., 1796, 'Sur les triomphes des Romains', in Holroyd, J. (ed.), *Miscellaneous Works*, Dublin: 123–48.

Grandazzi, A., 1997, *The Foundation of Rome: Myth and History*, Ithaca.

Hahn, F., 2015, 'The Obscene Songs', in Dutsch, D. & Suter, A. (eds), *Ancient Obscenities: Their Nature and Use in the Ancient Greek and Roman Worlds*, Ann Arbor: 153–74.

Hickson, F., 1991, 'Augustus *Triumphator*: Manipulation of the Triumphal Themes in the Political Program of Augustus', *Latomus* 50: 124–38.

Holloway, R., 2014, 'A Cover-up in Early Roman History: Fabia Minor and the Sextian-Licinian Reforms', *CJ* 109: 139–46.

Hopkins, J. 2016, *The Genesis of Roman Architecture*, Yale.

Itgenshorst, T., 2005, *Tota illa pompa. Der Triumph in der römischen Republik. Hypomnemata 161*, Göttingen.

Laqueur, R., 1909, 'Über das Wesen des römischen Triumphs', *Hermes* 44: 215–36.

Lundgreen, C., 2014, 'Rules for Obtaining a Triumph - the *ius triumphandi* Once More', in Lange, C.H. & Vervaet, F.J. (eds), *The Roman Republican Triumph: Beyond the Spectacle*, Rome: 17–32.

McCormick, M., 1990, *Eternal Victory: Triumphal Rulership in Late Antiquity, Byzantium, and the Early Medieval West*, Cambridge.

Niebuhr, B., 1832, *Römische Geschichte*, Berlin.

Osgood, J., 2014, 'Julius Caesar and Spanish Triumph-Hunting', in Lange, C.H. & Vervaet, F.J. (eds), *The Roman Republican Triumph: Beyond the Spectacle*, Rome: 149-65.

Östenberg, I., 2009, *Staging the World: Spoils, Captives, and Representations in the Roman Triumphal Procession*, Oxford.

Picard, G., 1957, *Les Trophées romains; contribution à l'histoire de la religion t de l'art triomphal de Rome*, Paris.

Pittenger, M., 2008, *Contested Triumphs: Politics, Pageantry, and Performance in Livy's Republican Rome*, Berkeley.

Popkin, M., 2016, *The Architecture of the Roman Triumph: Monuments, Memory, and Identity*, Cambridge.

Rich, J., 2017, 'The Triumph in the Roman Republic: Frequency, Fluctuation and Policy', in Lange, C.H. & Vervaet, F.J. (eds), *The Roman Republican Triumph: Beyond the Spectacle*, Rome: 197–258.

Richard, J.-C., 1990, 'Réflexions sue le tribunat consulaire', *MEFRA* 102: 767–99.

Richardson, J., 2008, 'Ancient Political Thought and the Development of the Consulship', *Latomus* 67: 627–33.

Richardson, L., 1992, *A New Topographical Dictionary of Ancient Rome*, Baltimore.

Ridley, R., 1986, 'The "Consular Tribunate": The Testimony of Livy', *Klio* 68: 444–65.

Rüpke, J., 2006, 'Triumphator and Ancestor Rituals between Symbolic Anthropology and Magic', *Numen* 53.3: 251–89.

Smith, C., 2006, *The Roman Clan: The Gens from Ancient Ideology to Modern Anthropology*, Cambridge.

Spierling, K. & Halvorson, M., 2008, 'Introduction: Definitions of Community in Early Modern Europe', in Spierling, K. & Halvorson, M. (eds), *Defining Community in Early Modern Europe*, Abingdon: 1–24.

Versnel, H.S., 1970, *Triumphus: An Inquiry into the Origin, Development and Meaning of the Roman Triumph*, Leiden.

Vervaet, F., 2014, '*Si neque leges neque more cogunt*: Beyond the Spectacle of Pompeius Magnus' Triple Triumph', in Lange, C.H. & Vervaet, F.J. (eds), *The Roman Republican Triumph: Beyond the Spectacle*, Rome: 131–48.

von Fritz, K., 1950, 'The Reorganisation of the Roman Government in 366 BC and the So-Called Licinio-Sextian Laws', *Historia* 1: 3–44.

Wiseman, T.P., 1995, *Remus: A Roman Myth*, Cambridge.

Index